## International Acclaim for *Curse of the Narrows*

"*Curse of the Narrows* is not unlike following news coverage of Hurricane Katrina: the account of the initial disaster holds us riveted. . . . There is a present-day resonance to all parts of this tale."
— *The New York Times*

"Powerful. . . . Mac Donald, a Halifax native, has crafted a fine account of the disaster, solidly balanced between the onrushing sweep of events and their growing impact on survivors and witnesses."
— *The Hamilton Spectator*

"Mac Donald's dramatic reconstruction of the moments leading up to and the days following the Halifax Explosion makes for powerful writing and even more gripping reading. She skillfully weaves together the horror and the heroism of those days with the human details of how ordinary people coped with disaster and extraordinary people arrived to help them through the worst of it; the result is a first-rate page-turner."
— Stephen Kimber, author of *Reparations* and
*Sailors, Slackers and Blind Pigs: Halifax at War*

"A compelling and well-written account, which adds to the growing body of work of the explosion and its aftermath."
— *The NovaScotian*

"*Curse of the Narrows* is a story of a forgotten tragedy, meticulously researched, and a reminder, if one were still needed, of the necessity to prepare for the unforeseeable as well as the foreseen."
— *Philadelphia Inquirer*

# Curse *of the*
# Narrows

Laura M. Mac Donald

HARPER
**PERENNIAL**

Published by HarperCollins Publishers Ltd, by arrangement with Walker Publishing Company Inc.

Art credits
Title page image: PANS. Pages 4, 18, 20, 43, 71, 73, 76, 85, 94, 96, 120, 123, 130, 131, 135, 146, 148, 156, 163, 175, 181, 186, 188, 191, 194, 210, 211, 213, 220, 238, 239, 248, 249, 276, and 277: PANS/NSRAM. Pages 54, 62, 67, 88, 127, 149, 197, 208, 217, and 258: Maritime Museum of the Atlantic. Pages 19 and 233: The Archives of the City of Toronto. Pages 24 and 243: The Duggan family. Page 116: The Dalhousie University Archives, Killam Memorial Library. Pages 143 and 236: Archives of the American Red Cross. Page 172: Boston Public Library. Page 181: *Halifax Daily News*.

First Canadian edition

HarperCollins books may be purchased for educational, business, or sales promotional use through our Special Markets Department.

HarperCollins Publishers Ltd
2 Bloor Street East, 20th Floor
Toronto, Ontario, Canada
M4W 1A8

*www.harpercollins.ca*

---

Library and Archives Canada Cataloguing in Publication

Mac Donald, Laura, 1963–
    The curse of the narrows : the Halifax explosion, 1917 / Laura Mac Donald.—1st ed.

Includes index.
ISBN-13: 978-0-00-639489-1
ISBN-10: 0-00-639489-2

1. Halifax (N.S.)—History-Explosion, 1917.  I. Title.

FC2346.4.M33 2004   971.6'22503   C2005-901676-0

HC 9 8 7 6 5 4 3 2 1

Printed and bound in the United States
Book design by Ralph L. Fowler

*For my mother, Dolly*

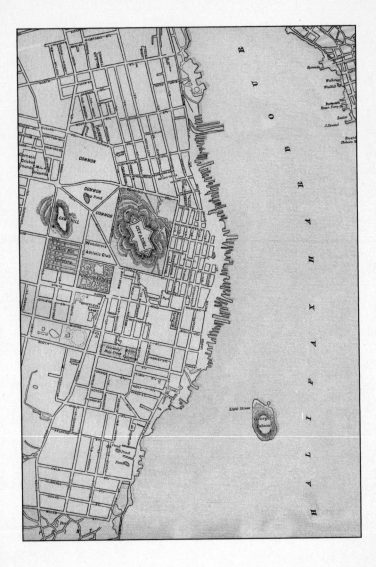

*Each December the people of Boston gather to witness the annual lighting of the Christmas tree. Some of them probably do not know why the people of Halifax send a tree every year or even that it is a gift from Nova Scotia. No one needs to know the story behind a tree to admire its beauty. But the people of Halifax know where it comes from and they remember the story.*

## A Word on Geography and Place Names

When I grew up, many Dartmouthians called the region Dartmouth-Halifax. Haligonians, as people from Halifax are known, called it Halifax-Dartmouth. In 1994 the two cities and much of the surrounding region amalgamated under the name of Halifax Regional Municipality (HRM). That did little to quell the burning fire of independence in every Dartmouthian's heart. I am sad to admit that I often failed to find a way to distinguish the two cities when writing but ended up putting my faith in the universal experience. If it is any consolation, there are a lot of people in New Jersey and Anaheim and Oakland who share our pain. I encourage them to appoint historians the minute anything interesting happens.

Regarding the North End: The neighborhood of Richmond began at North Street and ended at Africville. It was named after the Richmond Wharf, where sugar from Richmond, Virginia, was loaded not far from where the *Mont Blanc* exploded. In 1917, the neighborhood's main throughfare and only tramline was on Campbell Road, which along with Pleasant and Lockman Streets was in the midst of being incorporated into Barrington Street, creating one long street that ran from the southern tip of the city all the way north, parallel to the shoreline. To help retain the distinction between Richmond, where the worst damage occurred, and the rest of the city for readers unfamiliar with the city, I have chosen to use Campbell Road. There is also some confusion about the North End. In 1917 the North End referred only to streets north of North Street. Sometime after the explosion it became common practice to refer to everything north of the Citadel or Cogswell Street as the North End. I was also surprised to discover that at the time Halifax Harbour was often spelled Halifax Harbor. I have cleverly avoided arguments between my American publisher and my Canadian publisher, as well as with my family and fellow HRM-ers, by never referring to the harbor by its proper name except in the following sentence. It is now, and in my heart shall forever remain, Halifax Harbour.

# THE NARROWS, HALIFAX, NOVA SCOTIA
## December 6, 1917, est. 8:40 am to 9:04:35 am

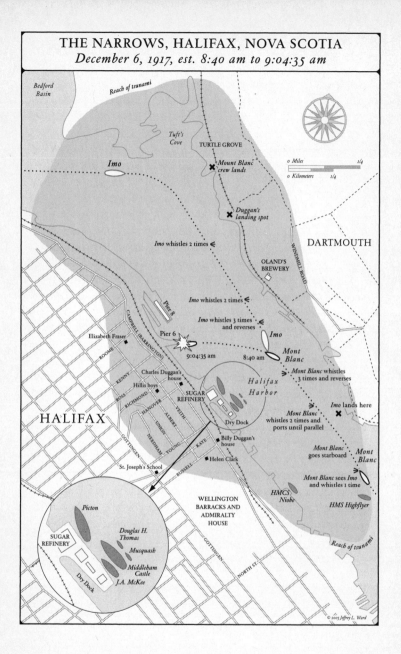

Bedford Basin

Reach of tsunami

Tuft's Cove

TURTLE GROVE

*Imo*

Mount Blanc crew lands

Duggan's landing spot

DARTMOUTH

*Imo whistles 2 times*

OLAND'S BREWERY

WINDMILL ROAD

o Miles ¼
o Kilometers ¼

*Imo whistles 2 times*

Pier 8

*Imo whistles 3 times and reverses*

Elizabeth Fraser

Pier 6

*Imo*

9:04:35 am

8:40 am

*Mont Blanc*

CAMPBELL (BARRINGTON)

Charles Duggan's house

ROOME

KENNY

ROSS

Hillis boys

*Halifax Harbor*

*Mont Blanc whistles 3 times and reverses*

RICHMOND

HANOVER

SUGAR REFINERY

*Imo lands here*

HALIFAX

ALBERT

VEITH

Dry Dock

*Mont Blanc whistles 2 times and ports until parallel*

GOTTINGEN

UNION

NEEDHAM

YOUNG

Billy Duggan's house

*Mont Blanc goes starboard*

*Mont Blanc*

St. Joseph's School

RUSSELL

KAYE

Helen Clark

*Mont Blanc sees Imo and whistles 1 time*

*Mont Blanc*

Picton

SUGAR REFINERY

Douglas H. Thomas

Musquash

WELLINGTON BARRACKS AND ADMIRALTY HOUSE

MONT ST.

HMCS *Niobe*

HMS *Highflyer*

Dry Dock

Middleham Castle

J.A. McKee

GOTTINGEN

NORTH ST.

Reach of tsunami

© 2005 Jeffrey L. Ward

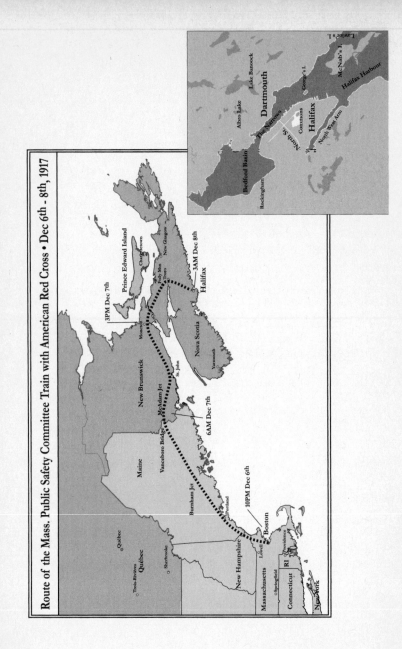

Route of the Mass. Public Safety Committee Train with American Red Cross • Dec 6th - 8th, 1917

# Contents

Contents

# A Short History of Halifax

*Three times a bridge over these waves shall rise,*
*Built by the pale face, so strong and wise,*
*Three times shall fall like a dying breath,*
*In storm, in silence, and last in death.*

WHEN I WAS A CHILD growing up in Dartmouth, Nova Scotia, my father used to tell me the legend of an ancient Mi'kmaq Indian curse. The Mi'kmaqs, the original settlers along the northeastern coast stretching from Maine to Quebec to Nova Scotia, had long ago left Turtle Grove on the Dartmouth side of the harbor, but they were alive and ferocious in my childhood imagination. I was convinced that if I looked hard enough I could see the mythical angry brave of the legend fighting the tide like Cuchulain. Dartmouth and Halifax sit on hills on opposite sides of the harbor. Our house sat near the top of the Dartmouth side. Sitting in my backyard high above the harbor, I would squint my eyes at the blue-green waters past where I imagined Indians used to build their wigwams on the Dartmouth shore. On summer nights, sleeping in a tent in the backyard, my sister Jennifer, who loved to terrify us smaller children, would whisper that the brave was going to find us in our tent and slaughter us. "Listen. You can hear the sound of the drums coming closer." Then she would lower her voice. "Bomp, bomp, bomp, bomp." It had more to do with Hollywood stereotypes and white paranoia than it did with the men and women we met selling porcupine-quill boxes at GooGoo's gift shop, but we loved it.

Over the years I heard different versions of the curse, but the one I remember told the story of a brave hiding in the woods and watching as his wife waited near the shore for her lover, a British soldier stationed in Halifax. As the adulterous couple slipped away in his canoe, the husband chased them across the harbor's tapered neck—the Narrows—before they disappeared into the night. When he caught up to them, he avenged himself by hacking the soldier to death. With his final blow the moon came out from behind a cloud and revealed the butchered body of his wife. In despair, he cursed the white man from ever bridging the Narrows. It was one of those stories that managed to insult everybody: The wife was unfaithful; the brave a raging lunatic who could not control his emotions long enough to even kill the right person; the British soldier an imperialist buffoon who took what he wanted. But we loved to hear it. Why? Because two bridges had fallen over the Narrows and we were waiting for the third.*

The first bridge collapsed in a hurricane in 1891, six years after it was built. Two years later, its replacement mysteriously fell "in silence" during a summer night and washed out to sea with the tide. The city did not build a third bridge until 1955, when they opened a handsome steel suspension bridge called the Angus L. Macdonald. Although it did not span the Narrows, but a spot closer to the outer harbor, city officials invited Mi'kmaq elders to perform a ceremony lifting the curse. Then in the late sixties the city began construction on the A. Murray MacKay Bridge, which did skirt the end of the Narrows. We waited with delicious anticipation, sure that it would collapse, but each day, it got longer and stronger until finally it opened. The first time we drove over what—for at least the next half-century—would be known as "the new bridge," my father pointed to the small cove past the anchorage.

"That," he said, "is where the Mi'kmaq settlement was before the Halifax explosion destroyed it."

I had never heard that before. The Halifax explosion destroyed the Mi'kmaq village? How could no one have told me that? In my six-year-old

---

*That this story did not feature a bridge did not occur to me until my editor pointed it out. After researching it, I found that the story originally featured the brave chasing the adulterous couple over a succession of canoes tied together—this was the first bridge to cross the Narrows. When he returned to Dartmouth he destroyed the flotilla and the bridge. (*Halifax Herald*, May 2, 1985) mind, the two legends—the curse of the narrows and the Halifax explosion—fused. Of course, I thought, the curse had already been sated. That explained why the new bridge was safe. (Even as a child I knew that it was not going to fall down.) Never mind that there was no collapsing bridge in the story of the 1917 explosion. And never mind the poem. The curse of the narrows was always about the water, the thin neck of water that separated the outer harbor from the Bedford Basin, Halifax from Dartmouth and the white men crossing it. Surely the Halifax explosion—the result of two white men making a fatal crossing in the Narrows—rent destruction enough to reverse any curse.

Standing today at the top of what used to be the neighborhood of Richmond, overlooking the Narrows, it is easy to imagine how the waterfront appeared on December 6, 1917. A massive dry dock sits where the explosive-laden *Mont Blanc* drifted into the wooden piers. The railyards are still there, dividing the port and the naval base from the neighborhood above. Men in dirt-toughened clothes still walk to work in the morning. Their children still run up Russell Street late for school, and all sorts of ships, including warships, still sail in and out of one of the deepest and best-protected harbors in the world.

The Mi'kmaq Indians called it Chebucto, for big. The French explorers named it *Baie Saine,* or Safe Bay. Both were right. The harbor is big and safe, and its shape, a lopsided keyhole carved into steep hills, makes it easy to defend in wartime and keeps its waters ice-free for commercial shipping year round. At the mouth of the harbor three islands divide the water into two channels. The eastern passage is sandy-bottomed and just three feet deep in places, so shallow that a warship trying to enter the main harbor through her unguarded waters would run aground. In contrast the western passage is wide and deep. Before World War I, the *Titanic*'s sister ship, the *Olympic,** easily passed through the western passage. Today it accommodates even the most colossal cruise liner. On the other side of McNab's Island the water rejoins but gradually narrows until it reaches a cul-de-sac called Tuft's Cove, an inlet tucked between what in 1917 was the Mi'kmaq village of Turtle Grove and a rounded peninsula protruding from the Dartmouth side (sometimes also referred to as Tuft's Cove). This wee bump of land forces the water into an angled channel a mere 480 yards wide, so narrow that a commercial spool of thread could stretch across it. These are the Narrows.

---

*Both belonged to the White Star Line, as did the *Runic,* later renamed the *Imo.*

For a sailor who does not know what is behind the hills, the harbor appears to simply end at Tuft's Cove. But the water does not end there. Instead, the Narrows open into a beautiful basin surrounded by hills so steep that the masts of hundreds of warships could hide out of sight of enemy ships patrolling the coast. The hills also protect the Basin's water from the weather, creating a safe haven in even the worst winter gales. Bedford Basin is Halifax's greatest secret, its wartime asset.

HALIFAX KNEW ALL ABOUT WAR. The city was settled in 1749 as a fort by Lord Edward Cornwallis, who was carrying out the assignment at the behest of Lord George Montagu Dunk, president of the Board of Trade and Plantations and second Earl of Halifax. When he sailed into the harbor with 2,576 Protestant settlers, they found nothing but trees and water. The unforgiving terrain must have shocked the settlers. No fields, no clearing, no gentle sloping hills, no fishing shacks, no signs of life—just hills and trees so close to the shore they seemed to grow straight out of the salty water. Worse were the steep hills that dominated both shores. Certainly they would offer safety, but when they built roads, they would build uphill.

Halifax seen from Dartmouth, 1917

When they built houses, factories, and walls, they would need to build into the hill. Farmers had to spread out to the other side of the hill where the peninsula turned to plateau. They would always be going up or down or around the hills.

Cornwallis saw it differently. For him the combination of hills and water offered the prospect of glory. Here he could develop naval dominance over the entire region. The settlers were barely off the ship and already Halifax's two competing ambitions—peace and war—were well established.

One hundred and fifty years later the rivalry was still entrenched, but the outcome was clear. The city's fortunes rose and fell with the tides of war. Halifax's privateers looted and plundered their way through the Seven Years War, the American Revolution,* the Napoleonic Wars, and the War of 1812, seizing French, Spanish, and Americans ships, sailors, and cargo. The question of their legality might best be answered by paraphrasing Benjamin Franklin's character in the play *1776*. Privateers are completely legal in the first person, such as our privateers; it is only in the third person, their privateers, that they become illegal. The privateers made some citizens enormously wealthy, and while they sailed in and out of port under the protection of the Royal Navy, the government began to plan new public institutions. Regal sandstone bricks replaced wooden shingles. A gorgeous formal garden was planted, which in the spirit of a young democracy was called, simply enough, the Public Gardens. In 1818, the lieutenant governor, a professional soldier returned from Waterloo, took the profits from turning a Maine port they had seized in the War of 1812 into a British Customs house and founded a secular university. By accepting all suitable applicants regardless of religion, Dalhousie College provided the city not only with lawyers, doctors, and professionals but an atmosphere of cautious tolerance that counterbalanced the regimented military attitude of the British.

In 1835, the courts tried and upheld the right to freedom of the press. Then, in 1848, Nova Scotia, with Halifax firmly established as its capital, called its first representative government to order, making it the first self-governed colony in the British Empire. It stayed that way until 1867, when it joined the Confederation as a province of Canada. Skeptics of the new

---

*Although initially sympathetic to the American colonies, the privateers joined the struggle against the revolutionaries after American privateers attacked them. For their part, the American privateers were much more effective than the newly formed American Navy. According to the U.S. Maritime Service Veterans, privateers captured more than eleven British ships for every one the Navy captured. (Privateers: 2283, Navy: 196)

country predicted that the lightly populated province would be unable to compete with Ontario and Quebec, but there was no immediate economic disaster. When it did come, it had as much to do with American politics as Canadian. At end of the American Civil War, Congress chose not to renew the Reciprocity Treaty that guaranteed North American free trade. In response, Ottawa imposed tariffs on U.S.-bound trade. It was a disastrous decision for Halifax. Her greatest opportunity lay in acting as a neutral go-between for Britain and the United States, a naval courtesan playing one rich and powerful ally against the other. The tariffs cut off access to both the U.S. and the U.K. ships that once stopped off in Halifax to unload or stock up on supplies. After that they sailed straight to Boston. Over the half-century of peace between 1860 and 1914, Halifax's waterfront did not receive any capital investment and started losing more and more business to Boston, as iron and steel ships overtook wooden ones.

With a shared heritage of English, Irish, and Scots, and a common history at sea, families were as often as not part of the cargo of ships running molasses, fish, and rum back and forth between the two ports. There were more Nova Scotians in Boston than anywhere else in America. And there were plenty of American descendants in Nova Scotia. After the Revolution, thirty thousand loyalists settled in Nova Scotia, leaving their brothers, sisters, and sometimes children behind. The Boston men, many of whom were Harvard graduates, became political and social leaders. There were soon as many Winslows, Wentworths, Uphams, Salters, Blowers, and Sewalls in Nova Scotia as there were in Boston and New York, although they were nowhere near as wealthy.

During the latter half of the nineteenth century, as the city's economy declined, downtown began to sink into a deep and foul slum. Most people blamed it on the unemployed sailors, who seemed to drink more and more as the nineteenth century progressed. Although alcohol was still technically prohibited in Halifax—in the nineteenth century Canadian communities were allowed to vote themselves wet or dry by referendum—Halifax boasted hundreds of taverns. Even shipowners who were getting rich running West Indian molasses bound for Boston rum manufacturers turned to the Temperance movement when they started losing profits because of drunkenness on their own docks. Much of the activity revolved around Sailortown, the nickname for the bars and bawdy houses on Upper and Lower Water Streets, which earned such a dismal reputation for encouraging deserters that the British and American navies designated it off-limits for enlisted men. Sailortown's more squalid companion, one known for its ready population of prostitutes, was called Soldiertown or Slumdom, a rough series of unpainted saltbox houses along the short blocks between Salter and Jacob Streets beneath Citadel Hill. It did not take much to drag a respectable but poor woman into prostitution. Any woman desperate enough to take a place in one of the boardinghouses in Slumdom and who slipped in the rent was soon encouraged to accept a visit with a sailor once or twice a month to make up the back rent. With even fewer opportunities than their white counterparts, black women opened their own brothels and girls who were brought up in whorehouses often remained in the family business. Women who were lucky enough to develop long-term common-law relationships with a soldier were called "soldiers' wives," and their serial monogamy was as despised by the city as it was by the military, both of which viewed it as another form of prostitution, and denied the common-law wives any legal standing no matter how long their relationship lasted or how many children it produced. Hidden behind and above the lively taverns of Soldiertown were small dank rooms without plumbing, crammed with desperate families, alcoholics, prostitutes, vermin, and thieves. The overflow melted out onto the streets, with men and women dotting the stoops like mushrooms. It did not matter how many times the patrol wagon moved them on; they reappeared within minutes. Among sailors Halifax was reputed to be one of the wildest seaports in North America; it had the added virtue of being one of the least violent. A captain who later commented on the generous support for Halifax called the port "a favorite station . . . not as if it were Cape Town, or Melbourne or Sydney." Rockhead Prison, which maintained a hospital for the city's indigent on the outskirts of town, went by its more common name: the Venereal Hospital. It was a long way from the bastion of civilization the early settlers had imagined.

Most civilians blamed the Royal Navy, which, as ever, was both Halifax's downfall and its salvation. As much as the locals hated its imperious officers, they basked in their association with admirals and royalty. (As its citizens liked to point out, Prince Edward himself laid out many of Halifax's streets and built its town clock.) They had grown so used to complaining about the Admiralty while at the same time admiring it, that when the Royal Navy finally packed up and sailed out of port permanently in 1906— leaving Halifax (and Canada) with a navy consisting of just one cruiser—it was a moment of both great pride and troubling self-doubt. As much as they resented the Royal Navy, Halifax's citizens believed it superior in every way to the Canadian Navy.

Nova Scotia's few successful entrepreneurs, such as Alfred Fuller,

Alexander Graham Bell, and Samuel Cunard, reasoned that the future lay in the open markets to the south. But Halifax's conservative atmosphere—its tolerance and liberal university, its preference for history over risk, and its rigid social class structure—was less suitable to entrepreneurship than to politics. In the forty years since Confederation, Nova Scotia had already produced three prime ministers: Charles Tupper, John Thompson, and Robert Borden. Borden would pay a lot of attention to Halifax, not only as his constituency but also because, in his third year in office, in 1914, a bullet passed through Archduke Francis Ferdinand's heart.

After Canada joined the war alongside Britain, tens of thousands of sailors began moving through port. Once again, the demand for prostitutes exploded and for a while the only passengers stepping down from the daily trains from Montreal and Toronto were young women wearing short skirts that highlighted their stockings and shoes. (The genteel ladies of Halifax still preferred a leather boot that covered the ankle.) The police filled page after page of their logbooks with complaints of public drunkenness, lewdness, and solicitation, as well as petty thievery and fights.

The citizens might have minded more if they were not making so much money. The harbor traffic rocketed from two million tons a year to seventeen million. For the first time in more than half a century there was plenty of work, but with one out of every four men in Halifax serving overseas, there were not enough men. Scarce labor was a worldwide phenomenon, as was a shortage of food and supplies that resulted in crippling inflation. To ease the labor shortage, women were offered positions in offices and behind retail counters—there were even two female doctors, one female psychiatrist, and more in medical school—giving women a new social mobility that quickly translated into political influence. Women were campaigning to win the right to vote, thanks in part to the efforts of the Women's Christian Temperance Union, which offered a neat bargain to politicians: it would soften its antialcohol and tobacco stance out of respect for the men going overseas, in exchange for the vote. Between 1904 and 1914, the Local Council of Women, a group of volunteer women, had been politicized, shifting its ambitions from getting schoolchildren to plant flowers to placing women on school boards, and when the city's working women made it known that they preferred factory work to domestic work, the Local Council of Women pushed for better training in hopes that it would increase and standardize women's wages. The war, the cause of some women's social downfall, turned out to be the path to respectability for others.

· · ·

IN THE FIRST YEARS of World War I, Halifax found itself at the center of a power struggle between Canada and Great Britain. The Admiralty had pulled out in 1906 but returned with the outbreak of the war, and the two navies argued as to who would run the port and how Canada would conduct her naval affairs. The Canadian Navy was put in the unenviable position of having all of the responsibility without any of the authority. Early in the war the Admiralty declared that German U-boats could not carry sufficient fuel to reach North American shores and insisted that the Canadian Navy concentrate on patrolling British waters instead of its own. In 1916, the Admiralty reversed its position shortly after *U-53* surfaced off the coast of Cape Cod. For Halifax, a fleet of wooden trawlers was retrofitted with guns and minesweeping equipment, but even finding men to crew the new ships was difficult. The British commander-in-chief at Halifax instructed the base to install a second submarine net between McNab's Island and Point Pleasant Park to deter subs from entering the outer harbor, a prescient decision.* In February 1917, the British government deciphered a telegram from the German foreign minister, Arthur Zimmerman, to the German minister stationed in Mexico, advising him that the Germans were going to introduce unrestricted naval warfare as of February 1, 1917, and ordering him to approach the Mexican president to ally Mexico with Germany against America. Until that time, America, as a neutral country, allowed trading with Germany and in some cases loaded goods into jumbo commercial German subs that passed the blockades undetected—a technical wonder. After receiving the memo, Washington abruptly broke off diplomatic relations with Germany. The evasive German submarines were recast as ominous and threatening. Two months later, on April 6, 1917, America entered the war. Almost immediately Halifax papers reported that mine-laying German submarines were racing across the Atlantic. The Admiralty, which had lost hundreds of ships early that spring, implemented the convoy system so that ships could cross the Atlantic together under the protection of destroyers. "The U-boats had much more difficulty locating a single group of ships than in finding a stream of vessels sailing independently and funnelling into constricted approach routes. U-boats proved reluctant to attack even a weakly escorted group." The success of the convoys, which departed from New York and Halifax, depended on secrecy.

*The first set, which was installed across the harbor from George's Island in 1915, protected the entrance to the Narrows.

Orders were kept to a minimum and sometimes left sealed until the last moment.

With the new submarine nets in place, patrol ships going back and forth outside the mouth of the harbor, the sudden appearance of American troops in port, and dozens of ships sailing out of the Basin escorted by British destroyers, the war dominated Halifax streets. It even threatened the sky. Since the war's onset, Germany had been experimenting with zeppelins, starting with bombing coastal towns and finally hitting London in May 1915. Then, in May 1917, the first airplanes began dropping bombs over Britain. The airplane, which until then had been a toy of the rich, revealed itself to be a new and deadly weapon that changed war even more than the submarine. The bombers terrified the British public, which had until then successfully relied on the channel for protection. The people of Halifax, who had already learned that fast technological changes could greatly shorten the distance between Europe and North America, believed that it was only a matter of time before a German bomber would cross the Atlantic. Blackout conditions were in effect.

Whispers of German sabotage spread up and down the waterfronts along the Eastern Seaboard. People told stories of German sympathizers in the United States injecting army horses with glanders, an infectious disease that could kill a horse within a week. Other horses arrived too weak to walk because their food had been contaminated with anthrax. Over the previous three years, American papers had reported dozens of accidental explosions that had eaten through millions of dollars' worth of arms destined for Europe. As early as January 1915, the German ambassador to America received orders from the German undersecretary to find ways to disrupt shipping, particularly to Canada. A month later, a German officer named Werner Horn set a bag of dynamite on the Vanceboro Bridge and lit the fuse. Although it was just a short truss bridge connecting the wilds of Maine to the wilds of New Brunswick, the Vanceboro Bridge provided an important shortcut for shipments linking the factories of Montreal and Toronto to St. John and Halifax. Washington's refusal to extradite Horn made the Canadians furious—they were calling for the death penalty—but when he was finally sentenced to jail, the incident faded from the papers.

A year later it was America's turn to worry when a powerful explosion, the brainchild of a German saboteur, went off at Black Tom Island, New Jersey, the last stop for munitions ships headed overseas.* In the wee hours

*Currently Liberty State Park, New Jersey.

of Sunday, July 30, 1916, fire ripped through cases of explosives, mortars, and shells until the whole warehouse burst into a crescendo of noise, light, and dust, which lit up the New York night skyline in purples, yellows, and greens. The blast rolled through the newly vulnerable streets of New York as menacingly as invading tanks, shattering window after window in the factories on the narrow streets of Lower Manhattan. As far away as mid-town, a water main burst and flooded the streets, while closer to Black Tom, bullets and shrapnel sliced their way through the Statue of Liberty for twenty long minutes.

Six months later the ambassador's men struck again. On January 11, 1917, the Canadian Car and Foundry Plant, a munitions plant in Kingsland, New Jersey, broke out in another fire that consumed the plant and its munitions. The U.S. Department of Justice acted, assigning domestic sabotage to the Bureau of Investigations, which, much to the relief of the public, determined that both explosions had been accidents. Despite the mistaken conclusions, port workers up and down the coast thought they knew an inside job when they saw it. Residents of Halifax, the last shipping point for the Canadian and American navies, the home of the Royal Navy in North America, filled with commercial and enlisted sailors from America, Japan, China, and the West Indies, kept their eyes trained on the sea and the sky for anything unfamiliar.

DARTMOUTH DEVELOPED IN MIRROR image to Halifax, their reflections literally joining somewhere in the middle of the harbor. While Halifax's downtown developed under the watch of Fort Citadel, Dartmouth grew up around the Shubenacadie Canal, an old Mi'kmaq water route that led from the harbor across the province to the Fundy shore. Encouraged by the success of the Erie Canal, the citizens began to envision a fast and easy shipping route to New Brunswick. Dartmouth needed the route more than Halifax because its shoreline was plagued with a series of shoals that made it more suitable for pleasure crafts and fishing than commercial wharves. From 1826 to 1831, Dartmouth watched with great anticipation as engineers joined the waterways through a series of contiguous locks, the last of which was located close to Dartmouth Cove. During the first winter, ice burst an upper lock, releasing a downstream tide that destroyed the half-million-dollar investment. Rumors that the canal would be restored emerged as fast as they faded, and businesses, churches, and houses continued to spring up parallel to the canal from Banook Lake to its mouth near the ferry terminal.

Without a decent shipping link for the next forty years, the population fluctuated and the city built as many churches as it did factories. Solutions such as a bridge across the Narrows were proposed but rejected until the nineteenth-century, when the railroad took over as the new transportation hope. Instead of building a link between Dartmouth and Windsor Junction, where the rail turned off to Halifax, Dartmouth opted for the bridge, which promptly collapsed. Unable to attract the businesses it needed to thrive, the city began to develop in other ways. Summerhouses with gingerbread accents and screened-in porches dotted the hills near the Mi'kmaq village at Turtle Grove. Lawyers, entrepreneurs, industrialists, and writers built genteel estates overlooking the harbor. Dartmouth, for all its attempts to industrialize, was starting to think of itself as a sporting town. And, naturally, sports in Dartmouth included water. A rowing club popped up on the north shore. Sailboats and canoes were overwintered in barns. By 1885, tennis was popular enough that St. George's Tennis and Quoit Club opened. In winter, skating and sleigh rides and the new indoor skating rink took over from swimming and rowing. But even as early as 1917, hockey was already the great Canadian obsession, and Dartmouth considered itself an integral player in the game's development. Although there was a debate as to the origin of hockey, with Brits claiming it as their game, the locals believed that it grew out of a Mi'kmaq ball and stick game played on ice. With British soldiers on one side of the harbor and Mi'kmaqs on the other, there was probably some truth to both stories. Still, local players refined the game, replacing the erratic hurley ball with a round slice of wood they called a puck. But the real change came in 1861 when players asked a local rivet-maker to design a better skate. Block skates were awkward contraptions made from iron blades bolted to wood that skaters strapped loosely onto boots. They often fell off and were hard to stop. Starr Manufacturing developed a blade that clamped onto boots and stayed there. It was also curved slightly at the front, giving the skater more control and the ability to stop sharp. The Starr Acme skate became an international favorite, selling in the millions, and, much to the dismay of the citizens of Dartmouth, the skate became known around the world as the Halifax skate.

Two cities on either side of the same body of water made for a natural rivalry. For Dartmouth, which was struggling to make the transition from summerhouses to subdivisions, the rivalry was particularly intense. An 1896 item in the Dartmouth paper reported on the competition. "About ten years ago the Chebucto team organized. They were mere boys gathered together on occasion to play the Halifax Wanderers. From that day to this, a

Dartmouth team had been defeated only once by a City team." Perhaps the most telling part of the rivalry in this editorial was not the hockey but the reference to Halifax as the City. Capital *C*.

Without a cheap route to Halifax's markets or the railyards, Dartmouth's chocolate-maker, rope-maker, rivet manufacturer, and sugar refinery found themselves spending on shipping any savings they made on land and labor. Instead of infusing the city with life, water was drowning Dartmouth. Until a permanent ferry and the railway turned things around in 1896, water made Dartmouth a difficult place to get to and an easy place to leave.

When the rail link was built, businesses finally began to prosper. Starting at the old Park School atop the Dartmouth Common overlooking the ferry, Windmill Road ran north past Crathorne's Mill, the new French Cable Company offices and wharf, and Oland's Brewery to the Cordage Company. Graceful Cape Cod houses were crowded out by cheaper saltboxes. White post-and-rail fences and delicate wild-rose hedges were replaced by row houses built straight onto the road. Near the northern end of Windmill Road, new streets sprouted off to the sides, encroaching upon the ancient Indian community at Turtle Grove, which was slowing being forced out. The city's first car dealership had opened, and fifteen men applied for taxi licenses. Cars, which had been banned from the road just eight years before, now careened around the horses, carts, and wagons in the streets. Sidewalks were the city's new priority, as well as schools. By the time war broke out, more families were finally moving into than moving out of Dartmouth.

BY 1917, THE REALITIES of the Great War—the horrible conditions, enormous losses, incompetent leaders—overshadowed petty rivalries everywhere, shattering the very notion of tradition and history. Men who had marched off to war with optimism and idealism returned home destroyed by their own illusions. They were not meeting their enemy face-to-face on the field but throwing anonymous grenades from vermin-infested trenches. After experimenting with other gases, the Germans perfected mustard gas earlier that year. It produced horrific results—blisters, bleeding, and extreme pain as soldiers tried to breathe with swollen, cankerous bronchial passages and lungs. Afflicted soldiers took up to a month to die excruciatingly painful deaths, as much of their viscera liquefied. The war, men quickly learned, was neither romantic nor particularly well run. The very machinery had changed—the shells, the torpedoes, machine guns that shot six hundred rounds a minute—were designed not to kill a single man but to rip and shred and obliterate. It was not uncommon for tens of thousands of men to die in one clash. At Vimy Ridge, the battle in which Canada declared itself a nation by recapturing a piece of the Western Front from Germany, more than seventeen thousand troops died. At Passchendaele, Canada took over from British, New Zealand, and Australian troops who had been fighting for four months and who had already lost one hundred thousand men. Within a month Canadian soldiers had captured the town and gained access to the German submarine base, adding fifteen thousand more dead. France had lost in excess of a million men; Germany too. In Russia, which lost closer to two million men, the revolution put King George V's first cousin Czar Nicholas under house arrest—he too would soon be dead—and newspapers across the world printed the Bolsheviks' startling political pronouncements on their front pages.

Not only were borders being reexamined, cut up, and rearranged, but the war was ripping into every aspect of culture. Sexuality and Freud were oozing into everyday conversation. People such as Virginia Woolf and James Joyce poured out paragraphs of broken narratives that flooded the pages with a new self-consciousness. Picasso's *Les Demoiselles D'Avignon,* which had shocked people a decade earlier with its fractured picture plane, looked conventional compared to Marcel Duchamp's dadaism, which turned the art world upside down with an inverted urinal. In Italy, the futurists produced works enthralled with speed, machinery, and warfare. Even everyday objects gleamed like machines as the handcrafted sensuality of art nouveau gave way to the broken lines of factory-produced art deco.

Halifax was suspicious of change. Parlors were still cluttered with Victorian lace, heavy furniture, picture wires, fringes, and wallpaper, although the waterfront looked different. Steel destroyers docked next to schooners along long wooden wharves stuffed with supplies, coal, and grain. Modern shipbuilding facilities were in place, thanks to two million federal dollars. Even the Royal Navy and its attitude were back training thousands of sailors and shipping out even more soldiers. The population could not have been happier to see the navy's trucks and touring cars rattle over the cobblestone streets. The whole place smelled like salt, tar, fish, and war. Peace was nowhere to be seen and, once again, Halifax was thriving.

*Chapter One*

# Wednesday

A T A FEW MINUTES past four on the afternoon of
Wednesday, December 5, 1917, a pilot boat outside
Halifax Harbor swung away from an outgoing
steamer and pulled alongside the *Mont Blanc*. Daylight was already failing
and Francis Mackey* knew that he would not have time to pilot the *Mont
Blanc* down to the Bedford Basin that night. As the smaller boat sidled
alongside, Mackey reached across the water, gripped the rope ladder, and
pulled himself up. That gap, that short space of sea between leaving one
ship and standing on the other, was the most dangerous part of his job.
Ropes broke, and when they did pilots such as Mackey were never seen
again. He clasped the ladder tightly as he scrambled up the side of the hull
and pulled himself onto the deck, where Captain Aimé Le Médec met him.
Although Le Médec was only thirty-nine, his sixteen years at sea read like a
map of red wrinkles. Mackey was the same. At forty-five, he had already
spent twenty-four of his years on the water.

Mackey told the captain that he wanted to sail to the examination boat
near McNab's lighthouse before he decided whether or not to anchor for
the night, but Le Médec had difficulty understanding his rapid speech. Although he had studied English for his captain's exam eleven years before, Le
Médec was self-conscious about speaking it; he was badly out of practice.

*Pronounced MAC-kee, not mac-KEE.

"I don't speak very good English," he told Mackey as they walked across the deck.

When they reached the bridge, the two men took their places on either side of the whistle cord. Alphonse Serre stood at the wheel. Second Lieutenant Joseph Leveque sat to their right, monitoring the telegraph station, ready to transmit orders to the engine room. When Mackey shouted out an order, the captain translated it into French, although the crew understood port, starboard, astern, and all the regular directions in English, just as Mackey understood *à la droite* to mean to the right. To prevent confusion Mackey supplemented his orders with hand signals, indicating that he wanted the ship to drop anchor south of the lighthouse. As the *Mont Blanc* slipped across the mouth of the harbor in the sunset, Mackey glanced at the bow where canvas straps bound nearly five hundred iron barrels to the deck.

"We are all explosives," Le Médec explained as they waited for the examination officer to board. With his poor English it almost sounded like an apology.

Examining Officer Terrence Freeman watched the *Mont Blanc* approach from the deck of the examination boat. He noticed her color first.

"War-color gray," he said to himself. Even the words sounded depressing. When she finally anchored, he sailed to her side in a lighter and climbed aboard. Once on deck, he was relieved to see Mackey because the captain's English was limited. Freeman asked to see the manifest. Le Médec handed him the papers. As Freeman scanned the lading list, he realized that he had never seen a cargo like this one. Despite the increase in wartime traffic, Halifax rarely received ships carrying high explosives. As far as Freeman knew, the *Mont Blanc* was the first one scheduled to sail all the way to the Basin. As he read further down the list, Freeman reached the benzol and monochlorobenzol, both petroleum products, which carried their own dangers. The combination struck Freeman as dangerous. "I knew it could do some damage all right." But since the war's outset, higher risks were more acceptable. Twenty minutes later, Freeman finished signing off and handed the manifest back to Le Médec, but he addressed his comments to Mackey.

"She can't go in until morning."

Although there was still some sun left in the sky, the gates were closed. He was referring to the two antisubmarine nets that were installed across the mouth of the harbor and on either side of George's Island. The chief examining officer changed their schedule every day, opening and closing the gates intermittently to allow scheduled ships in and out while preventing

German U-boats from slipping into the outer harbor. Both gates closed for the night at sundown and although it was only 4:30 p.m.—still thirty-six minutes before the official sundown—the sun had already slipped behind the hills. Underneath the cold water between Point Pleasant Park and Mc-Nab's Island, a diagonal mesh gate anchored to the harbor floor by three-ton concrete weights slammed shut for the night, sending a shiver down the buoys that marked its presence. The *Mont Blanc* would have to spend the night outside the gates. Freeman gave them their instructions before returning to the examination station.

"Stay at the anchorage until morning and then proceed up the harbor at the usual time if you do not hear from me."

Although Mackey's house was just across the water in Herring Cove, the pilot decided to spend the night on board. Downstairs in the cabin, Le Médec introduced him to First Officer Jean Glotin, who spoke fluent English, and who told him about their arrival in New York on November 9. The authorities had directed them away from their regular berth and instructed the *Mont Blanc* to dock at Gravesend Bay in Brooklyn. They knew something was up when the Board of Underwriters provided the ships' carpenters with a plan to line every inch of the holds with wood and ordered them to use copper nails. Copper nails were used to prevent accidental ignition of a flammable cargo because they did not spark when struck. As soon as the stevedores finished the holds, which were designed to be hermetically sealed when closed, police officers arrived and surrounded the ship, and soon barrels, kegs, and cases began arriving by lighter from across the bay. These were no ordinary munitions. These were high explosives. Never mind the U-boats: All that it required to send them to their death was a heavy storm or a sudden load shift. To a sailor who spent his life surrounded by water, accidental death meant drowning; fire was neither his specialty nor his fate. Yet in New York the crew watched with dread as stevedores wearing canvas slippers loaded the cargo into the holds below deck.

On Friday, November 30, while the stevedores tied down the last of the benzol, Le Médec and an interpreter returned to the British Admiralty Office in search of convoy orders. Inside the office, he handed the papers to Commander Coates, who opened the heavy registration book to the page where Le Médec had signed in. He compared the new papers to the original information.

"Is this the speed of your ship?" Coates asked, referring to the new documents.

Le Médec had originally put down eight knots as their average speed, but

The only known photograph of the *Mont Blanc*

when he returned to the ship, he reconsidered after checking the log from Bordeaux. It was his first voyage and he was still getting used to the *Mont Blanc*. At 3,121 tons, she was a heavier weight and class than his two previous vessels. She was also older, with a résumé that included sixteen years at sea as a commercial freighter. Her steel hull was 320 feet long, 44 feet 8 inches wide—a big ship—but she was slow.

"No, I don't think I will be able to maintain the speed of eight and a half."

"Can you maintain two hundred miles a day?"

"In very fine weather I probably would be able to."

"I will have to see about that." Coates asked them to wait and stepped briefly into his superior's office before returning. "You will proceed to Halifax for convoy."

"Supposing I cannot make this speed?"

"The convoy officer at Halifax will furnish you with a route in a sealed envelope, which you are not to open unless you lose the convoy. This envelope will contain the route if you lose the convoy and have to go alone."

Le Médec did not want to make the voyage unescorted. The German U-boats were more adept at finding and attacking a single ship crossing the Atlantic than a well-armed convoy. Plus this was his first time carrying high explosives and he knew almost nothing about them. He did not know that picric acid was the primary ingredient of the shells exploding across Europe or that dry picric acid was extremely sensitive to shock. All he knew was what someone told him about TNT—take care not to strike the wharf too hard or the whole ship could go up. And even then he did not know whether or not that was true. Certainly, no official from the Admiralty or the owners, the French Line, had advised him how to handle the cargo. What Le Médec did know was that he did not want to cross the Atlantic without a destroyer to defend him. He returned to the *Mont Blanc* as the stevedores finished strapping the barrels to the deck. On December 1 at 11 p.m., the *Mont Blanc* slipped out of New York harbor in the dark. Five days later they made Halifax. The weather had been lousy, the ship slow.

As Glotin talked, Mackey took out a cigar and began to light it.

"You can smoke in here but not outside," Le Médec warned him, adding that cigarettes, lit or unlit, were banned from the deck. Matches too. He told Mackey that there was no alcohol on board either, although the store's list of supplies revealed that they had bought thirty dozen bottles of vermouth in New York. Perhaps the Frenchman did not consider fortified wine to be alcohol, or maybe it was for medicinal purposes—wormwood, the principal ingredient in vermouth, was used as a tonic against intestinal worms.

In peacetime a ship carrying such a dangerous cargo would have flown a red flag as a warning to other ships and would have been instructed to dock in the outer harbor. The *Mont Blanc* would not have been allowed as far as the Basin, but since Canada had entered the war with Britain in 1914, the harbor rules had changed and the British Admiralty had taken charge of all

The harbor at Halifax

naval traffic. The red flag, or the red burgee, as sailors called it, was reclassified as optional during wartime, and for the *Mont Blanc* to fly it on the other side of the submarine nets where German U-boats patrolled the coastal waters would be unnecessarily risky. "It would be suicidal—giving information to enemy agents." The men settled in for the night.

LOCKED ON THE INSIDE of the gates, in the southwest corner of the Bedford Basin, Captain Haakon From paced back and forth on the bridge of the *Imo* as the sun sank behind the hills. The *Imo* was supposed to have been en route to New York already, but the coal supplier had arrived two hours late and they were still loading. Pilot William Hayes, who was supposed to sail the *Imo* out of harbor at 3:00 p.m., confirmed what the captain already suspected: The gates were closed. Hayes told him that he was going home for the night but that he would be back early in the morning. Captain From let him go. There was nothing he could do about submarine nets.

Another night in port was hard on the men. The law that sequestered neutral crews—those on hospital and supply ships such as the *Imo*—was meant to prevent spies from influencing them while in port, because neutral ships had access not only to the Allies' but to the Axis's ports. The Commission for Relief in Belgium was founded in 1917 after the British implemented an effective naval blockade against the Germans, which inadvertently cut off Belgium and Northern France from their food supply. The German army, which could barely feed itself, refused to help the civilians. Millions of people were starving. Herbert Hoover, then a mining consul-

The antisubmarine nets running between Point Pleasant Park and McNab's Island
circa World War I

tant who helped stranded Americans return home after the war broke out in Europe, was appointed the commissioner for relief in Belgium and negotiated with both the Germans and British to allow their neutral ships past the blockades. Raising over $1 billion from around the world, the private charity managed to deliver just enough food to keep the population alive, but after the Germans announced unrestricted submarine warfare in 1917, the situation worsened again when Germans began seizing the Belgian Relief shipments. For the *Imo*, the result was a couple dozen men who never knew if their cargo would reach the Belgians or the Germans and who were stuck onboard ship for months on end. Only the captain could go ashore, but even he was only allowed to visit the Customs Office. Docking next to a busy port full of seafront bars, women, and rum made the ship even more claustrophobic. At least the *Imo* was allowed alcohol onboard. On their last crossing out of New York, Captain From had signed out seventy-one bottles of whiskey, wine, claret, gin, and liqueur. Officially, the liquor was meant for visitors, but as a neutral ship the *Imo* was not allowed visitors aside from naval officers. Captain From ordered the crew to be ready to lift anchor in the morning and retired to his cabin, where his dog greeted him.

AS WEDNESDAY'S FINAL RAYS dipped behind Citadel Hill and shadows lengthened across the city, Captain From's agent, George Smith, who was still working in his Pickford & Black office, looked up and saw William Hayes step out of the tug. That meant the *Imo* had not sailed. Hayes stuck his head in the office as he walked by.

"I'll be down at 7:30."

Smith put in an order for a tug in the morning.

At the mouth of the harbor near the lighthouse, Terrence Freeman signaled the chief examining officer, Frederick Wyatt, that the *Mont Blanc* had arrived and that it was carrying explosives. Not receiving any special instructions, he thought no more about it.

As night settled over the water, residents across the city pulled blackout blinds over their windows and closed the curtains before turning on the lights. In the South End, professionals, merchants, and respectable middle-class families sat down to supper in their dining rooms while their servants ate in cramped back kitchens. Students who lived near Dalhousie campus sat in long rows at tables in their dormitories. Downtown, Christmas trees were starting to appear in windows, and the store displays and newspapers were packed with toys and gifts. Along Albermarle, which the city had optimistically renamed Market Street, streetwalkers in gaudy clothes slipped into damp doorways of the blind pigs* and bawdy houses that polluted the neighborhood. Soldiers and sailors began arriving in cabs and by foot, their boots springing up the stairs to hidden dance halls, poolrooms, and brothels. Further north in Richmond Hill, a working-class neighborhood overlooking the Narrows, twenty-year-old Charles Duggan finished ferrying the last workers to Dartmouth from the dockyards and tied up the *Grace Darling,* a long low wooden trawler that looked something like an elongated Cape Anne with a sharp bow and a flat stern. Six square windows on either side emphasized its oversized cabin where the passengers sat. The *Grace Darling* was the latest addition to the family ferry business—their first motorized ferry—a sign that the Duggan family was prospering.

Charles Duggan climbed the steep block to Campbell Road in the dark and entered the house on the corner, 127 Campbell Road, a two-story, semiattached saltbox built into the hill. From the rear windows, the family could see across the Narrows to Tuft's Cove where the ferry docked on the Dartmouth shore. Inside, Charles's wife, Theresa, whom everyone called Reta, was playing with their four-month-old son Warren. His parents, Susie and Charles Sr., lived there as well, along with Charles's younger brother and sister, Vincent and Evelyn. They were a close family, and even the older siblings who had married and left home lived nearby with their own families. Charles Sr. and Susie, who was born in Ireland, married in 1880. Charlie had some success as a fisherman. "They were a two-boat family." Alma Duggan and her husband Patrick Gallaway lived next door in the other half of the row house. The eldest Duggan, Billy, had finally moved back to Halifax from Dartmouth and had taken over the old family apartment at 29 Campbell Road, just two blocks south.†

Billy was famous in Halifax and Dartmouth. Despite numerous hockey teams and attempts to form professional leagues, hockey was not the cities' most popular sport. That title was reserved for rowing. Canada's first recur-

---

*According to wordorigins.org, blind pigs got their name from the practice among American taverns, which were prohibited from selling drinks by the glass, of supplying their customers with a complimentary drink if they bought a ticket to see exotic animal exhibits. Policemen, many of whom attended while off-duty, turned a blind eye.

†When Campbell Road became Barrington Street these addresses changed (to 1329 and 1229 Barrington, respectively).

ring competition, the annual Halifax Harbor Championship, was inaugurated in 1858, and it attracted not only local rowers from both sides of the harbor but rowers from across the country. In 1883, rowing provided Canada with its first world champion in sports, Ned Hanlon, who popularized the sliding seat. Before Hanlon, rowers had been unable to find a stable method to push off their legs to reset the oars. There were experiments with ball bearings, which burst into flames, and greasing rower's pants with lard, which was as messy as it was unreliable. Others had tried the sliding seat, but Hanlon took to it, practicing in Lake Ontario every day until he was convinced of its superiority. Billy Duggan, since his start in 1900, had won five major championships and hundreds of medals and ribbons. His biggest rival appeared near the end of Billy's rowing career. The Billy Duggan–John O'Neill rivalry was a favorite in Halifax-Dartmouth. Their most famous race was in 1904, a year after O'Neill beat Billy in the Natal Day harbor races. O'Neill was favored to win again in 1905, but Billy kept him waiting in his scull for twenty minutes. It was a cold day, overcast, and O'Neill was cranky and complained that Billy was keeping him waiting on purpose to stiffen his muscles. The crowd did not care. O'Neill might have been the reigning champion, but Billy was the local favorite, especially in Richmond, and he did not disappoint. He was ahead from the start, and by the time he passed the finish line eight thousand people were on their feet screaming and waving. The loss cost O'Neill his place at the Canadian championship.

Later that summer Billy traveled to Boston, where the *Boston Globe* featured his photo under the headline "The Halifax Sculler," noting that he was not the favorite. That was reserved for a hometown boy from the Boston Amateur Athletics club, but Billy's long, sure stroke rowed him "to a standstill." The win made Billy even more famous in Halifax. He traveled throughout New England and Canada, but in the end it was O'Neill who won the North American Championship in 1908. The two men raced once more that year. Over ten thousand spectators turned out to watch Billy lose by less than a foot. It was not surprising. Billy did not have a coach and he did not train. What he did have was a wife and six children to support. He had met Lottie Sawlor at a dance at the Armouries. Her brothers, Owen, Albert, and Percy Sawlor, were all popular rowers who founded the first rowing club in Dartmouth—North Star. Lottie and Billy married on December 5, 1903. If people wanted to see Billy row after his retirement, all they had to do was walk down to the foot of Stairs or

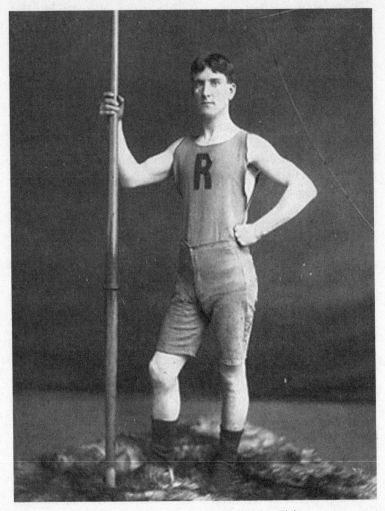

Billy Duggan in his uniform for the Resolute Club

Hanover Street and ring the bell. The champion himself would row them across the harbor.

Billy would have been arriving home from patrol on a minesweeper outside the harbor. He had just enlisted in October. His daughters Lydia, Irene, Bessie, and Helena probably helped out with the supper because

Lottie had to take care of the boys, baby Gordon* and five-year-old Kenny. Billy's family had been haunted by illness. Two other daughters had died earlier that year from tuberculosis. The elder girl was a teenager who worked in the Moirs' Chocolate Factory. The second, Alma, named after Billy's sister, was barely two years old when she died that spring. And now Lottie had developed a terrible racking cough that she could not shake. Elsewhere in Richmond, two other Duggan sisters, Ellen and Sarah, prepared supper—Sarah at the northern end close to Africville, a black village on the other side of the hill overlooking the Basin; Ellen in her house on North Street, closer to downtown and to respectability. There were Duggan families all over Richmond. Everyone knew them—at least anyone who took the ferry, and that was pretty nearly everyone. Charles took his place at the table. As with many Richmond families, Wednesday's supper would be the Duggans' last.

*The sex of baby Duggan remains unclear. He was listed as a boy named Gordon by the Halifax Relief Commission, but Helena later claimed the baby was a girl.

*Chapter Two*

# December 6, 1917

*Winter Morning*

THURSDAY, DECEMBER 6, 1917, began like any other clear winter day in Halifax. A light haze rose off the Narrows and disappeared into cold blue. The northern light offered no soothing tones, no coat of sticky yellow veneer to soften its landscape. Quite the opposite. White light stripped away the luxury of finishing layers, scrubbing everything raw. Shadows were crisp, full of blues and purples that outlined the world with a stark clarity. Three days before, the winter's first sleet storm had downed telegraph lines along the Nova Scotia–New Brunswick border, but the sun quickly melted whatever snow was left. Abrupt changes in temperature were nothing unusual. Like everything in Halifax, it all depended on the mood of the North Atlantic and the offshore weather patterns that blustered around her gray-green waters. The weather could change for the better or worse at any moment and with as little warning.

The Thursday morning papers were filled with news of the war. The *Daily Echo*'s headline ran "Enemy Massing Guns and Men on the Asiago Front for a Renewal of Heavy Offensive," while the *Herald*'s bold type read "Germans Start New Offensive to Take Venice." Although the names sounded exotic and far off, the people of Halifax paid close attention. Sitting on the edge of the North American continent, a base for the British, a stopover for the Americans, and overflowing with international war supplies, they worried that they would be the first place the Germans attacked.

The Pickford & Black tug carrying William Hayes onboard pulled up alongside the *Imo* just after 7:30 a.m. Then the tug turned slightly, heading her nose toward the southwest corner of the Basin where the neutrals docked. Slightly past the entrance to the Narrows, a curtain of haze hung from both shores, filtering the view of the outer harbor and the rising sun. The surrounding hills were still unpopulated enough to take on the dark-green cast of the evergreen trees, despite the smattering of summerhouses, cottages, and the Africville homes. Andrew Johansen, the captain's steward, noticed the approaching tug and walked down the alleyway that cut across the bridge deck. He knocked before opening Captain From's door.

"The pilot is coming."

Captain From picked up his coat and passed into the alley, leaving the steward to deal with his dirty washbowl, dog, and unmade bed.

OUTSIDE THE HARBOR, the *Mont Blanc* was already under sail, traveling about twenty minutes behind an American tramp steamer, the *SS Clara*.* She had arrived, picked up a pilot, and cleared examination all before 7:00 a.m., and now Le Médec and Mackey stood on either side of the whistle cord on the bridge, watching her green stern pass through the antisubmarine gates and into the outer harbor. Alphonse Serre, the wheelsman, stood behind them listening for orders through the open window that separated the pilothouse from the bridge. He glanced at the landscape outside the two portholes on either side of the wheel. Entering a harbor stream, they sailed not by compasses or charts but by landmarks, using buoys, hills, chimneys, and wharves as reference points. When they approached the gates, the channel narrowed and Mackey ordered down the speed. The shipping lanes were clear, except for a British destroyer anchored diagonally across the eastern channel and the ferries slipping out of their wharves, but he wanted to go in slowly.

*John Griffith Armstrong first identified the SS *Clara* in his 2002 book *The Halifax Explosion and the Canadian Navy*. I see no reason not to accept this identification and have referred to the *Clara* throughout as the green American tramp steamer mentioned in the trials.

"Half-speed."

"*Demi-vitesse*," Le Médec repeated to Leveque, who tapped out the order on the telegraph.

Downstairs in the machine room, the telegraph tinkled above the hum of the engines. Louis Brun received it and read it back through the speaking tube to Leveque.

"*Demi-vitesse*," Brun confirmed.

"*Bien*," Leveque replied.

Brun picked up a piece of chalk and recorded the order on the wall chart as the *Mont Blanc* sailed through the nets into the outer harbor.


ON BEDFORD ROW, the fifteen-year-old clerk, Edward Beazley, stood in front of the board at the pilotage office. The *Imo* was still listed with a Wednesday 3:00 p.m. exit time, although Hayes had come by at the end of the day to tell him that he would take her out Thursday morning. Beazley dealt mainly with agents, matching pilots to ships and keeping track of their hours. If a ship was going out, he liked to match her up with the same pilot who brought her in. If he could not get the same pilot, he would assign whoever was available, tracking who piloted what on the pilots' cards and on the big chalk chart on the wall. The pilots pooled their money, each taking home an equal share. Since the start of the war, five pilots had left Halifax, leaving the remaining fourteen pilots to work overtime. Mackey had pulled in as much as a thousand dollars in a single month, although most months averaged $400–$500, still an enviable salary in what had been a cash-strapped harbor.

The pilots had the best jobs in port, well-paid, respected, switching from ship to ship, but they earned their money. Many people who lived in the streets overlooking the water did not even know that they existed, assuming that captains brought ships in and out of port, but in Halifax, as in most ports, the law required a local pilot to helm any ship over a certain tonnage while in harbor. Pilots navigated a lot more than traffic. It was tricky work to come between a captain and his crew, particularly when they did not speak the same language. Pilots had to know the mechanics of different ships of different classes, even different command styles—not everyone steered the same way. Most ships in an English port used English command regardless of the crew's native language, meaning that if the pilot called starboard, the helm was turned port and the ship would turn starboard. In the Norwegian and American system, they had recently changed to the terms right and left—right being starboard and left being port. Communication was meant to be fluid, flowing easily between pilot, captain, and crew, as well as between ship and shore, where men scheduled incoming and outgoing vessels. On the water, men such as Francis Mackey and William Hayes saw beyond the surface. They knew its depths, its shoals, its currents, and whether the tide was working for or against the ship. They knew how fast the water ran and where it was safe and where the rocks could rip open a hull like a strawberry. The only thing they could not see through was fog, and in Halifax, there was plenty of fog. The waters outside the harbor, just minutes away, could easily turn to fog, rain, or drizzle while the city stayed bathed in sunlight. Even a simple pickup rendezvous could be dangerous if it was foggy. Despite whistles, flags, and shouting, enormous ships could stay hidden behind the gray curtain until they suddenly loomed above the pilot boat like a skyscraper. And so, like police officers and firemen who trusted one another to ensure their safety, the pilots banded together. Despite the eightfold increase in traffic, the number of pilots remained steady. Every day Halifax's fourteen pilots and eight apprentices jumped from ship to ship, hanging on to those rope ladders as if they were life itself. If the public did not recognize their work, so much the better: It meant they were doing their job. The Canadian Navy, not even ten years old, tried to break their stranglehold by introducing new men trained specifically to navigate Halifax, but the pilots fought them off with a sneer. They had spent their whole lives sailing these waters. They had no time for prairie sailors. What captain worth his stripes would trust his crew and his vessel to a man who had learned the sea at a desk?

On May 4, 1917, when Chief Examining Officer Wyatt requested that pilots inform his office of outgoing single ships, the pilots complained that it took too long to get him on the phone and the pilotage authority instructed Beazley to take care of it. He was supposed to keep the chief examining officer informed when a ship was sailing out, but Beazley did not like calling over to the office on the *Niobe,* a former cruiser and headquarters for the Canadian Navy. Chief Examining Officer Wyatt and his assistant Roland Iceton both paid attention and wrote down the names when he called, asking him to repeat the names once or twice when they could not keep up— Beazley spoke fast—but whenever clerks answered the phone, they sat in sullen silence until he finished rattling off his list. On a busy day he gave them fifteen or sixteen ships. Surely they could not write as fast as he talked, and by July he had the impression that not only were they failing to record the names and times, they were making fun of him. He felt a little hurt.

They had no call to treat him like that. Beazley picked up the eraser and wiped the *Imo* from the wall. A new day required a new chart.

Bjarne Birkland, the *Imo*'s third mate, was trying to live up to Beazley's confident swipe by organizing a group of men to hoist the anchor. Luckily, the captain had dropped only one anchor when they berthed; the section designated for neutrals was not crowded and it did not matter if they swung a bit astern. As they heaved up the chain, the anchor lifted out of the water and sent a salty stream back down over the hull before it clanked into place below the hawser pipe. Once they made open water, they would draw it up the rest of the way. Second Mate Peter B'Jonnas chanced to look up from the growing pile of chains just as Hayes climbed over the side and walked up to the bridge where the captain was waiting for him.

By 8:10 a.m. the *Imo* was gliding toward Tuft's Cove. Her decks were empty. Most of the crew were below deck eating breakfast. Wheelsman John Johansen, who had been helping with the anchor, was back at the wheel, zigzagging the ship around the merchant cruisers waiting to depart overseas. Every few seconds he caught a glimpse of Captain Hakron From pacing back and forth on deck beside the pilot. Captain From was a terse man—he said few words to the officers and even fewer to the crew—but he was nowhere near the worst of captains. He did not mistreat the crew, as some did. Still there were rumors. There was talk that Captain From had thrown a lawyer through the door of his cabin when the lawyer dared to board and serve him papers that claimed he had skipped out on a service bill. In August, nine men had deserted when they picked up a shipment of Manitoba wheat in New York. Someone had told Johansen the captain did not always pay, but Johansen did not give the matter much thought. As long as he was paid on time, it was of no concern to him.

As they approached the entrance to the Narrows, just past Pier 9, the *SS Clara* approached the *Imo* on the port side close to midchannel. Hayes grabbed the whistle and blasted it once. The *Clara*'s pilot, Edward Renner, answered with two. Hayes understood. The *Clara* did not want to cross port to port, as regulations demanded. Technically it was illegal, but entering the Narrows was tricky—an outgoing ship had to aim across the entrance to round the neck, then make a hairpin turn back and sail down the Halifax side. To make regulation, Hayes had to either change his course early or stop to let the *Clara* pass. The *Imo* was already sailing a day late so he reached out and yanked twice on the whistle cord.

Renner was pleased. "One meant he wanted to come starboard, I answered with two and he answered with two meaning he would go port; we passed starboard to starboard." He knew that she was just about to enter a thick haze, and he wanted to warn the pilot that the *Mont Blanc* was hidden in the mist behind him. Although he was not sure who was working the *Imo,* Renner cupped his rough hands over his mouth and called up toward the *Imo*'s open bridge.

"Keep a good lookout. There is a ship coming astern."

A man leaned over the bridge rail and shouted back. "What did you say?"

William Hayes, Renner thought, recognizing his voice. He leaned over and picked up the megaphone. "A ship is following right behind me."

Hayes waved in acknowledgment.

"Steady on a little port," Hayes called.

Johansen looked past the *Clara* and saw a tug carrying two scows starting to cross the Narrows. He turned the wheel and the *Imo* moved closer to the Dartmouth shore. Although mostly everyone spoke Norwegian, the ship was piloted in English by English command, as was Captain From's habit with a mixed crew. Johansen was familiar with all the systems. Only twenty-four, he had already been at sea for ten years. He spoke English well, having trained with a U.S. engineering unit, although Captain From probably hired him because they shared the same hometown, Sandefjord, Norway. The thirty-nine-man crew were nearly all Norwegian, although there were a few Swedes, Danes, and Dutch, too. Like many of the men from Sandefjord, Johansen had started on whaling ships and graduated to commercial steamers. When the war broke out, he was sailing with the American Navy.

Farther down the harbor on the Halifax side, the 229-ton tug, the *Stella Maris,* rounded the southern tip of the dry dock, pulling two heavily loaded scows laden with stone pieces headed for the Bedford Basin. On the bridge, Captain Horatio Brannen stood talking with his second mate William Nickerson and his son, first mate Walter Brannen. Nickerson was acting as boatswain. He had tied the scows, or barges, tightly to the tug and to each other so that Walter, who was on the wheel, could make a neat turn into the harbor from the dock. As soon as they straightened out, Captain Brannen ordered them released, and Nickerson climbed down to loosen them. A former English wooden gunboat, the *Stella Maris* was 120 feet long. Her two scows were 20–30 feet each, and when Nickerson loosened the ropes between them, that added another 150 feet, making her 415 feet in total— with such a long haul as theirs, they had to move slowly and carefully. They were taking their normal route, traveling a sluggish four knots toward the Basin and keeping to the Halifax shore before swinging her nose east just north of the sugar refinery, where they would cross to Dartmouth. They had not yet noticed the *Imo* coming out.


THE *MONT BLANC* WAS somewhere past Sandy Bottom near the foot of Morris Street in Halifax when Mackey ordered the engines stopped to allow the passenger ferries to cross. Their upper decks were crowded with students, office workers, and laborers taking in a bit of sun before the workday began. The Halifax-bound ferry crossed closest to the *Mont Blanc,* but it was the Dartmouth ferry that Mackey watched. Her wharf was more southerly and easterly, and if he did not take care, she could enter his path on her way back. There were no official rules about the ferries or other local boats aside from the "Rules of the Road," but the pilots tried to respect the ferry schedule, even though the ferries were often more agile than the steamers the pilots were navigating. Mackey waited until the Dartmouth ferry bumped against her wharf to ensure that he could get above her line before they pulled out.

"Full speed," he called out, and the *Mont Blanc*'s engines vibrated back to life, but as soon as they cleared the docks, he ordered the engines back to half. Glotin, who had been on the lower deck supervising the boatswain's work, returned to the bridge as the *Mont Blanc* passed North Street. He and Mackey had spent much of the last night talking. Mackey pointed out the great gray hulk moored off the navy docks over their port side. She was a burly old British cruiser with three massive stacks, two masts, and a mass of ropes, cables, guns, and lifeboats percolating out of her decks. She would be the *Mont Blanc*'s convoy escort to France.

"The *Highflyer,*" Mackey told him. "She is a celebrated ship. She sank the *Kaiser von der Grosse.*" Glotin knew the story. In 1897, the *Kaiser Wilhelm der Grosse* was the first of only fourteen passenger liners built to accommodate a fourth stack. She was as powerful as she was luxurious, and on her first crossing she set speed records, but when the war started, she was retrofitted as an armed cruiser and sent off in search of British ships. She had already sunk two when the *Highflyer* set out in search of her. Somewhere off the Canary Islands the *Highflyer* tracked her four stacks into port, where she stopped to refuel and demanded that the liner surrender. When the German captain denied the request, the *Highflyer* turned her guns against the great converted liner and the four stacks sank low in the smoke until she disappeared underwater.*

Mackey ordered their ensign lowered in salute as they passed the *Highflyer,* and instructed the captain to port the wheel, shifting the bow slightly starboard to bring the *Mont Blanc* more in line with the shoreline. On the deck of the *Highflyer,* the signalman waited to see if her crew would dip her ensign in response to the French ship. She did. He waited until he could read the name on the passing vessel's stern. The *Mont Blanc,* he wrote in his report. It was 8:30 a.m.

As the *Mont Blanc* was approaching Black Rock buoy on the Dartmouth side and aiming for a new buoy that marked a shallow area known as the twenty-four-foot patch, Mackey ordered the engines to slow. They were entering the Narrows, and while there was no official rule, it was common practice for ships to proceed slowly. They hugged the Dartmouth shore, sailing well under the harbor's five-knot speed limit. Mackey scanned the water for other ships. He sighted the *Stella Maris* carrying a load of stone past Pier 9, but it was what was behind the hills that interested him. Two tawny-colored masts glinted in the morning sun above the hills. The masts were creeping toward the guard ship in the Basin, still almost a mile away, but it looked like she was heading out. Mackey kept his eyes on the masts.

The *Stella Maris* had moved 150 yards off the dock and was heading toward Dartmouth when Nickerson brought Captain Brannen's attention to the *Imo* entering the Narrows. At first they could not make out her color, but as she emerged from the haze, they made out the whole of her starboard side with BELGIAN RELIEF spelled out in block letters. Captain Brannen gave the steamer a quick study. She was big, which would make her a slow turner. She was light, too, floating high above her waterline with her propeller sitting up in the water, giving her little purchase for quick turns. There was not enough time for the Belgian to correct her course without cornering his scow and dumping their cargo.

"Haul her in closer to shore, there's a steamer coming down," Brannen told his son. The Belgian seemed to be coming at them at a pretty good clip, judging by the foam at her bow. He turned to Nickerson and scowled. "She is going as fast as any ship I ever saw in the harbor."

---

*Although Mackey could not have known it, the German captain had opened the seacocks and ordered the vessels scuttled rather than face defeat.

Walter Brannen rounded the wheel and turned the *Stella Maris* back toward the Halifax shore.

From the bridge, Hayes watched the tug turn. He saw no need for the *Imo* to change course if the *Stella Maris* was going to go around him.

"Port and steady," he ordered.

WHEN THE *IMO* FINALLY revealed herself by sailing into the Narrows, about three-quarters of a mile from the *Mont Blanc,* all Mackey had to see were her four masts. The *Imo.* He knew that Hayes was onboard because he, Hayes, and Captain From had shared a tug the previous afternoon, and From had complained that the coal ship was late. He surmised that they had not made the nets. Mackey had taken the *Imo* out once or twice before—she was an easy ship to sail—but he did not like the looks of the foam at her bow. "Quite a ripple." He blew a single blast to get Hayes's attention.

"Slow," he called out. Le Médec translated and Leveque sent the order down to the engine room. By now the *Mont Blanc* was well past the twenty-four-foot patch buoy, closer to the French Cable Wharf.

"*Lentement?*" the third engineer answered.

"*Bien.*"

IN THE SOUTH END of the city, few were aware of the events in the harbor. Morris Street, like many streets in the city, was filled with those trying to get to school or to work on time. Fourth-year English students Jean Lindsay and Claudine Noiles buttoned up their winter coats and stepped outside the Halifax Ladies College into the sun. "It was a beautiful, sunny, warm day, more like September than December." The girls' first class at Dalhousie University was at ten o'clock, but they had made plans to study in the library beforehand. With their arms wrapped tightly against their books, the two girls turned the corner onto Morris Street toward the library.

A few blocks west, on the corner of Robie, fourteen-year-old Everett Covey shuffled back and forth on the sidewalk waiting for his friend Ginger Fraser, who was late. The boys said a quick hello and then set off toward Morris Street School. As they passed the Victoria General Hospital, doctors, nurses, and attendants, including Assistant Pharmacist Bertha Archibald, were running up the front steps to take over the day shift. Archibald was prepared for a busy day because her boss, Dr. Charles Puttner, was acting superintendent while the chief was attending a convention in New England. Inside she called out hello to her friend nurse Charlotte Flick, and the two women stood around the high dispensary counter chatting. Down the hall in the scrub room, Dr. George Murphy stood underneath a skylight in a clean surgery gown, sudsing his hands in and out of the hot water and soap before wiggling his fingers into his heavy rubber gloves. On the other side of the wall, three nurses and the anesthesiologist prepared the OR, checking and rechecking supplies and equipment.

IN THE NORTH END, the streets were in the lull after men had reported for work at the railyard, the dockyard, the printing plant, and the foundry, and before the children had left for school. At Wellington Square, a unit from the British Empire Force, or BEF,* was already marching while other cadets made their way to their classrooms. The streets were lined with rows of wooden saltbox houses, some of which were divided into flats, others housing a single family. On the hills, the houses were more diverse, larger, and more spread out. Empty lots, chicken coops, a horse, or even a cow in a sideyard broke up the residential rhythm. Cars were becoming more common, but because it was market day, hay wagons filled the streets. Inside the houses, elementary-school students gathered their books and winter clothes, preparing to leave for school, although the school bells were anything but uniform. Catholics started at one time; Protestants another; boys at one time; girls at another. And girls like eight-year-old Helen Clark, a Protestant who went to a Catholic school, started at a different time altogether. Helen lived on Russell Street with her grandmother, where she was staying while her mother was in Boston. Her father, a druggist, lived in Kentville, seventy miles south of Halifax. She stood in front of the mirror adjusting the new red plaid bow that her mother had slipped inside her last letter from Boston.

DOWN OFF THE NO. 4 dock, Fred Longland reported to the *Niobe*, an eleven-thousand-ton cruiser converted to a training ship that was the anchor of the young Canadian navy. Permanently docked at the waterfront, the former cruiser had the capacity to house a thousand men plus training

---

*The BEF was made up of British men living in America who volunteered to serve.

facilities, the office of the chief examining officer as well as Customs, so the *Niobe* was an important feature on the Halifax shoreline. Longland was pleased to find his old shipmate Chippy Carpenter sitting at the draft officer's desk. After a brief chat, Longland glanced out a porthole and noticed the *Mont Blanc.*

"There's no doubt about the nationality of that vessel; look at the size of her flag," he said before bounding up the stairs to the deck where he could get a better view.

ON THE *IMO,* JOHANSEN was having trouble finding the landmarks he normally used because the ships were docked three or four deep and he could not tell one wharf from another. Instead he used the twin hills of Fort Needham and the Dartmouth Commons, confirming his position in relation to the silos of the Acadia Sugar Refinery. On Johansen's last voyage to Halifax, they had changed course to starboard as soon as they left the Basin, using the silos to guide them back to shore from midchannel, but the *Imo* was already quickly approaching the sugar silos past Pier 6 and still had not turned toward Halifax. Hayes blasted the whistle twice. As a wheelsman, Johansen was paid to look, not to listen, but he could not help but glance around to see why Hayes was whistling. All he saw was the *Stella Maris* turning back toward Halifax, but when he looked over the wheel and squinted down the Narrows, he noticed a steamer emerging from behind the bow of the *Highflyer.* He had not seen her a minute ago, and yet there she was heading straight toward them with only four or five hundred yards separating them. Captain From saw the same thing and crossed the bridge to take a position between Hayes and Johansen.

"She is coming pretty fast," Hayes said to Captain From.

On the *Stella Maris,* Captain Brannen shot a look to his son at the wheel, as if to confirm that the whistle was not meant for them, and said, "It would not be for us in the position we're in," before turning to look past the scows in search of another ship. Second mate Nickerson followed his glance but had a hard time seeing because of the glare. The captain had better luck, catching a glimpse of the *Mont Blanc.* "It must be for the vessel coming up."

THE WHARVES NEAR THE dry dock were packed with ships. The coal carrier the *J. A. McKee* was closest, waiting for repairs. Next to her was a cargo ship, the *Middleham Castle,* which had also been in for repairs and was preparing to return overseas. Next to her was an old trawler turned minesweeper, the *Musquash*, and the Dominion Coal boat, the *Douglas H. Thomas*. Most of the crews had come up on deck when they heard the whistles. Daniel McLaine, the master of the Dominion Coal tug, nodded to his chief engineer, John Rourke. McLaine also thought the *Mont Blanc* was coming in fast. "That ship coming up the harbor has a lot of headway on her." Ships like the *Imo* with the more common sharp bow did not create as much foam at low speeds. Not realizing that the *Mont Blanc* had a bluff bow, which parted the water like heavy velvet curtains sending out long folds on either side, they misinterpreted the foam as evidence that she was speeding. Rourke walked over to where the captain was standing and, looking over the captain's shoulder, spotted the *Imo*. He thought the Belgian was also coming out quick for such a tight strait.

"They seem to drive very fast in Halifax Harbor."

Others thought the two-blast whistle peculiar as well; heads all around the harbor lifted. Although they had been paying no particular attention to the whistles, they recognized something out of the ordinary. It was one of those moments when a disruption in routine called attention to itself without immediately revealing its nature. The commander of the naval tug *Neried*, John Makiny, stood on the outside upper end of his tug watching the *Mont Blanc* pass his bow. He had plenty of experience on the Narrows and could see that the *Mont Blanc* was well on the eastern channel, and, being unable to make out the *Imo*, Makiny could not figure out why she was whistling and went back to work.

ON HANOVER STREET, Charles Duggan's day was already half over. He rose with the dawn to ferry workers back and forth to the docks. When he crossed the dining room, something gave him pause. Curious, he moved closer to the window. He had watched over the traffic on these waters his entire life, and it took him a second to recognize something he had never seen before. His wife Reta slipped in beside him, standing in front of the window as the two steamers approached each other along the inward lane of the Narrows. The Belgian was sitting high in the water, passing right in front of Hanover Street, but she looked to be outside of her lane—closer to Dartmouth than to the sugar refinery. The Narrows were tricky that way— a ship had to head almost straight across them to leave the Basin, but then needed to turn hard to starboard to reach the outgoing lane. International law required ships to stay on the starboard or right side of their respective lanes, much in the same way cars navigated the road, but the Dartmouth shore was shallower, so the center of the channel was not necessarily the center of the Narrows—no problem for a one-tonner like the *Grace Darling* but a challenge for commercial ships. The Belgian should have veered back toward Halifax by now, but she held her course. From Hanover Street he should have been able to see a bit of her port bow, but she was flat on her starboard side. Worse, she had raised foam, and looked to be fast closing the distance between them. It would be a dangerously tight passing in an already crowded harbor.

MACKEY THOUGHT HE KNEW what was happening. He could see that Hayes had passed a ship on the wrong side up above the Narrows, and from that unfamiliar angle the waters looked wider than they were. Further into the passage, he found the waters narrowing more and faster than he expected. The *Imo* was almost to the brewery wharf already. Mackey could see that she was in ballast, her cargoes empty, and her waterline flirting with the air. Both ships were nearly halfway into the Narrows. He decided on caution.

"Stop the engines," Mackey called, and, for the second time that morning, the engines shook the *Mont Blanc* until they silenced. He ran through his options. "I was not in a position to let the anchor go owing to little flood tide and swinging my ship crosswise in the channel, either out in the channel or swinging her stern ashore, and having on a load of explosives, I did not want to put her ashore, and if I had reversed my engines I knew she would slew ashore; I would have brought the tide on the starboard quarter and put her ashore, besides being crosswise, so I decided when I gave this second blast so as to attract his attention and see if he thought he was making a mistake." The *Imo,* he could see was still heading straight for him.

"Mind your port helm, starboard a little." By nosing in even closer to the Dartmouth shore, he hoped to make it clear that he was continuing as he was on the Dartmouth side of the channel and the *Imo* should turn starboard also. He asked the captain to repeat the whistle and Le Médec blew a single blast. The *Mont Blanc* got her answer as she drifted past the foot of Jamieson Street in Dartmouth. It was a double blast.

MAKINY LOOKED UP FROM the *Neried*'s deck for the second time in as many minutes. He finally saw why the *Mont Blanc* was whistling: A Belgian ship was way out of her lane. No wonder the Frenchman was making noise. When he heard the *Imo* respond again with two straight blasts, meaning she was going port, he could not help but watch. That was an unlikely call. Quite irregular. The Belgian had not deferred to the French ship, as required by law. Whoever whistled first controlled the navigation, and the French ship was most clearly in her correct lane and the Belgian was not. He picked up the binoculars and sang out to the others onboard.

"Come and watch the strike. There is going to be a beautiful strike here." He lifted his glasses for a better view. "Boys, there is going to be a head-on here."

They were still watching on the Dominion Coal boat too.

"They are getting kind of nervous aboard the French ship," Rourke said to Captain McLaine. Neither had heard the *Mont Blanc*'s first whistle, and they thought the *Mont Blanc* was answering the *Imo*.

"There is going to be a collision," McLaine answered as the water between the two ships closed. "The Frenchman has given a cross signal. Cannot be averted."

A cross signal meant that one ship answered the other in disagreement— in essence ignoring the other's intention. By law, when a cross signal was given, both ships were supposed to stop immediately. The *Highflyer*'s yeoman of signals, Thomas Roberts, was standing on the aft deck when he noticed that the Belgian Relief ship was steering a direct course for him. That was unusual, especially since the *Mont Blanc* was already close to shore and without room to maneuver. He thought that she would risk grounding if she went any closer to shore. On the bridge, Signalman J. C. Sibley looked on as the *Imo* stayed her course. Perhaps it was time to report the situation to the officer on watch. Sibley approached Lieutenant Richard Woolams, who had been walking the port quarterdeck in the morning sun since the *Mont Blanc* dipped her ensign.

"Two ships are about to collide near the Basin, sir," Sibley told him.

"Who is it?"

"The *Mont Blanc* and a Belgian Relief."

"I'll be there at once."

Sibley returned to the bridge. Woolams crossed to the starboard quarterdeck to watch as the two ships seemed to melt into one another.


MACKEY COULD NOT BELIEVE what he was hearing. Or that William Hayes was piloting that ship. That is not your order, he said to himself.

Everything suddenly appeared too close. The two bows were now only a ship's length apart and still sailing, although the empty hull of the *Imo* towered over the lower, heavily weighted *Mont Blanc*. Mackey knew that he could not take the *Mont Blanc* any closer to shore without risking grounding the ship and sending a shock through the explosives. He had to cross against regulation and he had to do it fast. There was no choice. The other steamer had cut her engines but was still moving under her own weight. If he could straighten the *Mont Blanc*, he could rack her up parallel to the Belgian Relief.

"Bear all to the left."

He grabbed the whistle cord and yanked it hard twice. Even at this slow pace, sailing only under her own steerage, the *Mont Blanc* answered her helm and her bow swung toward Halifax until she stopped parallel to the *Imo* with fifty-five yards between their bows. Mackey and Le Médec stood overlooking the ships from the right side of the bridge. For a brief moment, their parallel decks formed a massive metal platform as wide as two ice rinks and the length of two football fields. Le Médec relaxed his grip on the railing. It was over. Close but over. He looked across the deck to the front panel and read her name. The *Imo*, he repeated to himself.

Just as the two men thought they were out of danger, the *Imo* blew three blasts. Hayes was throwing her into reverse. The decks shook a moment before the engines took hold. Even those who did not hear the order understood what the vibrations meant. Le Médec and Mackey knew what the *Imo* appeared to have forgotten: Without a load, the *Imo* sat high with her bow nosing pertly out of the water—the propeller would be useless to control her. The *Imo* would never answer her helm; she could not answer her helm. The bow would turn toward the *Mont Blanc*. Le Médec raced through the packing job in his mind. "I knew that in the No. 2 'tween decks was the TNT and that was a dangerous explosive I had heard in New York, which would explode under the least shock, and I wanted to avoid the collision taking place on this hold so that the impact would not be on that particular hold." Mackey was thinking the same thing.

"All astern!" Mackey shouted, but Le Médec was ahead of him, yanking the whistle three times and shouting the order in French. They had to protect hold no. 2 from damage, but the engines barely had time to engage. For thirty seconds, Mackey and Le Médec stood on the bridge, the whistle swinging helplessly between them as the *Imo*'s white bow skimmed across the water toward their hull. Mackey looked down at the wake rising from the *Imo*'s starboard quarter. Bubbles appeared, burst, and then reappeared only to burst again, filling the air with a frothy popping sound. If there were even ten more feet of water, she might make it, but it was too tight. "The collision was unavoidable. . . . She did not swing very fast but you could see her swing." The *Imo*'s sharp bow with its dangling port anchor plowed into the *Mont Blanc*. It ripped through the metal sheeting near the waterline, torquing the *Mont Blanc*'s struts as her nose pushed nine feet inside and sent a shock rippling through both ships as if they were making a hard docking. "Quite a crash . . . heard all over the ship . . . A good hard crack."

Sailors ran to the *Mont Blanc*'s foredeck to check for damage in the holds and saw the bow crushed inside the no. 1 hold—they missed the TNT—but as soon as the ships released, a menacing roar greeted them. The *Imo*'s engines had finally engaged. The crew felt the ship's deck shake—the *Imo* was full speed astern and backing out. Sailors stood at the *Mont Blanc*'s rails, screaming, waving their arms, signaling the *Imo* to stop, but it was too late. Like an awkward, uncertain elephant, the *Imo* attempted to back up, slowly extricating her bow with a grinding scrape. The anchor was caught on one of the thick plates near the bulwarks that protected the holds. Its double-riveted seams held strong as the two ships gnashed against each other and filled the air with the whining and crashing of metal rending metal. Finally the plate buckled and ripped off its sheeting, releasing the anchor and the *Imo*'s bow. Her sudden withdrawal sent the *Mont Blanc*'s bow pivoting toward Pier 6, pointing directly toward Richmond.

"Stop the engines," Le Médec shouted.

As she floated toward the pier, Le Médec and Mackey leaned over the side to check the damage. A hole sliced through the no. 1 hold from the waterline up to her rail. What they could not see was that somewhere below the deck, the bow of the *Imo* had crushed a few loose grains of dry picric acid. As it withdrew, the combustible powder burst into ant-sized fires. They might have burnt themselves out if they had not found an invisible trail of monochlorobenzol vapors that had escaped from the barrels on deck. They ignited almost instantly. The first indication that there was a problem was a gentle white puff followed by black smoke.

"Fire!"

*Chapter Three*

# Black Smoke, White Smoke

I T WAS IMMEDIATELY EVIDENT that this fire was more intense than the usual coal fire. What started out as small flames at the bottom of the rip in the hull, stirred itself into an ugly red and black brew that soon overtook the side of the ship, the forecastle, and her derricks. As the stench of burning benzol—an oily, exhaustlike smell—wafted across the water, spectators along the shore began to fear that the steamer was carrying petroleum, a danger in a crowded harbor because the fire could spread quickly and the ship might have to be sunk. Even if they could put out the fire, the water would be polluted for months, if not years. There was also, of course, a slim chance of explosion, but most people discounted it. More likely, the ship would burn itself out, especially if she came to a stop midchannel, although, judging by her speed, that seemed unlikely. No one could agree what propelled the *Mont Blanc* forward; some thought it was the force of the strike; others thought that they saw her propeller rotating; still more, erroneously, thought it was the tide. Whatever it was, the *Mont Blanc*'s fiery bow drifted across the harbor toward Halifax's Pier 6 with what appeared to be a pilot's precision.

Across the streets of Richmond, children stopped to watch. People were drawn to their windows. Whole families such as the Duggans stood in windows mesmerized by the flames leaping up the side of the ship and across the fire decks. Charles and Reta stood in the window with the baby. His parents, William and Susie, came in from the kitchen, as did Warren and Evelyn. The two ships were now moving away from each other and smoke was starting to collect on the *Mont Blanc*'s foredeck. The seven Duggans stood in different windows, chatting, calling out to each other, and speculating about the flames. Fires by the coal loaders were common. The embers often ignited the old wooden wharves; the firemen were there every other day, but it was unusual to see a steamer as big as the *Mont Blanc* burning. A fire in the harbor was not something to be taken lightly, especially during wartime. Realizing that he might be able to help, Charles grabbed his wool jacket and cap and ran across the railyards to the dock.

Two blocks south on Barrington Street, Lottie Duggan wrapped up her newborn son and put him on a chair in front of the stove to keep him warm. Her daughter Helena had just set off to St. Joseph's School, but three other daughters, Bessie, Lydia, and Irene, were still at home, as was her five-year-old son Kenneth. Bessie and Irene were planning to skip school that day to go over to the Barracks and watch the soldiers. The family had just moved from Turtle Grove, and soldiers were still exciting to the children. In Turtle Grove all they had were farm animals, which they kept

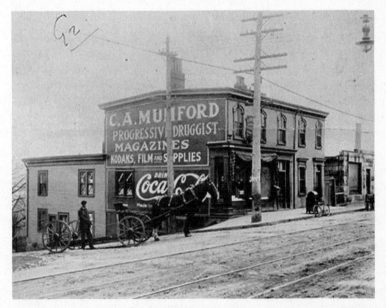

Southeast corner of Campbell Road (Barrington Street) and East Young Street before the explosion. Charles Duggan lived a block north and Billy Duggan a block and a half south on the same side.

to supplement their income. When they moved to the new apartment in Halifax, they had to give up not only the animals but also the extra space. Eight of them now crowded into one apartment overlooking the graving dock and the *Niobe*. That morning Billy was eighty miles out at sea on *P.V. VII* searching for mines. It was dangerous if boring work on the minesweeper, which was nothing more than a converted Menhaden fishing boat, an old wooden trawler with a couple of twelve-pound guns mounted to its front decks. All day long, they sailed up and down the harbor entrance dragging long lines with blades behind them, searching the ocean floor for anchored mines. When they found one, the blade would slice through the chain until a mine popped up to the surface like a rubber ball. One of the enlisted men would then shoot at it until it detonated. Billy received $25 a month in extra danger pay; with six children he needed every penny.

Between the two Duggan homes, Constant Upham watched as the *Mont Blanc*'s deck turned to flame from the window of his grocery store. Upham, who owned one of the few telephones in the neighborhood, picked up and dialed Chief Edward Condon. The Upham store was just behind the sugar refinery, giving Upham a clear view of the fire.

"A ship is on fire," he told the chief, indicating that it looked more serious than a simple coaling accident. He hung up and called several more firehouses. They all knew him. He often called when the loading docks went up. Within minutes several fire bells—each unit had a different bell— were ringing all over the North End. Anyone who looked out the window to see why so many bells were ringing saw a black, turnip-shaped cloud floating two or three hundred feet in the air. Others did not notice anything unusual, not the acrid smell, not the smoke funnel, not the fire bells, and many mothers went about their morning routine. Incredibly, some students, such as Helen Clark, walked to school oblivious of the disturbance at the foot of Richmond Hill.

TO THE SURPRISE OF Mackey and Le Médec, the scene on the *Mont Blanc* was one of controlled excitement. Within seconds, the fire forced the crew on the foredeck back toward the bridge. Sailors stood at the bottom of the stairs anxiously awaiting Captain Le Médec's orders. By the time Second Officer Glotin stepped onto the bridge, a low flame was curling all the way across the forecastle, feeding off the heavy benzol vapors. At the stern more barrels were strapped down, and the men knew that even a single errant spark could trap them in the middle and separate them from the lifeboats. The fire had already cut off any access to the anchors and the water pipes below, rendering the fire extinguishers useless. It did not make much difference—Le Médec knew that throwing water onto an oil fire would only spread the flames on deck, and there was no way to get water into the no. 1 hold where the fire had started. They could not even lower the anchor because they were cut off by the fire. The smoke was already so thick that Glotin could no longer see the gash where the *Imo* had struck. He found Le Médec and Mackey aft on the bridge. He called across to the captain on the other side of the chartroom in search of orders.

"Wait," said Le Médec. He turned to Mackey. "Is there anything we can do with the ship?"

"Look out for your boats," Mackey told him.

Le Médec leaned over and called to Glotin, "Leave the ship."

The men below him on deck were awaiting his instructions. He repeated the order to abandon ship. It was all the men needed to hear. They stormed past the bridge to the lifeboats, where each had an assigned spot. Their faces strained with controlled anxiety and impatience as they waited for sailors to prepare the lifeboats. Leveque stood up from behind the telegraph and left the bridge. Serre moved to join him but Le Médec stopped him.

"Set the helm amidships."

Serre straightened the wheel, locked it in place, then bolted down the stairs after Leveque, leaving Mackey, Le Médec, and Glotin alone on the deck. Le Médec ordered Glotin to oversee the lifeboats while he and Mackey remained on the bridge. Mackey would claim that he gave a last order to put the engines full speed ahead in an attempt to force water into the holds, but later both Le Médec and the chief engineer, Anton Le Gat, denied hearing his order. As it was, both men were surprised that the ship had not blown up already.

As the *Mont Blanc* drifted toward Halifax, the *Imo* fell in behind her and, at least from shore, appeared to be following the steamer. She was having trouble maneuvering in the Narrows and had put the ship into forward then reverse several times as she tried to turn back toward the Basin, but her bow was still pointed toward the wharf at Lorne Athletic Club. Sailors on the *Imo* who rushed up to deck after they felt the queer twisting stutter of the collision lined the deck watching the flames. Second Mate B'Jonnas debated whether or not the *Mont Blanc* could possibly be carrying explosives when the third mate interrupted him to report that he had checked the forepeak and that it was dry. The fire had changed dramatically since Birkland had gone below. The height of the flames alarmed him and he argued with B'Jonnas that the Frenchman might indeed be carrying munitions. Why else would the *Mont Blanc*'s crew be preparing their lifeboats?

B'Jonnas disagreed. "It was impossible for him to have any ammunition or explosives or else he would have the red flag."

Many others around the harbor who were unaware of the wartime changes wrongly assumed the same thing. *Imo* Steward Andrew Johansen, who initially returned to the captain's quarters after the collision, walked along the rail carrying the captain's clean water pitcher. He leaned over to inspect the damage, but all he could see were two punctures in the hull near the anchor. It did not look too bad. He turned to check on Captain From—as his steward he felt a certain responsibility for the captain's well-being—but the captain appeared unperturbed. He was just returning to the bridge from the forecastle and he stood in conference with the wheelsman and the pilot. Things seemed calm, aside from the telegraph ringing fore and aft, and Steward Johansen felt confident that everything was all right. Even when he saw the sailors on the other ship rushing to the lifeboats—the *Mont Blanc* was at most fifty yards away and he could make out the men perfectly—he thought that they were only worried that their ship would sink.


THE *STELLA MARIS* WAS just entering the Basin when the crew heard the crash. They stopped and turned to see what happened. "We saw white smoke, thought it was steam, then black smoke, then flames and more black smoke." Captain Brannen ordered his son to a small cove in the Basin on the Dartmouth shore where they could anchor the scows, and took the wheel from his son. Walter rushed down to the deck to unravel the fire hose and prime the pumps. Nickerson pulled in the scows as quickly as he could, while the others anchored and detached them. What little wind there was carried the black balloon of smoke down the Narrows and toward them. Brannen thought that the French ship would need help putting out the fire and evacuating her crew, so, finally freed of the cargo, he turned the powerful tug around and raced back up the Narrows toward Pier 6 with its fire hose shooting water over the side.


AT THE WEST STREET Fire Engine House, thirty-six-year-old Billy Wells jumped to attention when the Box 83 fire alarm rang. As the driver of the *Patricia*, the city's only motorized fire pumper, he liked to reach the fire before the horse-drawn trucks. Even better, he liked to race his brother Claude, who drove Chief Condon's new McLaughlin Buick roadster. It was not important that Claude normally won—the fun was in getting there—but just as he was putting on his gear, Billy remembered that it was Claude's day off. There would be no race, but he could still arrive before the other crews.

While the men raced to take their places on the back of the truck, the chief remained in the station, pounding on the bathroom door. A firefighter had come to work sick that morning. He said it was the flu, but the chief was unsympathetic. In a town like Halifax the flu might be the flu or it might be the rum. The chief, reluctant to wait any longer, left in disgust and took his place beside Billy in the *Patricia*. They rushed out of the station, sirens screaming. By the time they reached the corner of Gottingen and Gerrish Streets, a part-time fireman named Albert Brunt was waiting to jump onto the back of the truck. He had heard the alarm when he was pushing his paint cart along Gottingen, and thinking that they would need help, he had parked his cart and stood on the corner. He could see the *Patricia* barreling down Gerrish Street and moved closer to where it would take the corner, running alongside the truck for a couple of steps before leaping onto the running board and grabbing the rail. His hand slipped and he skidded off the sideboard as the truck swung left onto Gottingen. Brunt tumbled onto the street. Billy Wells could hear the other men laughing at Brunt, who was sitting upright in the middle of Gottingen Street watching the *Patricia* drive away.

GLOTIN RETURNED TO THE *Mont Blanc*'s bridge to report that the crew was ready.

"Has everyone been taken to the boats?" Le Médec asked.

"Yes."

Below them, Herbert Whitehead from the Canadian Navy pulled alongside the *Mont Blanc* in the duty boat. He stuck his megaphone out the wheelhouse window to offer the men gathered around the lifeboats a ride to the Basin in his boat in case they were in danger, but, watching the crew, he came to the conclusion that they were not panicked.

"Jump into my boat," he shouted, but the men either did not understand or did not care to join him. In their hurry to abandon ship, a man cut the cross ropes on the starboard side and the lifeboats dropped overboard and splashed into the water empty. Sailors streamed over the side, down the ladders and ropes. By the time Le Médec and Mackey arrived, the starboard lifeboat was already full and drifting away from the steamer. Or maybe the steamer was moving. Mackey could not judge because the smoke obscured his view of land. They crossed to the port side, where the remainder of the crew bobbed around in the lifeboat waiting for the officers. Glotin climbed down the ladder while Le Médec slid down the rope. Mackey thought he would be the last man on the ship, but once the captain reached the lifeboat, it occurred to him that he had not seen Chief Engineer Le Gat. He asked if anyone else had seen him.

"He is in the engine room," someone shouted.

Le Médec grabbed the rope ladder and began to climb but Glotin, who was still on his way down, reversed direction and went up ahead of him. The engine room was just at the top of the ladder. He shouted through the door leading to the upper rooms.

"Come up on deck."

Chief Engineer Le Gat and his third engineer, Louis Brun, had been awaiting the order three decks below in the engine room. Le Gat knew that they could not save the ship. The seacock was on the other side of the engines. It would take five or six hours to dismantle the engines before they could even open it. Sinking the ship would take another two hours. They were lucky if they had minutes with their cargo. Le Gat finished lifting the safety valve on the starboard boiler and signaled to Le Brun that they could leave. They passed the chalkboard on their way out. *Demi-vitesse* was the last recorded order.

Once on deck, Glotin, Le Brun, and Le Gat slid down the rope while Le Médec remained at the top of the ladder so as to be that last man onboard, but instead of climbing down, he stayed on deck. Without his coat and captain's cap he could have been any sailor, except perhaps for the flat expression of shock on his face. Glotin chased after him, but Le Médec was insistent. He should stay with the ship. Glotin argued with him, pointing out that the men were safe and there was nothing they could do about the explosion that would surely ensue. If the captain could not help the people in the city, at least he could see his crew to safety. Le Médec relented briefly and took a few steps down the ladder, but balked and again climbed back onto the deck. He repeated that he should stay on the ship, but Glotin thought this was a useless sacrifice and took Le Médec by the arm and steered him to the ladder. "I forced him, taking him by the arm to the ladder." He spoke in a firm but soothing tone, reassuring Le Médec that there was no use in him dying. The French was lost on Mackey, but whatever

Glotin said calmed Le Médec and together the two men climbed down the ladder, Le Médec leaving last. Once in the lifeboat he took command.

"Get away from the ship," Le Médec ordered, and one of the men picked up an oar, pushed them off the poop deck, and they crossed the stern toward Dartmouth at a fast chop.

Mackey stood and scouted the shore for a good landing spot. He pointed toward the Duggan ferry dock at Turtle Grove. It was close to the ship and there were plenty of trees to offer protection. Mackey looked around at the approaching vessels, desperate to warn them; he could just make out a couple of tugs and a naval lighter approaching from the east. One tug was close enough that he recognized Captain T. A. Murray, who was in charge of the slow convoys. Mackey shouted at Murray to take them in tow, but Murray did not seem to hear and switched directions. The other tug came close enough that Mackey could read the name—the *Ragus*, the sugar refinery tug. *Ragus* was *sugar* spelled backwards.

"She is going to blow up," Mackey screamed, but the tug ignored him and headed across the harbor toward the fire. "Nobody could hear. Too much racket." The *Mont Blanc* was approaching the end of Pier 6 as surely as if Mackey were on board guiding her.

"Go away. Go away," Mackey screamed. He waved his arms to get their attention. "Go away." Some of the men in the lifeboats joined him, yelling in French. As they passed by the *Imo*, Mackey noticed the scratches along her waterline with detached interest before trying again.

"The ship is going to explode." His voice passed undistinguished into the smoke.


RALPH SMITH, a marine engineer on the repair boat *Jutland*, watched the man in a peaked cap with a gold band waving his hands and screaming. The *Jutland* had been following about half a mile behind the *Mont Blanc* since they had left Bissett's Wharf on their way to the Basin, where they were scheduled to work on three ships. They were already late because they had stopped to witness the collision. Smith turned to watch another man waving his hands over his head. There it came again. "Explosion." It was the only word he could make out, but, satisfied that the lifeboats would reach the Dartmouth shore, he did not bother to chase after them. Instead the *Jutland* circled around the stern of the *Mont Blanc* to get a better look at the damage, but the dark smoke frightened him. He turned sharply to avoid getting trapped on the wrong side of the fire; a ship could get lost in smoke that heavy. As they passed into the Basin, Smith looked back at the steamer drifting toward shore. He assumed she was full of oil.

"It is a pity to see her sink. Why did they not try to beach her?"

By the time Charles Duggan, at the helm of the *Grace Darling*, approached the *Mont Blanc,* the big ship was drifting toward Pier 6, the over-sized J-shaped wharf that jutted out just below the freight shed. He had tried to get out to help the crew disembark, but arrived too late. "Before I had got half way to the French boat, her deck load had caught fire and the men of her crew were spilling over the side like rats." The fire was intensifying, with unusual colors that were made brighter by the backdrop of black smoke. Duggan felt a shock of heat hit his cheeks as he drew closer. Without a strong breeze, the smoke hung around the harbor. It was not dry like wood smoke, but dense and sticky, surrounding the *Grace Darling* like a sugary fog. The cabin grew darker as he sailed closer and the oiliness choked the air from his lungs. It was hard to see or breathe. He turned off his engine and kept his eye on the steamer's decks, still hopeful that he could help in some way, but the decks were deserted. The *Mont Blanc* must have looked enormous at that distance, a sheer gray metal wall with an eerie quiet at the stern and hissing steam shooting out from beneath the gash on the blazing bow. He turned to look behind him and saw the rowboats racing toward shore and the gray silhouette of the *Imo* retreating the way she had come, across the Basin, but much slower. The rowboats, which were heavy and cumbersome, looked to be headed toward the ferry wharf. Duggan thought they might need help. Besides, he wanted to get away from the fire. As he started to swing off, the first of eleven explosions rolled across the harbor. The force of the rumble startled him. While he started out across the harbor toward the lifeboats, the *Mont Blanc* slipped in beside the wharf and, with a slight bump, grounded. At that hour of the morning, the harbor was in slack water, between tides. What little current there was finally took the stern and jammed it up against the wharf, leaving a quarter of the ship sticking out into the harbor.

Captain Brannen steered the *Stella Maris* straight into the heat. The hose was pumped and primed, with a jet of water shooting out the nozzle, but it seemed futile, and Captain Brannen worried that his wooden tug might catch a spark more than she could handle. They had moved off 150 yards when a rowboat with six or seven sailors hailed them. Commander T. K. Triggs from the *Highflyer* pulled himself onboard the tug and joined Brannen on the bridge. While they were talking, the *Niobe*'s naval lighter pulled up alongside and Albert Mattison joined them. They all agreed that a single hose was not going to stop the fire from spreading and the best route would be to tow the steamer back into the middle of the harbor, where the fire could be contained. "They wanted to have her stern pulled away from the pier—they were afraid the pier would catch fire." Once a fire like that hit wood, the whole waterfront could go up. By now the wharf was already smoking, and water along the shore where oil had spilled from the bow of the *Mont Blanc* was in flames, but the firemen could deal with the wharf if somehow the three men could deal with the steamer. Mattison and Triggs climbed down into their boats and Brannen ordered the crew to throw the rowboat a rope from the stern; they were going to tow Triggs, who wanted to tell Captain From to leave the area, over to the *Imo*, while Nickerson prepared the hawser. They looped the rope over the rowboat and towed the men close to the *Imo*, where they left them. The *Stella Maris* then turned toward the smoke and the *Mont Blanc*. Brannen's son Walter stood on deck and Nickerson, below, eased out the five-inch hawser from the no. 1 hold slowly—a fast-unraveling hawser could squeeze a man to death or rip off a limb in seconds if it tangled. Seeing the five-inch hawser come out of the hold, Captain Brannen ordered Walter to get the ten-inch instead. The five-inch was not strong enough to tow the *Mont Blanc* off the seabed. Walter leaned over and shouted into the hatch to get the ten-inch. The explosions were gaining strength until they rocked not only the pinnace and the *Stella Maris*, but, eventually, all the ships tied up along the docks. Rolls of gas rumbled their way up through the smoke and burst into flame midair. It was a fire unlike any the port had seen.

IT WAS 8:50 A.M. when the telephone interrupted Captain Superintendent Frederick Pasco's breakfast. Pasco was in charge of the harbor until the permanent captain superintendent, Edward Martin, returned to Halifax. By coincidence, Pasco, who was staying at Martin's official residence, had noticed the *Mont Blanc* earlier that morning when it passed the No. 4 dockyard and thought that she was "a fine big ship." Knowing that she was there to join the convoy, he thought nothing more of it and returned to his breakfast. He was still eating when a call was patched through from the *Highflyer*, alerting him to a ship on fire in the harbor. He phoned the dockyard first, but no one picked up because the dockyard did not open until nine. Eventually he connected with the *W. H. Lee*, a tug with fire pumps, and ordered them to assist with the fire. Then he tried the transport officer and the harbormaster, but the phone just kept ringing. The harbormaster's home line was busy. Pasco was getting impatient. He turned to the servant.

"Take the telephone and try and get the transport office. I must try and see what is going on outside."

"You can see it from the upper window—there is a telephone up there."

Pasco took the steps two at a time, leaving the servant to work the operators. He looked out the back window. "I saw the *Imo* motionless apparently across the harbor blocking the whole harbor right across and I did not see the other vessel and the *Imo* had apparently a certain amount of smoke coming from the fiddleys."

There is not so much smoke, he thought, and, feeling much calmer, he pushed his face sideways against the window to see if he could see the other ship. He was still watching when Lieutenant Poole called from the dockyard. Pasco ordered him to round up some tugs.

"Send the *Lee* and the *Gopher* and the *Musquash*—anything you have with pumps in case the fire is serious."

"I understand."

As captain superintendent of the dockyard, Pasco should have known that the *Mont Blanc* was carrying not only munitions but explosives—it was the first ship allowed down the harbor with a cargo of high explosives. He received the daily lists of incoming ships and cargo, but if he had been informed of the *Mont Blanc*'s cargo, he did not remember. Later, when he learned that the benzol was packed on the deck over the holds of picric acid and TNT, he was shocked. "I am surprised any ship would allow it to be loaded; I am surprised the people on the ship did not leave it in a body."

Pasco's subordinate, Chief Examining Officer Wyatt, was just outside the dockyard when he learned of the fire. He had left work early the night before to attend a party. Most nights Wyatt worked in the office until 9:00 or 10:00 p.m., and as the chief examining officer he was never really off-duty. He was always careful to leave the phone number of where he would be, but there had been no call that morning. Instead, as he crossed the tracks to enter the dockyard, he saw young Iceton huffing and puffing his way up the hill, shouting his name. Iceton, who had been on duty since the night before, had tracked the *Mont Blanc*'s entrance into the harbor until she had passed by their offices on the *Niobe*. He had gone out on deck to watch, and after the signalman handed him the message that she had passed, he considered himself finished with her because he was off duty at 9:00 a.m. When the fire broke out and he realized which ship it was, he stayed on duty.

When he finally saw Wyatt, he sprinted up the hill to inform him that the *Mont Blanc* had been involved in a collision, was on fire, and was drifting toward Pier 6, one of the most populated areas along the northern stretch of wharves.

Wyatt bolted, shooting past Captain Martin's house, where Pasco was on the phone, and down over the hill to the coaling wharf just south of the *Niobe,* where the *W. H. Lee* was docked on the other side of the slip. By the time he reached the wharf, he knew it was too late. The *Mont Blanc* was grounded and the fire was far out of their control. Aside from the French crew and Iceton, he was the only person who knew what was going to happen.

IN THE SOUTHERN END of the city, few noticed the ominous black cloud climbing into the blue sky. Stenographers smoothed their skirts and took their places at their desks, merchants lifted the blackout blinds from their windows and unlocked their front doors for business. In the North almost all work had stopped and the waterfront was trimmed with a festive ribbon of spectators as people went outside or climbed onto roofs to get a better view. Fort Needham Hill was packed with people watching the smoke, but the excited atmosphere was slowly turning to concern. No one had seen a fire like this one, aside from a few men who had returned from the front, and for them the fires and the stench of burning oil were all too familiar and frightening. Charles Duggan's family, except his wife Reta, went outside to watch. Down the street his sister-in-law, Lottie, moved to the upstairs bedroom and squeezed in between her daughter Irene and the large mirrored dresser beside the window. Just over the hill, workers from the sugar refinery climbed onto the roof for an unobstructed view. On Hanover Street, Reta watched from the back windows, but it might not have been the fire that worried her as much as Charles turning away from the fire. The *Grace Darling* was motoring across the harbor as fast as she could go.

Farther south, the Dartmouth ferry that Mackey had avoided was again crossing the harbor to Halifax. C. E. Creighton was on the lower deck when a man approached him and asked him where the fire was. Creighton had not noticed anything unusual, but looked up, saw the smoke, and suggested that they go up to the upper deck to watch. The two men climbed the stairs and stood on the starboard side near the ladies' cabin, looking north down the harbor along with the other passengers. All they could see was "tongues of flames running up through the smoke and we then supposed oil must

The *Grace Darling*, rebuilt after the
explosion, continued as a ferry until
the 1930s.

be burning. A tremendous column of smoke shot up the great height and
spread out in light fleecy clouds." A warship must have blown up, he
thought.

Daniel McLaine crossed over the *J. M. McKee* and climbed onto the *Middleham Castle* to get a better view. Twenty-two-year old Charlie Mayers, the
third officer of the *Middleham Castle,* was already on deck talking with the
chief steward. He was self-conscious about $75 tucked safely inside his
pocket. He was supposed to be delivering the money to the captain on
shore, but he stopped to watch the fire when he got to the deck. The fire
made him nervous. He had seen this sort of thing before, and he knew it
could end in an explosion, but his sense of duty was stronger than his fear,
and after a few minutes Mayers climbed down to the shore. Everywhere
around him men were rushing back and forth trying to help. He looked up
the hill and saw the fire truck *Patricia* speeding down Campbell Road, but it
did not reassure him. Sparks had caught hold of the freight shed's roof at the
end of the wharf, and as Mayers approached he got a better look at what appeared to be an increasingly volatile fire. "There was flames from the waters
edge up . . . right along the derrick booms and the falls that was on them.
The fire was too high, too queer with strange colors and flame balls. She was
shooting these balls of smoke up in the air and then the jetty was partly on
fire too. . . . Like a 12 pounder would go off in the holds, and after you
would hear the sound like a gun, then the smoke would go up and burst in
the air." Mayers was just three hundred feet from the fire, which he had to
pass to get to the captain, but the heat and flames were too much, and a
shiver of fear crept through him. The $75 and the captain could wait. He
turned and ran back toward the *Middleham Castle.*

Three docks south, Fred Longland stood on the forecastle of the *Niobe,*
hoping for a better view, but when he got one, he did not like what he

saw. He was not alone. Most of the men—a collection of sailors, trainees, and officers—assembled to watch. Their initial excitement soon turned to concern.

"Ship on fire" passed around the deck as more men gathered to watch. A low rumble was followed by a burst of smoke that quickly turned to flame. There's going to be trouble here, Longland thought to himself. Something on that ship's foredeck was feeding the fire and intermittently exploding into a pillar of colorful smoke. Each subsequent explosion rocked the *Niobe* and the surrounding ships as if there were a great winter storm raging off-shore. Longland stepped onto a bollard* and steadied himself by placing his hands on the shoulders of a chief petty officer in front of him. "They'll never put that fire out."

AS THE *PATRICIA* SCREAMED along Campbell Road, Billy Wells could see the *Mont Blanc* sitting alongside the pier, and, despite recognizing the danger, he could not help but admire the view. "The ship was almost along side the dock and the multicolored flames shooting from her decks to the sky presented a beautiful sight." The crisp blue morning sky took on a greenish-pink cast. Even the seawater behaved in ways most sailors had never seen before, hissing when it splashed against the forehold and sending up clouds of steam. A low roil bubbled around the ripped plates; the harbor was boiling. The color of the ship's plates soon turned from war-color gray to the purplish blue-black of mussel shells. Wells turned right toward the docks and the *Patricia*'s thin tires bounced down the rough hill as he maneuvered the truck through the crowd in an attempt to get as close as possible, but the heat was too intense. It evaporated not only the water around the ship's bow, but the protective layer of liquid from the firemen's eyes.

AS THE FIRE BURNED unchecked, eight-year-old Helen Clark turned the corner from Russell Street and crossed onto Albert Street. She liked to walk along a well-kept garden that ran the length of the block, and because she was a minute early, she had the luxury of looking into the garden and trailing her pencil through the round wooden pickets of the fence. Helen was

---

*A thick post or a low 7-shaped hook bolted to the deck and used for securing ropes or hawsers.

allowed the privilege of arriving at St. Joseph's Catholic School at 9:05 a.m., five minutes later than the Catholic children who started their day with prayers. At the corner, Helen turned left and ran up Kaye Street to St. Joseph's, never once noticing the fire and smoke raging at the bottom of the hill below.

The four Lloyd sisters—Dorothy, Dolly, Margaret, and Hilda—ran along Gottingen Street, late for school. Their slates bounced up and down on their backs as they turned the corner to Kaye Street, where they were confronted with the ominous cylinder of smoke rising from the foot of the hill. The air smelled funny. A disheveled woman ran toward them, waving her arms and screaming. The girls were frightened.

"Go back! Go back!"

The sisters stopped, unsure what to do.

Fourteen-year-old Frank Hillis was home with his brother Gordon on Richmond Street just above the cattle pens near Pier 6. Both boys had the measles and were restless until they noticed the collision and the fire's quick progress. The flames had climbed to one hundred feet within minutes. Their house was half a block above Campbell Road, only a couple hundred yards from where the burning ship grounded, which afforded them an enviable view of the events. When they heard the *Patricia*'s sirens in the distance, Frank turned to Gordon. His spotted red face was animated with the morning's unexpected diversion.

"The ship will soon get out. I can hear the sound of the fire engine coming."

Their mother entered the room. She was putting on her winter coat. Catching a glimpse of the fire through the window, she decided to join the neighbors outside.

"Don't go out of the house until I come back. I'm going to Mrs. Bowen's house."

She left the two boys and ran down the hill to her neighbor's, where she found her sister-in-law on the porch. Below them people dotted the top rail of the cattle pen and more were wandering around joking and talking. From the window, it appeared to Frank and Gordon that the adults were as happy as they were to be freed from the morning's routine.

IT TOOK THE LIFEBOATS less than ten minutes to cross the water from the *Mont Blanc* to the ferry wharf at Tuft's Cove. It was a low wharf, and the men scrambled onto it and ran off toward the railroad tracks. Mackey ran down the dock shouting out to the manager of the French Cable Wharf to take cover. It was possibly Mackey who ran past a young Mi'kmaq boy and passed along the warning.

"The ship is going to explode. Run. Run!"

William Paul recognized the panic in the man's eyes. He picked up and ran toward the community of wigwams and shanties called Turtle Grove to warn his mother.

As Mackey shouted, Le Médec motioned toward a grove of spruce trees above the tracks, where he ordered a roll call. Glotin ordered the men to stand by position, dividing the stokers, seamen, and sailors into groups as he did a head count. "No confusion. They obeyed as if they had been on the ship." Thirty-nine. They were one short. One of the sailors blurted out that one man had run on ahead as soon as they docked.

"Go out," Le Médec shouted, and within an instant the men scattered toward the wood. He and Le Gat stood on the railroad tracks trying to see the *Mont Blanc* through the smoke. They could only catch glimpses of her, not enough to even tell whether she had reached the other shore. Mackey thought he saw her ground. They turned and followed the crew toward a wooded area. Le Médec was satisfied that he had saved the lives of forty men.

Just as the lifeboats docked, Aggie March wrapped her baby in a blanket and carried her outside to watch the fire. She was surprised to see sailors running across her lawn toward the small wood that separated her house from Turtle Grove. A sailor shouted something to her as he passed, but she could not make out what he said. More sailors ran by her porch. Her daughter cried out when another barrel exploded, turning the sky bright green. The explosions were getting worse. That was the fifth or sixth one. She would have to go back inside if they continued, but the sky looked so strange, she felt compelled to stay and watch one more. The light was warm and diffuse, dustier than the clear northern light of most mornings. Another quick explosion shook the porch. She turned toward the door, but a sailor jumped onto her porch, snatched the baby from her arms, and took off, carrying the child against his chest as he followed the others toward the spruce trees. Aggie chased after him, running several yards behind him as he veered toward the thicket. When she caught up, he did not hand the baby back as she expected but threw her onto the ground. No sooner had she hit the soft earth than he jumped on top of her, holding the baby between them.

Mrs. Paul was inside her house when she heard her son William run screaming into Turtle Grove telling people to run away. She thought he was being foolish and ignored him, but William danced around screaming and shouting, trying to convince his mother he was not making it up. "A white man just warned me that the ship is going to explode."

His mother handed over baby Madeline to her other son, Blair, and went outside to shush William.

"Don't be so crazy," she told him, but he would not stop.

"Run away. Run away."

Mrs. Paul moved over and stood next to an elderly woman to see what was going on, but all they could see was a lambent smoke filling the sky with a warm and enticing glow. Behind her, Blair stood in the window with baby Madeline in his arms, curious to see what William would do.

"The ship is going to explode!" screamed William. As the boy jumped around them, Mrs. Paul and the old woman watched the flames shoot above the Narrows, their faces cast in pink and green. When William's mother finally pulled herself away and turned back to the house, the earth began to vibrate. It came up through their feet, humming like the noise of millions of wings flapping. William shouted, but his voice was drowned out by the buzz.

Barrels from the *Mont Blanc's* foredeck were hurtling into the air by some mysterious force, bursting first into smoke and then into fire with a great roar. More barrels ripped from their strappings and catapulted into the sky, sending a ball of smoke three hundred feet into the air before stretching into a sheet of lurid pink and green flame. Charles Duggan, who was not even halfway across the harbor, did not stop to watch. Barrels were popping off and splinters raining down all around him. A second and third explosion occurred in quick succession. He bent over the engine, coaxing it toward Dartmouth, a trip he had made so many times in his life, but the engine, deprived of oxygen, chugged slowly. As if she were some great beast that needed encouragement, he leaned over the wheel and rubbed the *Grace Darling's* side, pleading with her to speed him away. The explosions were coming faster and gaining strength, rocking the trawler more violently with each blast. He turned to check on the fire and saw the sky painted a garish candy-pink, like a child's drawing. The *Mont Blanc's* stern sank slightly in the water. "A lurid yellowish green spurt of flame rose toward the heaven and drove ahead of the cloud of smoke." Then came the most appalling crash he had ever heard. It was 9:04:35 a.m.

*Chapter Four*

# A Word on Explosions

I N 1917 THERE WERE only two types of explosions: deflagration and detonation. Deflagration is the cycle of burning and disintegration accelerated by containment. When
any fuel ignites, it gives off gas and heat, which further expands the gas.
What is commonly called an explosion occurs only when the gas runs out
of room to disperse and the heat and gas shoot outward in all directions in
an air blast that is much larger than its original volume. Containment is an
essential element of deflagration; even high explosives can withstand fire if
they are spread thin enough over a large area and the gases can expand
without interference. Detonation is different. It is faster, more powerful,
more difficult to attain, and therefore more rare. In simple terms, detonation is achieved when a shock wave travels through the molecules at a supersonic speed, rearranging the molecules as it passes through them,
releasing enormous volumes of energy and its by-product, gas. If enough
energy is created, the shock wave becomes self-sustaining. Deflagration is
measured in milliseconds; detonation by microseconds. Although the difference seems minimal, it is not. Deflagration travels at less than a mile per
second; detonation can reach up to five miles per second, faster than the
speed of sound. Because detonation is more economical energywise, the air
blast from a detonation is bigger and travels faster and farther than a regular
explosion, making a quick, loud clap as compared to the swooshing sound
of deflagration.

Explosives are classified by whether they have the ability to detonate as well as deflagrate. High explosives, such as picric acid and TNT, have the ability to do both, but low explosives such as gunpowder can only deflagrate. No matter how much heat or shock is applied, low explosives will never convert at the molecular level, unlike high explosives, which can be set off by shock as well as by heat under pressure. If a stevedore dropped a fifty-pound barrel of gunpowder, nothing would happen aside from noise. If he dropped a fifty-pound barrel of picric acid, it would explode. Of the five substances packed in the *Mont Blanc*'s holds, only two—dry picric acid and TNT—were classified as high explosives. Gun cotton and wet picric acid, which both contained 20–30 percent water, were classified as flammable, meaning that they would burn without exploding if heated. But there was a catch: If water in either the wet picric acid or the gun cotton evaporated, the substances were then reclassified as high explosives.

Since the start of the war, TNT, a yellow powder introduced in the late 1860s, was starting to eclipse picric acid as the most popular explosive. It was not as powerful, but it was more stable, easier to ship, and cheaper. TNT could boil without exploding, which simplified shell production. Unfortunately for the Allies, the Germans perfected its production first. The British were still managing with picric acid, another bright yellow powder. Until the middle of the nineteenth century, picric acid was used primarily as a commercial dye. The French figured out how to use it in shells in the 1880s, but it was the British who, after testing its detonation properties in a town called Lydd, produced and consumed the most picric acid, which in Britain was better known as Lyddite. It was a less-than-ideal substance. "It was difficult to detonate, particularly if wet, so that it frequently misfired; whole dumps of Lyddite-filled shells were liable to blow up if hit by one hostile shell; it produced very black smoke when it exploded, which made air observation on possible targets difficult; and it could not be melted with steam or hot water, which was the safest way of obtaining an explosive in its liquid form for pouring into shells. Nor was it particularly safe." Another complication was that it was an acid, meaning that if wet picric acid came into contact with metal, it would react by forming crystals of dry picric acid and therefore had to be stored in either special all-wooden barrels made with pegs instead of nails or specially lined kegs. Picric acid was so sensitive—it had a tendency to blow up when it wasn't supposed to and not blow up when it was—that it was banned from regular cargo on U.S. railroads unless shipped with expensive precautions. When detonated, both TNT and picric acid released an unusually high number of carbon molecules, resulting in a heavy black smoke and soot.*

Gun cotton was invented in Germany in 1845. It was essentially cotton fiber soaked in explosive chemicals and then dried. It was cheap and easy to use, but impossible to produce safely. In 1863, a British chemistry professor eliminated much of the danger by crushing the strands of fiber into pulp. This form of gun cotton "was so stable, in this condition, that it could be cut, turned or drilled by wood-working tools. It could, therefore, be produced in shapes very suitable for insertion into bombs, mines, and torpedo heads, or in standard shapes and sizes for use in quarries and mines."

The other substances, benzol and monochlorobenzol, were classified as flammables.† Both were liquid by-products of processing coal into gas, and although sometimes used for fuel, they were more commonly used in the production of picric acid. And, like picric acid, all forms of benzol gave off a heavily carbonated gas—more black smoke.

Every substance in the *Mont Blanc*'s cargo was engineered to blow up. What was surprising was not that the ship exploded, but that it took so long to explode. The first smoke, which many people reported seeing, started in the no. 1 hold when stray grains of dry picric acid were compressed between the two ships. That fire then ignited benzol and monochlorobenzol vapors that escaped from imperfectly sealed barrels on deck.

Monochlorobenzol was considered safer than regular benzol because its denser vapors did not stray too far from their source, but, ironically, this was probably the *Mont Blanc*'s downfall. The heavier vapors fell over the side when the ship was jarred after colliding with the *Imo*, leading the flames straight to the barrels of fuel on the forecastle deck. Within one minute, a long low flame cut off the bow from the rest of the ship. Eight to ten minutes later, flames were already starting to lick the masts. The heat was unbearable. By the time the *Mont Blanc* slid onto the shore at Pier 6, the whole of her metal hull would have been superheated with flames climbing one hundred feet in the air, and the smoke cloud reaching up to three hundred feet. The *Mont Blanc*, with 2,925 tons of explosives in barrels and kegs,

*TNT: $C_7H_5N_3O_{6(s)} \rightarrow 3.5CO_{2(g)} + 2.5H_2O_{(g)} = 1.5N_{2(g)} + 3.5C_{(s)}$
Picric Acid: $C_6H_3N_3O_{7(s)} \rightarrow 5.5CO_{(g)} + 1.5H_2O_{(g)} = 1.5N_{2(g)} + 0.5C_{(s)}$
†Although the common usage in 1917 was *inflammable*, I use *flammable* to avoid confusion.

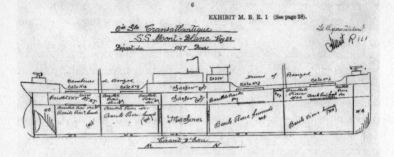

A drawing by Captain Le Médec of how the cargo was packed aboard the *Mont Blanc*

packed in hermetically sealed holds inside a super-heated hull, was now the most powerful bomb the war and the world had ever produced.

As the heat spread from plate to plate along the hull and the decks, the water in the wet picric acid and gun cotton turned to steam, further pressurizing the sealed holds. On deck, the benzol reached 176°F, its boiling point, and the iron barrels burst forth from their canvas straps and shot up into the air, only to be lost in the smoke. The monochlorobenzol took longer, but when it reached 296.6°F the barrels popped off the deck and exploded hundreds of feet above the ship. Some barrels landed in the harbor. Others came straight down, bouncing onto the metal decks. Whether it was this shock or whether the heated air in the holds was finally too pressurized, it is impossible to know. Either way, a keg of dry picric acid finally exploded, bursting open first the other kegs, then the no. 1 hold itself, setting off an air blast that rumbled through the TNT and across the machine rooms to the aft until it reached supersonic speeds and fully detonated the aft cargo of TNT and picric acid.

Altogether 2,925 tons or 5.85 million pounds of powder exploded, giving off over 9,000°F heat. The *Mont Blanc*'s iron hull shot up over a thousand feet, roiling within the initial flame ball until much of it vaporized. The anchor snapped its chain and separated, sending the 1,140-pound shank whirling through the skies over Richmond Hill and across the city for 2.35 miles, until it landed on the other side of the peninsula of Halifax across the Northwest Arm. The aft cannon shot off the stern and arced over the harbor and Dartmouth's North End for three miles, landing next to a small lake. As the cloud lifted and cooled in the clean air, white-hot fragments of the *Mont Blanc* showered down across the streets of Halifax-

Dartmouth. What was left of the boiling benzol rose into the air with the cloud and combined with the carbon particles given off by the explosives to create a slick black rain that fell across parts of both cities for as long as ten minutes.

On land, the sound arrived first. It rippled through the earth at the punishing speed of 13,320 miles per hour—twenty-three times the speed of sound. Depending on how far away people were, survivors perceived it as a rumble or a boom. Those who were close, such as the Mi'kmaqs at Turtle Grove, described it as a buzzing sound. People as far away as 225 miles, in Cape Breton and Prince Edward Island, reported hearing a low boom. Later that afternoon, when the crew of the *Wave*, a fishing boat, arrived at Boston's Finn Pier, they asked if there had been an explosion. They claimed to have heard a low boom rumble across the sea. Some people reported hearing two blasts, but what they actually heard was the air catching up to the sound. "The concussion went right in you, like right in, you could feel it. You could feel it! Blowing!" Others, such as Jean Lindsay at the Dalhousie library or Pharmacist Bertha Archibald in the South End, heard a noise ten seconds before the windows shattered. In Dartmouth some people counted forty seconds. Ginger Fraser's classmates at Morris Street School reported that their eyes were suddenly forced opened wide by the air blast. Lottie Duggan said that her house just flew apart all at once.

The air blast blew through the narrow streets, toppling buildings and crashing through windows, doors, walls, and chimneys until it slowed to 756 miles an hour, 5 miles below the speed of sound. The blast crushed internal organs, exploding lungs and eardrums of those standing closest to the ship, most of whom died instantly. It picked up others, only to thrash them against trees, walls, and lampposts with enough force to kill them. Roofs and ceilings collapsed on top of their owners. Floors dropped into the basement and trapped families under timber, beams, and furniture. This was particularly dangerous for those close to the harbor because a fireball, which was invisible in the daylight, shot out over a one-half- to three-quarter-mile area surrounding the *Mont Blanc*. Richmond houses caught fire like so much kindling. In houses able to withstand the blast, windows stretched inward until the glass shattered around its weakest point, sending out a shower of arrow-shaped slivers that cut their way through curtains, wallpaper, and walls. The glass spared no one. Some people were beheaded where they stood; others were saved by a falling bed or bookshelf. It pierced the faces and upper chests of anyone unlucky enough to still be standing in front of a window. Many people reported passing out. Many others who had watched the fire seconds before awoke to find themselves unable to see.

Every building within a mile was severely damaged. Houses out of range of the flame ball still caught fire when their stoves overturned. Others toppled under the blast. Stone foundations crumbled as quickly as the thick concrete walls of the Atlantic Foundry. In Dartmouth, Oland's Brewery, the Ropeworks, the Richmond Refinery, and French Cable Co. all collapsed. The shanties and wigwams in Turtle Grove were obliterated. In Halifax, all the buildings within half a mile of Pier 6 were demolished en masse. Pier 6 itself disappeared entirely above and below the water. Pier 8 was gone from the water up. The rail shed on Pier 9 shattered. Past that three miles of rail track was intertwined with the wreckage of 374 freight cars and 100 passenger cars. The air blast ripped up the wires of the Canadian Government Railway telegraph line between the North Street Station and Rockingham, totally demolishing the train shed, the cattle pens, and the repair buildings, and wrecking the automatic signal system, killing fifty-five railmen. Telephone lines, the tramways overhead, and the electrical lines were all ripped up. Upended lampposts sent a tangle of live wires across houses and into the streets.

As the air blast spread over Richmond Hill and North Dartmouth, it took everything it could with it, including the air, leaving behind a vacuum that exploded stoves, radiators, furnaces, and large cupboards. Piano keys burst out of windows and fell into the streets. Mailboxes exploded. Downtown, doors and plate-glass windows exploded outward as the higher air pressure inside the buildings sought to equalize with the lower air pressure outside. In many houses with storm windows, the upper two frames on the inside exploded when the air blast passed through, then the bottom two panes burst on the outside when the air rushed to fill the vacuum. The air blast weakened as it hit the top of the hills on either side of the harbor, but still moved with deadly force. It lost some of its strength when it hit the Citadel but was still strong enough to blow doors off their hinges and windows out of their frames as it spread across the peninsula and finally out to sea.

THE LAST THING CHARLES Mayers remembered was the first officer of the *Middleham Castle* shouting "Look out." The blast then picked up Mayers and tossed him through the air. At the top of Fort Needham Hill, it dropped him onto the ground over a mile away from his ship. "I tried to throw myself back and could not. . . . I remember hitting something with my left side. I remember meeting pieces of timber and wood; I was quite conscious; I felt the water. I thought I was under the bottom of the sea somewhere. Everything went black. I was wet when I came down . . . I had no clothes on when I came to except my boots. There was a little girl near me and I asked her where we were. She was crying and said she did not know where we were. Some men gave me a pair of trousers and a rubber coat." Other people reported the same thing—being picked up and dropped off gently on the top of the hill up to a mile away from where they stood. Once again, Halifax's curious geography had protected its citizens. The hills absorbed much of the force of the air blast and the wind slowed as it hit the top of the hill, dropping passengers gently to the ground despite having carried them to great heights. If the ship had exploded on flat terrain, they certainly would have been killed. The hills also protected the neighborhood on the other side of Richmond, saving many more lives. As the normally humid Nova Scotian air condensed in the high-pressure zone, those caught up in the blast were suddenly drenched with rain.

A length of chain whipped through the military hospital for returning soldiers on Pier 2 and the buildings on Pier 3 were torn in half. On Pier 4 where Canadian naval headquarters were on the *Niobe,* whole buildings were flattened. Fred Longland, who had wisely commented to his friend that there was little hope of putting out that fire, never got to hear the reply. A "blinding flash, an awful shudder and a bang" interrupted him, and he thought the whole world was coming to an end. Next came a brief but ominous stillness followed by a vicious metal windstorm made up of rivets and jagged steel that thrashed across the *Niobe*'s decks, cutting into anything in its path. Longland lay half-conscious on the deck as a heavy chunk of metal swept across the bow and hit the foremost funnel, completely flattening it. More debris hit the other funnels, sending more metal showering onto Longland. He had to get off the deck, but sailors were everywhere, hiding in corners, taking cover under whatever would shelter them. Some were even hanging down the ventilators. With his arm pressed against his head for protection, Longland ran the length of the deck toward the aft companionway, where he could hide safely behind the armor, but before he reached the deck, a tsunami swept over the *Niobe,* listing the ship and slamming Longland onto the steel deck. When the ship righted itself, he crawled to the aft deck. Others were not so lucky. The bodies of nineteen men lay scattered across the *Niobe*'s deck.

As the air blast expanded, the gases began to cool, and a wind rushed back toward the harbor, smashing through any windows left intact on the southern walls and finally knocking down any weakened houses left stand-ing on Richmond Hill. The wind picked up the debris and swept across the neighborhood in a swirling hailstorm of fragmented wood, glass, and iron. Two small tornadoes touched down near the Protestant Orphanage. When it was over not one of the twelve thousand buildings within a sixteen-mile radius was left intact. Over three-quarters of them had lost every pane of glass. Sixteen hundred houses lay in splinters. Windows all across Halifax, and through much of Dartmouth, were broken. Doors hung off their hinges. Chimneys were twisted or toppled, rendering the houses that sur-vived cold and vulnerable to fire. Nine thousand people were homeless. Six thousand were injured. Almost two thousand people were dead—one out of every thirty people.

IN THE HARBOR, THE heat of the explosion was so intense that a twenty-foot radius of water around the *Mont Blanc* instantly evaporated. As the air pressure pushing outward from the ship diminished, water from all over the harbor rushed into the void. The volume was so great that it sucked the wa-ter from other shores until men as far away as the dry dock and Tuft's Cove were shocked to see the harbor floor exposed. As the waves surged back to-ward Pier 6, they collided with such force that a geyser shot out of the har-bor up into the sky. The higher it rose, the more water it pulled from the opposite shores. When the geyser finally collapsed under its own weight, this sudden addition of water destabilized the harbor the way an ice cube dropped into a glass momentarily destabilizes a drink. A semicircular tsunami rippled outward across the harbor, picking up more water and force until it was twenty feet high. The wall of water picked up bits of metal, swept men off decks, broke mooring lines, and spit ships aside as it sped outward to the Basin and the sea. The worst of it hit Tuft's Cove, where it crashed over people, trees, and houses. A man on the Dartmouth side watched the buildings collapse in a wave. "Like a grain field in harvest before a gust of wind."

Along the docks, the wave lifted the tug *Hilford* out of the harbor and left her stranded on top of Pier 9. The *Imo* spun around across the harbor until she landed in Dartmouth Cove with her stern partially underwater. It took the *Curuca*, a British supply ship, across the harbor and sunk her in Tuft's Cove, killing forty-five of her crew. Ships floated aimlessly in the harbor, their mooring lines snapped and trailing. The *Middleham Castle*, which had just undergone repairs at the dry dock, was a twisted wreck and minus a funnel. The tug *Douglas H. Thomas* was peppered with holes where bits of the *Mont Blanc* had punctured her. She eventually sank. Another ferryman, George Holmes, who was crossing in the other direction from Charles Duggan, was picked up and deposited on Hanover Street below Duggan's house.

Underneath the water, two divers had just entered the water near the *Niobe* when the explosion took place, reporting "a sense of oppression" as the force rippled through the water, tossing the men until their air lines became entangled. The air lines led to a pump, an oversized wheel on the surface that required four men to deliver a constant air supply. Two of those men were dead and a third incapacitated by the blast. Walter Critch and Frank Gammon, who had been helping the second diver down the ladder, awoke twenty feet away. Critch ran to the shed where the pump was and found it intact, if buried underneath the shed's roof, and began to pump with one hand while holding up the debris with the other. Gammon ran back to the ladder and saw the divers below him tangled and exposed to the air where the water had receded to the center of the explosion. Realizing that the men were already struggling to breathe, Gammon jumped down the ladder and smoothed their air lines until the thin stream of air Critch was producing entered their suits. Gammon then rushed the men in their heavy awkward suits and helmets back up the ladder, anxious to get them out of the harbor because he could see the

The tug *Hilford* (left) tossed on top of a pier by the tsunami

tsunami heading down the harbor toward them. The two men barely made it onto the dock when the wave hit.

It took two minutes for the wave to reach the entrance to the Basin, five to hit George's Island, and eighteen minutes to reach the Northwest Arm, petering out the farther it traveled away from land and taking almost two hundred men out to sea with it. Altogether there was almost $35 million in damage.*

CHARLES DUGGAN WAS APPROACHING Tuft's Cove when he looked over his shoulder to check on the fire. He did not see the explosion or the fireball or the cloud of smoke, but he saw the tsunami. The wave smashed over the *Grace Darling*. "I myself was thrown into the harbor and engulfed in a swelling, roaring mass of water which closed over my head and drove me toward the bottom like a stone." The 40°F water shocked him awake and he bounced up through the green water, surprised to be alive. When he turned around to see what had happened, he saw another, even bigger wave filled with dead fish and debris surging toward him. This second wave slapped him so hard that he tumbled to the ocean floor and lost consciousness. On the Halifax side, the water smashed over the Duggan ferry wharf and ran up the shore all the way past Lottie Duggan's yard at Young and Campbell, sixty feet above sea level. In Dartmouth it went all the way up to Windmill Road. Finally it picked up Charles Duggan, swept off his outer clothes, and carried him to an empty field just north of the French Cable Wharf, where it deposited him, unconscious and facedown, in his underwear.

*Approximately $420 million U.S. in 2004 dollars.

*Chapter Five*

# Minutes Later

THE AIR WAS THE color of bruised plums. The first few moments were marked by a still silence until survivors' memories returned and they relived the moments preceding the explosion. Then came the clatter of people pulling themselves free of the debris. The lucky ones lay stunned on open ground. One thousand people lay dead in the streets with thousands more unconscious beneath the rubble. People who rushed into the streets discovered the neat line between public and private obliterated by splintered wood, bricks, broken wires, and chunks of metal. The dust and smoke floating through the air made it hard to breathe. Groups of dazed survivors wandered outside to assess the damage, while men who worked along the waterfront tumbled over the wreckage to get to their homes on the hill above them. It was hard going. Cars were overturned, horses dead. Lampposts all over the neighborhood were broken in half or leaning dangerously, with live wires snapping over the wreckage. Along the lower streets, where the tsunami had engulfed buildings, water dripped from the eaves as if it were a spring thaw. Boulders from the harbor were left exposed along the muddy shore. Other buildings were already on fire. Inside the houses, hot coals spilled onto wooden floors, but many people were too shaken to act and the fires took hold. Survivors complained that they had trouble thinking clearly, their brains and their bodies deadened to sensation while still more showed no reaction to stimulus at all.*

Near Pier 6, steam rose from the *Mont Blanc*'s metal plates, which had been scattered across the shore. Carbon particles coated everything, including the survivors. Mixed with the oily residue of the benzol fire, the black soot seeped through all layers of clothes and covered their skin so completely that initial witnesses who saw the survivors walk out of the neighborhood assumed that something had happened to the black community at Africville. Ironically, the hills that segregated Africville from the rest of the city offered that small community some protection from the blast, and while it was damaged, it was not nearly as decimated as Richmond.

But the first reaction to the devastation—even by those who watched the *Mont Blanc*'s barrels explode and crash onto the deck, who watched the flames turn the sky strange colors—was to search for the German plane that had dropped the first bomb on North American soil. Even the military was unsure of the cause for the first hour, and sought to establish whether they were under attack before sending their men out on rescue missions. The city was so conditioned to believe that the Germans could strike Halifax that they did not make the connection between the burning ship and the explosion. "Because at the time everybody thought it was a bomb from the Germans—you know—from an airplane. . . . They just said well, the Germans are here and somebody said there's going to be another one. . . . When my friend fell over the bank instead of running to help her I thought she was being shot at and I had better get out of the way of the shooting. . . . I ran out and I said, 'The Germans got us! The Germans got us!' . . . I couldn't get it out of my mind that they had come. I was hysterical if they mentioned a German."

The cloud rose straight for two thousand feet until the wind pushed it southeast. Fifty-two miles out to sea, the USS *Tacoma* was on the return leg of its third transatlantic escort and was not scheduled to stop in Halifax, but upon seeing the cloud from that distance, Captain Powers Symington thought something must be wrong. Half an hour behind it came the USS *Von Steuben*. Watching the billowing cloud from the bridge, the captain as-

---

*This is a common reaction to trauma, particularly head trauma, that usually lasts at most three to four days. People in Halifax complained that it lasted seven days for them, and their doctors noted that it was not until the eighth day that their wounds began to heal and facial expressions reappeared.

The *Patricia* before the explosion

sumed that something extraordinary must have happened. Both ships sped off toward Halifax.

The first thing fireman Billy Wells noticed after the explosion was that he was standing naked far above where he had parked the *Patricia*. He did not know what had happened to his clothes. He did not know what had happened at all. A large portion of the flesh on his right arm was missing. Another slice of sheared-off muscle hung limp from exposed white bone. He checked his other arm as if it meant nothing more to him than a desk or a table. Not only was his hand intact, it was still holding a piece of the *Patricia*'s steering wheel. The ship must have exploded. He looked down the hill to check for the chief, but was shocked to see a wave filled with boiling water and chunks of wood and metal rising off the harbor and smashing over the piers and railyards. He could not outrun it, so he let it wash over him instead. When it receded, he was lying in a field even farther away, but now his arm was throbbing. He looked over the empty piers. No firemen. No truck. No burning pier and no ship. "The sight was awful, with people hanging out of windows dead. Some with their heads missing, and some thrown onto the overhead telegraph wires." He did not know it at the time, but the rest of the eight-man fire crew, including the chief, was dead. The only other man who had survived was Albert Brunt, the volunteer firemen who had slid off the truck on Gottingen Street. Constant Upham, the grocer who alerted the fire department to the fire, was also killed instantly. The back of his handsome grocery and supply store was ripped off its frame. Upham's body was never found. Most people assumed it washed out to sea. Still clutching the partial steering wheel, Billy Wells headed toward Campbell Road and, he hoped, a hospital.

In the harbor, the *Stella Maris* was floating helplessly, nearly destroyed. Nineteen of her crew, including Captain Brannen, were dead. His son Walter had been blown into the hold on top of Nickerson but was not injured aside from bad bruises and a punctured eardrum. Commander Triggs and his crew, who had taken a boat from the *Highflyer* to help assist the *Mont Blanc*, were killed instantly, as were most of the men on the steam pinnace from the *Niobe*.

On the hills surrounding the harbor, over seventy children were entirely orphaned. They lost much of their extended families too. Other children who were the only healthy members in their families acted as adults, making all the decisions until they arrived at the hospital. On Richmond Street, the house collapsed on top of Frank Hillis; however, it was not the rumble or the bang that impressed him, but rather the sound of breaking glass. His brother Gordon was blown straight through the window and into the yard. Frank was trapped underneath the house until his father found him. George Hillis passed many wounded people lying in the streets begging for help as he ran home but he could only think of his own family. He pulled Frank out of the rubble by his arm, which had a compound fracture. Frank's other arm was badly cut and bleeding and his eyes were so badly damaged that he could not see. Next door at Bert Hillis's house, George's brother, things were worse. The house collapsed on top of Bert, his three-month-old daughter, Jean, and his five-year-old son, Laurie. George pulled his nephew Laurie from the wreckage too, but his skull was badly smashed. He held him in his arms until he died. Bert's wife, Helen, who had gone down to the Bowens' with her sister-in-law, was killed instantly. George and Bert's brother, Frank Sr., the president of Hillis & Sons, died when the blast slammed the door to the company vault shut and trapped him inside. They found his body the next day. At the Hillis foundry, two out of three employees were killed when the molten lead spilled over the floors and the walls shook to the ground. At the factory, a separate building, only three workers, who had been sent on errands, survived. Who died and who survived seemed to be random. Although young Frank's mother, his aunt Helen, and neighbor Ethel Bowen were all standing on the same verandah, only Frank's mother lived. Ethel Bowen was nearly cut in two by a doorjamb, while their mother was thrown into the street and pinned to the ground by a lamppost. Helen Hillis was found dead on the corner. This pattern was repeated all over the neighborhood. A man standing next to his friend would live while his friend would die. Some people standing close to the ship walked away, while those high on a hill died on the spot. People quickly gave up trying to make sense of it.

SIXTEEN-YEAR-OLD ELIZABETH FRASER arrived at her house on Roome Street shortly after nine. When she was thirteen, Elizabeth had left school to support the family and was employed as a domestic worker at the time of the explosion. No sooner had she arrived at work and started preparing a stew for lunch than she awoke in the yard, confused. People were screaming, and everyone she saw was covered in blood. Looking south, she saw the fire start to take hold near her parents' house on Roome Street and she started running, but found it tough to see through her tears. On Gottingen Street she passed her father. "I saw my poor father, down on all fours crawling like an animal, moaning and crying, but I did not stop. I had to get home even

The debris cloud rising from the harbor, as seen from the Northwest Arm

though I expected to find them all dead. My path was strewn with debris of all sorts, fallen wires and trees, and even dead bodies." When she arrived home she found her mother, seven sisters, and an aunt lying on the ground. She did not see her brother Arthur. The women appeared disoriented, unable to answer her questions, barely able to speak. The house was flattened.

"Mother, where is Arthur?"

Maude Fraser pointed to the ruins. Elizabeth ran.

"Arthur? Arthur?"

Elizabeth listened. She thought she heard something stirring underneath, but it seemed impossible that he could have survived. There was nothing left. What could she do? The answer was plain enough. Nothing. She turned to her mother but stopped in horror. "I saw my aunt, who was expecting a baby, dragging her little six-year-old boy by the hand. Her eyes were both blown out of her head and she was telling him to hurry; he was dead but she did not know." Elizabeth's aunt Sophie lived almost directly across from Pier 6 on Campbell Road. Every house on her block collapsed instantly, only to be submerged by the tsunami and its runoff. Besides Colin, the dead child Sophie was dragging with her, she lost her seven-year-old son James and her four-year-old daughter Margaret. Her husband James, twenty-three, was serving overseas, and without a husband, her first thought was to make her way up the street to her brother-in-law, but Arthur Fraser Sr. could not help her. He could not even stand.

Elizabeth sat with her sisters, trying to comfort them. They huddled together in the smoke, watching for hours as men ran past them, escaping from the burning piers and railyard at the foot of the street. Women walked up the street without seeming to notice that they were wearing their night-clothes or dustcaps, if anything at all. Cut and bleeding children wandered through the neighborhood, looking for their brothers and sisters. The Richmond Street School at the bottom of the hill was demolished, but luckily classes did not start until 9:30 a.m., so most of the children were still at home or outside when the air blast hit. Only two were killed. Eventually soldiers on horseback began to appear on Roome Street.

"Leave your houses. Head to open ground."

The Frasers, in too much pain and unwilling to split up, ignored the warning and remained in front of their house.

At St. Joseph's, Helen Clark had just sat down next her deskmate Frances Hayes when the classroom grew dark and she heard a deep rumbling thunder. "Like the thunder was taking place alongside of you instead of up in the sky." She was partially right. Thunder was coming through the ground, not through the air, as she thought. When Helen turned to look outside, expecting to see rain or hail or, perhaps, the season's first blizzard, she was shocked to see the windowpanes bend toward her like a jib sail extended in the wind. She wrapped her arms around her face and ducked just as the thousands of glass stilettos shot across the room. When the noise stopped and the shaking subsided, Helen raised her head, unaware of the blood running down her face. She and her deskmate bolted out of their chairs and ran for the door. "The ceiling above gave way at one corner and down two sides of the room, hanging like the flap of a great envelope and spilling out children from the room above." But even without light she recognized the stern grip of the Sister who grabbed her and Frances by the wrist and admonished them

"My heavenly God," she said. "The Germans have arrived. Get down on your knees girls."

Helen looked down the length of the dark hallway where a white alabaster statue of the Virgin swayed back in forth in a ghostly blur. Praying, she realized, could wait. "I clutched madly at her habit and beads, and she let go." The hallway was in ruins. Ceilings and floors had collapsed, but luckily the piano had fallen straight into a hole in the floor. Helen stepped onto it, testing it to see if it would hold her weight. It did. She bolted across the old varnished wood and leaped through a window to the schoolyard, landing in a "little heap of old snow in the corner by the steps." It was not cold at all. Not even sitting in the snow. Helen did feel tired, though. She laid down her head, resting her bloodied forehead in the melting snow.

Charles Duggan's nine-year-old niece, Helena, awoke in the basement on top of all that went before her: flooring, beams, bits of glass, paper, and plaster. She sat up and looked around for her classmates, but found she was alone in the dark. The last thing she remembered was the roar and then the feeling of the floor rising up from beneath her, but she did not spend much time wondering what had caused her fall; she just wanted to get outside. A dusty sunbeam lit up a length of banister and Helena strained forward to grab it, but her legs were trapped. The banister was only inches outside her reach. She tried again, this time wiggling her torso free of the wreckage until her fingers brushed against a spindle. That was all the encouragement she needed. She heaved forward and wrapped her fingers around the wood, kicking her feet free until, at last, she could climb over the wreckage toward the light. She popped her head through the hole. Teachers and children were running around her, some in the direction of the front entrance, others to the back. Anxious to join them, she pulled her knee onto the edge and dragged herself forward before jumping up and running to the front door, but a teacher turned her back, shouting that the front steps were unsafe. Helena followed the students from the second floor who were pushing each other down the back stairs and scattering outside. Once outside, she saw the smoke overhanging the harbor and reasoned that whatever happened, happened to the whole neighborhood. Her three sisters, her little brothers, and her mother were all at home on Campbell Road. Her father was at sea on the minesweeper and would not be there to help. She ran straight across the St. Joseph's schoolyard, past injured schoolmates, toward Young Street.

Nora Faulkner, a girl from Russell Street, had a deep gash in her neck and blood was seeping into the collar of her school blouse. A Sister pulled a handkerchief out from the wrist of her tunic and offered it to her.

"Here's my handkerchief, put it to your neck."

Nora took it and held it against the wound, but within moments it was saturated. The Sister looked frightened.

"Nora, go home if you have one to go to."

Nora, dazed and unaware that she was not wearing a coat, ambled off toward Russell Street after Helena, passing her neighbor Helen Clark, who was still passed out in the snow. Younger children were streaking around the yard, looking for someone to tell them what to do, but still nervous about leaving the schoolyard without permission. A teenager, Gus Crowley, lay in the field next door, where he had landed after being blown out of

St. Joseph's School destroyed. Helen Clark jumped from the second story.

the street. He watched the school flatten slightly, its middle bulging before collapsing. Injured children ran over to him.

"Where will we go mister?"

He had no idea where they should go. Looking down Kaye Street, it seemed as if the whole city were gone. He gave them the same advice he had been given so often since the war started.

"Stay clear of the buildings."

Dorothy Lloyd and her sister Dolly arrived at the school grounds panting and out of breath, asking about their sisters Margaret and Hilda. The four sisters had been caught up in the blast, which then dropped them briefly to the ground. This did not strike Dorothy as nearly as unusual as the long pieces of tubing tumbling above them.

"Dolly, look at the stove pipes flying in the air."

"Those aren't stove pipes," Dolly corrected her. "They're sailors."

The wind then picked up the four girls again, but this time it separated them. Dolly and Dorothy woke up in the middle of a vacant lot surrounded by a flock of dead birds. Margaret and Hilda were nowhere to be found. Dolly began to cry, but Dorothy grabbed her and pulled her off toward St. Joseph's. When they reached Kaye Street for the second time that morning, the nuns were carrying children into the yard. Some were dead. Dorothy spotted her deskmate laid out on the ground and stood staring until a nun noticed her. The nun was covered in blood too.

"Go home, girls."

Dorothy took Dolly's hand and they backed away, then turned to run, one hand still firmly grasped in the other.

Two men approached Helen Clark to see if she was alive, but their shouting went unanswered. She heard them but could not find her voice. They shouted again. Her right arm shot straight into the air, and a man lifted her out of the snow. Her hair was matted with glass, plaster, and with some sort of tar. Fresh rivulets ran over the dried blood that covered much of her face and neck. Pain shot through her legs when she stood up and she lurched to one side. Maybe it was from jumping out the window or maybe something had hit her—she had no idea; it just hurt. The man checked to see if she could walk. She could. When he was satisfied that she would not faint again, he straightened her plaid bow and left her to walk back to Russell Street alone. She tried to pray but worried that "Now I Lay Me" was not sufficient for such an event and settled on repeating the part of the Lord's Prayer she did know.

"Our father who art in Heaven . . . Hallowed be thy name."

She could not finish the prayer. As soon as she said the word *father*, she began to get upset. "I yearned for father. . . . I thought Kentville was on fire too." The blood caked around her eyes only let in a pinhole of light. She had trouble making out anything dark, but she could see white things. The picket fence that she had passed on her way to school stood out, and although it was smashed and on the ground, she was grateful that she could use it to orient herself. She was on Albert Street. When she hit cobblestones, she knew she was on Russell. The sight of a severely wounded naked man walking toward her did not faze her. He was covered in blood except for shavings of skin that stuck out from his flesh "like the curls of wood a plane makes on a board . . . the white flesh showed through wherever there was not a curl." He stopped and asked her for directions, but she did not recognize the street name. She ran down the hill sobbing. Her grandmother, Minnie Clark, and her aunt Hilda were standing at the gate, watching the children come down the street, looking for Helen. Minnie recognized her by the bow. She rushed over to Helen, took her by the hand, and sat her down next to a tablecloth that she had tied up like a hobo. Wrapped inside were all of her best dishes. Minnie rushed back inside one last time to find her teapot while Helen lay on the ground looking at the neighbor's house. "It was burning furiously, and from one of the windows I saw one of those red-haired children waving and screaming." Minutes later her grandmother returned with a silver teapot suspended in her apron. It was too hot to carry by hand. "In a little while the coal cart came by. It was two-wheeled and drawn by a horse. It was painted green and had big white letters on its side, spelling C O A L." Minnie picked up Helen, lifted her into the cart, and told the driver to take her to the hospital.

HELENA DUGGAN WALKED DOWN Russell Street too. It took a lot of effort to control her legs, which were desperate to sprint past what she saw on the ground. She feared tripping, afraid to touch the ground or anything on the ground. A girl close to her in age lay in the gutter, decapitated. At another house, a young girl tried to rescue her mother, who was hanging from a lamppost, tangled in a wire. Other women, or, worse, their body parts, hung from wires, trees, and windows. Individual fingers and feet were strewn all over the street. Almost everyone Helena saw was bleeding, and each time she passed an injured child, she could not help but think about her three sisters, her little brother, just five, and her new baby brother Gordon. Her mother, Lottie, was a petite woman who had been sick for much of her last pregnancy, worn out by a persistent cough. She had been confined until the last week of November, but was still weak. Helena fought off a rush of panic and sped down the hill, taking everything in, the naked men, the wounded, and the dead. Her legs broke into a run despite her determination to walk. The fires, she noticed, were spreading. The calm air kept the flames straight and low to the ground, but minor explosions sent sparks jumping across yards and streets, igniting houses lucky enough to have survived the blast. Wires snaked around, cracking and popping. Sparks burst out of their broken ends and fizzled into steam and smoke. She could feel herself start to panic, but she struggled to stay calm by talking herself into slowing down. A small black dog ran around the legs of a man stuck under debris, rushing forward and back, barking excitedly. Horses galloped through the streets without riders, some dragging empty hay wagons behind them, while others were already manned and carrying the dead and wounded to hospitals. At the bottom of the hill, Helena finally started to run, but a soldier grabbed her and yanked her to a stop. Helena did not look at the soldier. Instead, she pursed her mouth and peered at the house across the street. "That's my house right there," she said, pointing. "And that's my sister hanging from a beam. We've got to get her some help."

The soldier turned. The house was in splinters, but at the side he could see a twelve-year-old girl suspended from a beam. She was badly cut where her arm was hooked on a metal stake. He let go of Helena and hurdled over the debris toward the twelve-year-old Irene. Her eleven-year-old sister Bessie ran over and grabbed Helena and screamed that the rest of the family was underneath the house. Helena ran to the pile and started removing the rubble. Within minutes they found five-year-old Kenneth, who darted out from underneath some plaster after they pulled a board from the pile. He was stunned and bleeding. Bessie told him that they had to find their mother and Lydia.

As the soldier worked to free Irene, the three children tossed board after board into the muddy yard. Kenneth's pudgy hands grasped bits of plaster and lath, and he found his mother, Lottie, first. Bessie and Helena ran to help, grabbing at the boards that trapped her in the basement. As Lottie climbed out, Helen noticed a gash starting somewhere on Lottie's head, continuing across her forehead, down her right side, and stopping where her nose joined her cheeks. She was dizzy and disoriented. All she could remember was the house bursting out from around her. The girls got her seated safely before they went back for Lydia. When they found her, she too was badly cut.

On the top of the wreckage, the soldier tightened his grip around the beam while wrapping one arm around Irene's legs. The girl's face was cut and her arm ripped open from where she was caught on an iron spike. He had to lift her up to free her. Irene, exhausted and confused, fell from the beam and the soldier caught her and pulled her tight against his body. He saw her face, pale and frightened white. As he carried her to the ground, Irene's head fell back, exposing a long shard of glass protruding straight from her throat. He carried her to the yard, careful not to put any pressure on the wound. The other girls surrounded him, checking to see if Irene was conscious. Helena wanted to pull out the glass, but she could not get a grip on it—it was stuck in an awkward place—and it slipped from her grip each time she tried. They decided to leave it.

Lottie had been standing at the window watching the fire, but she was convinced that it was the mirror that cut her, not the window. Helena did not care what had cut her, she just wanted to get away from Campbell Road. The fires around them were getting closer. Flames licked the sides of Upham's General Store. Lynch's Bakery was burning. Farther down, near North Street, a telephone pole and a crushed streetcar blocked the road, as if marking the doomed entrance to Richmond. Lottie told them to go to St. Joseph's. Someone at the church would help them. Bessie and Lydia put their arms around their mother and Irene, and lifted them from the ground. Helena held Kenny's hand and led the family up the steep climb toward St. Joseph's, sticking to the center of the street to avoid the sparks. "We had her by the arm, taking her up to Russell Street, and both sides with wires and screaming and fire." Lottie was still dazed, and as they walked up the hill she quieted her two-year-old Alma, whose hand she thought she was holding. Helena watched in discomfort, knowing that Alma had died two months before. At the top of the hill Helena turned to look behind her. She could barely believe what she saw. The Richmond Printing Plant, a tall brick building, was a ruin. "I could see right through it, and that sort of shocked me, it made me confused." When they reached St. Joseph's, they found it deserted, with its roof and two walls collapsed. Helena sat her mother on the Glebe's fallen gatepost and looked around. There was nothing left of the neighborhood. She had no idea how to find help—her mother needed stitches and the glass had to be removed from Irene's neck. Her mother asked her for some water and Helena searched through the broken dishes, looking for a container. Finding a mug intact on the ground, she dipped it into a puddle and handed it to Lottie. Instead of drinking it, Lottie poured it over her head.

"Don't do that. Don't do that," Helena and Bessie screamed, and took the mug away. The wound in Lottie's head was so bad that they could see inside her skull. After resting briefly, the Duggans turned the corner to Gottingen Street, but got only three blocks toward the Admiralty Grounds before they rested again, this time on the curb. Soldiers soon appeared with gray blankets, and although the Admiralty House was being used as a hospital, there was no invitation for them to enter. It was already overcrowded. The four girls, Kenny, and their mother wrapped themselves in the gray wool, afraid to move.

As the neighborhood slowly cleared out, groups of soldiers appeared and began to evacuate whoever was left. On Roome Street soldiers with a horse-drawn wagon discovered Elizabeth Fraser and her family still sitting on their steps in the cold. They lifted the seven girls, one by one, into the wagon. Then came Arthur Sr., Maude, and Aunt Sophie with Colin. Elizabeth, unhurt, climbed aboard. The wagon picked up more casualties as they went along, trailing blood behind them all the way to Rockhead Hospital. A churchlike stone building with a tower rising from its center, Rockhead was also a prison, but since its construction in 1859, it had served the greater purpose of providing health care and shelter to the city's indigent. As the wagon approached the hospital, Elizabeth saw that eight elegant Romanesque windows extending two floors across the face of both wings were filled with the silhouettes of soldiers trying to nail woolen blankets across the cavernous frames. Once inside, the only light came from the flames of two old lanterns. There was just enough light to reflect shimmers from the glass sprinkled over the beds and the floor. The ward reeked of plaster and smoke, but this did not bother the Frasers, who made space for themselves among the injured. "We were like lost sheep, bewildered and did not know what might happen next."

AT TURTLE GROVE, William Paul's mother awoke on the ground. Heavy drops of rain fell over her face but instead of running down her cheeks like tears or water, the liquid stuck where it landed. A baby was crying. It sounded muffled, as if she were swaddled too tightly. Mrs. Paul stood up, her dress hanging off her in strips. It was dark; smoke obscured the outlines of the buildings and she could not see her house. The women who had been standing next to her lay on the ground decapitated. Mrs. Paul cocked her ear to listen for the crying Madeline, but every few seconds something crashed out of the sky and exploded next to her. It was hard to concentrate. She shuffled over to a pile of timber that she only then recognized as her house. Again the baby cried. She bent over to toss the wooden planks, but her pregnancy made it difficult. Each time she pulled off a piece of wood, the howls got louder. She dug faster until she exposed part of the stove. It was intact and upright on its curled feet, but the oven door was ajar. Mrs. Paul pulled open the door and looked inside. Baby Madeline was lying on top of a bed of hot coals. The back of her swaddling was scorched and her back burned. The side of her face looked crooked too, but she was screaming vigorously. The cries were a good sign. Mrs. Paul tried to comfort her, while she continued to search for the boys. She found Blair lying in a ditch, one arm and leg nearly cropped off, but he was alive too. Moments later she was astonished to see William walk out of the smoke unhurt. He ran to her. Sickened and stunned, she looked around for help, but could not see through the dusty blue air. Every few seconds they could hear things fall out of the sky and splinter on the ground or splash into the harbor. She wandered off toward the shore. She wanted to know what was causing the noise. At the water's edge she could see small wooden barrels raining down onto the water; others smashed open on the rocks. She looked up to the blackened sky, convinced that the world was ending. She dropped to her knees and prayed. William stood behind her, watching as a sticky black goop collected over her broad back. When the smoke lifted and part of the sky cleared, he tapped her on the shoulder. She opened her eyes to see patches of blue in the sky and chicken legs scattered across their yard.

Madeline's cries drifted over Turtle Grove to the field where Charles Duggan lay halfway between the Grove and the French Cable Wharf. His jacket and pants were gone and his long woolen underwear weighted with cold seawater. He rolled over and looked across the harbor in search of his ferry, but he could neither see nor breathe in the black smoke, and he collapsed.

ON THE OTHER SIDE of the field, the crew of the *Mont Blanc* gathered. They had barely made it to the woods before the ship exploded. When the sailor on top of her stood up, Aggie March found herself and her baby safe. He had saved both their lives.

The smell of spruce awakened Mackey. He and Le Médec had been thrown to the ground and knocked unconscious by an uprooted tree that pinned them to the ground. When they awoke they had to pull themselves out from beneath the heavy branches on either side of them. The captain was so stunned that he did not recognize Mackey. Mackey's head was aching and he had a slight bruise on the side of his nose, but, other than that, all he was missing was his cap and half of his rain jacket, which had been sheared off below the waist. The crew were all mostly uninjured, except for four men, one of whom was badly hurt. One man's arm was broken, and he was bleeding. Le Médec joined them and they staggered up the hill together toward Windmill Road, where they stopped a car. "I met a car and I asked him to bring me and I entered in the school where men was wounded." Mackey walked on alone. He made his way down to the Dartmouth ferry where he met Captain Peter Johnston, the superintendent of lights and buoys for Nova Scotia. Johnston had been on the ferry along with three hundred other people when the explosion hit. The ferry had jarred, then the windows crashed. The captain thought it was a stray torpedo, but then a strange rain started, which no one could identify.

Johnston gestured a hello to Mackey. Mackey, Johnston knew, would know what was going on in the harbor. Just to see Mackey at the Dartmouth ferry was an indication that something was seriously wrong.

"What caused the explosion?"

"The ship I was on exploded," Mackey said. As they waited for the ferry, Mackey told him the story of the crash in the Narrows. Once in Halifax, he reported to the Pilotage Authority.

WHEN CHARLES DUGGAN AWOKE the second time, the smoke had cleared slightly. He could make out a scattering of wreckage at the end of the field, 150 feet from shore. At 36 feet and weighing over a ton, the *Grace Darling* was "no mere rowboat," and it took Duggan some minutes to understand that the wood all over the grass, and all over him, was his beautiful new trawler. He tried to shake off the creeping nausea. His head felt thick, as if he had taken too much of the bottle or slept too long in the afternoon, or both. His limbs and feet felt heavy and clumsy. He knew that he was on the Dartmouth shore, and he recognized Black Rock Point to his right. Just offshore, the Belgian Relief ship, the *Imo,* sat grounded and on a list with her four masts pointing toward Dartmouth Cove. The last time he had seen her, she had been heading back into the Basin, two hundred yards away. It did not make sense. A ship like that weighed over five thousand tons. How did she get to Black Rock? He tried to stand up, but his legs trembled and he dropped back to the ground. He could not determine how long he had stayed there. It could have been a minute or an hour. He just wanted the dizziness to pass. He closed his eyes, conscious of the land beneath him.

Why was everything so greasy? So black? He lay there breathing, concentrating on moving his hands and feet. He had to open his eyes to see if they were responding. He drifted into unconsciousness again. When he awoke a third time, he realized that the daily clatter of the dockyards was gone: The booming voices of supervisors, the megaphones, the clanking metal of the shipyards were all silent, replaced by a thin, broken wail. The horrible noise carried across the water to where he lay outstretched in the field. His family, including his new wife and his infant son, lived only one block from where the French steamer had grounded. He had to get back home to Hanover Street. Duggan stood, still dizzy and bruised, but this time his legs held.

A short, steep hill led up to Windmill Road. From there he would have to walk two miles to the ferry, but his body refused to cooperate, his limbs swinging without permission, his knees crumbling with each step. The grass was slick, wet, black. He fell every couple of steps. His thoughts came and went, one unattached to the other, all equally slow. His chest weighed down on his lungs, as if trying to keep them from expanding, making the climb even harder. The trees on either side of the road had been blown out of the ground, but in different directions. On the southern side they faced Windmill Road with their roots exposed to the harbor, while on the northern side, their branches pointed down the hill.* The trees closer to the harbor's edge were already burning, their sap crackling as flames burned through the bark. To his left, Duggan could make out the outline of what used to be Oland's Brewery, now a crumpled heap of ruins. The redbrick smokestack of the Cordage Company, which normally towered over the neighborhood, was dust. Turtle Grove was on fire, the wigwams and rickety huts gone. He closed his eyes and concentrated on the hill, trying to think who could help him. He would stop at Baxter's, a store on the corner of Windmill Road. He stumbled over wreckage, falling forward onto the road. The urge to lie down washed over him, seducing him with the promise of rest and relief. He fought the sleepiness, opening his eyes and using his numbed hands to push himself off the ground, but his legs refused to support him. Using his arms, he pulled his legs along behind him. The store was not far now. Somebody there would help him. His eyes were bright and wild, like those of a feverish child. He crawled the last yards to Baxter's

---

*The same was true of houses in Halifax. "Those houses South of North Albert Street were blown down the hill, which is towards the explosion, while houses to the north of the street were blown in the opposite direction."

doorstep, but inside the counter was empty, the former proprietor, Jannette Baxter, dead. As he pulled himself across the doorsill, he felt his resolve slip away and he rested his head on the wooden floor. The dry heat soothed him. Unable to resist any longer, Charles closed his eyes, once more unconscious and oblivious of the flames creeping up the walls around him.

Charles did not know it, but lying near the fire was exactly what his body needed. Numbed from hypothermia, his blood had rushed to his heart to protect it. The fire coaxed the blood back into his limbs, but it was the smoke that woke him. As flames climbed over the shelves and display cases, the smoke filled the room until the prostrate Charles awoke, coughing and spitting. His hands and feet tingled. He stayed low to the floor and crawled back the way he had come, but this time his body responded to his commands and as soon as he was on Windmill Road, he was able to stand. When he looked back, he was surprised to see that Baxter's Groceries was almost completely engulfed in flames. He started to run.

Charles could not make sense of the damage that lay in front of him. Across the street, the newly built Emmanuel Church was a heap of planks and glass. Women and men dragged themselves through the streets, carrying their children and dodging wagons that had already started to collect the injured. Twisted bits of the *Mont Blanc,* scattered over the streets, made the run treacherous. Sailors from the *Niobe* passed by him, carrying the injured to

Oland's Brewery on the Dartmouth shore, not far from where Charles Duggan landed

open ground. The smell of burning wood filtered through the more acrid smoke coming from the harbor. Charles staggered along, coughing and falling when his legs got too weak. He avoided bodies stretched across the sidewalks; body parts were everywhere, but it did not occur to him that they were dead. He passed them casually, his mind unable to absorb the obvious, thinking that they were asleep or unconscious. His wet woolen underwear weighted his limbs even more, and as he walked farther from the fire, the wool stiffened with cold and chafed against his skin. In the minutes after he left Baxter's, he felt strong, but the effort to run soon cost him. The desire to sleep, the symptom of a concussion, returned again, and he found himself once again on his hands and knees, crawling down Windmill Road amid the confusion. Looking out to the harbor, Charles glimpsed a small boat bobbing up and down near the water's edge. Two men stood waving their arms and screaming for help. They had no paddles or oars. He knew that if they caught the wrong current they could drift out to sea. If they caught the right one, they would hit the shoals and they could walk to shore. It depended on the harbor tides. So much in his life depended on the harbor. It brought Billy medals and ribbons, recognition, pride, and a wife. It brought his father a career. Gave the family their position in Richmond. Bought them a new house. Everyone knew the Duggans. Of course, there were a lot of Duggans to know: auctioneers, steamfitters, mechanics, firemen, and, naturally, rowers. Charles grew up on the water, rowing families back and forth to Dartmouth, listening to their stories and telling a few of his own. He loved to talk, joke, tell stories. He was a risk taker, a gambler, a joker who knew his neighbors by name and now, he thought, by their screams. He could not get their cries out of his head.

The little boat drifted farther away from shore. Normally he would rush to their aid, but he turned his head and kept walking. Everywhere he looked people needed help. Himself included. His mouth was dry, as much from the shock as from the dusty air. He stepped over more bits of metal. How absurd it was to step over bits of a ship that he had been close enough to touch in the harbor just minutes before, a ship he had watched sail into the Narrows. The Narrows. The Duggan house on Hanover Street was barely a block from Pier 6.

At the intersection of Windmill Road and Water Street, Charles passed Park School. The city had already decided to replace the old wooden building, but the explosion expedited their plans. The spire that held the school bell was missing, the windows smashed. Gangs of young boys tramped around investigating the damage. Farther over the hill to the east, near the top of Victoria Road, dozens of people crouched down in the bushes waiting for another explosion. From the top of Water Street, Charles had an overview of the calamity below. Stores along the waterfront were abandoned, the windows smashed, their window displays covered in glass. All the food on the shelves was contaminated. Christmas turkeys were laced with glass shards. The wounded—a ragtag collection of men, women, and children—milled about Queen Street where Dr. Dickson had pulled his dining room table outside. He had been ordered to evacuate because of the threat of an additional explosion, but rather than desert his patients, he had moved everything outdoors. He opened up the table, extended its many leaves, then covered it with a white sheet. A light wind gently picked up the corners and set them back down again as Dickson worked. As soon as he finished one patient, he hurried the next off the grass and onto the table.

The businesses Dartmouth had fought for and fostered were ruined. The chocolatier John P. Mott & Company, Starr Manufacturing along the canal, its competitor the Atlantic Foundry, and the molasses plant had all collapsed. But Charles cared only about one business, and from where he stood, he could see that it was operating. The Dartmouth ferry was chugging across the harbor. Charles ran down the hill, determined to make the next crossing.

Since 1913, the Dartmouth Ferry Terminal had sat at the foot of Portland Street. From the outside, its peaked roof, tower, and delicate weather vane looked more like a church than a ferry terminal. Maybe that's because it was the center of Dartmouth life, with everyone from children to soldiers to freight shippers to farmers using it to get back and forth between the two cities. Fortunately the ferry, which ran a diagonal route across the outer harbor and back, absorbed the shock of the explosion without incurring damage, aside from broken windows. With only light damage, the ferries continued to run all day, although the crowds were much heavier on the Halifax side—people trying to get home to Dartmouth complained that they waited for hours because workers and volunteers had to wrestle a dead horse from the dock. When they finally dragged the corpse to the side, passengers ran up the stairs to the port side where, once they were on the harbor, they had an unimpeded view of the North End. Many passengers were students who had been sent home. They pressed against the rail, jockeying for better views of the fires. "A novel and dreamlike experience it was—death, destruction and fire all around and here we were, not as other people, but sailing smoothly across the harbor, intact and let out of school early."

On the Dartmouth side, families stood behind the tall ferry gates at the passenger exit, scanning the faces of exiting passengers to find family members who had left that morning. Many would remain there all day. It was easy to tell who had been through the explosion and who had not by their appearance. Some of the passengers wore clean winter coats and boots. Others, like Charles, arrived "half-denuded." Their faces were all either pale white or covered in soot. He pushed through the turnstile. No charge. After the ferry emptied, the gates opened and he walked across the soft wooden planks and climbed the stairs to the deck. Even from that distance, he could see that the North End was in worse shape than Dartmouth. As they pulled out, Charles heard cries drifting through the smoke from Richmond, and the sound chilled him. "Probably the cries I heard were that of my own people."

Billy Wells

# Chapter Six

# Far from the Harbor

P EOPLE WHO COULD NOT see the harbor assumed that wherever they were was the center of the disaster. After they stepped outside and saw that the surrounding buildings were also damaged, they usually assumed that only their neighborhood was afflicted. Aside from the people in Richmond, it was hours, even days, before people learned that every building in the city had been damaged. Tucked away in the South End, far from the inner harbor and the fire, the mood was first bewilderment, followed by shock, and then excitement, but as the day wore on and more wounded arrived in their neighborhoods, the mood grew somber. Residents began to grasp that this was not just a morning or afternoon event. Something irrevocable had happened to the city. As reports drifted in about people waiting outside hospitals and children without homes or even families, the sense of helplessness quickly gave way to the need to act. Halifax, with its rigid class structure—divided by religion, class, and country—briefly integrated. English Protestant mothers, who two days before would not have stepped foot in Richmond, suddenly welcomed poor Irish Catholic children into their homes. Whole families were invited to live in the parlors of wealthier citizens. Soldiers and sailors, who created so much moral apprehension in the middle classes, were transformed into heroes. They were important not only because they were organized and prepared, but because they did not have the responsibility of their own families. The very thing that created so much anxiety—their single status—meant that they were available to work long hours without distraction. Teenagers and young adults also proved particularly useful. They took instruction, worked for hours on end without sleep, and were free of the usual responsibilities. As one volunteer at Camp Hill Hospital noted, "It was amazing how useless the older people were in trying to help out in such a terrible emergency, and how wonderfully quick and bright the young boys of twelve to fifteen could be in lending a helping hand." The problem with the boys was that they had to overcome their attraction to excitement and adventure, and to realize that they too were needed.

At Morris Street School, teenagers Ginger Fraser and Everett Covey sprinted up the Y-shaped stairwell and slipped into the back door just as the bell rang. It was a drafty old school, but well lit because the upper half of the interior walls were glass. Their teacher, a young man they called Slacker because he had not enlisted, sat in the front preparing the lessons. Ginger slid into his seat next to Frank Lusher. Slacker started the lesson when Ginger noticed the paintings slanting off the wall. Then the floor began to shake. It reminded Ginger of when the physician down the street accidentally blew up his house.

"Doc's done it again," some of the boys shouted.

"The Germans have got us!" said another.

The glass walls crashed to the ground as Slacker jumped from his desk and leaped across the room to the door, ordering the students to stay calm and march to the basement. "I think that was the last time any one of us ever called him Slacker, and from then on we respected him very much."* The boys quickly formed a line, but stopped when they reached the stairs. Hot water was pouring down from the broken pipes across the treads and over the sides, sending wafts of white steam up through the stairwell. The line of boys, anxious to get out of the ruined classroom, bunched up against each other, but the girls, who had gathered on the opposite landing, knew exactly what to do. They often did it when teachers were not looking. The first girl lifted her skirt, hoisted her thigh onto the banister, and gripped the wood on either side. When she let go, she coasted down around the sharp bend and into the steam. At the bottom she jumped onto the first floor in a practiced landing. The boys followed. Down they went, girls on one side, boys on the others, swooshing past Slacker and disappearing into the steam. Downstairs, they filed into the basement and waited in the dark. When

---

*Ginger Fraser later learned that Slacker had tried to enlist but was refused.

nothing else happened, Ginger and Everett crept up the stairwell, shaking out the cramps in their legs. They blinked their way out of the front entrance and looked north where they saw the cloud rising over the Citadel. With the smoke rising behind it, it appeared to have been bombed. The boys could hardly believe their luck. Despite instructions to head straight home, they sprinted toward the Citadel, stopping here and there to inspect the damage. After they crossed Spring Garden Road, they ran up the side of the Citadel, hoping to find evidence to confirm their German bomber theory, but the cloud was farther north than they expected. Fire bells rang out from all the different neighborhoods, each with its own pattern, and the clanging bells drifted in and out of the constant scream of ambulance sirens racing along Brunswick Street. They had never seen anything like it. Thrilled, they ran down the hill past the old clock, down Duke Street, toward downtown. After years of watching the soldiers come and go and reading about the front overseas, the war had finally come to them. Their exuberance did not last. They stopped short overlooking the Grand Parade and City Hall, where trucks and wagons bounced over Barrington Street, leaving a dark trail behind them. It took Ginger a minute to recognize the cargo. "They were people, and had been thrown on these carts helter-skelter. No doubt some of them were dead, and blood was dripping from behind these carts and trucks."

"What happened?" the boys asked, but no one stopped to answer.

They cut across Grand Parade and turned left onto Barrington. The crowds were thicker here, with more vehicles arriving from the North End.

"What happened?" they shouted, but their voices were lost as drivers concentrated on the moving mass of carts, cars, and wagons jammed into the street together.

At Clayton's, a luggage store at the corner of Hurd Street, Ginger and Everett approached an old man standing outside the door.

"What happened?"

"A ship blew up. Everyone in the North End has been killed."

The two boys looked at each other and then back at the man in bewilderment. Once they were out of earshot, they exchanged knowing looks. "That was hard to believe."

The two boys continued walking north, pleased with their skepticism. Farther up Barrington Street, they passed crowds of strange people dressed in rags going in the opposite direction. Men on horses galloped past, many of them wounded. What was left of the morning sky was growing darker, as it became obscured by black columns of smoke. At Cornwallis Street, the boys got their first glimpse of the ruined North Street Rail Station. The brick building was punctuated by rows of Romanesque windows and a regal tower topped by a dome, and a massive flag. To the back, the trains ran in and out of a latticework of glass and metal. Ginger stopped, stunned by the building's sudden absence. There was nothing left except for some brick and a gaping loss in the skyline. Steam wafted into the air from the rubble, filling the space with a ghostly palimpsest. Ginger loved the old station with its effortless glass roof. There was something stylish about the train station, something modern and elegant, so unlike other buildings in the city. He was sad to see it all ruined. He and Everett edged past North Street toward the Wellington Barracks, but a hard yank on their collars stopped them short. A uniformed soldier towered above them. He told them that the dockyard was on fire and the ammunition dump was in danger of exploding. Fear overcame their wanderlust. "We did not have to be told twice, and watched our chance to jump on one of the flat wagons going down Barrington Street. There were quite a number of people in it, some moaning and most of them bleeding quite badly." Their journey back was nowhere near as spirited.

*Chapter Seven*

# Scramble at City Hall

THE NEW CITY HALL was a jumble of peaked dormers, Romanesque windows, balustrades, columns, and towers that somehow sorted itself into an executive edifice. The lower level of cut granite and the top two stories of freestone suggested permanence, even gravitas, beckoning that great civic virtue—duty. A clock tower separated the east and west wings, but despite the belfry there were no tolls, no chimes, nothing as frivolous as a bell. The clock presided over the square and the time without comment. Its hands were locked at 9:05.

When Deputy Mayor Henry Colwell entered the Parade Grounds at 9:30 a.m., the rest of City Hall looked as if it had stopped at the same moment. The front entrance, which was usually the site of clerks skittering up and down the stairs, was deserted. There were no aldermen, no grumpy citizens paying fines. The windows were empty. Roosters crowing madly at the poultry show two blocks north scored the scene with an eerie soundtrack. Colwell, the president of a local men's clothing company and a city alderman, had been walking to work when the air blast forced him off his feet. Like so many others, his first thought was of his family. He ran back down Morris Street, rounded the corner to South Park, and bounded up the porch in search of his wife. She was shaken but unhurt. He relaxed just long enough to remember that Mayor Peter Martin was away from the city and that he, Colwell, was the senior official. Taking his hat, he rushed back outside and dodged through the women and children gathered along the sidewalks, investigating the damage to their homes. The closer he got to downtown, the more violent the damage, but more worrisome still was the "water spout"–shaped cloud erupting over the North End of the city, where his son was living at the Wellington Barracks.

Inside City Hall, paper was everywhere. Forms, receipts, brochures, and letters that should never have met mixed together on the floor like a bad guest list. Office doors neatly tipped into the hall in a row, abandoned by workers whose first impulse was, like Colwell's, to run home. It was the same across the city. Unless they were in the military or on a ship, most men abandoned their posts and went home. Grocery carts were deserted in the streets and stores left open and unlocked. The headphones of telephone operators lay cast off on empty chairs. Telephone and telegraph lines were down all over the city. Trams sat empty in the streets. Only hospital staffs worked continuously. Colwell walked the echoing corridors in search of assistance, but found only two men, the city clerk and Chief of Police Frank Hanrahan, who told him that Fire Chief Condon was dead and that the city's only fire pumper, the *Patricia,* was smashed beyond repair. Fires were

Halifax City Hall

breaking out all over Richmond. The gas main that supplied the North End was severed to prevent it from catching fire and exploding, but that also cut off the electricity. There was no guaranteed way in or out of the North End except on foot. Cars, wagons, and horses had to pick their way through streets cluttered with survivors, soldiers, debris, and fire. Drivers stopped repeatedly to drag wreckage from the road so that they could continue. Nothing in Colwell's life as a businessman or alderman prepared him to run a city that had lost its entire infrastructure in just over a minute. Hanrahan and the city clerk agreed that they needed help. The trio left the building and cut across the Parade Grounds to Barrington Street. At Spring Garden Road, they entered the Military Headquarters where they met with Colonel W. E. Thompson. Colwell told the colonel that he had two immediate concerns: heat and homes. It was a warm day, but it would get cold as soon as the sun went down. Thompson suggested that the military set up tents on the Commons. He offered mattresses and blankets as well as a group of soldiers to assist the wounded and to monitor the streets. Anxious to get back to City Hall, Colwell accepted the colonel's offer and left. The streets were busier, carts full of wounded already making their way to the hospitals. Outside of City Hall, a man approached Colwell and asked if he could be of assistance, handing him his business card. "W.A. Duff, Assistant Chief Engineer, Canadian Government Railways." Colwell invited him inside, and as they walked upstairs, Duff described to Colwell how he had spent the morning. Duff had already toured the North End, dropped off wounded at the Victoria General Hospital, telegraphed General Manager C. A. Hayes, who was in Moncton, to explain the extent of the damage and to ask for medical assistance for the city. When Duff described the scenes he had witnessed in the North End, Colwell realized that the city would be overwhelmed.

"For God's sake send out additional messages to the different towns of Nova Scotia and New Brunswick asking for further relief. And sign it the Mayor of Halifax."

The men did not know it, but another railman had already done that. George Graham, president of the Dominion Atlantic Railway, had been in his private railcar eating breakfast with his daughter when the yard rocked and shuddered. Outside almost four hundred ruined railcars surrounded him. Some were on fire, others tipped over, and others smashed flat. When he tried to send a telegram from the Halifax office, he learned that the wires were down, so he set off to Rockingham by foot. He counted twenty-five dead employees along the way.

Hundreds of rail cars and miles of railway were destroyed.

At City Hall, Duff was getting ready to leave Colwell and Hanrahan when a soldier came clattering into the room, ordering them to get out of the building because the magazine at the Barracks was going to explode. Colwell and Hanrahan dashed down the stairs, out the front doors, running straight into a swarm of people headed for Point Pleasant Park. The Barracks took up a large patch of land from North to Russell Streets between Gottingen and Campbell Road. The buildings were organized around an open square where the men drilled and trained. To the south sat Admiralty House, an official residence that had recently been turned into a military hospital. Along the rest of the perimeter were quarters for men, married couples, and officers, interspersed with stores, stables, and storage sheds. In the northeast corner, separated from the rest of the grounds by an iron fence, was the Barracks magazine, a small wooden shed half-built into the ground. Inside were hundreds of cases of munitions and explosives.

Cadets were waiting for classes to start, watching the fire, and listening to the band that was marching in the square, when the blast shook the buildings. A piece of metal pierced straight through the drum, but left the drummer unhurt. Alderman Colwell's son dove behind a tree and watched in disbelief as a metal hailstorm slashed through the air around him. The cadets inside fared a lot worse, and within minutes they were carrying their friends and teachers out of their classrooms and down to sick quarters. Officers lined up all the injured cadets who could stand and marched them to the hospital. Healthy cadets formed a unit and marched over to Russell Street, where they began pulling people out of the rubble.

Lieutenant C. A. MacLennan had been outside the officers' quarters with three others, investigating why so many fire bells were ringing, when he saw the fire. His blue eyes lit up in awe. "The best fire I ever saw in my life." The blast knocked the men off their feet. MacLennan, a small nimble man, jumped into the Barracks. When he climbed out, he found his three friends piled on top of one another on the lawn.

"My leg is all knocked to hell," said Lt. Harold Balcom from beneath the other two men.

An iron shard had passed through the back of his pants, ripping off the right pant leg but leaving his flesh smooth and free of blood. Still Balcom could not walk and was in terrible pain, so MacLennan ran up to the square, where he found a stretcher and packed Balcom off to the hospital.* Then MacLennan took over as the orderly officer. He stood in the middle of the square looking for the bugler, but he could not find him. He would have to call the cadets himself.

"Fall in Company B," he shouted, but his voice carried only far enough to attract a couple of boys. Some had blood running down their faces and hands. Others had more serious wounds and could barely stand. He told the cadets to call out with him.

"Fall in Company B," they shouted. This time more cadets appeared and took their place in line. MacLennan separated fifteen or sixteen uninjured men and ordered them to follow him on fire inspection. Starting at the officers' quarters in the southwest corner of the square, he led them through room after room. When they found stoves toppled over or loose coals on the floor, MacLennan left one man behind to shovel out the coals while he continued the search with the rest. Buildings all around the Barracks were starting to burn, but what caught his eye was a hole in the magazine fence. The culprit, a six-hundred-pound steel plate from the *Mont Blanc*, lay next to it. MacLennan squeezed through the opening and found the magazine shed in splinters. Inside the collapsed doorway, the air was overheated and dry, and he realized that a single errant spark could set off the whole dump. Alarmed, he climbed back through the fence and ordered three men to stand guard, but the soldiers, still worried about Germans, protested that they did not have weapons. MacLennan instructed them to use their fists if necessary. He sprinted up the hill to the officers' quarters and found a colonel on his knees attending to his injured wife. He asked for orders to deal with the magazine. If fire reached it, there would be a second, possibly more deadly, explosion. The colonel reacted angrily.

---

*Balcom later died from his wounds.

"To hell with the military magazine. My wife is bleeding to death. Get me a medical orderly."

MacLennan left the colonel and went to the square, where he collared eight Company B soldiers, marched them down to the magazine, and ordered them through the fence. It was a dangerous assignment and the young men knew it, but they followed MacLennan into the heated darkness. By taking baby steps with outstretched arms, they separated canisters and boxes of munitions from the wooden slivers piled all over the floor. The air was close and heavy, an indication that the surrounding fires were getting hotter. Realizing that it could take hours when they might only have minutes, MacLennan ran back up the hill to the square for a third time. He found a naval officer in charge of twenty sailors. Telling him that he needed the men to secure the magazine, he led them down the hill to the opening in the fence. At the door he gave them their orders.

"Get your kindling wood out of that and light no matches."

As the soldiers worked, MacLennan decided to inspect the grounds surrounding the magazine. His usual sentry, a young soldier named Eisner, joined him and they walked around the back of the shed. On the western side of the magazine, MacLennan and Eisner were horrified to discover smoke billowing from the heater house, a wooden shed connected to the magazine by a two-foot duct. The windows and doors had been blown out, and coals from the overturned hot water heater were already smoldering on the wooden floor. "An honest-to-God fire." With only minutes to stop the fire from spreading to the magazine through the duct, MacLennan ordered the sailors to scoop up the coals and remove them from the vicinity. Eisner rushed off to grab two chemical fire extinguishers stored nearby. He threw one to MacLennan and the two men squirted the smoldering floor with a spray of white chemical foam. A puff of steam rose into the air above the roof.

The stream of soldiers and sailors flowing out of the magazine with boxes of munitions caught the attention of survivors walking along Campbell Road, and a crowd gathered to watch. Everyone in the neighborhood knew which building was the magazine and everyone knew what would happen if it blew up. Standing in a group, holding their stricken faces in anticipation, they followed the soldiers' every move. From the crowd's vantage point on Campbell Road, the steam appeared to be climbing from inside the magazine. It was indistinguishable from smoke. An old man lifted his cane and pointed to the cloud. Someone shouted that the magazine was on fire. That was all the traumatized crowd needed to hear. Panicked and terrified that another explosion was about to occur, men and women broke into a run down Campbell Road. Hearing a hubbub, MacLennan turned from his work on the roof, where he was checking for sparks, and saw the last of the sailors squeezing themselves through the hole in the fence below him. Thinking that a fire must have broken out inside the magazine, he jumped down and tried to run, but he could not get past the other men crowding through the fence. Eisner ran past him on the other side.

"Where is the fire?" MacLennan shouted, confused because he did not see anything unusual.

"On the roof."

His heart beating faster than his legs could run, MacLennan scrambled onto the roof of the magazine but found no fire. He turned toward Campbell Road. It was as empty as the sky. Everyone had vanished, including his crew. Only Eisner and a couple of soldiers remained. Unaware that bystanders had misinterpreted the steam as smoke and were now running for their lives, MacLennan could make no sense of the sudden evacuation and still suspected that there was a fire somewhere in the shed. He jumped off the roof and inspected the shed's interior but again he found nothing. "An hour before I breathed normally." MacLennan, Eisner, and the other soldiers continued to separate the munitions, taking them outside and spreading them on the lawn.

Later that morning General Thomas Benson surprised them by wandering by and watching them for a moment. He looked calm and unfettered. He glanced around the magazine, the munitions scattered on the lawn, and gave an approving nod.

"Carry on."

They finished at 2:00 p.m. Afterward MacLennan's sentry Eisner collapsed in the worst case of shell shock MacLennan had ever seen, dissolving into a mass of tics and jerks, unable to control the muscles in his face and arms.[*]

Although the military never gave orders to evacuate and never predicted a second explosion, the panic and fear that overcame the crowd watching MacLennan's men soon spread to individual soldiers who, out of fright, repeated what they heard from civilians. Two men, Lt. L.L. Harrison and his father, who had been told there might be a second explosion, turned around

---

[*]This would be considered an acute stress reaction today, an indicator of a person's propensity to later develop post-traumatic stress disorder.

and drove down Barrington Street slowly, spreading the panic south as they went. They were not alone. Soldiers and policemen began going door to door, evacuating people, urging them to go south. Soldiers on horseback rode through the side streets, shouting. Men screamed at anyone they met along the way. A police car drove up and down the street, warning people to head south because the magazine might "go up any minute." The response was enthusiastic; the result miserable. Since the beginning of the war, people had been warned repeatedly that in the event of an explosion they should head to open ground. Thousands fled what little comfort their ruined houses offered and headed to city parks on foot, filling the streets and slowing down the cars and wagons acting as ambulances. Many people dragged or carried whatever favorite possessions they had managed to save. The majority of people from the North End went to the Commons, an expansive series of grass fields behind the Citadel between Camp Hill and Cunard Streets.

It was a grim parade. Soldiers walked among them handing out blankets. The lucky ones had winter clothes; the unlucky ones had nothing at all. Many were so covered in soot that they were unrecognizable. Survivors recognized each other any way they could, by teeth, clothing, shoes, or jewelry. Many were wounded and bleeding; others died on the grass. "One girl, when the explosion occurred, had evidently been interrupted in her dressing. Save for her corsets, she might be said to have been 'wrapped in thought,' but thus attired she started, valise in hand, and found herself on the Common, then thronged with a vast concourse of people. All of a sudden she seemed to realize her condition. Without a word, she sat down suddenly on the grass, opened the bag, and, taking from it all it contained, began with generous haste to complete her dressing. She had brought nothing with her except a pair of green silk stockings and a pair of white satin shoes. But, attired in these, delicate and precious garments, she continued her flight." In one corner, a group of nuns had formed a circle by holding out the sides of their habits and overlapping them. Dorothy Lloyd, who was reunited with her family after being blown off her feet with her three sisters on their way to St. Joseph's, ran over to the nuns and peeked through the habits. Inside the circle, a woman was giving birth.

PEOPLE IN THE SOUTH END of the city also got caught up in the parade. Jean Lindsay and her friend Claudy who had walked home from Dalhousie comparing damaged buildings and assuming that the people they saw in the streets—"men in trousers, pajama coats and slippers, women in kimonos, slippers and boudoir caps"—had heard about the windows crashing at the library, found the atmosphere more frightening an hour later when they tried to mail a letter. A crowd of people were running down Barrington Street toward Point Pleasant Park as a police car drove behind them, warning people to head south because the magazine might blow up. Jean and Claudy ran. Jean suggested they sit behind the fence near the tennis courts but Claudy would not stop running. Jean caught up to her and said they could sit in the cemetery, but Claudy told her that if the crowd was going south, so should they. "We finally landed up in the cut of the Terminals. . . . With every large puff of smoke we expected the explosion."

Ginger Fraser was also caught up in the evacuation, and ended up in Point Pleasant Park. "A large crowd of people was coming down to the Old Bath House, and there were quite a number of sailors who were taking the ferry across the Arm heading for Purcell's Cove to get away from another dreadful explosion." For the first time the boys worried about what was happening in their families and agreed to go home. Ginger, worried that his father would be angry with him, jogged over the Tower Road Bridge, but stopped when he reached the Stanhope Bakery, which was popular because of its brilliant Burlington buns.* Exhausted and worried, but not too worried to eat, he and Everett bought six for a dime. They ate three each.


ON BARRINGTON STREET, Colwell and Hanrahan were pulled along the narrow sidewalk by fear and the crowd until Colwell noticed that nearly all the people shoving past him had cuts on their faces and hands; the medical demands were going to be enormous. He stopped and grabbed Hanrahan, who agreed to risk the second explosion by returning to City Hall to make arrangements. They were pushing their way out of the crowd when Colwell heard a familiar voice calling his name. Former Mayor Robert MacIlreith and Lieutenant Governor MacCallum Grant waved at them. MacIlreith had been walking against the crowd since he left his house on the other side of the Arm and told Colwell that people all over the city were heading toward the outskirts—wounded, old, infirm, children, many of them badly hurt. Colwell greeted the two men enthusiastically and urged them to join him at City Hall for an impromptu meeting. Inside, the four men searched for a suitable space for their headquarters, stopping when they reached the

*Jelly doughnuts covered in confectioner's sugar.

southeast corner of the second floor, where they found a wide room filled with desks. The awkward counter that divided the room lengthwise was meant to separate the public from the civic servants, but at 11:30 a.m. politicians and citizens both convened an emergency meeting. Despite the chaos and urgency, Colwell insisted that they not break with protocol and called the meeting to order with the understanding that it was a citizens' meeting, not an official quorum. He then suggested that Lieutenant Governor Grant accept the position of chairman, which Grant accepted. Colwell took the role as secretary and, grabbing a paper and pen, took minutes. Colwell, Grant, MacIlreith, and five members of the council agreed on creating five instant committees: transportation, food, housing, finance, and mortuary. At quarter after twelve the meeting adjourned until 3:00 p.m. MacIlreith left the collector's office and turned into the hall, looking for men to fill positions on the new committees. MacIlreith was delighted to see his childhood friend Colonel Paul Weatherbe waiting outside to offer his services. Weatherbe was an engineer—exactly the sort of man MacIlreith thought could pull together an impromptu medical system. After agreeing to accept the position, Weatherbe got straight to work, dividing the city into districts and implementing a system of registration for doctors and nurses who arrived to volunteer. With so many people homeless, information management would be crucial. Nothing was more frustrating to those left homeless and separated from their family members than not having access to information. "Quick decision at the risk of occasional error was preferable, in the first hours, to extended deliberation and discussion."

After meeting with Weatherbe, MacIlreith left City Hall with City Engineer Henry Johnson and took a car to the North End to look for a suitable building for the morgue. Even after just a cursory tour through the outskirts of the worst areas, MacIlreith realized that they would need a lot of space and manpower to run the morgue properly. He had been the mayor in 1912 when he got the call that the *Titanic* had sunk off the coast and the unidentified bodies were being brought back to Halifax. They accommodated a shipload of 209 bodies in a temporary morgue, and it was then that MacIlreith and much of the city learned the importance of the little things—the details and detritus of everyday life. Clothing, jewelry, and even incidental items such as those found in pockets—a laundry tag or a receipt—could speed identification, but in a panicked or disorganized atmosphere, important clues could easily be lost. It was crucial that the identification process be organized and centralized. It would not do to have different undertakers following different procedures. Plus a centralized morgue would mean that people had just one place to go to locate bodies. Private mortuaries could take over after that. The two men stopped at three schools, the last being the Chebucto Road School, situated in the triangle between North Street, Chebucto Road, and Windsor Street.

Peaked roofs at either end demarcated the boys' entrance from the girls', making the three-story brick building accessible from different entrances. More important, it was structurally intact, aside from the usual broken windows and burst pipes. Inside, at the top of the stairs, a series of wide doors topped with transom windows led to classrooms that would make good offices. MacIlreith wanted to see the basement, and he and Johnson walked down a carved wooden staircase. What was left of the morning sun slanted through the open frames and lit up the pitted cement floor, which shimmered with sparkling glass. On the north and south walls, two sets of double doors with ramps offered access to the schoolyard. At the back, on the boys' side, the boiler took up most of one room while a smaller tiled room offered plumbing and seclusion. In between the girls' and boys' sides was a wide private area that offered some privacy for the morgue workers. Standing on the broken glass, looking around the gray basement with its broken windows, the men agreed that Chebucto Road School would do. There was no time to look at anything else. With that, they walked back into the light and rushed off toward City Hall to consult with the military. The whole trip had taken less than thirty minutes. By the time they returned, much of the Eastern Seaboard was preparing to come to Halifax's aid, thanks to the rail stations outside the city.

Minutes before the explosion, Vince Coleman, a telegraph operator, had sent to Rockingham the first notice of a munitions ship that might explode in the harbor, and although the train had already passed Rockingham, stations along the Truro line picked up the message. While not as dramatic as stopping a train, it was ultimately more effective. When the lines to Halifax went dead, his message rocketed from station to station. Operators and rail staff got out the word that something calamitous had happened in Halifax. Beginning at 9:26 a.m., other telegrams began flickering between Nova Scotia, New Brunswick, Ottawa, Montreal, Boston, and New York. At 10:20 a.m. the military censor announced that it had seized control of the Halifax wires. Otherwise, the information was sparse. The telegrams mentioned a collision, a possible fire and explosion, several deaths, and that the city was cut off from the rest of the world. "9:50 a.m. Montreal—Reports reaching telegraph companies here indicate that the explosion near Halifax has affected their dynamos. All wire communication with Halifax and outside points severed.

10:13 a.m. Boston—The Postal telegraph Company's lines also down. The local offices stated that Montreal reported no wires working east of that city. One report was that an explosion of a bomb killing a number of men occurred at 9:30 a.m. 10:27 a.m. New York—Halifax has been cut off from all communication with the rest of the world, either by wire or cable, according to officials of the Western Union Cable Company in this city. All land wires are down, and the plant of the United States Cable Company at Halifax has been so damaged by the explosion that it cannot be operated. 10:37 A.M. Ottawa—According to advices received here the Halifax disaster was due to the blowing up of a munitions ship in the harbor at eight o'clock this morning. All telegraph lines are down and the damage is very serious. It is believed a number of people near the scene were either killed of injured, including several telegraph employees."

Only one came from Halifax: "12:26 P.M. Halifax NS (via Havana)—Hundreds of persons were killed and a thousand others injured and half the city of Halifax is in ruins as the result of the explosion on a munitions ship in the harbour today. It is estimated the property loss will run into the millions. The north end of the city is in flames." Cuba received it first. They passed it along to Washington, which passed it along to the Red Cross office in Washington, which also received a telegram from its representative in the Department of the Military Relief who happened to be in Halifax. The Red Cross in Washington sent it out to their Eastern offices, including the Boston Metropolitan Chapter.

Earlier that morning in Boston, James Phelan, a private banker, received the telegram that George Graham had sent on the private banking wire after walking to Rockingham. "Organize a relief train and send word to Wolfville and Windsor to round up all doctors, nurses, and Red Cross supplies possible to obtain. Not time to explain details but list of casualties is enormous." Phelan called Henry B. Endicott, America's biggest shoe manufacturer and the chairman of the Massachusetts Committee on Public Safety. Endicott suggested that they go to the governor and the two men arrived at the State House around 11:00 a.m. From its home at the top of Beacon Hill, in John Hancock's old pasture, the State House was the definition of stately, meant to impress citizens without intimidating them, while doing exactly the opposite for the bureaucrats and politicians it housed. When Governor Samuel McCall read the telegram, he did not know what had happened or what Halifax needed, but he knew he had to act. He dispatched his own telegram, addressed to Mayor Martin. "Understand that your city in danger from explosion and conflagration. Reports only fragmentary. Massachusetts ready to go the limit in rendering every assistance you may be in need of. Wire me immediately." Expecting to hear back soon, he called a meeting of the Committee on Public Safety for 2:30 that afternoon.

The Massachusetts Committee on Public Safety was the first organization of its kind in America when it was sworn into existence on February 10, 1917. It was a great new experiment in public policy, the first version of a public emergency response unit, created when it became clear that America was going to join the war. The group of government and private citizens had organized themselves to work together not only to react to disasters, but also to anticipate them. Its members came from all facets of public and private life: transportation, medicine, military, agriculture, housing, and, of course, accounting. Governor McCall was adamant that the people of the Commonwealth would retain their standard of living despite the disruption of the war and the new presence of returning soldiers who were disfigured, debilitated, or institutionalized. He was sure of one other thing; it would not cost the taxpayers any more money. He was willing to call on patriots everywhere to assist in the war effort. He would send boys into the fields to work without pay, women to work making surgical dressings for the military, professionals to offer their services without charge, but he would not raise taxes. This last provision made the Massachusetts response even more incredible. The state was struggling with its own financial troubles caused by the disruptions of war. That it would respond to a disaster in another country, without even accurate information as to the nature of the disaster, without a thought as to cost, was testament to a combination of geography, shared history, and war jitters.

At the afternoon meeting, attended by one hundred men from across the state, Governor McCall asked the executive manager of the committee, Henry B. Endicott, if Halifax had sent a response to their morning telegram, but Endicott answered in the negative. There had been no contact with the city. He instructed Endicott to contact the Department of War and the Department of the Navy to see if they had any news. Endicott left to make the inquiry, but returned shortly to say that no one from Halifax had contacted either department. Colonel William A. Brooks, acting surgeon general of the commonwealth, stood up and suggested that, if they could get a train, he could dispatch a large corps of surgeons, doctors, nurses, and supplies within a few hours.

Although still unsure of what had happened, this struck Governor McCall as the proper course of action. After all, that was what the first telegram requested. The problem would be the train. James H. Huestis, from the Boston & Maine Railroad, stood and offered one of his. McCall asked if it could be ready by ten o'clock that night. Huestis promised that it would be waiting on the platform as soon as he could make the arrangements. Before the meeting dispersed, Governor McCall named the Honorable A. C. Ratshesky the commissioner-in-charge of the Halifax Relief Expedition, and promised him a letter of introduction to the mayor of Halifax. Abraham Captain Ratshesky was well known in the State Legislature where he had served as a Republican state senator. The son of two Jewish immigrants, he had opened a bank with his brother Israel that provided financial services to Jewish and immigrant communities that were disenfranchised from the established banking world. Earlier in the spring, to mark his fiftieth birthday, Ratshesky had opened a foundation in his name to provide these same citizens of Boston with grants to improve both their lives and their social standing. He also donated a building to the Red Cross so that the Boston Metropolitan Chapter could have permanent quarters. Ratshesky gladly accepted the position of commissionor-in-charge.

McCall dictated another telegram to Endicott. "Since sending my telegram this morning offering unlimited assistance, an important meeting of citizens has been held and Massachusetts stands ready to offer aid in any way you can avail yourself of it. We are prepared to send forward immediately a special train with surgeons, nurses and other medical assistance, but await advices from you." He asked Endicott to send it through the Navy, thinking that their wires might have better luck getting through to naval wires in Halifax. He was wrong. For much of the day, the city remained isolated from all communication.


EVEN BEFORE NOON, City Hall had already become the focus of its citizens. Volunteers appeared to offer their services. Drivers offered their cars. Families arrived looking for assistance. They needed everything: food, doctors, a place to sleep. All the while soldiers pounded away at the windows, covering each hole with tarpaper and beaverboard so that the night might be more comfortable for the workers and the throngs of families waiting in the hallways. There was only an hour or two of daylight left. At the 3:00 p.m. meeting MacIlreith reported the addition of Weatherbe to head up the medical team and the Finance Committee reported that the Bank of Nova Scotia had issued a line of credit for the city, but it was General Benson and

Rear Admiral Bertram Chambers who had the most to report. Initially, when they were still unsure if they were under attack, the military was scattered and concentrated on individual problems, but when they realized the extent of the destruction, they developed a broader response. By 9:40 that morning, soldiers piled up wagons and trucks with thousands of gray blankets that they handed out to survivors so quickly that many of the people fleeing the area out of fear of a second explosion, did so wrapped in wool. Over 150 men from the BEF were assisting the remaining firemen while soldiers kept watch over the entrance to Richmond to keep people from interfering with the rescue efforts. By noon, cooks were on duty preparing meals for civilians and soldiers alike while the 63rd and 66th Regiments were in the streets fighting fires, searching debris, and collecting the dead. Soldiers living in the huts on the Commons were evacuated and hot broth was already being served to anyone who asked. Four hundred tents, complete with floors, cots, blankets, light, and heat, were being erected on the Commons as Benson spoke, as well as a temporary hospital. They expected the tents to be available by 6:00 p.m. Benson also assured them that the danger at the magazine was over and that people had been sent back to their homes. Remarkably, the military accomplished this all without imposing martial law but in cooperation with the impromptu citizens' committee formed by Colwell. The closest they came to martial law was when Lieutenant Governor Grant approved soldiers to commandeer private vehicles to help transport the injured. Lieutenant Colonel Flowers had already assigned men to stand at the junction of Cunard, Agricola, and North Park Streets and seize any passing vehicles. Stanley Smith, a journalist covering the disaster from St. John, later reported on two incidents where drivers refused to cooperate with soldiers. "I asked him to remove the boxes from his wagon but he informed me that he had to take his horse back to the stable. It was no time for parley. My closed fist instinctively met the point of his chin and he sprawled on the ground. His boxes followed, then with the assistance of willing hands, several of the wounded were placed in the wagon and a new driver on the seat." In another case, a driver refused, pleading to keep his new car clean of blood. The soldiers left him standing on the street. But these were isolated incidents. Overall, people were cooperative once they understood how desperate the situation was, and if the seizures were illegal, no one ever challenged them. By nightfall the committee had gathered a squad of between 250 and 300 cars.

Satisfied that at least a transitional organization had been formed to meet the needs of the city, the men withdrew to begin work. Colwell slipped into the city auditor's room, where a long table with a telephone awaited him. He took some paper and a pen and started making calls. Aside from short naps in the city clerk's office and meetings, Colwell would stay at the table for four days and four nights.

# Chapter Eight

# The First Responders

ONCE THE TELEGRAMS of railmen George Graham, A. C. Duff, and C. A. Hayes went out requesting fire and medical equipment to be sent to Halifax, provincial mayors began rounding up volunteers. Ottawa's first notice of the disaster came from Hayes through the minister of railways. "Halifax is on fire. Sending special trains out of Moncton and any other city with fire apparatus and auxiliary outfits and picking up all fire apparatus between Moncton and Sydney and rushing them to Halifax."

The Boston Express, which had been running late, "felt shock of the explosion near Rockingham." Cars tilted as far as they could without falling over. When they righted, their windows were all broken. The conductor, J. C. Gillespie, inched the train as far into the city as he could before stopping at the Willow Park Junction, where he saw the first of the survivors. "Cold, barefooted and torn people." Without the wires and ability to communicate with his superiors, he took it upon himself to fill the train with wounded people whom he would take out of the city. A young girl whose last name was Currie got on the train after it stopped outside her house. Her grandfather wrapped her up in his coat and put her inside. "There were a lot of children and little babies crying and they didn't have any milk . . . Someone had a bottle of brandy and they brought it and gave a little bit to my brother in his bottle and a little to my cousin's baby in a bottle." At one o'clock Gillespie took the train filled with wounded to Truro, a town sixty miles away. Three children died en route. Major C. E. Avery DeWitt, a doctor who had been on the train from Wolfville that morning, joined Gillespie at Rockingham when he heard about the wounded. He made his way through the railcars, wrapping wounds in ripped-up sheets and giving those in pain a shot of morphine from the hypodermic kit he happened to have in his pocket. He worked his way slowly toward the back of the train, treating whoever he could. Outside of Truro just before four o'clock, his supplies exhausted, DeWitt learned that a doctor and a nurse had joined him at Windsor Junction, one of the stops outside Halifax, and had been working toward him from the opposite end of the train. When the train came to a stop, DeWitt was delighted to see his sister and his father, a nurse and doctor, respectively, enter his car. They had come to Halifax on a special train from Wolfville, and upon seeing the Boston Express leaving with wounded, had boarded to assist. After they loaded the patients into the Truro train station, the DeWitts learned that they were the only medical people left in Truro. All the other doctors had gone to Halifax, as requested. The DeWitts stayed with their patients.

All morning doctors' phones throughout Nova Scotia and New Brunswick had been ringing. The war had already drained the region of so many doctors that medical students were being put to work upon graduation and sometimes before. After rounding up medical personnel, the problem of transporting them to Halifax became the rail companies' responsibility. Train schedules were abandoned, passenger and freight trains canceled, and new relief trains improvised. Nova Scotia, Sydney, New Glasgow, and Truro—each sent one train. Hayes assembled a train in Moncton, New Brunswick, with a crew of engineers, superintendents, mechanics, doctors, and nurses. Three more followed. In Halifax the sudden rail traffic was almost impossible to coordinate. The four miles of railroad from Rockingham to the North Station were a junkyard of disjointed tracks, fused metal chunks, splinters, and broken glass. Whole trains lay on their side, their upholstery in flames and their metal frames still smoking from the heat of the explosion. At the Intercolonial Railway, George Graham ordered Chief Dispatcher M. M. MacLearn to find someone to take over the Rockingham yard and to handle the traffic. His Dartmouth manager and stenographer were dead. Some of his most experienced engineers had been killed on their way to watch the fire. Overall, 120 rail employees had been killed.

The only rail route into the city was through a new set of tracks that led to the Ocean terminals at the foot of South Street, more than five miles away from Rockingham, but it could not be used until a wire was set up to coordinate traffic. A group of Italian workers from Cooks Construction had spent the last few years chiseling, cutting, and blasting the tall granite canyon from the Northwest Arm through the grand avenues to the south-ernmost tip of Halifax. The South Cut or ocean line, as it was called, was scheduled to open in the spring, but it was, until that day, untested by the casual traveler. There was not even a terminal. Manager Graham knew that with supplies and relief coming into the city and with casualties trying to get out, they would have to open the South Cut. He just was not sure how. He asked the telephone company to get him a line. In Truro, dispatcher P. W. Caldwell picked up his orders.

"Get to Rockingham on the Stellarton–New Glasgow fire department special train at 12:30. Take over Rockingham traffic and the yards."

The Lulan left New Glasgow at noon and arrived at the Truro track a half hour later, carrying with her a load of eleven doctors, nurses, firemen, and an army commissariat in charge of the expedition's food. Dr. George Cox, an ocularist from New Glasgow, watched as the train pulled out at 1:05 p.m. Cox, forty-six, had been educated at the New York Post Graduate Medical School and the New York Eye and Ear Infirmary. After practicing for a year, he had returned to the Graduate Medical School to teach in a clinic he opened for the school. As much as he enjoyed the city's theater and concerts—he kept a collection of handbills in a scrapbook—Cox had an-other competing interest that he found impossible to fulfill in the city. Na-ture. No one was more "familiar with animal, bird, insect and marine life of Nova Scotia." His specialty was conchology, the study of shellfish. At twenty-six, he traded New York for New Glasgow, a modest mill town one hundred miles from Halifax, where he established a practice and married. He worked hard to save even a scrap of sight for his patients, because blind-ness was even more debilitating in secluded rural areas than in the city. Spe-cialists were still rare in cities and much more so in small towns, and Cox was soon traveling across the northern part of the province making house calls and operating on kitchen tables by kerosene lamp. As he traveled from town to town in the early years of the 1900s, he could not help but notice the rising number of tuberculosis cases. The damp climate combined with large families living in small houses and pervasive poverty was as fertile a breeding ground for TB as the slums of Boston and New York. To help ed-ucate his patients and the public in general, Cox and two other doctors published a handbook instructing parents on the causes of TB. So as to reach everyone they could, they translated it to French, Mi'kmaq, and Gaelic.

Cox did not expect to be working as an eye specialist once he arrived in Halifax. Judging by the numbers of doctors who joined the expedition, his help would most likely prove unnecessary and he would have wasted his day for nothing. He did not know what he would find in Halifax; he had only got the call that morning, and he did not speculate. Others on the train did that for him, each with a different explanation that ran from German bombing to an American ship that blew up. Some people boasted that relatives working on the railway had told them about an explosion. People outside the city claimed to have heard something from someone who worked on the telegraph. Still others had received phone calls from relatives who lived on the outskirts of the city. Still more, like Cox, had heard nothing until he was asked to help. All he knew was that they described the situation as a horrible disaster, which was enough for him to gather his tools and walk to the train station in the sun. It was such a warm, calm, winter day that even the word *disaster* seemed improbable. Still it could prove interesting. He had never worked under difficult conditions like those he expected in a disaster, and the possibility of a group of diverse patients needing immediate care appealed to him. As a man of science in a small town on the edge of the continent, he did not get too much variety, and although he loved his life as a country doctor, there must have been times when he missed the vibrancy of New York. To have so many patients at once could prove to be, strictly from a scientific point of view, a valuable experience. On a personal note, it might be quite exciting.

Doctors in Halifax quickly turned into patients themselves, none more famously than Dr. Murdoch Chisholm, "a noted surgeon" and a "grand old man of medicine," whose death was thought important enough to appear in the *New York Times* the next day. On Brunswick Street, at the southern end of the devastated area, Dr. Lewis Thomas walked into his waiting room. He did not understand how there could be so many patients. He felt almost peevish.

"Why do not some of you go to Dr. Chisholm? I cannot look after all of you."

A patient looked up, surprised. "We were in there but he's dead."

Dr. Thomas bolted out the door, leaping over downed wires and poles to get to Chisholm's open door, two houses down. He found Chisholm unconscious with blood spurting from a wound over his temple. Dr. Thomas pounded on Chisholm's chest, and not until the old man's rheumy blue eyes opened and he took a deep breath did Thomas begin to suture the wound. By the volume of blood pumping out, it appeared as if the temporal artery, which travels up the neck and splits just past the ear en route to the temple, was severed. It would be almost impossible to suture without proper tools because the artery acts like stressed elastic. The second it snaps, it withdraws beneath the skin and flattens out in an attempt to control blood loss. It was no use. All Thomas could do was use compression. He looked around for a clean bandage and wrapped it tightly around the elderly man's head. The old man already looked shrunken and weak; he resisted neither treatment nor orders to get to the hospital, and once outside accepted a ride on the back of a truck.

Doctors such as Thomas, who came through the explosion unscathed, had little or no time to attend to their personal or family needs before casualties appeared on their doorstep, demanding attention. Waiting rooms and hospital wards reached capacity in the first hour. Those working out of private offices, unaware of the extent of the disaster, could not understand why patients did not seek help at hospitals, and hospitals could not understand why other hospitals did not take more patients. Some physicians, such as Dr. Grace Rice, one of the city's two female doctors, remained in her office for days treating whoever appeared. Others who heard about the state of the North End from their patients made the difficult decision to shut their doors and join the centralized services at the hospitals. There were fourteen hospitals listed in the city directory, and at all of them doctors were faced with poor organization, few supplies, dirty working conditions, and a line of seriously wounded patients that snaked far past the outer doors. All hospitals reported broken windows, some lost power, others had no heat, and some had no staff or supplies. Many doctors worked straight through the first days, standing as long as sixty hours at a time before outside doctors arrived to relieve them. The fourteen hospitals—a combination of military, private, and public institutions—claimed just three X-ray machines—one in Dr. Ivan Mader's private clinic on Coburg Road, one in the naval hospital on Upper Water Street, which was destroyed, and another at the Victoria General Hospital.

The Victoria General was in the South End on Morris Street. Of all the hospitals, the Victoria General was the farthest from the explosion. Here Dr. George Murphy had finished scrubbing up outside the operating room when "a grating rumbling sound" unlike anything Murphy had heard before blew through the room. It frightened him enough that he went to the window to investigate, reaching it just as the crash came. The skylight above him imploded around him. Murphy held his hands over his head and bolted outside, convinced that the building was collapsing. Murphy and his anesthetist, Dr. J. F. Lessel, arrived outside at the same time. The two doctors stood on the lawn in their surgical uniforms and gloves searching the sky for a German plane. Murphy saw something more ominous, "a dense, greyish smoke rising like a giant pillar over the north end of the city." Murphy knew instantly that his surgical skills would be in demand, but when he pulled off his gloves he was surprised to see blood dripping from his fingers. His head was bleeding too. A low throb pounded at the side of his skull where, he assumed, something had hit him. He went back inside and showed the wound to a colleague he met in the hallway and who pronounced the head cut minor, but warned Murphy that his hand would give him trouble. A deep slice exposed the heavy tendon that ran from his index and middle finger to his wrist. "It made movement of that hand clumsy and painful during the days I needed it most." His next thought was for his wife. Although still dizzy, he ran three or four blocks to his home on Carleton Street, where his wife greeted him with relief and directed him to his waiting room, which was already full. Murphy spent the next hour treating the worst cases before ordering the rest to go to the Victoria General.

Pharmacist Bertha Archibald was in the dispensary when he returned. She was unhurt by the blast, but shaken by "an arrow-shaped spear of glass about nine inches long, driven well into the hardwood moulding" exactly where she had been standing. If she had not ducked, she would have been dead, but her concern did not last long. "Soon patients came in droves, some on foot and others brought in various conveyances. Presently the whole building was filled, every bed, every cot, every stretcher, then, when no more were available, the wounded and dying were laid gently on the floors of the wards. The halls, the offices and the basement . . . a dark dirty cellar. . . . Wagons laden with little children were brought to the hospital and everyone who could, lent a hand to get them into the building. Most of them were taken to Ward 45. Their little faces and hands were black from the powder fumes, and their clothes tattered and torn. One little fair-haired boy was handed to the Pharmacist, who rushed with him to the ward. He was sobbing bitterly for his mother. She deposited him and went back for another child. He too was sobbing. Two children had to be placed in each bed. The little fellows put their arms around each other and their sobs grew less and less as they comforted each other."

Archibald too cried for much of the day. The calm authority of the hospital had been overtaken by an ugly improvisation. The administrator was away, the chief surgeon had not arrived, and the wards were filled with people whom she could not even keep warm. She stood staring at an open window across from the dispensary, trying to figure out a way to cover it, when she caught sight of a man through the broken glass. "Someone walking, oh-so-slowly up the front walk, leaning heavily on his cane, resting every few steps." Dr. Chisholm entered the wide hallway, his step faltering, his neck stained with dried blood, and a tightly wrapped bandage circling his neck and head. She ran to the door to greet him. He asked for the superintendent, but she told him he was away. Then he asked for her boss, Dr. Charles Puttner. Archibald had no idea where Dr. Puttner was. Although he was the chief pharmacist, he was acting as the superintendent while Dr. Kenny was out of town, and she had barely seen him that morning. But Puttner was not her worry. Dr. Chisholm's face was pale and his knuckles whitened where he leaned hard on the cane. She worried that he was about to faint.

"Oh," he said. "Do get me a bed."

"A bed?"

Archibald did not know what to say. Dr. Chisholm obviously needed to rest, but she could no more come up with a bed than she could anything else in the hospital. The morning was not even over and the supplies were already disappearing. Almost everything was in short order, but beds were the rarest of all.

"There isn't a vacant bed in the place," she told him.

Dr. Chisholm leaned harder on the cane. Archibald zoomed through the rooms in her mind, moving up floor by floor. Where could she fit him? She had to put him somewhere. Everything was full, even people's offices. When she got to the top floor, she remembered the interns' quarters. She put her arm around the old man's waist and the two climbed up the stairs as the wind raced ahead of them. Minutes later soldiers ran through the wards ordering everyone to evacuate, but the staff ignored them and kept working. Out of courtesy and concern, Dr. Murphy skirted up the stairs to see Dr. Chisholm. He was already feeling his absence on staff. "We needed him badly, not only for his active participation in the work but for his sound surgical judgment." He found Chisholm resting on a bed, pale, weakened, and heavily bandaged. He explained that the dockyard was on fire and the military dump could cause another explosion, possibly as serious as the last, and that the military was asking them evacuate. He offered to have Chisholm moved outside to a field.

Chisholm waved him away. "I will stay where I am."

Dr. Murphy, amused and pleased by the old man's decision to stick with his staff, returned to the wards. Not one staff member left the hospital.

.   .   .

M.CHISHOLM M.D.

Dr. Murdoch Chisholm, a prominent
Halifax surgeon, in 1907

THE HOSPITALS WERE SO overwhelmed in the first days that all healthy
people who showed up were soon put to work. Some of the first people to
volunteer were students from Dalhousie College. Some of them had trained
as VADs, members of the Voluntary Aid Detachment of the St. John's Ambulance Brigade. VADs were required to report in the event of an emergency to Lady Divisional Superintendent Clara MacIntosh. By noon
almost half of the 129 VADs reported or were already in service. "Sixty-two
members of the V.A.D. organization had rendered first aid in arresting
bleeding, removing glass, plaster, and wooden splinters from wounds, applying dressings and fixing splints where they thought these were necessary." Other students, including Jean Lindsay's roommates from the Halifax
Ladies College, started turning up at Camp Hill Hospital and the Victoria
General within half an hour. Some arrived with medical training but many
had none. At Camp Hill Hospital a teenager, Marjorie Moir, was one of the
first to volunteer. It was 9:25 a.m. The modest two-story white hospital
buildings rose out of a gentle hill that sloped out of the west Commons on
the site where the British used to house and sometimes execute soldiers. To
the south was the cemetery and to its east the Citadel sheltered the hospital
from the bustle of commercial life that thrived on the harbor side as well as,

on that day, the explosion. The hospital had been built to consider patients' mental health, inviting the sun inside with oversized windows. Intended as a temporary convalescent home, it was built from cheap materials and was neither a full-scale hospital nor an emergency center. When it opened in September 1917, the construction still was unfinished, its grounds muddy and uneven. Its capacity was listed as 280, but only 170 beds were set up, and soldiers already occupied them. By the time that Moir arrived, the convalescing soldiers had deserted their beds and were helping to carry the wounded. Moir had to fight her way across the throngs of people wandering on Jubilee Road to get to the front doors. "It was so crowded with scared people that she could scarcely get through to go to the hospital." She approached the first doctor she saw.

"Can I do anything?"

"Come right along in here."

She took off her coat and hat and hung them in a small office. Then she followed the doctor to a woman lying on her stomach. Her calves were cut straight up the back. "As though some one had done it with a knife."

"Hold her feet."

Marjorie Moir looked down. The woman's feet were blackened and filthy. Still ignorant of the extent of the disaster, Moir could not help being appalled by what she saw. "I did not know people ever let themselves get so filthy." Ignoring her disgust, she placed a hand around each ankle to keep them stable while the doctor wrapped them with gauze.

"Are you a V.A.D.?"

"No, I'm just an ordinary person but I'm willing to do anything I can."

"Nurse!"

To everyone's surprise, a nurse appeared. There were only five assigned to the hospital that morning. He asked the nurse to put Marjorie to work. The nurse led her to the kitchen and had her clean off the white oilcloth that covered the tables and then assigned her to the sink, where she began washing dishes. It was not long before she was washing surgical instruments. Camp Hill, set up as a convalescent hospital, had no provisions for surgery.

Florence Murray, a plump, fair-skinned, third-year medical student, arrived just before 10:00 a.m. She had already bandaged people near her house on Robie Street before deciding to go to the Victoria General, when she noticed the convalescent soldiers acting as stretcher-bearers at Camp Hill, carrying people from the cars despite their own injuries. One soldier who could barely crawl was on the ground trying to help. Florence entered the ward on her right and found Dr. George MacIntosh, Clara's husband. He nodded at her to come in, and she began to assist while soldiers came and went, dropping off more injured until every surface in the room was covered with patients. Many moaned in pain, but there was little Florence could do. Eventually, a military nurse approached her with a syringe.

"Has your class had instruction in anesthesia?" Dr. MacIntosh asked.

"Yes sir," she replied, neglecting to mention that she was not present for that lecture. "In the army one doesn't explain. One answers questions."

"Go to the operating room and give anesthetics."

She reported to the OR, where a nurse handed her a tube of morphine pills.

"Use this until the morphia is exhausted."

Florence looked at the tube. Ten of its twenty-five tablets were gone. Seeing her apprehension, the nurse assured her that they had sent out a soldier to get more. "The first patient was six years old. Did a child require the same amount of anesthetic as an older person or should she have a smaller dose? I did not know." What she did know was that she should monitor the child's eye to see how the reflexes were reacting. After a couple of patients, she grew more confident in administering the morphine, but she still did not have a system for prioritizing patients other than offering anesthetic to those who cried the loudest. When patients learned there was a shortage of the drug, many refused.

"Give it to someone who needs it more."

When she ran out of morphine, the doctor asked her to go to the kitchen to get supplies. Water was everywhere, and it was hot. At least the furnace was working. Major L. R. Morse, the CO, was trying to improvise a device in which to sterilize instruments. In the meantime, Marjorie Moir was still at the sink taking anything the doctors needed and dropping it into boiling water. Pans, towels, even knives disappeared in the sink and bowls. Hot bricks were in the oven, the only available heat source for the patients lining the cold corridors. Florence picked up the tools the doctor wanted and made her way back through the crowd. She was relieved to find that the soldier sent out for morphine had returned, but he looked troubled. He had not been able to locate any morphine anywhere in the city. The rest of the patients would have to undergo treatment without painkillers until more arrived.

# Chapter Nine

# Duggan Walks Home

C HARLES DUGGAN, half-naked and still in shock, made his way off the ferry and through the crowd outside, grateful to be back in Halifax. Even though he had heard the screams and seen the ruins in the harbor, he was shocked to see the damage along the downtown streets, and he could not make sense of what had happened. His head still fell thick and uncomfortable, the way his body felt when he was exhausted from rowing. He turned onto Jacob Street and walked into a billiard hall. Duggan, who loved playing pool and cards, was a regular at McCartney's, and they invited him to come in and clean up. His underwear was frozen in some places, wet in others, and he wanted to dry them out. He took them off and hung them over the stove. Then he washed off the black soot from his face and hands. His hair was sticky with dirt and oil. He sat down by the stove to warm himself and listened in silence to the stories about the explosion. When the wool on his underwear started smoking, he put them back on and began the two-mile walk home.

At the North Station, soldiers turned him back. He walked ten blocks west to 188 North Street, where his sister Ellen, thirty, lived with her husband Howard Quinn and their two teenage children. Quinn was a cabdriver and that morning had been driving his McLaughlin Buick when soldiers commandeered it, forcing him to walk home. Their block of North Street was far enough from the waterfront to escape the fire, but whole sides of houses had been ripped off their frames like rotten shingles. A dense black smoke rose from the Dominion Textiles Factory, which the fire department allowed to burn unimpeded while they concentrated on fires that threatened to spread into other neighborhoods. For the first hours, fires burned without any interference until so many smokestacks rose above the hillside that they looked like masts in the harbor.

The Nova Scotia Car Company, a factory that took up most of three square blocks directly across the street from Ellen's, was smashed but had not caught fire. Ellen and Howard's house was not in much better shape. The windows and blinds were shredded, blowing in and out of the house with the slight breeze. The stove was a ruin, adding cold to the chaos. Both clocks were stopped at 9:05. The hanging lamp, worth over half a week of Howard's salary, was shattered, as were their good china and tea set. Ellen was alive and shocked to see her baby-faced brother, Charles, with his stained skin and filthy hair, walk through what was left of her front door in nothing but his underwear and boots, but her joy soon turned to dread. She told him that their mother Susie, their father Charles Sr., their sister Evelyn, their little brother Vincent, their married sister Alma, and Charles's wife Reta and their baby Warren were all dead. There was no word from Billy.

Ellen was luckier than Charles. Her children Kathleen and Jim were alive, as was Howard, although the Buick, one of the two cars Howard used

A destroyed tram and leaning pole marked the entrance to the devastated area at North Street.

to run his taxi company, had been seized. Charles and Ellen did not know it, but their older sister, Sarah Kirkpatrick, was alive too. She and her husband, Frank, and their seven-year-old son, Edward, lived at the end of Campbell Road close to Africville. Frank would have been at work at Reardon Paints on Argyle Street or possibly out on a job. Either way, he was safe. Sarah and Edward both suffered badly smashed and cut feet, and Sarah's back was also injured. Somehow the mother and son made their way across Richmond that morning and across the Commons to Camp Hill, where they would remain for the next three days.

Throughout the afternoon in Richmond, frantic mothers and fathers stood dutifully on their block, hoping that a missing spouse or child would return or that someone would tell them where they were. Others, who had already made their way through a series of hospitals without success, double-backed to their neighborhood for the second or third time in hopes of finding a clue. Tight groups gathered on corners, exchanging information. "Someone had just to say, 'She was seen being lifted into an auto,' or 'Your little boy was carried away by a sailor,' and the distracted husband or father would begin his search once again." Volunteers and soldiers continued searching for people buried in the rubble, carrying them to waiting cars on improvised stretchers—fences, wheelbarrows, boards—anything flat and strong enough to carry a body. The trapezoid-shaped square at the intersection of Young Street and Gottingen atop the burning neighborhood became a dropping-off point. Men carrying stretchers arrived at the top of the steep hills out of breath, but stayed only long enough to deposit their charges before turning around. Dray wagons, autos, and vegetable carts arrived from the south and the west to pick up passengers before turning south toward the hospitals. One soldier, Ralph Procter, who was on medical leave with a punctured lung and forbidden to lift anything heavy, made twenty-three trips back and forth to the hospital with injured people, including one child, just five years old and with a broken back. "Affected me far worse than anything I saw in France. Over there you don't see women and children all broken to pieces." On one trip, his windshield smashed when a house collapsed and a burning beam fell across the car. "I had swallowed glass, I was pretty scared." He continued driving for the rest of the day.

Lottie Duggan and her five children sat huddled in blankets on Gottingen Street until they got too cold to wait any longer. Still hoping that perhaps one of the priests or a local doctor or even Billy would come along to help them, they realized that they had to save themselves, but they were under the impression that the whole city was destroyed and did not know where to go. They were still sitting on the curb, watching soldiers come and go from Admiralty House, when a driver appeared with a half-full grocery wagon and offered them a ride to the hospital. Lottie, Irene, and Lydia were getting weaker as the day went on and Helena helped them climb onto the back while Kenny scrambled up by himself. At Camp Hill, the family made their way inside the clogged hallways with some difficulty. Exhausted, dizzy, and unable to think, Lottie fought off fainting. When they got Irene settled, Lottie lay on the floor while Helena and Bessie walked through the wards in search of a doctor, but everyone they tried was busy helping someone else. Finally they found a nurse who followed them back to Lottie. She examined the cut in Lottie's head and sewed it up quickly. "They didn't even clean out her cut, they had so much to do and they couldn't spend time on one." Later they found a doctor to examine Irene, who still had the piece of glass sticking out of her neck. He told Helena that she had done the right thing by leaving it in place; if she had pulled it out, she would have killed her sister.

The nurse brought the family to a tiny room, laid Irene on the table, and put a blanket over her. Lottie fell asleep on the floor alongside Kenneth and the girls. Helena kept an eye on Irene. Her dressing needed to be changed frequently and Helena worried that she was going to die.

Minesweeper *P.V. VII* experienced a slight jolt when the *Mont Blanc* exploded and the tsunami traveled out to sea, but without orders to the contrary, they continued sweeping. Later in the afternoon the radio crackled. "Get back. Halifax is destroyed." For Billy, the walk back from where the minesweepers were moored at the southern end of the city, past Point Pleasant Park, to the North End would have been like walking from sanity straight to the core of lunacy. He was allowed to enter the neighborhood because he was in uniform. The first sight to greet him would have been the abandoned tramcar and the lamppost tipped dangerously across the road. To his right was the Canadian Government Railway Yard, where fifty-five men had died. To his left the Wellington Barracks was broken but not burned, thanks to the efforts of Captain MacLennan. After the Barracks yard was Russell Street, where the houses were either on fire or already burned out. Helen Clark's home was in cinders. All the buildings were flattened and burned. When he approached his yard, Molly, their big white bulldog, greeted him with a howl. She whimpered and scratched against the foundation, crying and rushing toward Billy for comfort. "Shedding tears like a baby. Only the foundation was left, a burned out hole of debris and smoldering coal." Billy's car was ruined. Their furniture, Billy's medals and trophies, the children's clothes—it was all gone. Seeing no sign of Lottie or the children, he would have looked for the ferry, but open water stood where the dock had been that morning. Mud from the harbor covered the lower parts of the remaining docks and the land all the way up to Campbell Road. Where had it come from? The sugar refinery with its tall smokestacks was still burning. At Upham's Grocery, someone had stacked up a pile of coats and sweaters and left them in front of the store. Despite the cold, and even though many fleeing the neighborhood were in their underclothes or nightdresses, no one had stolen the coats. Billy felt sure Lottie and the children were dead. They were so close to the worst damage. He did not imagine that they could have survived. Around him soldiers in groups of twos and threes stacked bodies, which were starting to freeze, one on top of the other "like cordwood." Further along Campbell Road at Hanover Street he found his parents' house. Nothing was left there either except blackened ruins, mud, and splinters. Depressed, Billy headed toward Veith Street, where his mother's family lived, but Veith Street was in flames. His aunt's and uncle's houses were gone, the foundations filled with charred ruins and white-hot coals. He got his first good news when he ran into a friend who told him that he had seen Lottie with the children going off to Camp Hill. Billy turned back south and trudged toward the Commons. It was getting colder as the light failed. The wind was coming up.

THE LINE OUTSIDE CAMP Hill was long, dirty, and tired. Billy Duggan waited along with many of his neighbors to enter. He walked the hallways, stepping carefully over the mattresses in his heavy black boots as he

Bodies waiting to be identified at the morgue

searched the features of the helpless, soot-covered bodies strewn across the floors. He recognized many people, but no Lottie, no children. As he passed a small office with a switchboard, the memory of the ruined house and the howling dog haunted him, and he tried to prepare himself to learn his family was dead. He looked into the small room. A young girl lay still on the table coated in black. More children and a woman rested on the floor. Families were everywhere. He continued down the hall until someone called out for him to stop. He turned around. A little girl, a stranger, ran after him. She led him back to the switchboard, where, after a second look, Billy recognized a heavily bandaged Lottie stretched on the floor. She was weak from so much blood loss, her head throbbed, and her cough was aggravated by the dust and cold, but when she saw Billy walk by she had asked the girl to chase after him. Billy leaned over the little girl lying on the table. Up close he could see that it was Irene. She looked weak, but she was alive. Bessie was cut too, but not quite as severely. Helena, Lydia, and Kenneth appeared dirty and exhausted but healthy. Billy relaxed, relieved to find them alive. Then he asked to see baby Gordon, just three weeks old. It must have been an awful moment, the longest pause he ever heard. Lottie told him that they had forgotten the baby.

*Chapter Ten*

# Nightfall

A T 6:00 P.M., Harvey Jones, the editor of the *Daily Echo*, stood in the shadow of a row of stone buildings at the end of the Pickford & Black Wharf. He was waiting for the same tug that had dropped Hayes off at the *Imo* earlier that morning. Pickford & Black were the agents for many of the ships damaged in the explosion, including the *Imo*, and Jones wanted to be onboard when they did their inspection. It was dark, the city in blackout, and he could barely see in front of him. When the tug arrived, he climbed on carefully; the deck was slick from the black rain. Standing on the port side, looking to his left as the tug pulled out, the hills of Richmond soon came into view. Individual fires still burned, their flames teasing the night sky, but most smaller buildings—the houses, barns, and stores that he had passed so many times before when he covered stories at the dockyard—were burned out. All that was left was smoldering bright orange and red patches. A tree on fire leapt out like a character from a children's storybook. A slight pink cast could be seen toward the west, and aside from the rank odor, the air had the dry clarity of impending snow. He looked up at the sky as the tug labored through the black water. Even in a tug, it was rocky sailing. Debris bumped against the tug's nose and sides as they passed the docks. Ships were everywhere too, some on top of each other, others listing in the water, still others anchored in awkward spots. Whole wharves were gone, either smashed or burned. On the other side of the harbor, they could just make out the *Imo*, brooding and abandoned by the Dartmouth shore.

They pulled up alongside the *Middleham Castle,* and a couple of men scrambled aboard to search for corpses, returning shortly with a man's body balanced on a plank between them. They warned Jones that he would not want to see it. The men hoisted the plank over the rail and lowered it into the tug, but just as Jones thought it was safe, the board tilted to one side, revealing a corpse with a smashed skull. The brain rolled out and plopped down next to his feet. Jones looked away. His body felt heavy, and for the first time that day he felt tired.

After the *Middleham Castle,* they crossed the harbor to the *Imo.* Her four masts were intact, but the rigging hung limp and much of the middle deck was flattened. The bow was still light, resting slightly higher in the water. The last letters of Belgian Relief were underwater. Jones grabbed onto the freezing ladder and crawled up the side after the Pickford & Black men. As far as he knew, they were the first people to board the ship since it had left port that morning, and only their echoing footsteps answered when they called out. It was not true, of course. The crew from the *Highflyer* had come along and evacuated the crew shortly after the explosion, and they were staying onboard the destroyer until the military and the city decided if there would be an inquiry. Anxious not to be left alone, Jones followed the others to the bridge, nearly tripping over two dead men on the forecastle-head. He slowed his step, shuffling along with more caution. He could not make out much. When they reached the bridge, a man called out and they gathered around the lifeboat. It was the pilot, William Hayes. Jones could just make out the outline of a man crouched under the lifeboat, as if he were trying to protect himself. They stood in the moonlight, staring at Hayes's mute body, as if it could explain what happened, before turning toward the captain's quarters. Jones hastened to catch up, sandwiching himself between two men for safety and feeling his way through the dark passage with his hands outstretched. He took short steps because he dreaded tripping again. A tingle of fear spread up his neck. He was cold and, he admitted to himself, scared. All the excitement was gone; the adrenaline dissipated. "I was feeling kind of blue. There was nothing left to do now but clean up." The twisted metal creaked and groaned around them as if the ship itself were in pain. A sudden howl of agony and mourning sent another shiver up his spine. The fellow behind him bolted back to the tug, leaving Jones's back unprotected. Jones briefly considered joining him when the bellow sounded again from inside the cabin. The man in front of Jones grabbed the handle and threw back the door. From the darkness Captain From's dog lunged and then retreated in a menacing crouch, snarling and barking. The men backed into the corridor, laughing off their shock. The dog must have been locked away since morning. The cabin was a wreck, with the wood paneling strewn across the floor. When they tried to coax the dog outside, lowering their voices to a soothing murmur, the dog would neither leave nor let them in, crouching lower and pulling its lip back into a snarl. It's gone mad, Jones thought to himself. A soldier stepped forward and shot it. A quick yelp died in the darkness as the blast echoed through the *Imo*'s empty hull.

THERE WERE NO NEWSPAPERS that night. No radio. The hospitals and the morgue were still too busy to compile lists of who was where, and as night settled in more people arrived at City Hall requesting information about what to do, where to find their family, where to go for medical help. Most people were more desperate for information than for food, but officials had little news to offer them and many left with more cheese than information.

At suppertime, cadets, volunteer units of teenage boys, were called to duty at City Hall. Ginger Fraser got the word at 6:00 p.m. that night when a knock sounded on the front door. The soldier told Ginger's mother that all cadets had been ordered to report to City Hall immediately.

The *Imo* lying adrift. Note the puncture wounds in her hull, possibly made by the anchor. The *Imo* was thrown to the Dartmouth shore, where she remained for the winter.

Ginger had arrived home only a few hours before. The front door swung idly open.

"Mother. Mother?"

He ran into the living room, then halfway up the stairs, but no one answered, so he skittered back down the stairs to the kitchen. A slight wind blew in through the northern windows where the wooden sashes had been torn from the brick wall. The stovepipe was cracked in half and a dusting of soot covered the kitchen. The abandoned breakfast table looked like a macabre still life. A skin of black soot floated on the pitcher of milk, and blood was smeared across the table. "Then I really began to worry. I ran from room to room yelling my head off." He knew that the blood had to belong to his mother or one of his sisters.

When he heard voices drift in from outside, Ginger ran onto the porch only to discover that it was his neighbors, not his mother, as he had hoped. He asked them where everyone had gone, and they told him soldiers had come around to evacuate them to Collins Field on the corner of South Street. Relieved to hear that his family was just another among the crowds he had seen with Everett, he sat down on the porch. Mrs. Fraser and his sisters appeared on Morris Street soon after. Jean Fraser's hand was heavily bandaged. Ginger's mother told him she had been cut at the breakfast table.

"A nasty gash." She looked Ginger over for injuries. "Are you alright?"

"Sure."

"Well you had better find your Dad. He has been to your school and to the hospital looking for you. He met one of your schoolmates and he had said that 'Ginger was all cut and bleeding.'"

Ginger had not noticed that his hand was scratched, and the dried blood from where he had wiped his face made him look much worse than he was. His father arrived home shortly afterward, and Ginger was surprised when he appeared relieved to see him. He was convinced that he was going to get into trouble. They spent the afternoon sealing up the dining room for the winter.

Ginger, who was an officer, was not only pleased to get out of more cleaning, but was excited to be called upon to serve. With some pride, he changed into his uniform and made his way to City Hall, where he found autos waiting with the motors running, dropping off and picking up medical staff. The cadets were divided into three groups. The first group worked with the medical committee at City Hall. That day the military set up thirteen dressing stations across the city, which provided both immediate medical attention and a waiting area for those seeking hospitalization. Pools of doctors and nurses remained at the stations and whenever a call came in to City Hall, medical personnel were dispatched within half an hour. Cadets ran back and forth with addresses, names, and requests. The second group delivered food baskets to families who called City Hall. The third, and the largest, best-known group, were sent out as messengers. When the lines opened up, thousands of telegrams asking for information about relatives jammed the circuits. Cadets were sent to deliver them, but it was not easy work because many of them were for people in the North End. Old addresses had to be cross-checked with new. "At least two thirds of the ones we tried to deliver we couldn't because there was no house left standing there and nobody there. So we had to take them back to the telegraph office."

Ginger was assigned to deliver food. City Hall was crowded with volunteers, survivors, and people dropping off donations. Food distributors, farmers, and private citizens arrived with boxes of food that were sorted by type so that pickers could assemble balanced packages for delivery. All afternoon the food committee had sent out baskets of bread, milk, and butter to whoever requested one. They planned to open three other depots by morning to ensure that children had milk for breakfast. All night Ginger ran the baskets up and down the stairs, dropping off food to workers in the building and outside to the chauffeurs driving the medical staff around the city. One of the doctors who arrived at City Hall that night was Dr. George Cox.

Thursday night, as the Lulan rounded the Bedford Basin toward Rockingham Junction, doubts about whether Cox and the rest of the doctors would be needed passed into silence.* A thick, fawn-colored smoke obscured the view of the outer harbor and the Dartmouth shore. Shredded wood—remnants of wharves, houses, and boats—bobbed in unwelcoming gray-green water. The train ground to a halt alongside the station, and Cox gathered up his belongings and carried them outside. Neither an official nor a car appeared to guide them. After some discussion, his party agreed that they should walk toward downtown, but the winter light was failing and night quickly overtook them. Rockingham was the second to last stop on the North line, four miles from North Station and neighbor to Africville, an impoverished black community that had sprung up on the Basin side of Richmond Hill along with the railroad. This tiny village greeted them with what would quickly become the explosion's hallmark:

---

*It had taken four hours to make the sixty-mile trip from Truro.

Richmond in ruins

Tilted, windowless, and doorless houses stared at them like shell-shocked soldiers. Despite this introduction, Cox was still unprepared for what he would see when his party rounded the hill. Richmond was gone. And the detritus that replaced it no more resembled the neighborhood than a pile of unraveled wool resembled a sweater. They could make no sense of the geography because the order of streets was demolished, leaving them to grope about in the dark with only the jets of flame shooting out of basements for light. The party picked their way around the debris and the dead with little concern for themselves, the gentle moans, calling out from under the debris, a constant reminder that their suffering was incidental. As Cox passed the corpses of men stacked one on top of the other, he mistakenly assumed that looters had left them there. Dr. W. B. Moore, who had made the same journey two hours before, was most affected by the blackened tree trunks "standing, gaunt and spectral like, as it were, the outpost sentinels of their kingdom." The twisted and mangled landscape, intertwined with the half-dead and the still suffering, reminded him of the scenes in Dante's *Inferno,* which he had seen at a movie theater some years before. "The rows of blackened and often half naked and twisted bodies of the dead, through which we picked our way, made a weird and desolate

Neighborhoods were flattened, aside from the blackened trees.

spectacle, the depressing effects of which could only be understood by those unfortunate enough to witness it." Farther south, the party met a group of officials who sent them to City Hall, where Weatherbe assigned Cox to Camp Hill.

Cox rested as the party motored in silence past the darkened fields. As the car made its way past the protection of the Citadel, the wind buffeted the windows and a few snowflakes teased in and out of the low headlights. The moon, lost in cloud cover, provided no light, and the car bounced past the graveyard toward the hospital entrance in total darkness. When they arrived, the distant voices of soldiers and the soft murmur of conversation greeted them. Groups of three or four stood together wrapped in blankets, sheets, and military coats, children in their parents' arms, asleep. Others gathered at the entrance, pushing their way inside, frustrated by still more people trying to exit. Mothers stood holding the hands of tired children. Others roamed through the crowd, calling out unanswered names into the night. The same black soot Cox saw on his walk through Richmond reappeared, although some who had tried to clean their faces now wore a light gray smudge that further highlighted their lack of expression. As he stepped into the crush of sooty blankets close to the door, the soft murmur separated into whispers.

*Have you seen my father? . . . . A soldier told me that my wife would be here—he car-*
*ried my baby up Russell Street and that was the last I saw of him. . . . He's just two years*
*old. . . . The house is gone. I got my silver out. . . . Poor Aunt Hester. . . . We will find her,*
*my love.*

Taking a breath, he squeezed through what would have been the front
doors had there been doors. Single bulbs scattered along the hallway threw
pale light over the wounded lying in the corridors. A glance into the wards
revealed hundreds of people squeezed together on a carpet of mattresses
that covered the floors entirely. Men slept underneath beds, and whole
families gathered on a single mattress. The burned lay uncovered, unable to
bear anything against their raw skin. Fractures abounded and it was not unusual to see a foot or an arm facing the wrong direction. Onlookers trailed
one another down thin paths and across mattresses, bending over those lying on the floor, trying to distinguish a relative, a friend, or a neighbor. The
hospital seemed to have no order—children beside adults, dying beside the
scratched—few staff, and yet, there was no hysteria. Eyes sought out his as
he passed through the hall, but no one appealed for his help. Looking inside
an office, hoping to find someone in charge, he found people curled on top
of desks while still more slept underneath. The windows were covered with
boards and blankets, but the cold wind passed through like one more un-
wanted patient.

At the end of the hall, Cox turned into a spacious room where single
bulbs dangled over long tables on top of which lay dimly lit patients. It was,
he presumed, the dining room. Young women and teenaged cadets appeared and disappeared without comment, leaving Cox to make his way
through the wounded in silence. The next door revealed the kitchen. Here,
with some relief, he made out the silhouette of an acquaintance working in
front of a table. Others were operating mutely on the floor. With little discussion, Cox opened his bag, took out his tools, and started to set a broken
bone. It was just after 6:00 p.m.

Upstairs a young woman named Dorothy McMurray was trying to comfort forty injured patients. She had arrived at the hospital in the afternoon,
shortly after realizing that, as a VAD with certificates in nursing and first
aid, she was required to report for duty. Her problem was that she could not
find anyone to take her. She had tried to report to Clara MacIntosh, but
found Clara's house empty—MacIntosh was helping her husband attend
the wounded in the Commons. As she turned to walk down the stairs, cars
sped past her, carrying wounded to the hospital. She crossed the street, determined to report directly to the hospital. "After vainly trying to push my

way through the mobs to find somebody who could tell me what to do, I realized I was on my own and as I needed a pair of scissors to cut bandages I fought my way upstairs looking for them."

Upstairs, the halls were no better than the market on a crowded morning—people everywhere and no one serving anyone. She walked past the injured, poking her head into rooms on the lookout for scissors or any kind of useful supplies. As she approached a large ward near the end of the hall, a low sad moan from a side office caught her attention and she leaned her head inside. Forty people looked back at her. She glanced around the room, taking a brief survey—"a tangle of dental equipment and dental chairs." Many had open wounds without any kind of dressing at all. It occurred to her that some of them might be dying. She really did not know. It was a scene quite beyond her training and her years. She asked if anyone had been in to help them and they answered no. One person lay on the floor with her chest smashed flat. Another's limb was bent the wrong way. Still others appeared to be moaning themselves into unconsciousness. Although there was little she could do for them other than bringing them water and keeping them warm, Dorothy stayed with them until morning.

Downstairs, Cox looked around the room for an empty table but, finding none, squatted next to a patient on the floor. In the dim light he could make out plaster and glass on the floors. It was almost twelve hours since the explosion and some of the wounded, exhausted and depleted by cold and lack of food, fell asleep. Through the night, doctors tried to make out who was sleeping and who could be carried out on a stretcher. Cox got to work, setting broken bones temporarily, but without benefit of X ray it was little more than an educated guess. Almost all the patients had accompanying skin wounds. Young girls dropped hefty blue tablets of antiseptics into hot water and rushed their porcelain bowls through the wards trying not to spill them. Nurses—when available—dipped their cloths into the fresh bowls and scrubbed the wounds, hoping to separate the black dye and tar from the raw skin. Cox chose his cases based on the appearance of suffering, whether it was the wound itself or the intensity of groans. Through palpation, an examination by touch, he discovered hidden bits of metal, glass, and even household items deep inside the wounds. "One man yielded up from beneath his shoulder, a piece of the *Mont Blanc*, one pound . . . there was, strange to say, little infection, considering the dirty nature of the wounds. It is wonderful what good scrubbing will do and the face will do wonderfully." Incredibly there were no incidents of tetanus.

The eye and face damage was as varied as it was depressing, and there was no indication that it would diminish. "Here was the kind of thing one dreams about sometimes, enough cases to keep one going steadily for days and days ahead." All night Cox moved from his "heaps on the floor" to his colleague's table, assessing and operating on eyes. As soon as a wound was treated, soldiers appeared and removed the patients to private houses. No car leaving the hospital went empty and new patients appeared as quickly as the last left.

AT 9:00 P.M., LIEUTENANT Colonel Frederick McKelvey Bell, assistant director of medical services (ADMS) for the Canadian military, dictated a confident telegram to St. John telling them that he would not need any more doctors. As the ADMS, the military hospitals—Camp Hill, Cogswell, and the destroyed Pier 2—were his priority, but they were filled with thousands of injured civilians and that made it his job to figure out how to treat them. In his uniform, McKelvey Bell appeared to be an ordinary enough man, a thirty-nine-year-old surgeon who in the first year of the war left the quaint houses of Ottawa to enlist. There was nothing outstanding in his features—his short stature, or barrel chest, nothing unusual about his heavy mustache or dark hair shorn into conformity—to indicate that he could lead an emergency medical team with unfailing optimism and organization. If there was something compelling about his face, it was his dark blue eyes. They drooped a little in the outside corners, creating an almost permanent sympathetic expression. "His ability to make people relax under conditions that tended to tenseness was unfailing." But for all McKelvey Bell's diplomacy, he was unsentimental, efficient, and prepared. His experiences in France could not have been better training for disaster work. On October 3, 1914, McKelvey Bell embarked with the No. 2 Stationery Hospital to France, the first temporary hospital set up by the Canadian Army Medical Corps in Europe. For two years he oversaw the treatment of thousands of wounded soldiers carted off the fields and dumped at his door. He stayed until 1916, when he was detailed back to Britain after developing a case of phimosis, a tightening of the foreskin, which left him hospitalized for a week in England. He shipped home in April 1916 and in 1917 was appointed ADMS, District No. 6. He was well familiar with triage and building temporary hospitals out of derelict buildings and boxes, although when he toured Richmond he told a reporter, "he had never seen anything on the battlefront equal to the scenes of destruction that he witnessed in Halifax today."

Lieutenant Colonel Frederick
McKelvey Bell

McKelvey Bell had another unusual talent. He was a scribbler, a writer, a novelist, and an observer of subtle details in the midst of chaos. As a champion of the Canadian military, he was passionate about documenting and celebrating their work during the war. He crafted his experiences in France into a roman à clef that had been published earlier that year. It was already in stores—no doubt with a publisher dreaming of brisk Christmas sales. McKelvey Bell had already autographed copies for readers. *The First Canadians in France* followed two friends, Jack and Reggie, who helped set up and run a hospital in a fishing village three hours outside of Boulogne. McKelvey Bell's soldiers seemed to adjust to the war with great equanimity, tempered by alcohol and a jocular affection, although the French civilians were less accepting of the Canadians' crude manners and the indignities of war. His descriptions of people fleeing the battle of Ypres could have easily described the people fleeing Richmond earlier that day. "Feeble old men tottering along, tearful women carrying their babes or dragging other little ones by the hand, invalids in broken down wagons or wheel-barrows, wounded civilians hastily bandaged and supported by their despairing friends hurried by in ever-increasing numbers. Some had little bundles under their arms, some with packs upon their backs—bedding, household goods or clothes, hastily snatched from their shattered homes. With white terror-stricken faces, wringing their hands, moaning or crying, they ran or staggered in thousands. Their homes destroyed, their friends scattered or killed, death behind and starvation before, they ran."

He sent his first telegram to military headquarters in Ottawa Thursday night. He marked it urgent. "All hospitals filled to overflowing with wounded (stop) Interior Pier 2 Hospital Clearing Depot destroyed and useless (stop) Rockhead Hospital temporarily useless (stop) All other hospitals working well (stop) Every living man or woman being cared for (stop) Have brought in all available physicians, surgeons and nurses from outlying towns (stop) Plenty of medical supplies except antitetanic and anti-streptococcal sera (stop) Can you send two eye specialists from Montreal (stop) Approximately one thousand wounded in Military hospitals (stop) All going as well as can be expected."

He had grossly underestimated the numbers of injured. There were over 1,400 patients at Camp Hill alone. The Cogswell was full. The USS *Old Colony*, an American passenger steamer that the U.S. Army had acquired for the British Navy, converted itself into a hospital ship with the help of the USS *Tacoma*, the ship that turned to Halifax upon hearing the noise. The *Tacoma* arrived at 2:00 p.m., and after a brief visit with the authorities, its captain ordered his medical officer and his staff to take all their supplies and report to the *Old Colony*. The *Tacoma* crew scoured the city for supplies, taking enough equipment from a Coast Guard cutter, the USS *Morrill*, the Victoria General Hospital, the remnants of the Pier 2 Naval Hospital and their own ship, the *Tacoma*, to assemble two temporary operating rooms. Fifty-four wounded were brought aboard throughout the day. Seventeen died by midnight.

At 11:00 p.m., two hours after McKelvey Bell turned down St. John's offer to send more medical staff, he changed his mind and asked for more volunteers and supplies. Telegrams rocketed back and forth between McKelvey Bell and the offices of the Adjutant General in Ottawa. In Montreal, Toronto, and St. John, orderlies, military nurses, and blankets were packed onto trains with boxes of food and cooking supplies. Others, including the whole 159th Battalion, who were waiting to go overseas, were on standby orders, ready to take the first train east, but it was not an easy decision. Whoever he brought to the city needed housing and food, and the shortage of both was acute. There was another complication. A navy ship was headed to Halifax with a cargo of one thousand wounded Canadians, which meant that he had to get the civilians out of the hospitals by the time the ship docked.

Colonel Thompson was also worrying about the shortage of personnel. His soldiers had spent the day trying to keep citizens calm, first sending out blankets and then sending out men to disperse the people who had evacuated their homes, reassuring them that there would be no second explosion. He had also bought up the whole stock of tarpaper to prevent profiteering. Most of the soldiers he did have were still at work in Richmond, searching for survivors. He was understaffed and, with the windows and doors blown out of stores as well as houses, he was worried that the looters would show up after dark. "The whole city was open and our men were exhausted." He was at his desk trying to think of a solution when Rear Admiral Chambers, followed by two American officers, walked through the door. Chambers introduced Captain Moses from the *Van Steuben* and Captain Symington of the *Tacoma*. Symington stepped forward.

"Is there anything we can do?"

"Can you give me any men to patrol the streets?"

"Any number."

"Can you give me two hundred and fifty?"*

"Yes."

Thompson sat back in his chair, relieved that his men could get some sleep. They would need it with the amount of work they would be called on to do over the coming days. Outside, the temperature was dropping fast, and the staccato rhythm of hammering echoed through the streets as people rushed to cover their windows. In the North End, searchers bent low to shine their torches over the frozen basements filled with wreckage, but without proper light and equipment it was useless. "There were still moans and cries from shattered houses but there were little means of reaching the victims lying underneath." At 2:00 a.m. the rescue operation was called off. Aside from ambulances, soldiers, and sporadic snowflakes, the streets were deserted. The blighted city tried to rest as American soldiers patrolled the streets of Halifax.

AT 8:00 THURSDAY NIGHT, the phone rang at Dr. William Edwards Ladd's office in Boston. James Jackson, the division manager of the Boston Metropolitan Chapter of the Red Cross, identified himself and then asked Ladd to head up a hospital unit destined for Halifax on Friday. Ladd had been trained as a gynecologist, but since his graduation from Harvard in 1906, he had earned his reputation as a surgeon and had privileges at three hospitals, surgeons then keeping private independent offices and popping in and out

---

*Symington quoted two hundred in his report.

of different hospitals depending on the day. "A very unsatisfactory arrangement." He would have preferred to dedicate himself to one institution and one set of patients rather than run between three at the behest of other doctors who made the diagnoses. In 1910 when Ladd began volunteering at the Children's, he knew where he wanted to work full time. "The Children's was my very first and most permanent love." Ladd came to believe that many of the children he saw were neglected not only by society, and often by their parents, but by the medical community as well. Even small surgical interventions could effect positive results in both the child and later in the adult. He was particularly soft on the children with facial deformities, such as a harelips; he saw no reason why they had to go through life disfigured when surgery could reduce both the deformity and the stigma. He determined that as soon as possible he would devote himself to Boston Children's Hospital.

Boston Children's was a progressive institution founded by four doctors who, after serving in the Civil War, were each introduced to specialized children's hospitals in New York and Europe. Specialization was a new approach; more commonly children were treated as adults, if they were treated at all. These new institutions tailored not only their medicine but their whole establishment to the children's needs, right down to pint-sized furniture,

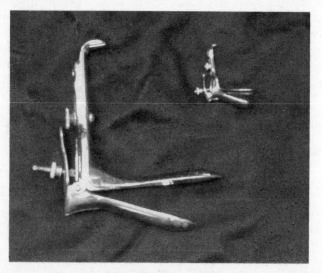

An adult and a child's speculum.

an approach that the doctors believed was missing from Boston's medical network. Certainly, many of the children's diseases in Boston could be prevented if the hygiene in crowded, ill-ventilated slums was improved, but the doctors identified another problem. More often than not, both parents of underprivileged children worked. If their children fell ill, the parents could not attend to their health. Put simply, the poor children needed a place to go if they caught something serious, which, because of where they lived, they most likely would. Founded in 1896, Boston Children's tried to accommodate their young patients in any way they could, and were unafraid of trying unconventional approaches to problem solving, such as keeping a herd of cows on the front lawn to ensure their children drank tuberculosis-free milk. It was the ideal place for an ambitious young surgeon.

In the early years, when Ladd volunteered at the hospital, children in other hospitals were still considered undesirable patients because, more often than not, they died. "Tuberculosis, osteomyelitis, syphylis, yellow fever, typhoid, malaria, and many bacterial infections were rampant and without good means of management. There were few useful drugs beyond digitalis, aspirin and the opiates. Insulin was unknown." Over the previous few decades, pediatricians had gained some acceptance with both patients and the medical community, but pediatric surgery was still controversial. In 1910, the survival rate of sick children was dismal; in surgery it was pathetic.

The cows grazing the lawn of the Boston Children's Hospital circa 1918. The hospital kept the cows to guarantee TB-free milk for children.

"Surgery was limited by the fact that intravenous fluid therapy was not yet understood and that there were no blood transfusions. When surgery was performed, speed was essential. Drainage of abscesses was the most frequently used procedure, although resections of tumors, hernia repairs, appendectomies and other operations were well established." Well established perhaps, but hardly successful. In 1910, appendicitis was the fourth-highest cause of death among children under twelve. "In most hospitals, the mortality rate for a simple colostomy was in the range of 90%." Doctors' inability to control the intravenous fluid therapy, also known as the fluid balance, was one of the most pernicious problems. A child's intake and excretion of fluids—primarily water, potassium, and sodium—was so delicate that a few drops either way could result in dehydration or shock, both of which resulted in death. No one understood how precise the fluid and electrolyte balance was in an infant's tissue. Instead, surgeons based their calculations on adult formulas, an approach that Ladd realized was hazardous for two reasons. The first was that the proportions were not the same in adults and children, much as a recipe for a cake for two and a cake for forty were not the same. The second was that babies needed precise measures of fluid. An adult could give or take a pint of blood without much distress. For an infant who weighed six pounds, that translated to a tablespoon. Even several extra drops of blood loss quickly became a severe health risk. Too much fluid created a similar risk. "The smaller the baby, the bigger the problem. The younger the baby, the narrower the tightrope." Without any means to control the fluid balance, surgeons were forced to work with greater speed, less accuracy, and, almost always, worse results. When by chance, skill, or luck a young patient survived a surgical procedure, the patient often succumbed to infection during recovery.

Ladd perceived other problems with childhood surgery. Even diagnosing a child required a different skill set. Children could not articulate their symptoms verbally, through inability, fear, or both. "The physical signs alone may be all that is available. . . . [The surgeon] must be able to gain the child's confidence or acquire the knack of performing the physical examination with sufficient gentleness to avoid frightening the small patient and thereby making his examination almost valueless." Surgeons needed to rely heavily on their own senses—smell, touch, and sight—to diagnose children and discover what the child could not describe. Ladd also complained that general surgeons took too many cases. If children's surgery were specialized, it would allow those surgeons a wider range of child patients with the same disease, giving them the opportunity to learn more about childhood diseases. Sometimes, Ladd saw only two or three cases of the same disease over ten years, too small a sample to draw uniform conclusions. Furthermore, adult-sized surgical tools were unsuitable for children, most being too bulky for precise work, especially on helpless, exquisite creatures such as infants.

Early on, Ladd suffered setbacks. After operating on three infants with intussusception, a painful condition in which one part of the infant's intestine blocked another and which usually resulted in death, Ladd returned to the pathology lab. "The autopsy table was his library." Working with his former Harvard embryology professor Dr. J. L. Bremer, Ladd examined the infants' colons to find a solution. They did. In his 1913 paper in the *Boston Surgical Journal,* Ladd reported that he and his chief surgeon Dr. J. S. Stone had cured ten times as many children with intussusception as had been cured in the five years before, dropping the mortality rate from 90 percent to 45 percent. Through pathology, Ladd recognized that diseases themselves were different in children, having not reached the later stages more familiar to the general surgeon. A child, Ladd later concluded, was not just a "diminutive man or woman" and that "the adult may safely be treated as a child but the converse can lead to disaster."

When Ladd later presented these views at the Boston Surgical Society, the most prominent surgeon of the day, the revered Dr. Edward Churchill, stood and sneered.

"Anyone who can work on a bunny rabbit can operate on a child."

Ladd never forgot the slight. Despite his affable manner, he was intensely competitive. During his studies, he rowed with the Harvard crew and his love of the sport and competition was so strong that he continued overseeing Harvard's training for four years after his graduation to ensure that they continued to beat Yale. Under his tutelage, they did not lose one race to their rivals. For the rest of his life, he kept a long oar above his bed. Ladd maintained his own physique long after he left Harvard. He stood six-foot-three, was slight but muscular, with "iron gray" hair and dark brown eyes. His voice was low and modulated, betraying the understated confidence of wealth—he arrived at work each day by limousine—but the attribute people usually noticed were his hands. "He'd pick up a baby and it fit right in his hand." "His hands were so large you could not imagine them inside a child." By the time Jackson of the Red Cross called Ladd's office on December 6, 1917, Ladd had risen from volunteer to the second-highest rank on staff.

The afternoon papers were full of the explosion. Thursday night's *Boston Evening Record* headline ran in large bold type: "U.S. Powder Ship Blows Up in Halifax Harbor; parts of City in Flames; Many Dead." In New York, the stock market closed weak, partially spooked by the news that the war had taken its first casualties in North America. Jackson explained the situation to Ladd in case he had not read the papers, and asked him to head a Red Cross relief expedition. Ladd agreed, asking what he needed to do. Jackson told him to round up thirty volunteer doctors and fifty nurses to to leave for Halifax the next morning. He promised to take care of supplies if Ladd came up with the staff, but Jackson did not think finding people would be a problem. The Red Cross had "an embarrassing numbers of letters from the Boston people ready to go anywhere or do anything." Jackson told him that the first group of Red Cross workers was leaving with the Committee on Public Safety even as they spoke.

THAT NIGHT TWO PULLMANS, a baggage car, and a buffet car pulled alongside the Boston platform. It was cold and the travelers bundled themselves up for what would prove to be a long train ride. Colonel William A. Brooks had gathered together thirteen medical professionals, members of the Massachusetts State Guard. The Red Cross, which had been working with the committee since its inception on a War Services program— exhibiting Red Cross films, war films, conservation messages, and organizing sing-alongs on the Boston Common—called Ratshesky and requested that six of its representatives, all experienced disaster workers, be allowed to join the train. Otherwise, they would have to wait for the train that Jackson was arranging for Ladd. Ratshesky invited them. After all, John Moors had been named head of both the American Red Cross in Halifax and part of the Aid Division of the Public Safety Committee. Four railroad officials showed up as well as five reporters from the *Boston Globe*, the *Associated Press*, the *Boston American*, and the *Boston Herald*.

The train pulled out of the station at 10:00 p.m. All along the East Coast, to Portland, Maine, Ratshesky wired Halifax without receiving a response, and settled instead for the tidbits of information railmen gleaned from the telegraphs. The train was on schedule throughout the night until thirteen miles outside of Waterville, Maine, at Burnham Junction, where it slowed to a stop. Ahead of them, men were cleaning up downed telegraph poles and a heap of wreckage where five freight cars had derailed. They waited for over an hour.

The Boston Metropolitan Division of the American Red Cross, including Dr. W. E. Ladd, arriving in Halifax

Over fifteen hundred miles away, off the coast of North Carolina, a heavy arctic wind was driving the warm Carolina air out to sea, where it met the Gulf Stream. The collision of warm and cold turned the wind into an enormous, fast-paced, low-pressure swirl that was gaining speed and moisture as it followed its usual route up the coast toward Nova Scotia. Meteorologists had two names for this winter-weather phenomenon. Some called it a Hatteras Low. Others called it an Eastern Seaboard bomb because, when it hit, it dropped so much snow so fast. With the telegraph line in the hands of the censor and the city services devastated, no one bothered to check with the weather bureau.

# Chapter Eleven

# Friday Night and
# Folly Mountain

OVERNIGHT THE TEMPERATURE in Halifax dropped over twenty degrees to 16.8°F. The wind picked up speed as it switched directions from northeast to northwest. The snowflakes that had been appearing sporadically Thursday evening began to thicken and stick to the ground. By late Friday morning the city was in the midst of a fierce blizzard. By noon the local weather office recorded the wind at gale force, forty to forty-five miles an hour, strong enough to snap twigs off trees. "It was a heavy damp snow that clung to the clothes, blinded the eyes, and made traffic well nigh impossible." D. G. O. Baillie, a sailor on the HMS *Isis*, a 5,600-ton British cruiser, arrived in the harbor that morning and recorded his first impression upon sailing into the port: "The mercury registered 20 degrees below, a pall of smoke hung over the ravaged city, and infernal gloom half-hid the remaining building so that at first we thought the whole town had been destroyed. We were anxious to make ourselves useful, and soon had every chance to do so, for we were ordered ashore to help in digging out the innumerable bodies known to be buried in the ruins. It was the kind of job that heavy rescue teams were trained to tackle expertly, with the added complication that everything was frozen solid, but we had no idea how to set about it. At first we stumbled about aimlessly over piles of masonry and shattered timbers. The bodies were frozen as stiff as any wood or stone so that often the unguarded blow of an axe or shovel would slice off an arm or leg. It was a gruesome experience and more than once I saw a shipmate turn aside to be violently sick. The cold was our worst handicap, for nothing kept it out, in spite of the hard physical work we were doing. Trying to keep my feet warm, I nearly lost a toe through frostbite, the circulation having been restricted by too many pairs of socks."

Captain Symington from the *Tacoma* recalled his soldiers at 8:00 a.m. and again offered his assistance to Colonel Thompson, who explained that they needed men to help build temporary shelter for the homeless. The weather was so cold that the tents set up on the Commons went unused. Symington offered more men. Working in crews of five, Symington's men walked through the snow, going house to house installing windows, covering holes in walls and helping anyone who asked. The blizzard swept through the harbor, which was already confused, with many of its ships tentatively anchored by moor lines that had snapped in the explosion. Normally, with advance notice of a storm, ships would have been sent down to the protected waters of the Basin, but that day, in the confusion, most were still in the outer harbor. An American steamer, the *Saranac*, grounded on McNab's Island. Symington sent his Coast Guard cutter the *Morrill* to help. After lunch, the steamship *Northwind* drifted into the *Von Steuben*. The antics in the harbor affected more than ships. "One of the dragged anchors took out the submarine cable connection between Halifax and Rye Beach, thus cutting communication through Boston to the Canadian interior. Farther to the north and east on Cape Breton Island, the storm tore down the landlines to North Sydney, closing access to that submarine cable as well. With the Halifax-Truro land line still down from the explosion, Halifax was temporarily cut off from all communication. Gangs of men working through the harsh weather were able to restore the Truro connection by 11:00 p.m. on the night of the storm, but in the meantime, thousands more unsent telegrams—including responses to anxious inquiries from Ottawa headquarters—piled up at the terminals."

The snow complicated everything on land as well. Relief workers deserted their cars and trucks when they could no longer climb the hills. Searchers' visibility was impaired. And although the majority of bodies recovered were frozen—there was no way to tell when they had died—there were some successful rescues. In the morning, seven members of 63rd Regiment answered the calls of Private Benjamin Henneberry next to the entrance to Mulgrave Park. Henneberry had just returned from the front, and was living on Campbell Road between Ross and Kenny Streets when the explosion flattened his apartment building. He pointed to the wreckage.

"I am sure I heard a moan a minute ago."

The snow muffled everything except the wind. Finally, they heard a child's whimper eke out from under the rubble. The soldiers attacked the beams and debris until they exposed an iron stove with its ash pan pulled out. When they looked underneath, the round, scared eyes of a toddler greeted them. She had been burned by the coals, covered in black soot, and cut on the face, but the ash pan had saved her from being crushed or frozen. Private Henneberry said it was his eight-month-old daughter Olive, and she was sent off to Pine Hill Hospital while the soldiers continued digging. The word spread of a baby found alive, and the hopefulness enlivened the morning search, but for Henneberry it was a terrible day. The soldiers quickly discovered five more of his children and his wife dead.

Henneberry's block was particularly hard hit. Adding in single boarders who rented rooms, at least forty-four people on Henneberry's block were killed, including three children of Sophie Fraser, his neighbor, and Eliza-

Volunteers and soldiers search the snow-covered rubble for survivors and bodies.

beth's aunt. When Elizabeth Fraser awoke at Rockhead on Friday morning, everyone on the ward was talking about the blizzard, but Elizabeth resented the talk because it reminded her that her brother Arthur, only eleven years old, was trapped there in the rubble, freezing to death if he was not already dead. She burst into tears.

"I'm going to find Arthur."

She ran toward the door, but an orderly stopped her and wrapped the warmest thing he could find, a cotton shirt, around her shoulders and head. Outside, she blinked in pain at the sudden whiteness. "Everything was covered with snow and ice. . . . it looked like the prairies, you could not tell one street from another." She headed down Gottingen Street toward downtown. She did not want to go back to the house. Arthur was probably in a hospital by now. What was the point of going home? A sleigh dragging a heavy load appeared on Gottingen. The wind caught its canvas and she could make out stiff beef carcasses frozen on the back. She chased after the driver asking for a lift. The Frasers grew up near Leaman's slaughterhouse, and carcasses were a far less disturbing cargo than what she had witnessed the day before. The driver, seeing the young girl with only a light shirt to protect her, slowed down and made room beside him, and the two slipped through the frozen streets in silence. Fires smoldered under the snow, melting great black rings around foundations. Piles of bodies sat covered along the side of the road, and the muffled din of soldiers chopping their way through the ruins clamored and faded as they passed. She could not get the image of people lying underneath the snow out of her head. At the end of North Gottingen, the driver drew in the reins and stopped the sleigh. Elizabeth thanked him and jumped into the snow, careful not to land too close to the runners. She did not know where to go and there was no one to ask. "Heartbroken and lonely, I had no idea what I was going to do." She rounded the side of the Citadel and turned onto Brunswick Street, walking past the town clock that overlooked the harbor from the foot of the fortress. Across from the Royal Artillery Park, Elizabeth noticed people entering the Grafton Methodist Church, and she slipped in behind them, partly out of loneliness, partly to get warm. Inside, a line of people moved through rows of ornately carved pews where wounded people were laid out. Elizabeth rushed to join the line of searchers, but did not find Arthur. Most of these people were not even as badly hurt as her father. A volunteer handed her a cup of hot soup and told her that they had taken the worst cases to the hospital. This information made her feel worse; she was surprised she could feel worse. She tried to take a sip of soup, but it would not go down. "I couldn't eat; I kept thinking of the dead out there under the snow and my little brother." At least the heat felt good on her hands.

CHARLES AND BILLY DUGGAN set out in search of their families on Friday as well. They did not have to go far. The Duggan house had been demolished but not burned completely through. Timber and wreckage were piled into the basement. Debris was everywhere. Alma's trunk full of baby clothes—she was expecting her first child—sat on the side of the road, open, its bibs and milk shirts frozen. Their mother Susie was lying half-covered in the snow with half her head blown off. They found the rest of the family outside, except Reta and Evelyn. They could not find either one of them. Finally they decided to dig in the foundation, pulling the frozen timbers apart and throwing them to the side until they found Charles's wife lying on the ground, their son held tightly in her arms. They were not allowed to take the bodies. The soldiers had to do that. Aside from the two children found alive on Friday—besides Olive Henneberry another baby had been found alive and warm, snuggled against a collie puppy—the situation grew more desperate as poor weather continued.

FRIDAY MORNING THE NEWSPAPERS finally managed to get out an edition. At the *Halifax Herald*, where the printing press had been damaged, they distributed a handprinted broadsheet that trumpeted, "Halifax

Half a mile from where the *Mont Blanc* exploded. Every house in the city suffered some damage.

Wrecked: More than One Thousand Killed in this City, Many Thousands are Injured and Homeless." Lists of names appeared under long columns titled "Missing and Dead." Another column of names was listed under "At Snow's Mortuary." Even the living had difficulty finding each other, so the papers opened their columns to information about survivors' whereabouts. A week later scores of queries continued to be listed by surname and age, with the majority of the listings requesting information about missing people. Many, such as Jessie Aitken, who had been standing below the Duggans' house watching the fire, later turned up on the list of the dead. Others would be reunited with their relatives, if not their parents.

AITKEN: Jessie Aitken, age 15 years, of 33 Veith Street is missing. Please communicate with Mr. William Aitken County Court House, Spring Garden Road, St. Paul 23S. She wore a dark blue serge middy suit, brown sweater and gray coat, dark eyes and black hair in braid. Was last seen at foot of Hanover Street and Barrington Street.

BAKER: Will Miss Grace Marguerite Baker who worked at Clayton & Sons please communicate with Alonzo Myers, Birchdale Hotel, St. Paul at once.

BABY: An unknown baby boy about seven months old, brown eyes and hair and uninjured picked up on Herring Cove Road on the day of the explosion now at the Infants Home.

COURTNEY: Mr. Joseph Courtney of North Sydney. Mrs. Courtney is in the city at St. Mary's Glebe.

FAULKNER: There is a little boy named Alfonso Faulkner at 51 Hollis Street who has no one to claim him and his parents and relatives can see him at this address.

The evening edition of the *Acadian Recorder* urged survivors to report to the city clerk's office.

1. That all parents or guardians seeking lost children and all persons who are housing lost children are requested to call at the City Clerk's office and register.

2. All persons who are homeless or who need shelter are also requested to register with the City Clerk when they will be assigned quarters as soon as possible.

3. All persons who are willing to provide accommodation for survivors are requested to file their names, together with accommodations available with the City Clerk.

4. As there will likely be a serious shortage of the available supply of glass all persons removing glass are earnestly requested to do so with as little breakage as possible. A large quantity of the glass required will be sizes as small as 8×10 and 10×18. If persons assisting in this way will telephone the City Clerk's office such glass will be sent for.

5. All persons removing sashes to have same made with small lights in order that small sizes of glass may be used.

6. All outside towns contributing relief furnish as far as possible the following articles: Glass, Beaver Board, Tarred Paper, Lumber, Putty, Bedding and Blankets.

7. Carpenters, glaziers, masons and plasterers are urgently needed and as quickly as possible.

The *Recorder* also reported that at the Relief Meeting that day Colwell and MacIlreith read out the telegrams that they received from across the country. The Duke of Devonshire, who was visiting Regina, Saskatchewan, got top billing.

"Regretting news, hoping for exaggeration, tendering sympathy and offering all aid."

At the Friday morning meeting, Lieutenant Governor Grant read more telegrams. In Clara MacIntosh's opinion, the telegrams served only to lengthen the meeting. Clara was a small woman with blond hair, big blue eyes, and a lot of pent-up energy that she wanted to put to use. Earlier that morning she could not stop thinking about the people she had seen on Thursday. Well aware of the stoic character of the city, she knew that some injured people would forgo hospitals once they heard that they were under-staffed. Still others, especially the older ones, might be alone in their houses with no one to help them. Others might be in shock and too stunned or frightened to leave their house. The MacIntoshes lived on the far side of the Commons, north of Quinpool Road. Thursday morning, Clara had still been in bed when five windows sprayed glass all over the floors. Her maid began screaming downstairs, and she ran down the stairs in her nightdress and bare feet to investigate. The house was badly shaken, and on the main floor sofas, tables, and chairs were crushed under the fallen plaster from the walls and ceilings. Almost immediately neighbors began knocking on the door, asking to see her husband, Dr. George MacIntosh, but when she tried the phone to call him, the line was dead. She did not know it, but he had already gone to Camp Hill. The people on the doorstep were already hem-orrhaging badly, and the worst cases collapsed immediately from shock. They had lost too much blood. She barely had time to dress before she be-gan to treat the people—as the lady divisional superintendent of the St. John's Ambulance Brigade, she was trained to respond to emergencies—but there were too many wounded. At 9:45 her husband walked through the doorframe—there was no door—and began to help stitch up the wounds. Shortly after, Lillian Giffen arrived in a shredded dress, her skin black. She had been kneeling on the floor with her elbows propped up on the win-dowsill with her sister and friend, watching the fire, when the explosion tossed her out of the house and pinned her against the Protestant orphanage fence. A telephone pole tipped over and trapped her there until her father rescued her. The blast shook the orphanage to its foundation, killing twenty-seven children. Mr. Giffen told her that her sister and her friend had both died instantly. All Lillian could think about was that she wanted to be clean.

"I want a bath," Lillian told MacIntosh.

MacIntosh explained that the house was damaged and, instead, offered the girl some clothes before setting her to work sweeping out the glass. When MacIntosh found a man with a working wagon, she sent him on a tour of the neighborhood to collect VADs and take them to the hospital, but, as it turned out, most had already set off for Camp Hill. Slowly, the MacIntosh house filled with people lying on the floor asking for water—even the furnace room was crowded. When a soldier appeared at the door and ordered them to evacuate, Clara, her husband, and a nursing officer carried those who could not walk across the street to the Commons on blankets and rugs, and continued to administer aid. "We spread a blanket about the centre of the common and sent Scouts to bring in the most urgent cases, which we treated until the danger of further explosion was past." At two o'clock a soldier told them they could go home. Dr. MacIntosh returned to Camp Hill. Clara went home, where she continued dressing cuts until eight o'clock, when patients finally stopped arriving at the house. Then she walked down Robie Street to Camp Hill, where she assisted until midnight. When she thought she was going to faint, she returned home and climbed into bed, but by then the phone was working and it rang continuously all night. More patients began arriving, and since there was no door, there was nothing she could do but see them. When a druggist she knew, Mr. Tremaine, walked in, she told him that she did not have the strength to stand. He brought the supplies to her bed and she dressed his wounds there.

When she awoke Friday morning, she was convinced that still more wounded remained in their homes untreated. Someone had to visit them. She tried to bring it to the attention of the mayor and the deputy mayor, but without success. Then she called Mrs. William Dennis, the wife of the local senator who also published the local paper. Agnes Dennis was the president of the Local Council of Women and active in charity and political work. Clara, who was not a member of the council, and who, outside of her VAD work, considered herself more of an artist than a politician, explained her idea that there needed to be home visits, a census of sorts.

"Why not go offer your services?" Mrs. Dennis replied, adding that there was an 11:00 a.m. citizens' meeting planned. To Clara, two hours seemed like an eternity, plus there were no cars or trams, but she agreed. She set off on foot, trudging through the snow past the empty canvas tents on the Commons. Downtown the banks were already open and the city back in business, as the least damaged stores began to open again, albeit with boarded-up windows. Grocers were particularly hard hit, with many of their supplies laced with glass shards. Food had to be thrown out and stores thoroughly cleaned, a difficult task without proper light.

Before the meeting started, Clara mentioned her idea to Archdeacon William Armitage and Lieutenant Governor Grant, and the archdeacon was supportive. She sat quietly as the meeting started. Lieutenant Governor Grant read through the telegrams telling them of trains already en route and offers of supplies and services. Then he reported with some pride on the solid state of mind in which he found the inhabitants of the Old Ladies Home, which he had visited earlier that morning. A short discussion followed about what to do with the inmates of the Deaf and Dumb Institution. When the fire department reported that the fires were under control, the room erupted into applause. Clara grew impatient listening to the self-congratulatory descriptions of how well the city was faring; it was perfectly obvious that people needed more help. Just as the meeting was about to end, she stood and offered to organize a committee of forty women who could systematically visit each house in the two square miles around Pier 6. There was no moving or seconding. The meeting simply continued. She sat mute, confused about the men's reaction to her offer.

"Am I to go on with this work?" she whispered to the archdeacon.

He endorsed her motion and authorized her to take over an office in City Hall. She turned to Miss Jane Wisdom, a social worker who had slipped into the seat next to her after the meeting began, and asked her if she would help. Miss Wisdom thought Clara MacIntosh impertinent to make a motion without first enlisting the help of Mrs. Dennis and her cousin Mrs. Edith Archibald, the senior community advocates, but she agreed. It was clear that things would be extraordinary now, including Halifax's strict social order, which would just have to give way to expediency along with everything else. After the meeting adjourned, the two women went down to the city clerk's office and began gathering volunteers. Miss Wisdom started by calling a secretary and by one o'clock they were ready to move. The city was already divided into areas for the upcoming elections, so MacIntosh's women set out in teams determined to visit each house in each area. "Teams of women with typewritten information slips, pads and pencils were ready to start out over the devastated area. The slips contained information telling those who were able to walk where to go for medical treatment, food, clothing, fuel, bedding, and shelter, and where to report their missing, etc. In the case of those who were not able to leave their homes, details of their conditions were brought back and reported to us. The facts reported were dealt with by Departments quickly organized to tabulate the different needs and send the information to the Committee in charge of each. These emergency workers were not only investigating, but giving relief as well, the teams conveying them often taking a supply of food and clothing." Clara MacIntosh remained awake and on duty at City Hall from Friday through Monday night.

· · ·

DR. COX GREETED FRIDAY morning at Camp Hill, exhausted but exhilarated. Overnight, doctors and nurses had arrived from New Brunswick and Nova Scotia, but, dressed in civilian clothes and without the benefit of nametags, it was hard to identify who was staff and who was visiting. Cox had heard a rumor about a train from Truro arriving in Halifax, but no one offered to help him. Twenty-two patients had died Thursday night. At 8:00 a.m. he grabbed a biscuit in the kitchen and set off to find the commanding officer, to whom he introduced himself and explained his credentials as an oculist. Cox suggested that perhaps he could take all the eye cases in one ward, since they needed immediate attention. The CO said he was welcome to set up an eye ward if he could find the space.

Cox made his way through the bracing air of the hallways, ducking in and out of hot wards in search of a suitable space. The hallways were brighter in the morning light, the outer doors reflecting the clean bright snow each time they opened. Two soldiers posted as guards tried to sort out who was volunteering and who had relatives inside. The chief nurse was trying to instill a system where volunteers reported to her first, so that she could not only account for them but assign them to wards that needed them the most. Her first concern was the kitchen. Their food supplies, she noted, were dwindling quickly. Many of the survivors' relatives were using the hospital as a restaurant, and Miss Ayre, the dietitian, was already having trouble keeping up with the demand.

The survivors crushed together on every surface, giving the heated wards a steamy heaviness that was alleviated only when the door opened to the drafty hallways. If the medical staff had a moment to worry about something other than their patients, it was the spread of communicable diseases. In one of the most crowded wards, Ward L, an older woman with pneumonia discharged long rattling coughs as if trying to dislodge tissue paper from her lungs.

Cox kept moving, looking for a space with enough light and space to accommodate patients and two operating tables. He bounded up the stairs and found himself standing at the end of another crowded ward. The white iron beds stretched all the way to the back wall, where there was a modest room minus its door. Inside he found the VAD Dorothy McMurray still cleaning and bandaging cuts. This room was just big enough. Together with "an old sergeant as orderly," "a fine military nursing sister," and the medical student Florence Murray, who had worked through the night administering chloroform, he rearranged the room, securing three tables. A single bulb jerry-rigged over the operating table was all the light available to them. The sergeant placed screens across the open door to shield patients from witnessing the operations. After the room was organized to his satisfaction, Cox walked the wards with the old sergeant in tow, picking out an hour or two's work. He checked first one eye and then the other by gently lifting their swollen lids, if there were any lids. "Eyelids were cut into literal fringes and in addition to removal of the ball, one often had to hunt among the swollen scalp to find material to reconstruct a set of lids. In many cases there were no more eyeballs. It was as if the ball had been laid opened and then stuffed with pieces of glass or sometimes crockery, brick splinters, and on palpation, they would clink. Pieces of glass were driven clean through the eyeball and one found it necessary to feel about in the orbital tissue before dressing the case. Pieces of glass as large as an inch square or larger were found." One of the difficulties in treating a damaged eye was that a healthy eye could develop sympathetic symptoms and deteriorate if the injured eye did not recuperate. Not wishing to risk a patient losing both eyes, doctors such as Cox, Mathers, McKelvey Bell, and Kirkpatrick, who all worked on eyes over the weekend, sometimes removed one eye in hopes of saving the second. In private practice Cox called on his most persuasive arguments to convince patients that enucleation was required, but in Camp Hill, the patients offered no arguments and few objections. Later Cox recalled the cooperation with wonder. "Everyone, when the case was briefly explained to them and the necessity of the operation laid before them, fell in at once and moved to follow me to the table. Whether it was the habits of discipline, the readiness to do what they were called on to do or suffering brought about among our people by the already long continuation of the war or whether it was the stunning appalling effect of such a sudden catastrophe—I do not know but I think it was both."

Behind the screen, Florence Murray applied the chloroform while Cox dropped a cocaine solution into the eyes of those who needed a suture or a foreign object removed from their eye.* When they ran out of cocaine solution, they used a spatula to wipe grains directly onto the cornea, although some doctors quickly discovered that cocaine was not strong enough for

---

*Murray was the hospital's official anesthetist, according to her autobiography. Cox says that he worked with a medical student, one in a succession of anesthetists. I have placed them together for brevity's sake. It is possible that his anesthetist was someone else.

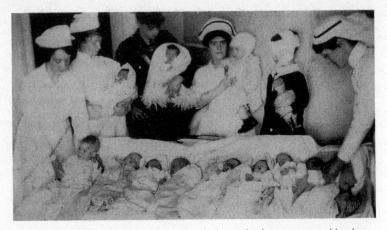

Babies without identification were taken to the hospital, where nurses cared for them until family members claimed them. Others were eventually placed in orphanages.

soldiers returned from the front. They needed chloroform.* Cox kept both cocaine and chloroform going at once. By the time he finished administering the cocaine to the simpler cases, the chloroform had taken its effect on the surgical cases. When he was finished operating, the cocaine would have numbed the eye and socket, and he worked on that patient as the nurse administered chloroform to the next.

Late Friday afternoon, eighteen-year-old Jack MacKeen drove up to the Camp Hill doors as he had been doing since Thursday morning, but this time he turned off his car and walked inside. He was the youngest of four children by the late David MacKeen—a senator and then lieutenant governor—and his third wife. He and his family had spent the last day and a half searching ruins and delivering survivors to the hospital, but the snow prevented him from driving any more. The ruts in the road were filling with

---

*Cocaine was first used as a local anesthetic in ophthalmologic surgery in Germany in 1880 after Dr. Carl Koller read Sigmund Freud's paper advancing the drug's properties. When he saw that cocaine had a numbing effect, he realized that it could prove to be more than an unpleasant side effect and began experimenting with it himself, promoting the drug as a safe method of anesthetizing the eye. Before cocaine solutions were available, eye patients were forced to sit perfectly still and not move their eye as doctors removed cataracts or foreign objects. In some cases doctors used assistants to hold the patient's head still.

ice and snow, and it was almost impossible to get traction on Richmond's steep hills. Once inside, MacKeen found Dr. A. C. Hawkins, and told him that he had taken a course in first aid. Hawkins pointed to a row of twenty-five people, and told him that they had had no medical attention. He asked MacKeen to try to clean their wounds as best he could.

Almost 250 people were squeezed into the musty ward built for 50. MacKeen made out his row of hunched figures and asked for supplies, receiving a yellow crystalline brick called iodoform, an antiseptic made by heating alcohol with iodine. A sweet, cloying smell wafted up from the bowl. He took gauze and bandages in his other hand, and made his way through the VADs and nurses to his patients.

MacKeen went straight to fireman Billy Wells, who was lying on the floor. It was Friday afternoon, and he still had not seen a doctor. MacKeen pulled back the blanket—the muscle between the area where the upper arm joined his shoulder was missing entirely. Wells had also lost a substantial amount of blood, and MacKeen worried that he was in danger of going into shock. MacKeen must have brought Wells to the attention of one of the medical staff, because he was instructed to use a newer, stronger treatment—Dakin's solution—a fluid made of diluted bleach and boric acid that was developed to treat soldiers' burns and gangrene in the field. Its success was not its power, but its subtlety. Stronger solutions like iodine and carbolic acid destroyed living cells along with the dead, whereas Dakin's solution separated healthy tissue from necrotic, speeding the recovery process. Another advantage was that bodily fluids did not dilute it, which was vital for burns and bloody wounds. MacKeen dipped a wad of gauze into the yellowish-green liquid and wiped the tar off of what was left of Billy Wells's shoulder.

At the front door, the medical student Florence Murray told the guard to let in the two girls who had come to volunteer. One of them was Jean Lindsay, the third-year Dalhousie student who had spent Thursday morning wandering around like a tourist looking at damaged buildings without any sense of danger until she was caught up in the evacuation to the South End. Although some of her friends had already volunteered, Jean refused outright: "I thought it was ridiculous sentiment and nothing more and what could girls do there, still more I, who hate all sickness." Friday morning a housemate named Margaret White convinced her otherwise. She told Jean that she had come home on an ambulance with three corpses, but after what she had seen the night before at Rockhead Hospital, "it seemed a small thing." Jean, who first tried to return home to Lunenberg but who could not get a train, canvassed the other girls to try to find someone to accompany her to Camp Hill, but anyone who wanted to volunteer had already left. Finally a girl named Abbie Hemphill said she would join her. Jean, dressed in a long skirt and a white middie blouse, named for its sailor collar, put on her green winter coat and bundled up against the snow, and the two girls trudged through the blizzard to Camp Hill, nervous at what they might find when they reached there. "The door was guarded for there was a crowd there almost fighting to get in to see if they could find missing relatives. Only a few were allowed in at a time."

Florence Murray took the girls to the matron, who assigned them to Ward L. Mostly Jean ran errands for caregivers and brought patients whatever they needed, which was, most often, water. The woman with pneumonia asked her for water and Jean attended her, pleased to be useful. The VAD who witnessed her act shooed her away, assuring her that the woman was dying and that there was no purpose in prolonging her misery by giving her water. Jean wondered if there was any point to her volunteering. "What sent me home however was orders from a woman in an elegant sealskin coat, doling out sweet biscuits and seating herself at each bedside in turn to hear the story . . . I thought she was just as well able to run after glasses of water as I was. That I was more suitably dressed was a witness to my sense not hers."

She and Abbie finished their shift at 6:30 p.m. Assured that all cars had been commandeered for ferrying patients and staff, they found an expensive-looking car waiting at the front door. Abbie got up her nerve to ask the driver for a lift home, but he coolly assured her that the car was in the service of its owner—"our sealskin friend's car." They walked in what they assumed was the direction of Robie Street, but the road was buried beneath almost a foot and a half of snow, and snowdrifts, which started at their knees and sometimes climbed thigh high, obliterated the usual landmarks. Two soldiers dragging a toboggan caught up to them and called out, offering them a lift. Grateful for any transportation, Jean and Abbie tucked their long coats around them and sat down on the toboggan with what little grace they could muster. The soldiers dragged the two laughing girls through the swirling snow in the dark past the cemetery fence to the corner. By the time the girls arrived back at the Ladies College, Jean's coat was so wet that the green dye had seeped through the lining and turned her clean white middie a pale shade of green. She minded, but not nearly as much as she would have two days before.

. . .

FRIDAY NIGHT, DR. COX stood dazed, watching as his medical student carefully poured two or three droplets of chloroform onto ribbed cotton gauze. Cox was preparing to remove both of a man's eyes. As the med student held the cone over the man's face, Cox turned to his other patient, the man's wife. He could save one of her eyes, Cox thought, if he took out the other, worrying about how a marriage could survive with one eye between them. "The double cases were particularly sad." He tried not to consider it; there were many terrible cases, some so bad they could not be treated. "In one poor woman the whole frontal bone had been chopped off and she lay there with her brain exposed, moaning until she died some twelve hours after. It was said that she was found in her backyard holding her headless baby in her arms."

Cox waited for the chloroform to take effect. Funny to think that his office, clean, empty, orderly, sat waiting for him back in New Glasgow. When had he left? That morning? The morning before? He longed for sleep. "But it was rather tough to knock off from being tired out at night for even a few hours knowing that there were still scores lying in the rows needing attention." He would have to go on still longer. Eye cases needed immediate attention, and many of them, Cox estimated, would not see a doctor for days. This explosion was, in his opinion, probably the worst eye disaster in history. He could not think of any other instance of damage on such a scale. At least he still had a supply of anesthetic and suture. Other surgeons had already switched to cotton thread and sewing needles. No one had any time to sterilize. Cox checked in with Florence Murray. She looked sleepy too. Adrenaline would last for only so long. By midnight Friday he had removed seventy-five eyes.

"If relief doesn't come soon, I shall murder somebody."

An angry scream jolted the staff. It came from a young woman at the end of the ward. She had been going on and off for an hour or more. Whenever staff approached her to investigate, she kicked them, howling so loud that she woke anyone fortunate enough to find sleep. She appeared sound enough to Cox. It was probably simple hysteria. He should, he thought, be grateful that only one person was in such a state, but instead he felt irritated. How difficult she was, healthy and unhurt, compared to the good nature of the injured, the sad mute faces so accepting of their grim fate. The easy compliance struck Dr. Moore differently: "The patients as a rule seemed stoical and stunned with the severity of the shock, few requiring anesthetics for things that could not be done in ordinary practice without them. The nerve centers both sensory and mental, seemed to be numbed, and while such a condition seemed to mitigate somewhat the horrors of acute suffering, yet it did not augur well for the future, and a larger mortality rate, and slower recovery might be expected than from injuries of similar extent under other conditions." Moore was right. Many patients remained stunned for a week. On the eighth day, patients reported that the sluggishness lifted and their faces reanimated. Only then did their wounds begin to heal.

Friday at six o'clock, twenty-four hours after he had arrived and thirty-six since he had last slept, Cox put down his scalpel. He had to sleep. A volunteer led him to a dark room reserved for doctors. It was probably the only vacant room in the hospital. He took a gray army blanket and stretched out on the floor in the dark. Trying to put the visions of waiting patients out of his mind, he fell asleep. Three hours later he was back in his improvised eye surgery. Every hour or two, he opened the screen to examine the 120 people awaiting treatment, traveling up and down the rows and tagging patients in order of priority. As more doctors arrived from outside, he noticed that some were duplicating his efforts, taking patients he had already handpicked, and he asked his assistants to devise a way to identify his patients. They came up with linen tags and a pen. After each treatment, a young med student dutifully took down the patient's name and address while Cox dictated the particulars of their injury, treatment, and future needs. The system worked. "In a day or so we had order. The rows of beds and cots began to look ship shape and gradually one began to see daylight."

THAT NIGHT ELIZABETH FRASER opened the church doors and walked onto Grafton Street. Almost sixteen inches of snow had fallen, making it difficult to walk where there were sidewalks and almost impossible where there were none. Only the most awkward pieces of debris identified themselves; the rest hid underneath the snow like rabbit traps. Tracks from cars and wagons provided a better path, but most had stopped running hours before, leaving only slight indentations in the snow. The town clock read eight o'clock. It would take hours to get back to Rockhead trudging through the snow. It was almost a mile and a half to North Street and another mile after that. The silver-white blur of snow enveloped her and stole whatever warmth she mustered from the walk. The shirt around her head and shoulders froze itself into an icy scarf, protecting her from the wind but not the cold. "My hands and feet were very cold, but I dared not stop." She tried to keep her hands tucked underneath her arms for warmth, but took them out when she lost her balance, which was often. She stumbled along in the darkness, numb with cold and grief. By the time she reached Roome Street, her only companions were the snow and the acrid smell of yesterday's fire. She stood in front of her house, terrified, trying to convince herself to act. "I stood for a long time, scared to death to move. It was so very lonely and there was a foul smell everywhere." She was barely sixteen and without a coat, but she refused to leave Arthur exposed to the snow or, worse, animals. She made out a bulky silhouette on the ground in front of her. She inched closer, leaning over to inspect it. A milky brown eye stared back. Elizabeth swallowed a gasp and backed away deliberately, every muscle strained in a desperate effort not to trip. It was a severed cow's head, probably from the cattle yards at the bottom of the hill, but this explanation offered no comfort. Absence overwhelmed her. She could not feel her hands and feet. She could not see a foot into the darkness. There was not even anything to hear aside from her own thoughts. Everyone was gone. No grinding metal from the railyard. No shouts from the piers or the ships. The harbor itself was mute. She thought of all the babies she had heard cry on Roome Street, including Arthur. Nothing. Then from her right, a horse chortled in the cold. It came from the bottom of the hill and was soon joined by the voices of soldiers. Elizabeth screamed.

"Go in there and see what that is; my brother is missing and I believe he is in there."

The soldiers pulled up beside her in a sleigh covered by a dirty tarpaulin and set off toward the wreckage. They were not gone long before one returned with Arthur in his arms. Elizabeth ran to him but they would not let her hold him. Her brother's skull was misshaped and his clothes frozen with blood. The soldier carried him to the sleigh. The other soldier lifted the canvas and he placed Arthur on top of other corpses before covering him. He told her she had to identify him at the morgue before she could bury him. Elizabeth chased after them as the sleigh started to slip up Roome Street. "How I ever got there I will never know."

The morgue had been centralized since morning. Within a couple of hours of MacIlreith's Thursday visit, trucks filled with soldiers, and supplies rolled onto the Chebucto Road schoolyard and began unloading wood, tarpaper, sealant, and supplies. The soldiers worked on the windows first, sealing out the weather, the light, and the curious all at once. They were worried about security. There were already reports of scavengers going through the wreckage stealing rings, money, whatever they could find. Inside, water from the pipes ran over the floor and dripped down the stairs.

The boiler could not be fixed, so they installed portable stoves instead. Downstairs in the basement they cleaned the glass and splinters from the floor as other soldiers strung up a series of bulbs from the low ceiling that, as the last window was covered, left the basement in "a restful half light." The plumbing proved to be a greater challenge, and soldiers canvassed the neighborhood for water for the next two days, walking back and forth from houses to the school, carrying buckets of hot water, if they were lucky, cold if they were not. Food was also problematic until women from the surrounding houses started to appear sporadically with trays of food that the soldiers, and then the staff, gratefully accepted. When engineers installed running water at the school, the Food Committee arranged for a military cook to take over the meals. That morning Colwell had sent word out through the 66th Regiment to the 250 soldiers, 30 men from Cooks Construction, and the private citizens who were still searching, that bodies should be delivered to Chebucto Road School. He also appointed Arthur S. Barnstead, whose father had overseen the bodies brought back from the *Titanic,* as chair of the Mortuary Committee. That morning Barnstead placed an ad in the papers instructing funeral directors to send all bodies there too. Almost immediately, vehicles, carts, horses, and wheelbarrows arrived, carrying bodies, pails, boxes, and tins. Soldiers directed drivers to the boys' side, where other soldiers helped unload.

"'What have you there?' asked a soldier, checking.

"'Nos. 12, 13, 14, 15, 16 and 17,' came the reply from the undertaker's assistant.

There were but two piles on the sled and the soldier asked for a check.

"'Here is No. 12,' said the assistant, 'and here,' indicating the other pile, 'is 13, 14, 15.'

"'And where,' asked the soldier, 'is 16 and 17?'

"'In that box,' was the reply, as the assistant pointed to an ordinary-sized cake box. 'They are the members of the Thomas family.'"

FROM THE START there were problems. Bodies arrived without any information or their tickets had blown off in the blizzard. Hospitals delivered bodies stripped of all identifying belongings and tickets. Soldiers made mistakes recording numbers from tickets to lists. One woman identified George Holmes, the ferryman, who had been found on Hanover Street. As she leaned over to check that it was indeed him, a slight moan escaped his lips and she jumped back. When they touched him, they realized he was

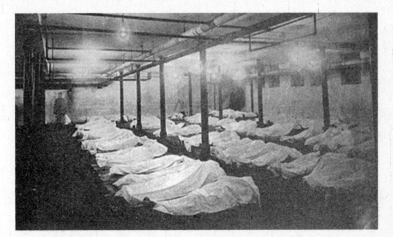

The basement at the morgue located in the Chebucto Road School

still warm. She insisted he be transferred to the hospital. In spite of individual setbacks, a system emerged.

Donald Morrison was standing on guard inside one of the doors, trying to ignore his rumbling stomach and the cold when Elizabeth arrived. His pants were wet to the knees and he had had almost no food or sleep since he awoke, floating in the harbor after the explosion. He spent the better part of Friday searching for bodies and carrying corpses into the morgue through the worst part of the blizzard. Morrison worried about looters, who visited under the guise of distressed loved ones, stealing whatever they could find. Stories were circulating about men who cut off fingers to get at rings and he had orders, which he meant to keep, not to let anyone in after 10:00 p.m. He did not want any more trouble from the kind of man who would steal from the dead. He tried to rest. He would have to work through all of Saturday too, but the thought of looters made him anxious, and he could not sleep despite his exhaustion. Outside Elizabeth Fraser approached the school in the dark, but a soldier stopped her, explaining that the morgue was closed and that she should return in the morning. She argued, but the soldier was unsympathetic. She ran around the school from door to door, pleading and banging on the door with her hand.

"Help. Help. Please help me."

Morrison looked up. The voice was too young, too desperate to be a looter.

"Oh please help. Will not anyone help me?"

He shouted through the doors that his orders were to keep the morgue shut after ten, but she pleaded with him to let her in so that she could identify her brother, stressing that he was just eleven years old. Morrison picked up the lantern and walked to the door. As he put the key in the lock, Elizabeth Fraser "tumbled into the room."

"Is my brother here? Please help me. I have looked everywhere and I cannot find him."

Morrison passed the lantern across her face. "She was sixteen or seventeen. Her face was dirty and tear-stained and she was wet and cold. She told me she had been looking for her brother for two days." Unwilling to add to her sorrow, he led her to the first row, lowered the lantern, and lifted the sheet. Elizabeth shook her head no. "Body after body we checked—some were badly mutilated—from time to time I stole a look at my companion but she seemed unaware of anything, working with a fervor that I had to admire. Cold, hunger—everything was forgotten." They shuffled along that way, Morrison lifting back the canvas, shining a light, and Elizabeth shaking her head no until they finished the row of teenagers. Just as they finished, the light from Morrison's lantern caught a stretch of canvas leaning against one of the columns. Elizabeth said that it looked like the same dirty tarp from the sleigh. "We went over to have a closer look." The body was tagged 611. Morrison pulled back the canvas. Elizabeth let out a short scream. She fell to her knees and embraced her brother's crushed body.

"I found you. I found you."

Morrison watched in silence. "She cried as I have never seen anyone cry before or since." When she was done she tidied his body, replaced the canvas, and stood straight. All at once she felt the cold and it occurred to her that she was not wearing a coat. As if suddenly awakened, she noticed that her hands, her clothes, everything was filthy, as stained as everyone else she had seen in the last day. She had not noticed that before, and it suddenly seemed important to be clean. She tried to think where she could go to wash, but there was nowhere. She thanked Morrison and told him she would return as soon as she could, as he led her to the door. In no time she was back with two men and a stretcher. "Under ordinary circumstances I would have been court-martialed but my C.O. only reprimanded me. I guess he realized I was only human."

THE BOSTON & MAINE chugged into McAdam Junction before dawn on Friday. It was a busy terminal on the Maine–New Brunswick border, where passengers normally transferred to local trains, but the relief train was going all the way to Halifax. A mix of Americans and Canadians met them on the platform, but they still had no real firsthand news from Halifax. Ratshesky grow more concerned. "The most we obtained were rumors, and the more we received the worse they sounded." Listening to the stories of people burned by oil, people blinded by glass, and itinerant families, he began to doubt whether the relief workers on the train were properly prepared. He sought out Major Harold G. Giddings of the Massachusetts State Guard and consulted with him as to his experience. Together they called a meeting of the doctors, nurses, and the Red Cross staff, where Ratshesky asked for an inventory of everything on the train, plus a list of supplies that they might need, keeping in mind the terrible stories of widespread injuries caused by fire, glass, and exposure. He worried that they were overreacting—in their experience anecdotes about disasters were usually exaggerated—but better to have too many supplies than too many injured. Wartime medical supplies would eventually find their way to good use if they were not needed in Halifax. The staff made their way to the baggage car to assess the inventory, and produced a list. The medical staff also came up with a separate list of things that they might need if the rumors of fire and flying glass were true. Ratshesky made a plan to buy these supplies in St. John, a small New Brunswick coastal city usually just two hours away, but the trip took longer than expected. At every local stop along the track from McAdam Junction to St. John, the platforms were lined with solemn-looking workers holding shovels, carpentry tools, and medical bags, hoping for a ride to Halifax. Ratshesky, seeing the worried faces, had to decide whether or not they should stop and pick the workers up. "I instructed those in charge of the train to fill every available space, giving doctors and nurses the preference." The Boston & Maine train, intended to make the fastest time on record to Halifax, was now a milk run, stopping at every town on the route. By the time they reached St. John, they were in the midst of the blizzard.

A prominent lawyer, King Kelly Esq., was waiting for them on the platform. Kelly confirmed the true extent of the explosion and the desperate condition of the city. It was worse than Ratshesky had imagined. All the disparate rumors they had heard along the run were true. Fires raged through two square miles of the city. Thousands were injured; thousands more homeless. No one knew how many were dead. Not a house in the city had all of its windows. And now bitter cold and snow. Ratshesky wired Endicott, who was working from Boston to send a trainload of glass, putty, and building materials. King's only good news was that a relief train from St. John carrying members of the Canadian Red Cross, who had left before the snow started, preceded them. Ratshesky handed King the new list of supplies they wanted and asked if he could get them. The first four items on the list—alcohol, iodine, cotton, and boric ointment—along with the rolls of adhesives and safety pins indicate that they were concerned about the volume of burns. The empty bottles, tins, and olive oil would have been used to create solutions and creams, again most likely for burns. The digitalis was used to revive weak hearts, while the ammonia and camphor were probably purchased out of a concern for the spread of pneumonia. Cocaine was used as a local anesthetic, while brandy was used to manage pain, although brandy also had the side benefits of stimulating the appetite and bringing on sleep. The atropine, which stopped salivation and any other volume excretions, was used in conjunction with ether and chloroform, both of which produced excessive drooling. In short, they were concerned about burns, pain relief, and respiratory diseases brought on by exposure and infection. They would need it all. Men from the press appeared and gathered around the two men, anxious to get a quote for the afternoon papers. Ratshesky spoke.

"Governor McCall has given me orders to go the limit in rendering aid and I shall. Just as soon as I can get detailed first-hand reports I will wire him fully because it appears now that tremendous assistance will be necessary. Arrangements were made last night with James Jackson, head of the New England Division the American Red Cross, to forward large equipment needed to supplement what we have here tonight aboard. The assignment of our staff and nurses will be determined after arrival at Halifax but the whole force will be placed as a unit under the direction of the Surgeon General. There is much to be done as reports show that not one-half of the terrible story has been given the world."

He addressed his next statement directly to the reporters and the people of Halifax.

"Will you please have the Associated Press say to the people of Halifax that everything that can be done in a great affliction has been ordered by Massachusetts and this is not the last relief corps that the State is prepared to rend. We shall be on the job tonight and our doctors and our nurses will stay on the job with those from nearby Canadian cities until the homeless and the hurt can see daylight ahead."

Journalist A. J. Philpott scribbled down the message and ran to transmit it to his editor at the *Boston Globe* before the train started again. He tagged on an extra paragraph at the end. "For hours today the relief train ran through a country foot deep in snow that whirled over the field in a cutting north wind. Railroad men said it was cold and raw at Halifax and that suffering was intense. The Massachusetts special had the right of way and made a record run on its mission of mercy." The normal passage was twenty-seven hours, but they intended to arrive in Halifax Friday at 8:00 p.m., cutting five hours off the journey. The Relief Special did have the right of way, taking advantage of its privileged status to pass the regular Boston train, but it would not make a record run.

IN ANOTHER PULLMAN, the director of the Halifax Relief Unit for the American Red Cross, John Moors, sat ensconced with others from the Boston Metropolitan Chapter, planning their actions upon arrival. The Boston Metropolitan was one of the first chapters to set up a Civilian Relief Committee, a volunteer organization made up of professionals trained to deal with emergencies. In April 1906, when the San Francisco earthquake killed 498 people and left 100,000 homeless and twice that many without food, President Theodore Roosevelt called the Red Cross to ask for their help, but no one in their offices had disaster experience. The organization was under new leadership and without the resources to manage such a large-scale event. They went anyway, and the experience convinced them that they should train others so that they could be prepared for disaster before it occurred. In 1908, they began training staff all around the country in principles of disaster relief, tailoring their response to the demands of floods, fires, industrial accidents, and earthquakes, which each demanded different responses. In 1917, the American Red Cross had dealt with enough fires, earthquakes, hurricanes, floods, and tornadoes to commission a small handbook called, simply enough, *Disasters*. They were correcting the proofs when they heard about Halifax.

The Red Cross divided disaster relief into two stages. The first was the emergency phase, which included providing medical treatment, food rations, and temporary shelter. The second was rehabilitation, which meant restoring people to the state they were in before the disaster struck by providing permanent housing along with enough life and career training to ensure that they could remain independent. "The welfare of the individual and that of the community are both bound up with the welfare of the family. That which threatens or weakens the family at the same time similarly affects them. Conversely that which helps or strengthens it strengthens and helps them. The first principle of disaster relief is that the family must be the unit of treatment. Whether the disaster victims number a few score or several score thousands they must be dealt with family by family. There is simply no other way."

Before the war, it was a radical idea for communities to prepare themselves for unseen events, but after being caught unawares in San Francisco, the Red Cross made disaster relief first a national priority, and then experimented with organizing local disaster relief committees. Boston and New York set up the first two committees. New York was already rushing the first of several trains to Halifax, filled with twenty engineers, doctors, nurses, $15,000 worth of tools, $150,000 worth of lumber, one thousand portable houses, and thirty thousand pounds of bandages.

The structure of the Civilian Relief Committees was tailored to the local community. "Within the membership of this committee a relief squad has been formed, composed of persons of technical training and experience who are pledged to active service in emergencies. Each member has a definite responsibility. One is responsible for keeping track of public buildings in different communities which would be available for sheltering refugees, or as relief headquarters; another, for furnishing emergency food supplies." In Boston, they had arranged contracts with milk suppliers and bakers to respond immediately if called upon. They organized a registration committee that carried thousands of preprinted cards that would be filled out by local volunteers, for each client, giving his or her name, old address, temporary address, needs, and services administered. John Moors had considerable experience with large-scale disasters such as the Chelsea, Massachusetts, fires (2,835 buildings destroyed and 16,000 people homeless), the Salem (Massachusetts) fire (1,792 buildings burned; 16,000 homeless), and the San Francisco earthquake and fire (17,450 buildings destroyed; 100,000 homeless). If their efforts were to succeed in a foreign city, the key would be speed, structure, and most important, diplomacy.

As they pulled out of St. John, a woman who boarded with some other Red Cross workers in St. John approached Moors and introduced herself as May Sexton, vice president of the Halifax Red Cross. The Halifax Red Cross was a candent tinderbox of suffragettes and political progressives, determined to drag the old city into the new century. The national executive of the Canadian Red Cross had gone so far as to chastise the unit for not having any men on its board. They appointed one man, made him president, and continued doing what they had been doing all along. Sexton was also part of the Local Council of Women and was fighting to get women the vote, but her personal mission was to open up the technical and trade schools to women so that they could standardize their wages. She saw no reason why carpenters were paid a living wage while seamstresses were not. She herself was a graduate of MIT, and her husband, an American whom she met at MIT, ran the Nova Scotia Technical Institute. Sexton was not getting the support she needed to open the technical schools to women. A royal commission ignored her suggestions, and then the war came along and everyone's priorities shifted. Sexton took up fund-raising for the Red Cross with her usual enthusiasm and efficiency, but ironically the war had already opened employment opportunities to women. Even the explosion gave one woman the opportunity to become the city's first female transit worker.

Moors was grateful to find such an important liaison even before their arrival, and asked her to join the discussion. Sexton explained her background and her husband's position at the Technical College. More important, she told them, he was also the vocational director in the rehabilitation work for returned soldiers, putting him in charge of fourteen hospitals along the East Coast. This was valuable information, and both Ratshesky and Sexton knew it. As the train rolled along, stopping and starting in the snow, they peppered her with questions. "Mrs. Sexton, knowing Halifax very well and being an officer in most of the important organizations in Halifax, and having a very special interest in the work of the Canadian Red Cross, was of unusual help in outlining for us the work of the various civic and philanthropic Organizations in the city, the names of their executives, the best members of the respective boards of directors, the functions of each of these organizations, and an appraisal of their worth. . . . Mrs. Sexton reemphasized the importance of Halifax as a military port, the center for Canada and the United States." The Bostonians did not seem to realize that, since American soldiers had started shipping overseas in June, many U.S. soldiers had stopped off in Halifax before going to or returning from overseas. This meant the possibility of hospital ships as well as local military hospitals. Sexton told them about the new convalescent hospital, Camp Hill Hospital, but warned them that Pier 2, the dockside hospital where ships usually sent their wounded, had been destroyed.* Sexton rattled off the names of citizens she thought would be useful. She also offered to introduce

---

*According to Murphy's report, Mrs. Sexton also told them ". . . of one very terrible tragedy of which there had been no newspaper mention. An English troop ship, loaded

the Bostonians to the public so as to best garner a good opinion of the outsiders and their relief effort. They agreed on their priorities: transitional housing for the homeless, care of the sick and injured, possibly a special committee working with children, and very probably a special medical social service, particularly for the handicapped.

While they talked, offshore winds buffeted the cars and piled snow into burdensome drifts that blocked the tracks. The engineers opened the gate and poured black shovelfuls of coal on top of their white-hot predecessors, sending billowing gray clouds from the smokestack. The engine barely had enough power to pull the cars through the drifts. The Red Cross added the weather to their list of concerns. It would make everything much more difficult, particularly if there were high numbers of homeless, as had been reported. Outside a fine black soot fell out of the smoke and drifted over the snowbanks as the engine labored through the countryside, stopping and starting as the drifts increased. By the time they pulled into Moncton Station in New Brunswick on Friday at 3:00 p.m., they were in a whiteout. The conductor asked to switch engines. They needed something heavier and with a better plow to make the rest of the trip. From his seat in the Pullman, Ratshesky could hear the clanking of metal as they made the switch. Even from his window he could see that the snow was much worse. He was afraid that they would not make it through. Snowplows could only do so much. If they ran into a snowslide, which happened when snow slid off a mountainside, dragging soil, rocks, bushes, and even trees onto the tracks, they could be stuck for days. As long as the snow remained dry and loose, they would be able to push through, but slides were denser and more dangerous. The pass between Moncton and Truro would be mountainous. More snow. They needed all the power they could muster.

Kate McMahon, assistant director the Home Service Department of the Northeastern Division of the Red Cross, settled in for another long night

with West Indian troops, stopped at Halifax. Two days out of Halifax the ship cast its rudder. This was replaced, only to be lost also. Then the ship was carried far north in a storm before a third rudder could be put in place. There was terrible exposure to cold on the part of the troops, so that many had their hands and feet frozen. The ship came back to Halifax, unloaded those in the most serious condition, and it was found necessary to amputate the hands and feet of approximately 350 of these troops. Mrs. Sexton said these maimed men were in one of the special vocational hospitals in Eastern Canada and were going through the same re-education work which held for soldiers who had actually been across and sustained disabling injuries."

onboard. They were already losing light and it was only 3:00 p.m. They would never make their 8:00 p.m. deadline. The train rattled as the first engine disengaged and the second engine took its place. McMahon took out paper and pen and began to write. "The Vice President of the Halifax Red Cross came aboard some distance below St. John and she at once took us under her wing. Her connections have made her a most valuable adviser . . . She has given us a confidential list of 'Who's who' and carefully instructed us on local points of possible conflict. We have held a conference practically all day and have our minds cleared as to first steps." McMahon also monitored the relationship between the Public Safety Commission and the Red Cross, reporting that relations were so far cordial and that Ratshesky had already donated $500 for their use. More ominously, as the train left the station, she reported on the rumors. "At every stop the size and consequences of the disaster increases."

LADD TOLD HIS STAFF to meet him at the Boston train station at 5:00 p.m. Friday, but as the Red Cross workers began to amass the supplies, they sent out word that the train would be delayed, and people were instructed not to arrive before 6:30 p.m. What postponed the train was the "wonderfully complete" Harvard hospital unit, as Ratshesky noted. The unit was meant to go overseas earlier that fall, but it was not fully assembled when the ships sailed. It was equipped with all the supplies required to set up a five-hundred-bed hospital base, including, among other things, surgical dressings, ether, iodine, carbolic acid, morphine, bandages, pajamas, sweaters, and convalescent gowns. This second relief train from Boston would be the only unit to arrive in Halifax with its own complete nursing staff of sixty-five women and five men.

As the winter light faded into night, the nurses and doctors began to gather on the platform where the ladies of the Red Cross Emergency Canteen Committee waited for them. The Red Cross still understood the value of a decent meal and wanted to ensure that no one started off what would surely be a cold and difficult journey without so much as supper. The problem of feeding both soldiers and workers had been with the Red Cross since its inception and, relief officials concluded, that it was more important to a successful venture than everyone, except the hungry, realized. The canteen ladies, many the wives of prominent men, unpacked oversized coffee cans and sandwiches onto a baggage cart that they had fashioned into a canteen. Trays of foods and drink were arranged across the top, offering a late supper of hot coffee, sandwiches, and doughnuts to the nurses and doctors who came clattering across the platform in their civilian clothes. Others, coming straight from work, arrived in their uniforms, starving and grateful for a bit of supper. Governor McCall's wife, Ella, dressed in a blowsy black hat and with her astrakhan collar pulled over the Canteen Committee's bulky canvas apron, picked up a tray and wove through the excited chatter, handing out coffee and sweets. After a round or two, she took a moment to pose for a photo for the local papers.

Head nurse Edith Cox crossed off names from her list of sixty-five volunteer nurses as they arrived. Added to them were twenty-nine doctors and fourteen civilians, including several Red Cross secretaries, over one hundred people in all, each of whom added to the confusion about departure times and who doubtlessly descended on Dr. Ladd, demanding to know the schedule, when his tall figure appeared on the platform. The atmosphere must have been something like a convention or a reunion—one hundred trained medical staff, most of whom knew each other, some meeting for the first time, leaving on an overnight expedition together. The months since America entered the war had been filled with anticipation and now, as the

Governor McCall's wife Ella as she appeared in the next day's paper after seeing off the volunteers with sandwiches and doughnuts

staff carefully boarded the train, the tension broke. Something had finally happened. It was almost a relief. As Ladd looked out the window at retreating Boston, he could not help but notice that it had begun to snow.


THE BOSTON & MAINE train—the first relief train—did not get far outside Moncton before the freight engine broke down. The relief workers ate supper and gazed out the windows as worried-looking men walked back and forth. The train was starting to feel worn out, its inhabitants cramped and cold, but after tedious hours of false starts, the engine's familiar growl resumed and jolted the train forward. Whatever speed they may have had was gone. "We came into full force of the blizzard. It was a nightmare." It would only get worse.

That night at the Chignecto Isthmus, the narrow neck of land that connected Nova Scotia to the mainland, they had to cross a swatch of the Appalachians that cut across the province. Like all mountainous regions, these hills were prone to deeper, more intense snowfalls, and the tracks began to disappear underneath drifts more regularly, forcing the engineer to stop. If it looked like loose powder, the train lurched backwards until the engineer gauged that he had enough room to get up some speed. Car after car jerked to an abrupt stop. The whistle blew and a genie cloud of smoke rose from the engine. The wheels slowly ground over the rails until it acquired enough speed to plunge through the drift, sending a shiver down the spine of the train and, most likely, its passengers. If they were unsuccessful the first time, the engineer again plowed a path by throwing the switch back and slamming the engine against the packed snowdrifts. Inside, the passengers grew used to the rhythm of jerk, stop, roll, jerk, stop, speed, and shiver. It went on for miles. In some spots as they squeaked through extended stretches of drifts, passengers looked up to discover snow scraping against their windows. It gave the cabins an eerie, otherworldly glow. When they could see out to the mountainside, everything was hushed and white, one form indistinguishable from another. Even the pine trees disappeared into the snow, their conical green cheeriness smothered in white monotony. The workers in Ratshesky's car decided to make it an early night. They obviously were not going to make it to Halifax on time, and if they arrived after midnight, they might be called on to work immediately. This sleep could be the last decent one they had for a week. They bid Ratshesky good-night and drew down their covers. Ratshesky could not sleep. He stayed up talking as the train inched its way through the night. Aside from the explosion, the Friday papers were filled with the news that America had declared war on Austria-Hungary and there was much to discuss. Wounded soldiers would soon be reappearing in Boston, demanding rehabilitation training.

On Folly Mountain, about a thousand feet up and seventy-five miles away from Halifax, the train stopped. This time it did not start again. It was as if the passage just suddenly ended there. The conductor, C. H. Trueman, and the general agent for Canadian Railways, C. K. Howard, walked back through the cars until they found Ratshesky. They said they could not go any farther; an enormous snowbank was blocking the tracks. Ratshesky was a patient man, but he did not intend to wait until morning. If snow was piling up so high that it could block trains, what was it doing in Halifax? Their train of workers and supplies was more important than ever. Even with word of replacement workers arriving before them from St. John and New Glasgow, the majority of relief workers would be exhausted by now. And so would their supplies. Ratshesky removed from his pocket the telegram that he had carried with him from Boston. It was from the Boston & Maine Railroad, and it asked for the special train to be given right of way over every other matter. "I pleaded with them to do everything in their power known to railroad men to clear the track."

People started to appear in the aisles, asking what was the matter. Why was the train stopped? Ratshesky reminded the conductor of the situation in Halifax. Surely there was a way to get through the drift. Outside a group of men with shovels stood in a halo of yellow light from the engine. The wind pierced ears and hands with shooting cold. Ratshesky spoke to them, detailing what he knew of the disaster. The homeless. The injured. The children. The weather. "The men, realizing this, and knowing that every moment was precious worked like Trojans." Shovels flew through the night air, sending snow off to the sides. When a section of the dark track was visible, the men waded up the hillside until they were safe. Over 135 tons of metal raced forward and slammed itself into the snowbank. It might as well have been concrete. The train stopped with a shudder. The engineer pulled back the engine several yards, then pulled the release. Steam jetted out from the engine, melting round caves into the snow and sending hot water trickling out onto the railbed as men scrambled down from their ledges onto the track. The snow was wetter now, and their shovels tipped with the weight as the men dumped the snow to the side of the track. The men attacked fresh areas until they could dig no more. Ratshesky watched with gratitude as the sweating men peeled off their outer clothes and then moved out of range on the hillside. They signaled the engineer. The engine shot toward them and drilled into the snow but only compacted the snow further, which made the digging even harder. Again, the engineer released steam, melting gaps into the drift before the men jumped onto the track and shoveled as long as they could. Again the men stopped to wipe the sweat from their faces and necks while the engineer backed up. By then most of the passengers were awake and in the aisles cheering them on, urging them to keep shoveling. An hour later the plow hit the snow again, but this time the engineer finally felt it shift, and he kept up the pressure until at first small, then larger clumps of snow began to fall aside and the plow broke through the drift, neatly dividing what was left in two. The passengers shouted out their approval when they felt the cars sliding forth, and they waved their arms in celebration as the train passed through the drift. The crew jumped off the embankments, ran after the train, and pulled one another onboard. As the train started to round the bend, Ratshesky looked behind him in satisfaction and was astonished to see the baggage car disappear completely behind what was left of the drift. Gradually, the volunteers returned to their cabins, but Ratshesky could not sleep. He and the Canadian Railways representative, C. K. Howard, talked as the train made its way over the fifteen miles to Truro and a new engine. The old crew would not see the train to its destination either.

With a new crew and engine, they reached Rockingham at 3:00 a.m. and were supposed to divert off the north rail to the newly open South Cut, but once again snow blocked their path. Ratshesky and Howard were still awake talking when the wheels locked and screeched to a stop. They pulled

A snow slide on Folly Mountain in 1905

back the door and stepped off the last stair into snow. The wind was quiet and the last of the storm had left only a gentle dusting on the wet hardpack beneath. The blizzard was over. It left waist-high drifts along parts of the tracks and the dockyards, but even layers of snow could not dampen the trace odor of fire and oil in the air. The two men walked the length of the platform alert to any signs of officials, but the night was as still as it was dark. No one had come to greet them, so they climbed back onboard to await the morning's snowplows.

*Chapter Twelve*

# Saturday

*Reorganizing the Relief*

AT 6:00 A.M. SATURDAY MORNING, the Boston & Maine train pulled out of Rockingham station in the dark. Doctors, nurses, and officials who appeared in the dining room looking for a breakfast were surprised to find Ratshesky and Howard still talking where they had left them. They teased the two officials for staying up all night, but the mood switched to somber disbelief as they caught sight of the landscape outside the windows as they passed through the newly opened South Cut toward the ocean terminal. "Fallen houses could be seen lying by the track. The face of the embankment along the water's edge was gone. One mighty gash had all the appearance of a shell crater in Flanders with the effect heightened by the huge pile of earth and stones which had been heaped up several yards ahead, the lip of the crater itself extending to the harbor front. One railway track, close to the edge, was badly damaged, and before we left the water front vanished altogether, the protruding rails left dangling over nothingness." They slowed to a stop at 7:00 a.m.

Once again Ratshesky and Howard, by now good friends, stepped off the stairs expecting a greeting party, only to be disappointed for a second time. Mrs. Sexton, who accompanied them, thought they were rather chagrined that no one had come to meet them and that the tracks, aside from a couple of trains, were deserted. There was not even a terminal, so the two men and one woman, three black dots in a white field, tramped past the nose of the train toward the building where the Canadian Government Railway had set up a temporary office and where, once inside, they introduced themselves to a solitary man at a makeshift desk. Mrs. Sexton recognized Mr. Hayes and introduced him to Ratshesky and Howard. He stood and offered his hand.

"Mr. C. A. Hayes, President of Canadian Government Railway."

On Thursday night when Hayes arrived in Halifax, he urged the phone company to string a telegraph through the South Cut so that the railroads could disembark trains there. Another railway loaned them a line to install a temporary connection to City Hall to keep Weatherbe informed of arrivals. All the railways canceled regular passenger and freight service to Halifax to open the rails for the relief trains rushing to the city. Trains from New York, Rhode Island, Maine, Toronto, and Montreal were already en route to Halifax. Ratshesky handed Governor McCall's letter to Hayes, who read it with great tenderness.

To the Mayor, City of Halifax, N. S.

My Dear Mr. Mayor:

I am sending Hon. A. C. Ratshesky of the Massachusetts Public Safety Committee, immediately to your city, with a corps of our best State surgeons and nurses, in the belief that they may be of service to you in this hour of need. I need hardly say to you that we have the strongest affection for the people of your city, and that we are anxious to do everything possible for their assistance at this time. Kindly express to the people of your city the very deep sympathy of the people of the Commonwealth of Massachusetts, and assure them that we are ready to answer any call that they may need to make upon us. Immediately upon hearing of the terrible blow dealt Halifax I sent the following telegram to you:

"Understand your city in danger from explosion and conflagration. Reports only fragmentary. Massachusetts stands ready to go the limit in rendering every assistance you may be in need of. Wire me immediately."

Upon being informed that the wires were out of commission, through the good offices of the Federal government at Washington this further telegram was sent you by wireless: "Since sending my telegram this morning offering unlimited assistance, an important meeting of citizens has been held and Massachusetts stands ready to offer aid in any way you can avail yourself of it. We are prepared to send forward immediately a special train with surgeons, nurses and other medical assistance, but await advices from you."

Won't you please call upon Mr. Ratshesky for every help that you need.
The Commonwealth of Massachusetts will stand back of Mr. Ratshesky in
every way.

Respectfully yours,
Samuel W. McCall,
Governor

P. S. Realizing that time is of the utmost importance we have not waited for
your answer but have dispatched the train.


Ratshesky was surprised to see tears spill across Hayes's cheeks.

"Just like the people of good old Massachusetts. I am proud of them. I
was born in that State, having formerly been a resident of West Springfield.
Anything I or my railroad can do is at your service."

Ratshesky asked that his new friend Mr. Howard be allowed to work
with him, and Hayes quickly agreed, offering them the use of the wire they
had to City Hall. Satisfied that they were in good hands, Sexton said she had
to check on her house before going to City Hall and set off toward home.
Hayes pointed out the window to a railcar on the tracks next to them.

"The private car of Sir Robert Borden, Prime Minister of Canada."

Ratshesky probably did not know it, but Borden was a native Nova Scotian and in the middle of a difficult reelection campaign. He had been in
Prince Edward Island when he got news of the explosion, and returned as
soon as the railways allowed, arriving in Halifax midblizzard. Hayes told
Howard and Ratshesky that he would inform Borden of their arrival and
the three men walked back down the snowy tracks. Minutes later, a well-
dressed man with a great shock of white hair parted down the center
opened the door and let himself into the Boston & Maine car. Both his
brow and nose were thick and straight and his full dark mustache stood out
in contrast to his white hair. Ratshesky recognized Sir Robert Borden, the
conservative leader of Canada, and was thunderstruck by his informal entrance. He jumped to his feet and welcomed him. Borden shook their
hands, thanking them for their quick response and telling them that they
were the first relief train to arrive. Ever the politician, he failed to add, from
America. Trains from across Nova Scotia and New Brunswick had been arriving since Thursday. Borden explained that he was on his way to City Hall
to meet with the Relief Committee, and asked them to join him. Ratshesky
requested that Mr. Hayes, Mr. Howard, John Moors of the American Red

Cross, and Major Giddings of the medical unit accompany them. Borden
agreed. They needed to gather as many capable people as quickly as possible. Even from the South End, six miles from the Richmond Hill, they
could see that reports of the devastation had not been exaggerated.

The men climbed into a car idling at the curb. Its seats were stained with
mud and blood, but the men showed no hesitation. The young driver explained that he had been running injured back and forth to the hospital
since Thursday morning when he learned the fate of his family, a wife and
four children—all dead. Ratshesky was taken aback by this quick and sad
admission. "It was a gruesome start." They drove off down Barrington Street
toward City Hall, barely a mile away, talking among themselves while the
driver jumped out to push pieces of wood, glass, tiles, and trees to the curb.
C. C. Carstens, the secretary of the Emergency Relief Committee, and another member, J. Prentice Murphy from Boston's Children Aid Society, decided to walk to City Hall to better assess the situation. The sidewalks were
crowded, but the mood was still somber, and many of the pedestrians they
passed had bandaged hands and lacerated faces. Soldiers were posted along
the streets and more flew past in cars and trucks. The buildings, they noted,
were damaged, but would survive. They were surprised, each time they
passed an office building, to see the lobby clock stood stuck at 9:05.

It was 9:00 a.m. when the car trundled over the blue cobblestones to City
Hall. Ratshesky looked up in dismay at the three rows of vacant windows,
surprised that this was where the relief effort was stationed. "An awful sight
presented itself, buildings shattered on all sides; chaos apparent; no order
existed." It might have looked worse than it was. Only one civilian and one
military hospital had been closed, and while the others were over capacity,
they were operating and, after the first twelve hours, with supplies. Doctors
and nurses were needed, but more were arriving and being assigned to hospitals. Looking at the pale, drawn faces of the relief workers, it was obvious
to everyone that the enemy they now faced was not danger but exhaustion.

Deputy Mayor Colwell was waiting for Borden and the Bostonians at the
same table where he had sat down on Thursday. Since then he had winked
out only two hours' sleep on the floor of the city's clerk's office. The room
was so crowded they could barely squeeze in. Eight women, including the
head of the VADs, Clara MacIntosh, were at the desk taking orders for coal,
food, oil, and blankets. "Our only orders were from Controller Murphy to
'give everything to everybody.'" Cadets ran in and out of the office, calling
out messages or grabbing slips of paper from one of the women at the desk
and rushing off to deliver them to another part of the building. Ginger was

Clocks and watches stopped at approximately 9:05. The seismograph at Dalhousie
recorded the time of the explosion as 9:04:35 A.M.

still there handing out food. "I never ate so much cheese in my life." On the
other side of the counter behind the row of women, several men worked
the phones, frequently shouting questions to each other from across the
room. Ratshesky learned that the mayor was out of the city and that Lieutenant Colonel McKelvey Bell was in charge of the medical relief. Premier
Borden pushed through the crowd to shake hands with two politicians and
three uniformed men, introducing them to the Bostonians and gathering
them together for a quick consultation. Ratshesky found the men
distracted—this was common after a disaster—and he approached them
with gentle suggestions. "We did not wish to appear as intruders." Carstens
also found the men distracted, but he was less surprised. "Overwhelmed
and conscious of their terrible responsibility, immediate details interfered
with long-range plans." Their eyes were red, their faces pale. Unlike more
isolated disasters, he reminded himself, these men had undergone shock
along with everyone else in the city. May Sexton, who arrived after checking in on her house, was also shocked by the agitated condition in which
she found the city leaders. "The straightest-thinking people were far from
normal." Ratshesky suggested tactfully that while the temporary committee
had bridged the first terrible days, they could now reorganize the relief effort
to make it more efficient. Moors suggested that perhaps a quieter building
would help, one close by but not as badly damaged or as busy. He did not
say so, but he also wanted to get the relief effort out of the political world
and into the hands of citizens. The American Red Cross experience was

that, in the initial period, community leaders usually bonded just long enough to address emergency relief, but without the introduction of a long-range plan, the effectiveness of relief efforts would quickly disintegrate as local interests reasserted themselves. A quorum of dedicated citizens was more effective, resourceful, and fairer than politicians who, at least in Moors's opinion, were more often than not useless. Someone suggested the City Club, an elegant three-story brick building just a block south, and everyone agreed they should go have a look at it. The procession of black coats, bowlers, and canes bobbed and slid their way across the Parade Grounds to a narrow path stomped into the snowy sidewalk.

The rooms inside the City Club were warm, dry, and quiet. The men gathered together to listen to Ratshesky, who informed them that Massachusetts would do what it could to gather supplies, raise money, and send special equipment.

"Speaking as a Representative of Governor McCall, I bring you this message from Massachusetts: 'Anything that you want for your people which we have or can get you can have. If anything is wanted from the American Red Cross or the Commonwealth of Massachusetts, our orders are to get it for you and give it to you. You have but to tell us what you want and it is yours.'"

He then introduced John Moors, who gave a sensitive and practiced speech detailing the Red Cross' record with disasters, including the Salem and Chelsea fires, and the San Francisco earthquake, and assuring them that the Red Cross' knowledge and expertise were at their service, but only at their service. Even when introduced by the prime minister, it was tricky business to enter other people's community, much less country, and tell them what to do, and he did not want to alienate anyone.

"We have come here to help you; anything that we have is yours; anything that we can do will be done. We are here to assist in every way possible and place our experience fully at your disposal. We've come to help but not to take charge."

They outlined their participation. The American Red Cross members would not serve on subcommittees, but act only as advisors. The management, the decisions, and ultimately the city were the citizens' responsibility, and although they usually discouraged the use of untrained workers to attend to those affected by disasters, they agreed that in this case untrained volunteers would be necessary. There were just too many people who needed help and would for a long time to come. Moors then outlined the plan that they had devised with Sexton on the train. He stressed three principles to which the Relief Committee needed to adhere.

1. Centralized financial control of all relief funds.

2. Centralized control of distribution and clearance of records.

3. The appointment of an Executive Committee and of chairman of the important committees from among the members of the Executive Committee.

Transportation was the first priority; they had to keep the people and supplies mobile. The others were finance, construction, relief, housing, medical, and warehousing. MacIlreith asked Moors if they could submit a plan by 3:00 p.m., and then suggested that the first order of action was a tour of the devastated area, but Moors declined, explaining that he preferred to stay behind to get the offices and committees organized in time for the afternoon meeting. Carstens, William H. Pear from the Boston Provident Association, and Murphy opted to tour the area by car. Ratshesky sent word to the medical staff on the train to report to City Hall, where they would be assigned hospitals, with the understanding that they would soon be recalled to work together as a whole: "In my opinion being that the greatest good could be done in keeping the unit working together and in establishing a hospital at the earliest possible moment." In order to meet this goal, Ratshesky suggested that perhaps they could establish a temporary hospital if there were a suitable building. McKelvey Bell suggested that they should walk through the city together and pick one out. Major Giddings, in charge of the Massachusetts State Guard Medical Unit, agreed. Several doctors who were present asked if they could join them, and together the men walked through the streets.

At the corner of Queen and Spring Garden, they stopped in front of a three-story townhouse with a winterized front porch and dormers. It was called the Bellevue Building, more popularly known as the Officer's Club. Not one window or door stood intact, and water flowed easily over the stairs from the attic. Incredibly, there were officers inside who assured them that they could make it habitable again. The men agreed that the Bellevue would be the first temporary hospital. Major-General Benson ordered the officers out of the club and called on the engineers and ordnance crews to assist in repairing the building, while McKelvey Bell sent for orderlies. By eleven o'clock a couple dozen American soldiers from the *Old Colony* appeared to offer their services.* The British military brought in bed tables, rubber sheets, dishes and cutlery, cooks, a kitchen detail, and supplied the hospital with food. The Massachusetts State Guard Unit cleaned the inside of the building while the U.S. sailors carried in supplies as they arrived and worked with the orderlies from the Canadian Army Medical Corps to organize the rooms. The Canadian Engineers and Ordnance Corps retrofitted the exterior structure. Together, the Canadian soldiers, the American sailors, eleven doctors, and twenty-one nurses removed all the furniture from the upper floors, sanitized the building as best they could, covered the windows with paper and boards, and installed an operating room complete with a hundred-bed ward.† Although the hospital would not officially be turned over to them until the next day, Bellevue put the word out that they would take patients and welcomed the hardest cases who had not yet been treated. By nightfall sixty patients had been bathed, had their wounds treated, and were lying in the beds.

IN THE NORTH END Carstens, Pear, and Murphy drove along Lockman Road. The street wound along the hillside twenty or thirty feet above the railroad, parallel to the water's edge, and as the car approached North Street the men noticed six or eight blocks of houses still standing, far more than they expected. They were pleased, thinking that perhaps the damage was not so extensive after all. In their experience of disasters, the damage was almost always overstated. A little farther along, as the road curved westward, they approached the ruins of North Street Station and then passed into Richmond. "Extending north from the North Railroad Station, there was complete and utter desolation. Houses, churches, buildings of all sorts had been shaken down and burned or else badly damaged and then destroyed by fire, ship docks and wharves destroyed or badly damaged, and there were piles of destroyed or partially destroyed freight cars and great masses of twisted iron and other metal strewn along the water's edge." They got out of the car with their earlier skepticism chastened.

George Yates, Premier Borden's secretary, stood to the north of the

---

*McKelvey Bell counted twenty American soldiers who assisted. Ratshesky counted fifty.
†The staff numbers are disputed. Ratshesky records that there were fifteen doctors and twelve nurses. McKelvey Bell claims twelve surgeons, ten nurses. Carstens claims eleven doctors and twenty-one nurses.

Bostonians looking over the flattened hill. He compared it to the front: "In the hard shelled towns of Flanders some walls do stand after the intensest bombardment." Everywhere he looked men heaved picks into the ruins and pulled out metal and wooden scrap until they were sure that no body lay there hidden. "With sledge hammers, pick axes, crow-bars and levers of all kinds, they tug at the twisted wreckage which they hurriedly throw aside." He watched an old man pick through the remains of a house, searching for bodies. Yates walked toward him, stepping over what had been a house, conscious of having reached the backyard without obstruction.

Murphy and Carstens looked across the harbor where the *Imo* listed mournfully. They looked for the *Mont Blanc,* but soon learned that there was little more intact than the front section of her bow, still grounded on the sand. Standing on the side of the road, overlooking the railway, they could see dozens of men working on the rail lines, frantically trying to reestablish the telegraph lines. A sleigh coming along Campbell Road stopped at one of the sites where a group of men had gathered. Prime Minister Borden stepped out and joined them, inquiring into their health and that of their families as a smaller sleigh with bodies piled high passed behind him.

Yates, Carstens, Pear, and Murphy gathered around a heavy oil delivery wagon. The oil tank had been thrown twenty yards up the hill. The two horses lay together, one cut in half, stretched across the other with its hind legs extending straight out from its back. They had obviously been thrown in the air, still tethered together, while the cart remained where it had landed, upside down. The whole depressing scene was covered in ice, literally freezing their last agonizing minute. The stillness and permanence of the horses struck Murphy, reminding him of equestrian statues gone wrong. Yates left the horses and returned to the old man combing through what had been his house. The man picked up an old cork leg and looked up to catch Yates's eye.

"That," he said, "belonged to the lodger down stairs. He won't need it any more. He was a railway man, and he lost his leg, and they put him on a crossing. He's gone. When my old woman heard that the boat might blow up she went up to the daughter's place on the hill there. You can see the place, still smoking, from here."

"Did she escape injury?" Yates asked, expecting him to say yes.

"Oh no. She and the daughter and four children were burnt up. It's funny I should find that cork leg undamaged, don't you think?"

The old man waited for an answer, but Yates could think of nothing to say. Instead, he watched two men walking down what was left of the street. One had a bandage wrapped around his head. "The other with hollow,

Prime Minister Robert Borden inspecting the damage

lack-lustre eyes, and blackened hands and face, carried a sack on his shoulder. It was of sinister shape and blood-stained." Yates thought that it was probably part of the man's family. He had already heard a story of a man carrying a box onto the train. Someone asked him what was in the box.

"That is all that is left of my wife and two children. I am taking them to Windsor to bury them."

Depressed, Yates crossed the street back toward the horses, anxious to get going. He did not need to see any more. He knew these streets well from Borden's campaigns, and their current state seemed unbearable. "I begin to feel that I now know what war must mean." He waited for the others next to a bundle of linen topped with a piece of linoleum ripped from someone's kitchen. Placed on top of that was a piece of scaffolding heavy enough to keep the linoleum down in the wind. The *Boston Globe* photographer who had accompanied them stood off to the side taking photos. Yates was curious as to what was under the linoleum, but he thought better of the urge and resisted. Still he wanted to see. Yates, after all, had been a newspaperman. He had lived through his own disaster when the London City Hall had collapsed on top of him and he had awakened some hours later in the morgue. He gripped the corner with his gloves and peeked under the linoleum. He found nothing but bedding. Relieved, perhaps embarrassed, he looked over at the photographer. Whether it was Carstens, Pear, or Murphy, Yates did not say, but someone let out a cry. They had pulled off the blanket below the linoleum. Yates turned in time to make out a quick glimpse of the blanket's inhabitant before turning away in horror. He cursed himself for looking. It was a memory he would prefer not to have.

On their way back down Campbell Road, a man flagged down their car and approached the driver's side.

"Are you going downtown? If so, would you call at the undertaker's and have them send out a sleigh. We have found two more." He pointed to a tiny bundle.

It was almost time for the three o'clock meeting. No one was more grateful to attend than Yates.


AT THE MEETING, IT was apparent to May Sexton that the men were not interested in the women's participation. When they announced the list of twenty people on the various committees, no women were included. Frustrated, Sexton stood up and addressed the men, trying to force them to either acknowledge or reject the trained volunteers.

"All the women's organized effort of the City is at your disposal."

To her delight, Moors accepted her offer with enthusiasm, calling on all of the women's organizations to participate. Sexton then suggested that they also create a medical services committee, reminding them that, in total, supplies for twenty-five hospitals across Halifax and Dartmouth were required. It would be no trivial effort. Mr. H. Milburne, a shipping agent from St. John and a Red Cross member, was named chairman. Sexton was made vice chair. They returned immediately to the Technical School and drew up a plan. "On the second floor of the Technical College over three hundred women sewed steadily for five days. Red Cross supplies, including aneasthetics and all kinds of sterilized dressings kept coming in from every branch in Canada and the hospitals soon found that the supply base filled their every requisition in short order. Apart from medical supplies the Canadian Red Cross supplied shirts, pillowslips, blankets, stockings, dressing gowns, children's garments, oil heaters, felt slippers, hot water bags, cocoa and many other articles."

Moors was pleased that their plan was adopted so readily, and that the

Sewing bandages at the Red Cross dispensary organized by May Sexton

committees were organized quickly and without politicking. Now they could concentrate on problem solving. Their immediate goal was to secure more blankets and enough milk for the children's breakfast on Sunday morning.

AT CAMP HILL, COX was still standing over the operating table. He had been at the hospital for forty-five hours, operating straight for over thirty. He was rationing the chloroform for use on the worst cases. On Saturday afternoon alone he removed twenty-five eyes and threw them into a metal surgical bucket on the floor. By midafternoon it was full. The medical student in charge of gathering information, who had served beside Cox since his arrival, gently put down his tags, smiled at Cox, and fainted. Cox leaned over the table and saw the young student lying in a heap on the floor, looking like the patients he had worked on since Thursday night. It seemed like weeks had passed since then. He requested a replacement.

When Jack MacKeen, the soldier who had attended to fireman Billy Wells, returned to the hospital Saturday morning after sleeping several hours at home. He was summoned to Cox's side. He made his way to the "busy eye ward," where he walked between the rows of patients with gauze over their eyes and linen tags pinned to their chests. He had heard the rumors about eyes being removed without anesthetic, which made him apprehensive. At the end of the ward, two soldiers picked up a man on a stretcher and carried him through the makeshift door. MacKeen followed them behind the screen, where he got his first look at Cox, who was standing over a patient on the table. His wavy hair, which he tried so hard to keep neatly combed and parted, had fallen into loose curls. His smooth broad face looked as haggard as soldiers returning from the front. Next to him on a chair was the man who had been carried in on the stretcher. Half of his face was chopped open. A nurse administered chloroform at the end of the table. One of the original five nurses, she also looked exhausted. Cox caught the teenager's glance at the surgical bucket and asked him to empty it. When MacKeen returned with a clean bucket, Cox ordered him to take charge of the tags, gathering the name and address of the patient, "the type of operations etc.," and they continued this way until sometime after supper when the nurse put down the chloroform cone. Her eyes looked heavy, as if she were having trouble making sense of the scene before her. She could not go on. Cox looked over to MacKeen and told him to take over.

The nurse showed him how to place a metal-framed cone strung with ribbed-cotton gauze over the patient's nose and mouth and then slowly drip the sweet-smelling chloroform onto the fabric until the patient slipped into unconsciousness. She monitored the patient's pulse and his eyes carefully. Administering chloroform was no simple matter. Only trained doctors were supposed to administer it, and in America they were already switching to ether, which was easier to control. The nurse left the teenage MacKeen and the soldiers lifted the man with a severely lacerated face onto the table. His nose hung upside down over his mouth and chin. Cox looked at him with curiosity. "Remarkable . . . the face had been cloven down slantwise from the bridge of the nose as if with a hatchet, going through the nasal cavities and antra and the whole flap hanging forward." He examined it from every angle, perplexed. What was left of the nose was swollen and inflated. The wound itself was clean. He picked up the flap and fit it perfectly onto the wound, but the man gasped for air. Cox pulled it back, fascinated. He had never seen anything like it, but he had an idea how to fix it. Cox fed a tube through each nostril into the cavity and sewed the whole nose back onto the face. It was the only thing that he could think would work. When he checked the patient several days later, he was pleased to find that it was heal-ing. "As if nothing had happened." The man could breathe.

THAT AFTERNOON THE COMMANDING officer, Major Morse, asked the VAD Dorothy McMurray to follow him on his rounds. He had great sym-pathy for the families in search of lost loved ones, yet people trooping up and down the halls and clomping over mattresses in wet boots were not helping the situation. Increasingly, the staff also began to suspect that some of the people in line outside were gawkers. Morse intended to create a list and post it outside, so that if visitors wanted to know if their relatives were inside, they could check the list rather than disrupt the staff and pa-tients. Reunions were as common as they were dramatic. A young mother who thought her small son had died was relieved to find him sitting up in bed at a hospital. When she rushed to him, his first words were "Oh, mother, it is so very dark." Only then did she notice the bandage around his eyes.

At the Pine Hill Hospital, Charlotte Liggins and her daughter were still looking for her daughter-in-law and grandchildren who lived on the same block as Benjamin Henneberry, the soldier who had found his baby Olive in the rubble. As the two women passed Olive, the toddler reached out to the two women and began crying and howling. Charlotte Liggins looked at the name attached to the bed and then to Henneberry.

"Oh, that's not your child. That's a Liggins."

She was right. Incredibly, the baby was not eight-month-old Olive but eighteen-month-old Annie Liggins. Henneberry, a young widowed sol-dier, was pleased that it was not his daughter. Bereaved of his family and on active duty, he was already making plans to place her with another family.

"What am I going to do with a baby?" he asked them.

Dorothy trailed behind the major for the rest of the morning and part of the afternoon. If patients could speak, the major asked for their name and address and to describe their injury as best they could; Dorothy carefully recorded their responses. As in the eye ward, some of the patients were al-ready tagged. When they were finished, Dorothy typed up the list. When she finished the last name, she was surprised to find that they had collected over one thousand six hundred names, an average of over five persons per bed. After the list was posted outside the entrances, the major ordered the hospital closed to the public and placed two guards on each set of doors. He

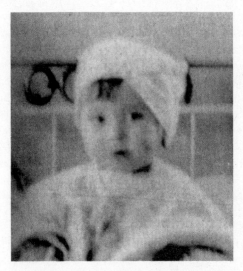

Annie Liggins, the baby dug out from underneath a
stove on Friday morning and identified as Olive
Henneberry. She later became known as
Ashpan Annie.

then forwarded the list to the newspapers, who obliged him by printing it
so that people could scan the papers instead of tramping around from hospital to hospital.

DALHOUSIE STUDENT JEAN LINDSAY returned to Camp Hill Saturday
night. She had tried to return to the hospital Friday night, but the snowdrifts were so bad that City Hall could not send a car to pick her up. She
tried to leave the city Saturday afternoon, but the tram to the northern train
depot was disabled. She convinced her friend Sally MacDonald to join her
at the hospital. "We got in without difficulty and reported to the matron
who was lovely and put us in Ward L." She flushed with pleasure when she
saw that the woman with pneumonia, the one she comforted with a bit of
water, looked much stronger, almost healthy, and certainly not dying as the
officious VAD had suggested. Even without the relatives marching up and
down the halls, the hospital was still crowded, and the patients seemed un-

able to sleep, especially the children, perhaps because of the rainstorm. Thunder and lightning started sometime after midnight, and the noise and unexpected flashes made the patients uneasy.* Jean paid particular attention to a little boy. "He was about 2½. His little face was cut and he was burned and injured internally. No matter how his hands were tied up, he would work them free and tear at the stitching on his face. His vocabulary was wonderful. He did nothing but swear furiously. When asked his name, his usual reply was 'Go to h—.' I got him in a better mood once and I thought he said his name was 'Tarlie.'"

Tarlie's real named was Charles Patrick Wiswell, and Jean had heard rumors that four or five of his siblings had been killed. She did not know if this was true, but she did know that no one had come to claim Charlie or even to visit him. Jean sat on Charlie's bed, encouraging him to sleep by holding his hands to discourage him from scratching off his bandages. Just as Charlie's eyes closed, the doctor and the matron appeared and Jean sat still, waiting for them to make the rounds. "I did not want to jump up for fear they'd think they got me to move on." The old nurse peered at the teenager through the chunk of glass missing from her lens.

"Sitting on patient's beds is not assisting in any way."

Jean dropped Charlie's hands and stood up, blushing. She did not want to explain. There was no point. Instead she turned to check on the stevedore, a burly man who had lost his teeth in the explosion. "He kept a feeding cup hidden under the covers for fear he'd lose it." As the ward quieted down, the girls gathered for lunch in the kitchen after midnight.

AT 2:30 A.M. MCKELVEY Bell dropped into his chair. A telegram had arrived that afternoon informing him that two eye specialists from the Royal Victoria Hospital were en route from Montreal by train. He wrote out a summary of the medical situation and telegraphed it to Ottawa. "Military Medical situation well under control (stop) five hundred patients Camp Hill Hospital, 200 Cogswell Street 100 Nova Scotia hospital Dartmouth (stop) Pier 2 and Rockhead hospitals being rapidly repaired by Engineers expected to be ready in a few days (stop) organized and opened new hospital complete

*Many survivors complained of being startled and frightened by loud noises for the rest of their lives.

today in Bellevue Officers Mess seventy five beds (stop) Handed this hospital over to Massachusetts Medical unit which arrived today (stop) Dozens of civilian practitioners arrive daily (stop) Many wounded in Private houses awaiting attention (stop) Can use fifty more nurses (stop) Washington sending twenty five today and St. John N.B. same number (stop) Patients in all Military hospitals getting good attention (stop) Plenty of medical stores for immediate needs but please rush antitetanic and antistreptococcic serum and other stores which we order (stop) Civilians organizing strong committee today medical officers will be needed if ship comes in with wounded (stop) Or may these cases be sent home immediately on arrival?"

AT 4:00 A.M. JEAN LINDSAY stood to one side of a nurse, holding the lantern as the nurse changed the dressings. At first it was going well, but when the nurse unwrapped an eye socket, nausea finally overcame Jean's good intentions. She passed the lantern to another volunteer and stumbled out of the ward and into a chair, unable to move. "No more dressings for me that morning." When the nausea passed, she made her way into the kitchen and took a cup of coffee, still smarting from the earlier scolding and her failure with the eye patient. Around dawn, as she prepared to leave, the matron returned to the ward and asked her if she could come back again that night. Relieved that she had been of some use, she agreed to work Sunday night and went off to breakfast, where she took a seat next to her friend Sally MacDonald, who was talking with another volunteer.

"How long have you been here?"

"Let me see," said Sally. "Why I came here Saturday night."

Something about the response struck Jean as odd. It took a moment for her to remember that it was only Sunday morning.

Life on the wards at the Victoria General was starting to return to normal as well, although Dr. Puttner had collapsed on the floor Saturday afternoon. They put him in the same room as the chief surgeon, Dr. Murdoch Chisholm, whose condition had improved since Pharmacist Bertha Archibald had helped him up the stairs after the explosion. When she entered the room, he was sitting up and reading the paper. "There, in striking headlines, was the notice of the death of Dr. Murdoch Chisholm—the old gentleman was reading his own obituary." His blue eyes peeked at her out from behind his glasses and he smiled with some satisfaction.

"That man Chisholm. He was quite a man."

The front entrance to Camp Hill, where the list of patients was posted

*Chapter Thirteen*

# Duggans Reunited, If Briefly

Ginger Fraser was still at City Hall late Saturday afternoon helping to hand out food when he spotted his father, walking toward him. Fred Fraser told Ginger that he had done enough and persuaded him to come home for a hot meal. "I was glad to go with him." After supper he returned to duty, but this time he met up with the rest of his platoon, who were gathered at Dee's Grocery on Hurd's Lane, where they were waiting for Ladd's Red Cross train to arrive from Boston. The boys hung around inside where it was warm. A couple of cadets sipped soda pop, but Ginger and his friends had their eyes on the cigars. He had never smoked before, but in his uniform, on duty, serving his city in its hour of need, it did not seem as far-fetched as it might have a week before. He put a nickel down on the counter and the grocer handed him a five-cent stogie. Biting off the tip, as he had watched other men do, he lit a match and dipped the other end into the flame. The smoke carpeted Ginger's tongue, tasting more acrid than sweet, nothing like the smell. He passed it to the boy next to him, who stole an experimental puff before passing it along to the next boy. Ginger was pleased to share it. His stomach churned and, for a moment, he worried that he might throw up. "That would be the first and last for a long time."

Around midnight, the train whistle called the boys to work, and the platoon filed out the door into the cool midnight air. Their breath trailed behind them as they ran to the freight sheds at the bottom of the street. Ladd's train had arrived. One group of boys was ordered to escort the doctors to the hospitals, while Ginger's group took others to the Carleton Hotel. By the time he was off-duty, the storm had started and he ran through the streets lit by lightning. The downpour was so heavy that drivers were once again forced to abandon their cars. On the Beaufort scale, which went from calm (zero) to hurricane (twelve), the overnight winds hit an eight. On the harbor, the long cold waves turned to whitecaps, picking up wreckage along the shoreline and carrying it out to sea. The snow and then the rain did have two beneficial side effects: The precipitation put out many of the remaining fires and it flushed away the soot. By Sunday morning, everything had been washed clean.

In the early hours of Sunday morning, Ginger slid between the cold sheets with a new appreciation for his bed. It would be his last sound sleep for a year. The next morning he was assigned to the morgue.*

SINCE FRIDAY MORNING, all bodies had been processed at the morgue under the supervision of Professor R. N. Stone, who arrived over the weekend from Toronto. Stone and his assistant refined the system of processing, identifying, and discharging bodies to ensure a smooth and accurate transition. Incoming bodies first went from receiving to a sergeant major, who tagged the body and wrote a brief description. Up until Stone arrived, soldiers only washed faces. Stone ensured that they washed the whole body and noted all identifying marks, not just the ones on the face. "No. 198 MALE—36–40 years of age. Black hair slightly bald on top. Full set of natural teeth. Muscular body. Vaccination mark on left arm. Tattoo mark on back of clasped hand underneath the letters 'H.M.' 'A.A.' and 'Forget Maggie.' Thin unlined, black trousers. One print black striped working shirt, marked on neck 'Adams, 844 Argyle St., Glasgow, Scotland.'" Two soldiers removed the clothing, washed the bodies, and oversaw the ticketing of personal items. Sgt. James Burpee, a Canadian conscripted out of California, compiled the list of items associated with each body. Once they were recorded, these items were gathered into small gray bags tagged with the number of the body. "No 480 MALE— . . . Four large keys on ring similar to those used on steamships. Three steel keys and two Yale keys on smaller ring. A piece torn from a calendar for November 1917, with the date 19th

---

*In his account Fraser places the morgue at St. Joseph's. I have placed him correctly at Chebucto, the only place where bodies were identified.

crossed out with pencil. Small empty leather card case. Small coin case, empty. One black handled penknife, two blades, one broken. Crucifix and R. C. emblem. One black and white handkerchief marked 'P.L.'" Then, when a body was identified, a committee of eight led by Stone checked to ensure that the identification matched the records. Even the smallest mistake could lead to longer suffering for families and prolong the time the body spent in the morgue.

Stone established an embalming room in the tiled room in the basement, where he first embalmed children, then adults. Archibald MacMechan, the official historian of the disaster and a member of the Medical Relief Committee, visited the embalming room. "It is a mysterious, awful place. Thick steam-clouds limit the vision to a few inches. Through the mist loom up the indistinct contours of nude corpses above which ghoul-like figures bend with eerie implements and vessels." When bodies were registered and cleaned, they were carried into the room, placed on a pallet, and covered with a simple cotton strip. Upstairs in the office, soldiers, stenographers, and cadets moved through the desks freely. Clothing lay in heaps along the children's desks. "The attendants are very pale and tired, with low-pitched voices, as if always ready to answer the same hopeless question. Yet some of the stenographers are giggling, and a box of chocolates is being passed

Mortuary effects: The details and detritus of everyday life became enormously important in helping identify bodies.

around." An oversized chart of where bodies were laid out took up most of one wall. Male and female—each had a section—as did children. Outside, hundreds more waited next to the piles of coffins. Just that afternoon soldiers found another seventy-three bodies tucked safely away in a skating rink, abandoned by earlier searchers.

Searchers were escorted by soldiers from the BEF, who let them in one by one, careful not to let in too many at once. They asked people who they were searching for, their sex and age, and then provided them with an escort who lifted the cotton sheets. When a positive identification was made, either Stone, Williams, or Donald McRae checked the records for accuracy and wrote out a death certificate and a burial permit, before moving the name to the list of identified, which was published each day in the newspaper. All death certificates were signed at Chebucto Road, but then, if the family wished, the body would be sent to a private funeral home for preparation and a service. If the family could not afford a private home, they could leave the body at Chebucto Road, where it was transferred to a coffin. At times as many as seventy soldiers worked at Chebucto Road, while another twenty to fifty worked in cemeteries around the city, pitching their shovels into the frozen ground. The morgue opened every day at 9:00 a.m. and closed at 10:00 p.m., when the staff, cold and, most likely, depressed, left for a night's sleep before returning the next morning. This continued for three weeks. By Christmas, over eleven hundred bodies had passed through its doors.

IT WAS STILL RAINING on Sunday morning when Ginger reported for escort duty. It was a nasty walk to Chebucto Road. By noon, over an inch of rain had fallen over the frozen city. Silver-white pools of slush backlogged street drains and flooded the roads. It was miserable until the sun broke through sometime after noon, when the temperature sprinted up thirty-five degrees to 50°F as if it were an early spring day. Already soggy snowbanks shrank in the sudden heat. "The streets were waist deep with semi-liquid snow, whilst small rivers rushed down many of the streets. If anything was required to add to the discomfiture of the unhappy town this was the last straw." In the back room where the embalmers worked, the white steam hissed from pipes and tubes, adding to the close, humid climate. On the public side, the cotton strips covering the bodies showed dusty smudges from the footprints of searchers; crowds tracked in as much soot and mud as soldiers washed off. No matter how bad the weather, the line was always the same. It was easy to tell who came from Richmond by their clothes. Some were still dressed in soldier's coats—gifts left over from Thursday. Others managed to borrow clothes from relatives and, judging by their ill fit, inappropriate style, and bright colors, some had already made their first trip to the clothing depots.

The morgue struck everyone differently. Some were fascinated. "I can see the little things would impress you when you're a child. Buckets of water with disinfectant in it. . . . I remember this man—he had a sledge hammer in his hand." Some returned every day in search of a loved one. Others, the more tentative ones, found they were unable to withstand the demands of identification. "Some of the bodies had no heads at all. He thought he would recognize them from the clothing. So he said, 'No, let's get out of here.'" Still more felt drawn to it, out of curiosity or morbidity construed as duty. "My older sister took me, she said do you want to come, and I said I don't want to go but there might be somebody we recognize, some body." Some went out of consideration for another family member, trying to save them from the gruesome experience. "So he went out, he wouldn't take mother anywhere. He wouldn't have her nowhere. He said I just want you to stay home; I'll do this."

Ginger entered the morgue with a heavy step. "The basement there was quite a sight; quite a sight to see." The drafty room was left unheated to discourage bacteria, making it as damp as it was cold. The sound of the rain pelting against the boarded-up windows drowned out the low murmur of searchers and soldiers. He led searchers down into the freezing basement and across the cement floor to the children's area or to the male adults or to the old men or adult women, offering what consolation he could. Up he lifted the cotton strips to show them what was left of their families. "And he said, to me that looks like that would be him. Look at the shoes. . . . That's him. Oh, now I know, she said, turn the sleeve over, that's mine. That's him. How did you know? Because, she said, that's where I patched it. That's my work. People identified relatives and neighbors by whatever scrap of familiarity they could find. They were so covered up that she just knew her mother by her mouth and a mark that was on her face."

Ginger was working when Charles and Billy Duggan arrived at the schoolyard with Alma's husband Patrick Galloway. Charles was now staying with his two sisters on Creighton Street. Like many others, he still had no clothes other than what he had after the explosion, and was either in his underwear or had borrowed something from his brother-in-law Quinn. Billy did not have anything other than his uniform. The brothers might have had some hope that their younger sister Evelyn survived. The morning's paper said she had been carried to the Victoria General alive. In a final indignity, the *Morning Chronicle* listed seventeen-year-old Vincent as Vivian. Lottie and the children's names appeared in the column under "Camp Hill Hospital." Helena and Bessie were still there too, and they spent their time exploring the hospital until they were scared off. "One doctor had a bucket and he was fixing this man and he took one eye out and it rolled around in the bucket, and that's the last we ever looked again." Lottie's head injury was serious; she was still dizzy and weak. The doctors refused to discharge her, despite their desperation for beds.

Charles, Billy, and Patrick moved up the puddled schoolyard toward the door. The mood in line was one of suspense. Talk was minimal. Many people had made the trip before. Others came twice a day to search the three hundred bodies on display. Bodies that were found on Thursday and early Friday sometimes took the longest to identify because they had been found before the Mortuary Committee standardized the system. Although those bodies might have been found and identified almost immediately, they were often moved and sometimes lost. When they finally did make it to Chebucto Road, they most likely arrived without tickets or identification. Billy and Charles left no record of how many times they visited the morgue. It might have been their first time, it could have been their fifth. Whichever it was, the brothers waited with Patrick until a soldier or a cadet met them at the door and asked them how many, their ages, and sex. Their list was a long one. They walked out of the sunlight and down into the gloom.

Billy Duggan set off in search of his mother while Charles went to the section of younger women, in search of his wife Reta. Instead, Charles found his younger sister, the seventeen-year-old Evelyn. He had last seen her at the dining room window as he ran out the door and down Hanover Street to the ferry. She would have seen him approach the *Mont Blanc* and his hasty retreat across the harbor. That was when they would have known something was wrong. His father and possibly all of his family would have been watching, not the fire, but the *Grace Darling* chugging across the Narrows.

Farther down the room, another escort pulled back a sheet and Billy nodded. It was his mother, Susie Hinch Duggan, fifty-three. Patrick Gallaway identified his pregnant young wife Alma Duggan, twenty-six, and her fifteen-year-old brother Vincent. Alma's body was badly burned. M. Keating, a neighbor, identified Charles Sr. When Charles found his wife Reta, she was still holding the baby tight to her chest. Soldiers often reported finding women with their children. The mothers and their children affected many people at the morgue, including Donald Morrison, the young soldier who had helped Elizabeth Fraser find her brother Arthur. "One of the sights I shall never forget was that of a mother with two children. She was holding them so tightly that even in death we couldn't part them. We were ordered to bury them like that."

The Duggans were a well-known family, and they were most likely one of the families that people whispered about, using them as a barometer against which to measure their own loss. Even the papers acknowledged the family's devastation. "While going through the ruins on North Gottingen Street yesterday a reporter met David Hinch who had lost four of his own family and many family connections. The Hinch family has been one of the best known in Richmond for years and have taken prominent part in sport, with the Hinch Lavers crew in aquatics, and the Richmond tug-o-war teams of which David Hinch was the well-known coach. The present calamity has left the family almost extinct with about a score and a half of relatives losing their lives. The reporter expressed his sympathy to Mr. Hinch and the unselfish character of the man was found in his reply that he was no worse off than others. It is just such type of man was to be found in Richmond and which has made them so highly esteemed by their acquaintances. Another prominent Richmond family that has suffered most severely is the Duggans. William Duggan the well known oarsman lost father, mother, brother, sister, his own child, and others of his immediate family. The Duggan and Hinch families are connected by marriage and 52 relatives of the Duggan's were lost in the disaster."

For weeks the papers were filled with terrible stories of loss, but as time went on, the reporters seemed to exhibit loss-fatigue and then guilt over the fatigue. Even the survivors displayed guilt because there was always someone who had lost more. Two characteristics appeared repeatedly—the sufferers' quiet acceptance, as evidenced by David Hinch, and the fear that readers might gradually becoming inured to suffering. On December 21, 1917, the *Amherst Daily News* ran a short article interviewing an unnamed sailor. "Sad stories are such common things these past few days that it almost seems as if the heart could not again be stirred. But some tales have such outstanding points of grief that they lacerate afresh. This poor young sailor, himself but twenty-three, who found the headless burned body of his young wife of twenty-two in the ruins of their little home and later discovered the severed head of the one he loved so dearly, somehow appeals even though the heart seems dead within from the accumulated horrors. Of the poor soldier whose wife and two little ones are missing and who says in a woe-deadened tone, 'I am all right. I've got to where I can eat now, but I can't sleep. I don't mean to be selfish. I know that others have as much trouble and more, but after all this is my own family, and I can't rest for thinking of it.' No one who has heard these stories direct from the sufferers can ever forget or ever get out of touch with humankind again."

Holiday parties were canceled and socializing simply stopped. Everyone was either working or recovering. As Christmas approached, the mood was somber, but the population proved to be easily agitated and excitable. People were still convinced that the Germans were responsible for the explosion. Three days after the explosion, the police had rounded up sixteen Germans who had registered with military intelligence.* A week after the explosion, the *Morning Chronicle* printed the story of the McCall house in Dartmouth. On Friday morning before the blizzard started, an all-white dove flew in through the window and landed on the shoulder of one of the children. When Mrs. McCall held it, it made no attempt to struggle or resist and she had the impression that it was tired. As she examined the bird, she found that its feet were bloodied and raw. "A little metal band encircled one of its feet, and fastened to the metal was a strip of celluloid bearing the numbers 29–29." Rumors immediately spread that the bird was carrying a message in the tube. Another story particularly exploited the tension in the community. An unconscious man awoke in hospital and asked the nurse if it was December 20 yet. She said no.

"Thank God, then it has not happened yet."

He then slipped back into unconsciousness, but the damage was done. A rumor that Halifax would be bombed again on December 20 washed over the population and for a second time people deserted the city.

The Fortress Intelligence Unit, the local military intelligence that was investigating the source, posted a warning in the paper. The punishment was so draconian that it sounded like a rumor itself. "Every effort will be made to find out and punish the originator but everybody is warned that in repeating such wild rumors they become liable to a sentence in the penitentiary." It would not be the first time the military used a false impression to control the population. On the first Saturday after the explosion, Colonel Ralph Simmonds was put in charge of the patrol overseeing the devastated district and joked to a colleague that he had shot a looter. To the

*Since the start of the war, a group of German military men had been living in a prison outside the city.

colonel's great delight, the story was repeated not only around the dinner table but in the papers. In no time everyone knew someone who heard about a dead looter. Simmonds did not bother to correct the impression. "Kept people away like the plague." The morgue was particularly vulnerable to looting. They even had trouble with their own staff. Sergeant Burpee, who was in charge of the bags of personal effects, stole $200 on Christmas Eve, which he spent on a drinking binge that continued until authorities threw him in jail.

Those working at the morgue, including Ginger Fraser, did not enjoy their job, but recognized that it had to be done. "I'll admit I did not like this job too much, but someone had to do it, and I was willing to do anything to help." He lasted only two days before he requested a transfer because of recurring nightmares. "I would see the sheets rising up and the dead people pointing their finger at me. My Dad wakened me two or three times a night. He said I was yelling my head off."

Sunday afternoon, after the last sheet was replaced, Charles, Billy, and Patrick climbed the heavy wooden stairs to the office, where they sat amid the children's desk, the chart on the wall, and the boxes of chocolates, and swore to the positive identification of their mother, father, brother, sister, wife, and child. Professor Stone or possibly Professor McRae would have signed seven death certificates, writing their names beside their numbers. Alma, 1249; Reta, 1250; Warren, 1250; Charles Sr, 1251; Susie, 416; Evelyn, 435; Vincent, 133. Billy, the eldest son, the man "with arms like a blacksmith," would have taken the papers and the three would have left together, grateful to escape. Twenty-year-old Charles Leo Duggan, married just seven months, a father for four months, walked away from Chebucto Road School a widower and an orphan.

# Chapter Fourteen

# The End of Emergency Relief

John Clark
Halifax Hotel
December 9, 1917

Dear Will,

Have just returned to the hotel from Hillis's. Helen is getting on fine. Ma and Hilda have only a few scratches but will not leave Mrs. Boyles at present. Frank's lady has been found this P.M. They found Bert. His whole family is wiped out. They will all be buried together. Mr. Hillis's wife is a patient on "Old Colony" US hospital ship in harbor. Geo Harris, his baby and father-in-law killed. His wife Ida not expected to live. All the Uphams but one gone. Not a house standing north of Barracks or sugar refinery. Gone as well, Kaye, no house or any building on it. Dry dock left standing. I came in on the special train with doctors and nurses from Kentville. Arrived Africville 2:30 and had to walk down. Could not tell where Russell Street had been located and when I located Wellington Barracks there was only a little brick and cement left. No house standing on Russell Street. I then made for school at top of hill and that was demolished—children killed and many of rest badly injured. Helen got clear by jumping out second story window. The teacher who held her and another child was killed in front of her eyes. Also the other kiddy. Her playmate. Helen then made for home which had already collapsed and was burning. Ma and Hilda passed up through the Admiralty grounds. When they got there they found they had to leave. They got some sailor to carry Helen to Dockyard Hospital to have her head dressed but when they reached there, they were bringing out the dead and wounded. Helen then was put in a dairy cart and started for Admiralty House via North Street. Ma and Helen going up thru Admiralty grounds. When they got there they found they had to leave on account of danger from the magazine and Helen with the others was taken to Camp Hill Hospital. Ma and Hilda then lost her and had to the search the hospitals till 5:30 before they found her. They then had her removed to Hillis's. Friday I had myself to give her chloroform as we could only get our Doctor MacAuley, Nita MacDonald's husband, who has been the last two years in Kentville and he had to put 34 stitches in her head. But she is getting along nicely. Ma, Hilda and Helen have only dresses they started in as house burnt down. I have hopes they will get the insurance. I gave Ma $100 on Friday and we'll see what we can do for the winter later. Wired you, Winnie, Allan and cabled Charlie. Winnie, I think, is on her way home. I thought that Hilda could stop with Mrs. Hillis for a few days, then they could got to Norwich for Xmas and New Years. And then we could make further arrangements.

I had sent Ma $100 beforehand and she left it in her desk. That seemed to worry her the first day more than replacing any other loss. Helen's head is badly cut but fortunately her eyes are alright and she says she can now tell Joyce what war is like. George Harris and another man were on verandah of the Lorne Club and their bodies were found on Gottingen Street. Almost every pane of glass in city is gone. Massachusetts Relief train arrived Saturday morning and two from New York, Washington tonight so should get things straightened out a little.

Your brother,
John

Jean Lindsay woke Sunday night in time for supper. It was, she knew, her last one at the Ladies College for some time. School was canceled until after the holiday and a proclamation in the paper ordered everyone who could to leave the city. The food supply was low. Like Jean, many of the people in Halifax were originally from small towns in the province and could easily board with relatives while the relief continued. Jean's father had finally got a call through from Lunenberg and insisted that she return home—her family had heard wild rumors—but she told him that she had promised to work a last shift overnight at Camp Hill, a promise she meant to keep. It had only been four days, but she was a different girl from the one who had thought volunteering was "ridiculous sentiment." She left shortly after six in the dark. "I sallied forth. The rain had washed the snow from the car tracks. It was no longer raining and the walking fairly respectable. Opposite the Technical College cars came from three directions. I couldn't move without going into the slush, so I signalled the one coming up the hill."

"Are you going in the direction of Camp Hill?"

The driver dropped her off at the hospital door at 9:00 p.m. There were still eighty people on Ward L, although, Jean noticed, a woman with a terrible case of pneumonia had died the night before. Still uncomfortable with illness and deeply unsentimental despite her willingness to volunteer, Jean felt relieved. "She greatly disgusted me the night before. I was glad I was late." The ward and the weather were calmer, allowing the patients deeper sleeps. When Jean heard that plenty of nurses and drugs would be there in the morning, she decided that it was indeed her last night. At dawn she met with the matron. "She thanked me for coming very nicely." Standing on Robie Street in the dawn, Jean was relieved to see a tram trundling down the street toward her. She left the city that afternoon.

ALL DAY SUNDAY AND Monday, relief trains that had been held up first by snow and then by the rain arrived from Boston, New York, Philadelphia, Washington, Montreal, and Toronto. The State of Maine Unit alone brought 110 doctors, 4 nurses, and 10 civilians who were assigned to convert the Halifax Ladies College into a temporary hospital. Electric services had been restored in much of the city, and tram service—eight cars in all—had made it back onto the tracks after losing service first in the explosion, then in Friday's snowstorm, and again during Saturday's rain. Outside of Richmond and Dartmouth, which still had not restored the line across the harbor, telephones were ringing again. For the doctors and nurses who arrived Sunday, food was a problem. Ladd's group finally asked if someone could help them get tea, and three volunteers offered to take them home and marched 108 men and women through the streets, stopping milk wagons and grocers along the way to buy milk and bread. "Bostonians very appreciative." The relief workers had to call around to local restaurants to arrange for breakfast for the workers, settling on the Tally Ho, which soon became the unofficial hangout of the Americans.

John Moors informed McKelvey Bell that more supplies, including twenty-five thousand blankets, were leaving Boston that day. A private citizen, Captain Eugene O'Donnell of the U.S. Steamboat Inspection Service, had organized a ship, the *Calvin Austin* from the Eastern Steamship Company, after Boston received a telegram from MacIlreith on Friday. "Citizens deeply appreciate your Governor's offer of assistance. Particularly need glass, bedding, blankets, clothing, boots, rubbers and surgical dressings. Will wire later as to further needs." The biggest donations were the loan of the blankets from the U.S. Army, four thousand sets of women's underwear, winter clothes, and 1,486 cases of window glass. The night before, dozens of women had stood outside the Red Cross offices in Boston sorting and packing the cargo by category until boxes filled the street. At the last moment Endicott rounded up $10,000 worth of milk, bread, crackers, and canned food in case regular shipments were unable to get through. The *Calvin Austin* and its captain were used to sailing to Nova Scotia from the many blueberry runs the ship made between Yarmouth and Boston. Lowbush blueberries, or wild blueberries as Americans called them, were smaller—just three-eighths of an inch in diameter—and tarter than the highbush berry that came earlier in the American season.* Starting at the end of July, ships would line up in Yarmouth to cart away as much as one million pounds of the tiny berry.

McKelvey Bell told Moors that a trainload of three pounds of the disinfectant carbolic acid, over 1,000 pounds of gauze bandages, 194 forceps, 72 scissors, 200 silk ligatures, thousands of assorted tubes, and 7 brandy bottles were already rushing express to Halifax. What the two men did not know was that both shipments would be delayed by yet another snowstorm. The *Calvin Austin* was forced to sail into shelter at Yarmouth to wait out the rough weather, but even in that out-of-the-way fishing port, women from the Canadian Red Cross appeared and asked to board so that they could continue organizing the cargo while the ship sat out the storm.

McKelvey Bell assigned Ladd to St. Mary's College, a boys' school near the corner of Windsor Street and Quinpool Road, a few short blocks from the morgue. After a brief icy ride through the streets—for a third time cars were deserted along the sides of the roads—Moors accompanied Ladd to inspect the building. What the explosion started, the blizzard finished—two sides were almost completely destroyed, with the floors covered in ice and snowdrifts, but that aside, the staff from the school were still working there. Ladd and Dr. John Balch wandered inside, despairing at the conditions.

---

*Ninety to 150 cultivated blueberries make one cup, as opposed to 350 to 450 lowbush berries. Lowbush blueberries are also healthier because the anthocyanin, which gives blueberries both color and flavor, is found in the skin. The smaller the berry, the more skin per berry. They also leave pie-eaters with bluer teeth and tongues.

Loading boxes of supplies into a train in New York

"The windows were practically all gone, snow lay on the floors and stairways, either as it fell or melted into water, which lay an inch or so deep on the floors . . . Debris was everywhere." The rooms were not the spacious wards of hospitals but cut up into cramped spaces, which would require more nurses. Ladd was not worried about the nurses, he had a surplus, so many that he had assigned some to Dr. E. A. Codman at the YMCA, but the frozen floors were a serious menace; invisible glass shards lay camouflaged under the ice and water, which would slow the restoration work. The school was not ideal, but with one roomy, sunny area on the south side, they felt confident they could turn St. Mary's into a working hospital. Within the hour, soldiers had evacuated the building and were shoveling debris. Before he left, John Moors suggested that Ladd and his colleague Dr. Balch join him and McKelvey Bell later that night at the Halifax Club. As he crossed the frozen lawn back to the car, he could see patches of yellow and green grass peeking through the soggy snow. The frozen sod made a crunching noise as if each blade of grass bending underfoot were protesting.

After he was gone, Ladd and Balch took off their jackets, and Ladd, with his big gentle surgeon's hands, picked up splintered wood and swept out the rooms alongside the soldiers.

After it was too dark to work, Ladd, Balch, and Codman met with McKelvey Bell. "We had a pleasant and helpful chat during the evening." McKelvey Bell informed them that the Bellevue had officially opened at 9:00 p.m. that night, admitting sixty-six patients, and Ladd determined to visit it in the morning to inspect their setup. After the meeting McKelvey Bell returned to work, satisfied that unless the ship of one thousand soldiers docked in Halifax, the medical situation was in hand. More doctors and nurses were arriving tomorrow, and gradually local doctors and nurses were being sent off to sleep. If anything, the problem was now too many medical staff and volunteers.

MONDAY WAS A TURNING point for those involved in the emergency relief. By the end of the day, five temporary hospitals plus two more in the neighboring towns of Truro and New Glasgow were siphoning off patients from the military hospitals. The first temporary hospital that opened, the Bellevue, was easy to identify with the American flag overhanging Spring Garden Road and Canadian Army Military Corps orderlies unloading patients from the back of heavy trucks. Their first American patient was scheduled to arrive Monday morning. After Captain Thomas Harrington, the physician-in-chief of the Massachusetts State Guard, learned that a patient at Camp Hill shared the same hometown—Lowell, Massachusetts—he went through the hospital in search of her. He found her in Jean Lindsay's ward. Martha Manter awoke there thirty hours after the explosion with no memory of what had happened. Early that morning Captain Harrington gently sledded her across the city in the brittle cold, mindful not to aggravate her injuries with a bumpy sleigh ride. Drs. Ladd and Wollcott were there when the sleigh pulled alongside, watching as Harrington jumped out and carefully lifted the new patient from the back of the sleigh and carried her up the stairs. Martha looked up at the flag flapping in the wind above her and began to cry.

"What is the matter?" Harrington asked, thinking that he had hurt her.

She dropped her head low and whispered, "The sight of the American flag was too much for me, and I could not control myself. It looked so good to me."

.  .  .

The first emergency hospital, the Bellevue,
run by the Massachusetts State Guard Medical Unit

AFTER TOURING THE BELLEVUE, Ladd and Wollcott returned to St. Mary's, where they found soldiers sawing beaverboard on the lawn, their warm breath frosting up the brittle air. The forecast called for another storm and the twenty Jackies* from the *Old Colony,* the Canadian engineers, and a smattering of NCOs pushed to weatherproof the school before the snow started. The windows on the northern and eastern walls were already covered in board, but almost half the windows on the southern and western sides were intact, providing their largest ward with pleasant natural light and good circulation. Ladd was pleased. It began snowing around 2:00 p.m. as Ladd and the soldiers sprinted up and down the steps, unloading boxes from the back of the truck. They carried in an enormous amount of sup-

*Jackies,* a diminutive for Bluejackets, was the nickname for American soldiers, derived from the American Revolution, when they wore blue jackets in contrast to the British, who wore red.

Soldiers loading patients into the third emergency hospital, St. Mary's Boys School, run by Dr. W. E. Ladd

plies, the most anyone had brought for a single hospital. They had everything they needed except beds.

The work continued as the storm buffeted the walls and the thin beaverboard windows. As the afternoon light faded, Ladd oversaw the acetylene gas lamps and portable tables being set up in the operating rooms while the soldiers installed temporary plumbing, including water closets, slop sinks, and a hot water heater. The beds sent by McKelvey Bell arrived later, and the gas lamps cast the rooms in a warm yellow glow as soldiers assembled them. By Wednesday one hundred patients filled the wards, while doctors and nurses attended to outpatients on the other side of the building. When Moors came to visit on Wednesday, even he was surprised by the transformation of the wrecked school into a well-organized hospital. "It was pleasant to see Dr. Hugh Williams in shirt sleeves working over a wounded patient and to feel that with him, Dr. Balch, Dr. Ladd, and the others, the unfortunate people being rapidly brought in from the military hospitals on stretchers and looking very forlorn were to have the best treatment which Massachusetts could afford." That was just as well because at St. Mary's, the one hundred patients were some of the most difficult cases, aside from the eye injuries. Many were burned, and without constant treatment in the first days it would make their dressings difficult to remove. The children were the worst, especially the burned babies who arrived parched, in pain, and oozing serum and blood. "There were also many cases of burns where dry absorbent cotton had been applied. I specially remember a small boy, whose face was very badly burned. Dry cotton was all over that child. Finally, the doctor said there was nothing to do but to take him to the operating room and etherize, and have the dressing removed." Ladd requested that an X-ray machine be sent from Boston. Without papers or policy or political maneuvering, he was suddenly the head not only of his own hospital but of North America's first pediatric surgical ward. He had all the patients he needed. And as he was known to do in Boston, Ladd stayed with them as long as he could, seeing them through not only their surgery but throughout their recovery. He was the last American doctor to return to Boston, and when he left he took something with him. Ladd finally understood how to control the fluid balance in children. St. Mary's Hospital did not lose one patient.

Over the next week, the other four hospitals—the Bellevue, the YMCA, the Halifax Ladies College, the *Old Colony*—each absorbed hundreds of patients from Camp Hill and the Cogswell, freeing up many of the exhausted local nurses and doctors so that they could finally get some rest before returning to their private practices or to the hospitals for regular shifts. For those who were not hurt badly enough to stay in the hospital, the thirteen dressing stations were still open. There doctors and nurses attended to 3,755 wounded people.

Throughout Monday trains full of volunteers arrived from western Canada as well as a Red Cross unit from Rhode Island and a Christian Science train from Boston with clothing, food, and $10,000 cash. This last train also included an additional thirty doctors and nurses from the Red Cross, an irony that newspapers across North America could not help but note, since the Christian Scientists preferred prayer as a treatment over medical science. The *Chicago Post* called it "a strange contradiction" and the *Daily Times Journal of Ontario* referred to it as "an unusual spectacle." The Christian Scientists saw no great irony in the combination—they had been actively involved in relief since the war's inception—and reported the journey as "happy and harmonious" and resulting in at least one possible conversion and a stream of checks from their members to their war committee. "I enclose one dollar for the Halifax Relief Fund. It is very small, but I wanted to add this to the collection taken Sunday, for which I was not prepared."

The Rhode Island Unit was particularly difficult for McKelvey Bell to place. A full unit of fifty-three nurses, fifty doctors, a pharmacist, and one volunteer worker jumped off their train wearing homemade green brassards. The train had left without being able to obtain the usual Red Cross armbands, and so on the journey the nurses tore down the green curtains in the Pullman and, ripping up a white sheet, fashioned Green Cross armbands for their unit. The people of Halifax, with their English, Irish, and Scottish heritage, mistook the armbands as signifying the presence of the Irish Red Cross. McKelvey Bell and Moors told Rhode Island that there was no hospital for them, but that rumors persisted of people stuck in their houses without relief. The nurses agreed to a canvass, unaware that a blizzard worse than Friday's was on its way. Between 2:00 p.m. and 5:40 p.m., five and a half inches fell, drifting up past the nurses' knees, and when they returned to their train, both wet and frozen, they expressed their displeasure to Major Garry Hough, who ran the unit. The canvass of 147 houses, in their opinion, had been unnecessary. Clara MacIntosh and her VADs, as well as the nurses and doctors at the dressing stations, had already done the job for them. "No instances of neglect could be found."

On hearing this news, McKelvey Bell suggested that they visit Dartmouth, and that night a party of nurses and surgeons crossed the harbor but soon returned, saying that they had found a charming little hospital filled

One of the thirteen temporary dressing stations where patients could receive treatment

with doctors hard at work. Their colleagues seemed pleased but puzzled by the sudden appearance of the Rhode Island delegation, and assured them that they did not need help. Dartmouth asked for no assistance from their Halifax counterparts and set up their own relief commission, run by former Mayor Arthur C. Johnstone. To unite with the better-organized and -funded sister city would have made more sense, but the rivalry and independence was too ingrained. Dartmouth's relief remained independent until August 1918.

The Rhode Island Unit never did seem to find its place in Halifax the way that other units had. On Tuesday some members continued the canvass in the North End, while nine nurses and eight doctors were assigned to Camp Hill, but found their services were not needed there either. Without its own hospital, the unit would move to the Bellevue; the Waegwoltic, a private club converted to a convalescent hospital; the Infirmary; and the YMCA. Despite being bounced around and their initial feelings of dissatisfaction, the unit worked steadily until December 23 along with the State of Maine Unit.

On Tuesday, May Sexton's Medical Supply Depot at the Technical College, which had already organized donations, ordered drugs, and taken drug requests, opened officially. During the first week alone, doctors went through $2,000 worth of instruments and $8,000 worth of drugs, dressings, and equipment, aside from what the American and Canadian Red Cross brought with them, as well as the drugs, utensils, supplies, clothing, and footwear that local chapters from across Canada continued to send. One of the few things that they were still short of was pediatric instruments—no doubt the request of Ladd. Commercial trains that brought food into the city were still not allowed on the tracks, and there was much discussion about how to get safe milk to the children.

MONDAY MORNING AT 6:30 a.m., one of the eye specialists that McKelvey Bell had requested, Captain Frederick Tooke, MD, stretched his small, well-shod foot down to the ground from the bottom step of the Montreal train. Again overnight, the temperature had dropped a dramatic forty degrees, from 54°F to 14.6°F, before climbing a quick eighteen degrees back to freezing. A bitter wind swept up the platform and fluttered Nurse Etter's cape as she and Dr. Tooke stood gape-mouthed, staring at the twisted metal beams of the North Station. The bulk of the ruins remained where they had landed after the air blast. The removal work, the arduous process of carting away all the wreckage from the neighborhood, which would consume so much of 1918, had not even begun. Dr. Tooke sketched the scene: "The day was dark and cold and the details of the city could scarcely be made out. The roof of the Canadian Government Railway Station had fallen in, innumerable cars and trucks were wrecked on the sidings, and we were compelled to make our way through a sea of broken glass and over countless obstacles, chiefly wreckage and coffins. One could not begin to count the latter. The sense of depression was almost unbearable. Not a sound could be heard, railway trains were not running . . . electric cars had been suspended, one could not even hear a motor horn. The streets seemed to be empty. The silence was intolerable and Halifax at first impression seemed to be in fact a city of the dead."

Although Tooke was too old for active duty, he reenlisted in the Canadian Army Medical Corps at forty-two, but his usual work was more mundane than taking dramatic train rides. His sole duty consisted of checking the eyesight of newly enlisted soldiers on a part-time basis. When his assistant director of medical services for Quebec had called and ordered him to Halifax on Saturday, Tooke had filled his satchel with velvet-lined leather cases of surgical instruments, slight ivory sticks with thin steel wires sticking out of one end that were so pretty and delicate they would look equally at home in an lace factory as they did in a surgery. He made his way down the hill to the train station in the snow. Montreal was just starting to get the blizzard, and as he brushed off the snow from his coat, he looked around for the nurse that the Royal Victorian hospital had sent to assist him. Coincidentally, or perhaps luckily, the ophthalmologist's hazel eyes scored a perfect 20/20. When he located Nurse Etter, they boarded the train to Halifax in what Tooke considered a long and tedious train ride. With one glance at the ruined neighborhood, all of Tooke's complaints about the ride evaporated. That short span of air from train to the platform demarcated comfort from—from what? He was not sure. It looked as if they were in a war zone—everything shattered except the record cold temperature.

At City Hall, Tooke registered, and he and Nurse Etter set off to Camp Hill by car. The drive through the center of the city was nothing like they had seen in Richmond. Certainly windows everywhere were boarded up, but the trams were running, the stores were open, and people walked the streets, at least until the snowstorm started at noon and shut down the city once again. Camp Hill, sitting slightly above the surrounding fields, also looked more cheerful. The windows, Tooke noticed, were all new, recently repaired. Soldiers guarded the newly improvised outer doors, and Dorothy

McMurray's list of patients was still posted, if somewhat more tattered. The corridors were free for walking and, while hundreds of patients had been removed, the wards were still overstuffed with nine hundred to a thousand patients, although they now all had clean clothing and bedding. A fluent staff of volunteers worked alongside the soldiers cleaning sheets, washing dishes, and feeding patients. The organization and particularly the cooperative staff impressed Tooke. "Mistress rubbed shoulder with maid and char-woman, all imbued with the same desire to help." He and Nurse Etter followed a volunteer through the corridors into the eye ward where over 120 bandaged men, women, and children crammed together. Most, he could see, would require major surgery. Much of the work looked crude to him, the stitches ripping through the thin skin around the eyes, but he recognized that the effort was enough to save the eye. "Practically every face wound was septic; nay more, each was welling out with a copious purulent discharge while other wounds appeared almost to be gangrenous. An earlier attempt had too often been made to bring the edges of these tears together by sutures, the stitches invariably sloughing out at one side, leaving the adjacent tissue more necrotic. The faces appeared as though some filthy septic claw or rake had been dragged over the face as deeply as it could penetrate." At the end of the ward, Tooke slipped behind the screen, where he discovered Cox still standing and still operating under a single electric globe. A wave of blood seeped up the edge of his cuffs like embroidery. Cox looked up. His face was pale and ageless. Tooke could not judge how old he was, fatigue so erased the particulars of his character. Forty-five? Sixty-five? Tooke glanced into the surgical bucket; its contents stared back. A weak smile passed over Dr. Cox's colorless lips. He did not think it would ever end. He held up his scalpel.

"I have done so much work my instruments no longer cut."

Tooke told him to go to bed and Cox obeyed. "I was tired and had had enough of a good thing for once." He did not have much choice. He had been working for eighty-four hours without a break, aside from the two hours' sleep on Friday night and three hours on Sunday. Jack MacKeen, with whom Tooke boarded, and VAD Dorothy McMurray were relieved to see the new doctor. "Eyes were being removed without anaesthetics." Tooke immediately immersed himself in his new patients, moving from patient to patient, examining their wounds and their treatment. There was much work left. They were still removing as many as fifty eyes a day. Later that day, Tooke received notice that enough anti-tetanus serum had arrived to be administered to every patient. He was relieved that there was no

Public posters and flyers were one way of keeping the public informed.

tetanus, gangrene, meningitis, or serious infection. "In many cases it was marvellous how intense had been the injury inflicted upon one lid while the underlying eyeball had not been disturbed. On the other hand it was equally to be wondered at how often an eye was picked out by glass while the lid remained uninjured. . . . Any attempt at bacteriology would have been a burlesque. We made the best effort at asepsis that was possible under the circumstances. I could vouch for my instruments and dressings through Miss Etter's care. I could not employ rubber gloves as I abominate them in eye work. Perhaps there is a certain unrecorded virtue in the frequent application of 'Queen's Laundry Bar . . . Perhaps it was because I used strong bichloride till my hands began to cut, perhaps it was both; but more probably because our luck was with us."

THE NEXT DAY, AFTER a long sleep, Dr. George Cox visited his patients one last time. He had arranged to transfer some of them to a temporary hospital in New Glasgow, where he could continue to treat them. Cox picked his way through the smoking foundations of Richmond. Everywhere he went white-hot coals, stored in the basement for winter, glowered through the ruins, sometimes the only indication that a house had once stood there. Everything was gone—not a house for blocks except the twisted trees at once ashen and frozen. As he passed the ruins of the Hillis foundry, a piece of paper with writing caught his eye. Curious, he bent over to pick it up. It was a postcard addressed to a neighborhood address. A local man leaned over and read the name.

"The inmates of that home are all gone," he told Cox.

Somewhere in France, September 16, 1917

My dear little girl—Your little loving letter received and I am thankful to know you are really well. Pray for the day when your daddy will come home to you and mother. Your loving father with lots of kisses for you and baby Joe.

Cox flipped it over once or twice as if trying to decide its fate before putting it in his pocket and resumed walking to the train home.

MONDAY NIGHT, after a long day of registering outside medical staff and organizing the discharge of civilians to the temporary hospitals, McKelvey Bell stamped the snow off of his boots and walked into his office, where he sat by the flickering flame of the coal lamp and typed a telegram to military headquarters in Ottawa. "December 10, 1917 [10:30 p.m.] Please stop any more doctors or nurses from coming unless by special request from me. (stop) Supply already in excess of demand. (stop) Medical situation well under control. A.D.M.S. No. 6 (stop)"

*Chapter Fifteen*

# Cap Ratshesky Says Good-bye

Life in Halifax began to seem a little more normal by Monday, when mail delivery and gas service resumed in neighborhoods outside of Richmond. At City Hall it took Colwell, who was still sitting at his desk, two hours just to open the explosion-related letters. In the devastated area, the military continued to patrol the streets. Only those with a special pass were allowed to enter the area to ensure that searchers could continue their work free of sightseers. Rumors proliferated. One was that Mi'kmaqs had paddled over from Turtle Grove and looted the wreckage, even though the village had been destroyed and eight of the thirty-eight Mi'kmaqs were dead, many more injured, and the rest homeless. It made no sense, but the story flourished. Elizabeth Fraser, who buried her brother Arthur over the weekend, returned with a pass to see if there was anything that could be salvaged from their house. She kicked around in the snow until she stubbed her toe against the heavy family Bible frozen in the ice. She dug it out and set it aside, freezing her hands as she pulled it free. To keep herself warm, she chipped away at the snow with her feet until one of her boots snagged on a coil of leaves and twine twisted in a loop. She leaned over to investigate. It smelled familiar. Tobacco.

"That is just what poor papa wants."

She yanked the tobacco rope free of the ice and wrapped it around the Bible. Together they weighed over twenty-five pounds. She had to stop and rest many times, but just the thought of giving her father the tobacco kept her warm. "I had a heavy load but I felt happier than I had been for days. My father was very pleased with the tobacco, and it lasted him until we had a home to move into."

Even residents with passes were sometimes mistaken for sightseers and chased away. Colonel Simmonds, who was put in charge of the devastated area, as Richmond was soon known, was working just north of the Duggans' house when he noticed a boy around thirteen years old poking around some ruins with a stick. Simmonds spoke sharply.

"You, what are you doing there. What is your name? Show me your pass."

The boy turned his head to look at the colonel, revealing the inevitable dull look of survivors. "My name is Thomas Walsh. I live here. My father was buried the day before yesterday at Mt. Olivet, my brother and sister are in the hospital and the rest of my family is buried—" He pointed the stick toward the charred wood. "There."

The colonel cleared his throat, trying not to let the boy see his tears. Unable to speak, he walked away, conscious that he, himself, was the first person he had seen cry since the whole miserable experience began.

For the next week soldiers sent between fourteen and twenty bodies a day to the morgue, after which they concentrated on charred remains and bones until the search ended on January 11, 1918. Stories of survivors continued to pop up in the papers. Monday morning, a paper reported that a man wedged between two fallen girders had awakened when rescuers

**City of Halifax**          *No.* 15264

# Pass for Devastated Area

*Allow Bearer within Devastated District*

NAME _A. J. Johnston_

**FRANK HANRAHAN**
**Chief of Police**

A pass to the devastated area signed by Police Chief Frank Hanrahan pulled off the top beam. He jumped up, shocked to hear that he had sur-vived an explosion, fire, thunderstorms, and a blizzard, and had been un-conscious for over four days.

Stories about animals also circulated. One dog remained by its master's body until soldiers carted him off to the morgue. Other animals escaped the explosion and found their way home. "I had a little brown color dog and that use to follow dad down to work and dad had to shut him up in the railway station, so he wouldn't run out barking and getting hit by the trains that come. So he had it locked up in his office down there. And old Jacky—that's the dog—I think it was the next day Jacky came home. But he was no longer brown he was black. How he got all covered with soot and dirt and somehow he got wiggled out of the office that collapsed and he wiggled out of there and got home." Some pets, such as Billy Duggan's bulldog Molly, slunk around the wreckage of their house, reluctant to leave. As soldiers pulled wreckage out of collapsed foundations, terrorized dogs and cats leapt out from underneath and skittered away. It was un-pleasant business, but they were getting hungry and the area was littered with remains. Loose dogs were shot on the spot, and people were asked to keep all animals out of the area. On Monday when the secretary of the So-ciety for the Prevention of Cruelty to Animals learned of the problem, he wrote to a committee member, volunteering to assist with abandoned creatures. The Massachusetts Chapter sent a check for $1,000 plus two workers to assist the SPCA in putting down injured animals and sheltering orphaned pets. They also rounded up livestock and tried to return them to their owners.

WITH THE MILITARY CONTROLLING the streets, the cleanup under way, and volunteer medical staff supplementing the local doctors, both Deputy Mayor Colwell and the mayor of Dartmouth, Edward F. Williams, agreed that the problem now was no longer manpower but money. On Monday, they published an appeal, asking the rest of Canada for assistance. "The Capital City of this Province has been overtaken with an appalling disaster. You will see the Public Appeal for help in the Press. The Province of Nova Scotia, while doing its full duty in the emergency, nevertheless in-vites, and will welcome, the most generous aid from the sister Provinces." Donations began arriving immediately through churches, the Red Cross, and individuals—one woman offered to record a tribute song that she would sell to raise money for the indigent—but the biggest donors after the

Canadian government were other governments. Britain and America each contributed $5 million.

When MacGillvray told Moors that they estimated they needed $15 million to restore the city, Moors thought the sum ludicrous, but in the end MacGillvray underestimated by $20 million: Total material losses reached $35 million. Federal government and shipping losses, including railways, comprised 42 percent of the losses. Dwellings accounted for 24 percent, furniture 13 percent, manufacturing and merchandise 17 percent, and churches 4 percent. As private donations began to arrive, the American Red Cross was pleased that the politicians did not try to divert any of the incoming monies. "Further inquiry leads me to think the city government is in most departments very lax but not very wicked. All the city governments where I have seen relief work, San Francisco, Chelsea, and Salem, have been incompetent or worse, yet except for spasmodic efforts at San Francisco no real attempt has been made to get political hands on the relief funds and apparently none is being made here." They centralized the American and Canadian donations that weighted down mailbags. When the Boston Symphony announced a benefit concert featuring the famed soprano Nellie Melba* and the Austrian violinist Fritz Kreisler, the show sold out in the first day. A riot nearly broke out when the Eastern Steamships Company organized another blueberry ship, the *Northland,* to carry stores to Halifax. The company called in the police to control a crowd that answered a call for donations. Despite the chaos, even the most modest of gifts were accepted. One tiny boy with the toes out of his own boots offered an official a bit of wrapped chocolate.

"Give this to some poor Halifax kiddie."

The official did one better and delivered it to the mayor.

"A poor woman brought her mite, one shirt washed and neatly ironed. A factory girl brought three pairs of stockings. Then several wealthy women drove to the dock in their automobiles and taking off their fur coats gave them to the shivering women of Halifax." More important was the shipment of ten trucks sent by the Massachusetts Automobile Club, whose president, J. H. MacAlman, was a member of the Public Safety Committee. An hour before the *Northland* sailed, MacAlman appeared at the State

---

*For whom Peach Melba and Melba toast are named. Melba is the diminutive of Melbourne, where she was raised.

House and spoke with Endicott, who was arranging the committee's actions from Boston.

"Mr. Endicott we bought the trucks we hired ten first class chauffeurs to go with them and train the Halifax boys and if you'll break down certain stiff laws we'll send gasoline enough along in them or being carried on them to run 'em for awhile."

The trucks' arrival in Halifax turned into a miniparade, as they drove through the streets to the cheers of the people.

BY TUESDAY the relief effort and the city were starting to stabilize. Moors convinced Ratshesky that the Public Safety Committee should stop sending all supplies unless the Red Cross made a specific request. By Thursday, December 13, the situation was well enough in hand that Ratshesky, the Massachusetts Public Safety Committee, and the State Guard felt comfortable returning to Boston. On Wednesday night, Lieutenant Governor Grant threw a dinner party in their honor, with McKelvey Bell, Bob MacIlreith, General Benson, and Rear Admiral Chambers in attendance. Grant thanked Ratshesky and the people of Massachusetts by reading a resolution passed by the Halifax Relief Commission.

"That the heartfelt thanks of the citizens of Halifax, as represented by this Executive Committee, be telegraphed to the Commonwealth of Massachusetts for their overwhelming sympathy, most generous gifts of relief supplies, the sorely needed services of doctors and nurses and hospital units, and especially for the thought of accompanying said gifts with the services of A. C. Ratshesky, whose generous and expert advice have greatly helped to solve many of our problems, and whose sympathetic activity and tact will, we trust, soon assist us to bring comparative order out of the chaos resulting from the terrible loss of life, crippling of the living and terrible devastation of our city."

The next morning, minutes after 8:00 a.m., Ratshesky and the Public Safety Committee gathered one last time in front of a group of reporters. Standing on the platform by their train, Ratshesky held up his hand to indicate that he wished to speak. The crowd quieted and the reporters took out their notebooks, scribbling to keep up with his long good-bye.

"Gentlemen, the resolution passed by your committee at its session yesterday afternoon so appealed to me that I felt before leaving the city of Halifax I should make the statement how glad I am that the Commonwealth of

Massachusetts has been of assistance to you in helping in this disaster befalling your city. In my letter of introduction, His Excellency Governor McCall of Massachusetts instructed me to do anything and everything that was possible to alleviate the suffering and distress in the different departments in which I have gained experience in the crises in other cities.

"It is fair to state that the different committees that I have come in contact with are so organized that after a few days they will be in fairly perfect running order, and will be able to handle the large volume of affairs that will come before them. While it may from time to time appear as if the overlapping of work does exist, it will not take long to unravel each case as it comes up, and make possible co-operation by each committee through the executive.

"I wish to state that the men who have charge of the committee have shown that interest and willingness which augur well for the success of the work. They have been willing to listen to suggestions and have applied themselves in such a way as to bring to the situation that business judgment which must prevail to bring about a satisfactory result.

"I wish to thank Premier Borden, Governor Grant, General Benson, Mayor Martin and all members of the general committees and citizens for the great assistance which they have afforded in the creating of organization.

"I wish to acknowledge the fine co-operation of Colonel McKelvey Bell and his department in the ready and hearty assistance afforded the medical men of Massachusetts, culminating in the establishment and maintenance of Bellevue Hospital. I am quite sure that Major Giddings and his staff of doctors and nurses are deeply grateful to him for all the attention and thought that he has given, and if the hospital has proved the success which has been set for it by all who have been close to its work, I feel that Colonel Bell and his staff should participate in any praise that is given.

"I wish to extend thanks to the officials of the railway and telegraph companies for their co-operation and assistance to the Massachusetts unit, and for the magnificent service that they performed, although greatly hampered in their operations.

"I also wish to thank Mr. A. S. Busby, Chief Inspector of Customs, and Mr. A. S. Mitchell, Collector of Customs for the Port of Halifax, for the extreme courtesies extended to the Massachusetts unit relative to customs. The newspapers and their staffs have our sincere thanks for their kindness and attention.

"What Massachusetts has done is symbolic of what it stands for—not only to help its own citizens but to help all those, who may need assistance—and when the word came that Halifax was in distress, she could not do otherwise than help. The hearts of her People have gone out to your citizens, not only in her generous supply of clothing, food and money, but, better than all, in that fine sentiment of affection for the People of your city that will bring about a strengthened friendship that will last for generations to come.

"I am proud of what my State has done. I am also proud of what your citizens have done, and sincerely trust, when your city is once more established on more normal lines, that Halifax will be a bigger and better city. God bless you in your endeavors.

"I have authorized the Massachusetts-Halifax Relief Committee to enter my Personal subscription for the sum of $1000."

WITH THAT, RATSHESKY SAID his last good-bye and climbed onto the train. The mood onboard was filled with camaraderie and excitement. When they rolled into Boston on Friday afternoon, they were delighted to finally find a reception party waiting for them. A government official collected their luggage and whisked them off to several waiting cars that drove them straight to a luncheon at the Algonquin Club. Here they supped with Governor McCall, informing him that in the last stretch of the train ride the men decided to form themselves into a group called the Massachusetts-Halifax Relief Associates. Ratshesky was pleased not only by the initiative, but with its spontaneous birth. At last, when the tea had grown cold and the early winter sun started to fail, the Massachusetts-Halifax Relief Associates returned to their homes confident that their last week had been one of their best.

The next day the Halifax papers reprinted Ratshesky's speech alongside many tributes to the Bostonians and Americans who traveled to Halifax. They would repeat the accolades a week later on December 21, the morning after the Halifax Medical Society threw a dinner in honor of all the outside medical staff who arrived by train.

Some reports about the medical response that appeared in the Halifax papers tended to highlight the efforts of volunteer doctors and the Canadian military while ignoring the local doctors who worked constantly over the first weekend. Even the Americans noticed that they were singled out at the expense of their colleagues in Halifax. Dr. Codman was so embarrassed by the amount of attention he received that he wrote to say so in the New Year. "I have never received so much undeserved credit as I have for my

Halifax trip, for all the real work was done by you people in the transformation of the Y.M.C.A. Building into a hospital. People persist in giving me
credit of having done something which I am quite conscious is merely an
expression of their ignorance of the real facts." Codman had been in charge
of the YMCA, which had been originally opened as a dressing station. By
Monday afternoon, soldiers had managed to transform the gym into a 166-
bed ward, including building a long wooden ramp that descended gradually
across the gym so that patients could avoid a steep stairwell and be wheeled
in smoothly.

As for the Red Cross, they were uncomfortable with the perception that
all the American medical staff who arrived in Halifax were working under
their supervision. This discomfort seemed to stem from two concerns, the
first being financial responsibilities of the Red Cross and the second whether
they could be held responsible for other volunteers if a mishap occurred.
People in Halifax believed that all five medical units were under Red Cross
auspices, but in reality there were only two: the Bellevue and St. Mary's.
On New Year's Eve, when people began to complain about the bureaucracy
behind the relief, a situation the Red Cross found embarrassing, a colleague
wrote to Moors that Ratshesky left at precisely the right moment "from the
point of view of successful publicity just as it is well in a drama to let the
curtain go down at the climax." But Moors knew that the climax was
merely the uncomfortable transition from emergency relief to rehabilitation. It was not a moment that survivors enjoyed and, as Dougall
MacGillvray would soon come to understand, the head of the rehabilitation
was often the most unpopular man in town.

*Chapter Sixteen*

# Playing Solomon

D OUGALL MACGILLVRAY WAS made chairman of
the Rehabilitation Committee on Wednesday, December 12, but it was immediately apparent that
this rehabilitation effort would be different from the American Red Cross's
other experiences, which were in keeping with their belief that relief was not
about replacing what was lost but about providing the means to replace loss.

It is the province of emergency relief to provide for immediate, common
needs. The promptness and completeness with which they are met are the sole
tests of efficiency. The province of rehabilitation is to help each family meet
the needs peculiar to it and return to its normal manner of life. Its efficiency is
tested by the degree to which it succeeds in accomplishing these results.
Emergency relief plans and acts to meet present needs, rehabilitation plans and
acts for ultimate welfare. All disaster relief should be a process of evolving from
dealings with its victims en masse to treatment of them as individual
families . . . need, not loss, is the basis of relief; there must be the fullest
possible utilization of community and family resources for self-help; accurate
determination of need, family by family, is the only basis for a just and effective
distribution of relief; in addition to needs which can be met by money gifts,
there are others which can be met only by wise counsel and devoted,
intelligent personal service.

—J. Byron Deacon, *Disasters*

Judge Robert Harris, a Supreme Court judge who was briefly the head of the Finance Committee, expressed to Moors privately that he thought the people deserved more than the usual housing and vocational training. Moors and Harris had met at the first meeting at City Hall, and since then Harris had been advising Moors. Harris told him the story of a car conductor he knew, a middle-aged man who had just finished building a house for his family for $4,000. The house was now demolished and his life savings wiped out. It struck Harris as unfair that a family could be ruined by a war-related accident. It was no act of God; the state should be responsible. When Moors checked with MacGillvray about whether it was fiscally possible, MacGillvray surprised him by assuring him that between Britain, the federal government, and private donations, compensation could be made. It was the first time in the American Red Cross' experience that people would be compensated monetarily for disaster-related losses.

Moors and MacGillvray put forth their best plan, a series of committees and subcommittees under the control of the Rehabilitation Committee. MacGillvray wrote letters to his counterparts in San Francisco, Chelsea, and Galveston, asking about rehabilitation, and invited Christian Lantz, who was in charge of Chelsea rehabilitation, to come to Halifax to consult. It took some pressure from the American Red Cross to persuade Lantz to come; he was one of the few people who did not immediately offer his services. Perhaps only someone who had chaired a Rehabilitation Committee could appreciate the difficulty of trying to rebuild a city to its citizens' satisfaction. It was an organizational nightmare. Old committees had to be dissolved, new ones formed, and the public kept abreast of the process. Almost immediately there was conflict between the Information Committee, the Registration Committee, and the Application Committee about who would maintain the records and how to merge existing case files. Fire Insurance Companies requested that they control their own committee. Life Insurance Companies complained that no one had contacted them, and collected their own information, which they then supplied to Registration. MacGillvray resigned on Christmas Eve, replaced by J. H. Winfield, the general manager of the phone company. Once again information management was both the biggest hurdle and the public's greatest frustration.

In an unfortunate coincidence, the day the Rehabilitation Committee began its work the survivors' began to shake off the numbness so often observed in the first week. The calm, accepting demeanor began to crack with the return of feeling. Wounds, which had been slow to heal in the first week, began to improve. And with the pain, came voices. Suddenly, everyone was dissatisfied. Clothing quickly became the focal point of their complaints. Much of the clothing that arrived in the first shipments was secondhand and worn past decency. Worse, there were not enough clothes suitable for mourning. "One young woman who went to fetch her widowed mother from hospital found her in tears, holding the brightly coloured outfit she had been given. The girl rushed out and, with the last of her money, bought her a black dress." The Red Cross was not surprised by the city's sudden irritation. They expected this phase—in fact, it was considered a sign of health—but that did not mean they were pleased with how the clothing department was run. "The whole department remained a sore spot and was little short of an outright scandal for a long time." Not everyone had a bad experience with the clothing. Children lucky enough to receive clothes from one American town found secret treasures such as perfume, teeny boxes of talcum powder, and toys hidden in the pockets. Helena Duggan, who was billeted with a Mrs. William Eaton until Lottie got out of the hospital, was thrilled when Mrs. Eaton returned from the Green Lantern Building Clothing Depot with an imitation sealskin coat, probably the most expensive piece of clothing Helena had ever owned.

ON MONDAY, DECEMBER 17, the Rehabilitation Committee took its first step toward restoring the city's independence by replacing food rations with a weekly food allowance that could be spent at local stores. The allowance provided people more choice, while it restored the local economy. Although not as vital as in the first ten days, when they distributed over 100,000 loaves of bread and an average of 16,000 rations daily, the food depots remained open, distributing vouchers and registering people for relief. By January 10, when the food depots closed, 5,000 people had signed up. Those who registered broke down into 861 families and 189 orphans. Their problems were overwhelming. Everyone needed not just food and clothing, but furniture, heat, medical treatment, and funeral services. Even when families were left intact, they were often forced to live out the winter in one room, and it was not unusual to find three or four families together in a house without proper windows, ventilation, furniture, or even heat. Accommodations were so scarce that Cora Hotchkiss's family lived in an abandoned railcar until March. They soon discovered they had neighbors in other railcars. Families who left the city, as mandated by City Hall, soon learned that they could not return because there was no housing, which put their jobs at risk and further jeopardized healthy but homeless families.

Moors was impressed by the subtlety of some of the problems he witnessed in housing problems. "Perhaps it is worth noting that at San Francisco, Chelsea and Salem the line of demarcation between families burned out and families not burned out was a sharp line of demarcation, whereas at Halifax everybody suffered somewhat, and the lines of demarcation were not easily determined."

Home visits continued regardless of where people lived and how many committees were dissolved or merged. Miss Ruth Emerson of the Social Service Department of the Massachusetts General took over the medical social service with five other social workers from Boston and Jane Wisdom from Halifax. Anyone ready to leave the hospital—except the blinded, who had their own committee and workers—met with a medical-social worker, who sent their data along to the Rehabilitation Committee. Social workers made home visits too. Each day for months they sat next to beds, at kitchen tables, and in railcars, filling out forms with the names and ages of children, types of injuries and how they got them, job history, and whether or not they could return to work. They collected information about salaries, domestic losses, funeral costs, and insurance claims as well as determining immediate needs. In the early days, their recommendations usually called for supplying common but important items such as clothing, footwear, mattresses, and blankets. Later on, the claims were more involved, with housing, furniture, heating, and medical follow-up taking top priority.

Using the family as a base unit created a plague of organizational problems. The files sometimes were either divided or consolidated when families were separated or reunited. Should a mother-in-law be included in her married daughter's claim? Should two shattered families, related by a dead relative but sharing a house, be treated as one family or two? It was endless. When Josie Crighton, the elocution teacher from the Halifax Ladies College, stepped down as Jane Wisdom's assistant in July, she left behind a four-page document explaining how files were classified, numbered, reclassified, and renumbered. The files were thick with repetition, but as imperfect as the system was, the medical social services workers achieved McKelvey Bell's goal of emptying the military hospitals—only sixty civilian patients remained in military hospitals by New Year's. But by then the ship of one thousand Canadians wounded in the war had been diverted to St. John, New Brunswick.

On New Year's Day, Mrs. Hilbert Day, a native Haligonian transplanted to Boston, returned to assist with the medical–social services work. With McKelvey Bell's assistance, she read through 3,000 medical records and flagged 261 cases that dealt with individuals who were not blinded but who would most likely be handicapped for life. Half of the cases were caused by simple fractures and deep wounds. Burns, septic wounds, amputations, compound fractures, paralysis, and psychological problems made up the rest. In his report on the medical services, McKelvey Bell concluded that the military's presence in Halifax was vital to the relief, especially on the first day. "Had such a disaster occurred in any part not well organized for relief work and without military assistance, the number of deaths and suffering would have been tremendously increased." In March he submitted his suggestions to improve response in future disaster work, suggesting that volunteer groups be organized under a central emergency response plan, equipment be standardized, medical equipment be kept ready in standardized containers, and that the ADMS be put in charge of the medical efforts from the outset.

DISPLACED CHILDREN PROVED TO be a particular challenge for social workers because they could neither register themselves nor provide much more than their names and, if lucky, former addresses. Plus children were scattered all over the city and, in some cases, the countryside without anyone to supervise them. The lucky ones, such as Helena Duggan, remained in the hospital with a parent for the first weeks, but other children fended for themselves in a confused and confusing atmosphere. Their care was in no way centralized; no one knew where they were or what kind of treatment they were receiving. In the first rush to get people to the hospital, some children were shipped outside the city without their parents' knowledge. A week after the explosion, thirteen-year-old Fred Kidd, who was treated at Pine Hill Hospital with other children, found himself on a train to Campbelton, New Brunswick. As New Year's approached, officials informed them that they were to be permanently distributed among farm families in the area, but Kidd, one of the older children, objected. His mother had been pronounced dead after being dug out of the wreckage, but she surprised doctors by waking up in the hospital later in the day, and Fred had no intention of losing her a second time. The other children stood by Fred and demanded to return home. In January, the officials capitulated and loaded the children onto a train to Halifax. Kidd was reunited with his parents, who were already living in one of the temporary apartments built on the Commons.

The priorities of the Children's Committee were to stabilize the existing children's homes, locate missing children, determine the needs of those affected, locate their relatives, and supervise their permanent placement with either families or friends. Committee members soon realized that they needed to build new institutions to house orphans. Dr. Ladd, always an advocate for those who could not speak for themselves, suggested that more shelters with fewer children in each one would be more comfortable for the children, even if they were more difficult for the committee to arrange. The chairman of the Children's Committee, E. L. Blois, who was also the provincial commissioner for dependent and neglected children, did not like the Red Cross' interference and refused to have any Americans work on the committee. For their part, the Red Cross found Blois inflexible and went so far as to call him jealous of the rehabilitation workers—not all of whom were American. Blois did not need their approval. As soon as a child was labeled dependent, he switched roles and invoked his power as the provincial commissioner and denied the Rehabilitation Committee any involvement. This was not just a political matter. Once a child was turned over to the province, there was no way for the medical-social workers to follow up, so the child was visited by yet another series of new social workers and required to repeat the same painful information again—the exact thing the rehabilitation workers sought to minimize.

Overall, the committee dealt with 500 children: 70 full orphans, 200 hospitalized, 120 who had lost their mothers, and 80 who had lost their fathers. Of the 120 children who had lost their mothers, only 9 had fathers in Halifax. The fathers of the other 111 were all serving overseas, making their children orphans, at least temporarily. A neighborhood woman unofficially adopted Cecilia Brogan when her grandmother decided to send her to an orphanage, even though her son-in-law, Cecilia's father, was serving overseas. Celia never saw her father again.

Generous offers to adopt children arrived daily from across North America. Many informal adoptions were already in motion as children moved in with relatives and neighbors. "There was a tiny little baby in the dance hall. Bertha wanted to go into nursing and later she said, 'My, I would like to take that little fellow home.' She went home and asked her mother and they took him home and adopted him." Some children complained they were sent to live with people looking for servants, not children. Blois insisted that all adopted children remain within Nova Scotia. If children did eventually move out of the province, the Relief Commission kept track of them through their pension.

Many injured, homeless, or orphaned children spent Christmas in hospitals and in temporary shelters where volunteers arranged for them to receive gifts.

Unclaimed children continued to appear in the papers daily. "Out at 617 Robie Street, a little boy with light hair and dark brown eyes, aged about 2-$\frac{1}{2}$ years. He can give no account of himself or his people other than that 'Daddy is at war.' He was found near Richmond. Some poor man overseas is probably being harassed with fear and it may be that a distracted mother is awaiting news. This is written in the hope of reaching somebody who may recognize the baby from the description given." Lottie Duggan, who believed that her baby had died in the fire—there were only embers left when they finally went back to look for her youngest—decided not to search even after unclaimed babies were advertised in the papers. Others were haunted by missing children and continued to look for them for the rest of their lives. One mother, Charlotte Moore, lost three of her children, aged nine, five, and six months. She "traveled for years to different parts of Canada and even to Massachusetts—to wherever she heard that children had gone. 'Maybe they are living with someone. If they are, I hope she is being good to them. . . . Had I known they were dead, I could have put my mind to rest.'"

.   .   .

THE OTHER GROUP THAT required specialized care was the blind. The initial estimates of five hundred blinded was revised dramatically downward. Many people who lost their sight in the immediate hours after the explosion found their vision returned after the irritation and swelling subsided.

"A joint committee of the American Red Cross and of the Halifax School for the Blind was appointed for the purpose of studying the eye conditions and the needs of the patients and for devising immediate and permanent care, training and education for the sufferers. . . . They urged strongly the need of follow-up work of those who were in danger of losing the little sight they had left, and the establishment of a clinic for those who would return for treatment. At their suggestion, Miss Lotta S. Rand of the Massachusetts Commission for the Blind was invited to go to Halifax for three months at the expense of the Red Cross for the purpose of directing the follow-up work and devising further means of training and education."

Out of the 5,923 eye injuries reported, only 16 people lost both eyes, 249 lost one. When the Red Cross and the Victorian Order of Nurses conducted surveys of eye injuries on January 1 and April 9, 1918, respectively, they were surprised to find their numbers matched exactly—totaling 691 people with ongoing eye injuries. By April almost one-quarter of those people had healed. One-fifth were blinded in one eye but in good health. Of the 41 fully blinded people, the majority were women between the ages twenty-one and forty. They were the ones people remembered, the ones who provided the central image of the explosion: women standing in their windows mesmerized by the pink and green skies and lurid flame balls before the final blast.

In the spring, the School for the Blind arranged for classes in reading and writing Braille. Many of those who had been blinded had already lost contact with former friends, and the social aspect of the classes proved to be an important tool in combating their overwhelming feelings of helplessness and loneliness. After students learned to read and write, they learned to use typewriters, tune pianos, cane chairs until, in some cases, they were able to return to their previous jobs. The Relief Commission also paid for children to board at the School for the Blind, where in many cases they adapted faster than their parents at home. Women took classes in sewing and teachers visited them at home to teach them how to run their household. The Halifax-Massachusetts Relief Committee provided them with washing machines, bread machines, and sewing machines. One woman was trained as a hairdresser and by the end of 1918 was working at a salon. As the rehabilitation process got under way and the medical demands trailed off, volunteers began to return home too. The X-ray machine that Ladd had brought from Harvard was sold to the Canadian Red Cross, which donated it to Halifax. The twenty-five thousand blankets were sent back to the U.S. Army, and hospitals were closed or turned over to local doctors. John Moors left as early as December 18, 1917, convinced that the rehabilitation effort was in good hands. The Maine and Rhode Island units left December 23. Only Ladd's unit stayed until January 5. The American Red Cross briefly considered putting him in charge of the rehabilitation altogether, but decided that he did not have enough experience. When he returned to Boston, he was allotted two beds at the Boston's Children Hospital, from which he created North America's foremost pediatric surgical ward.

On January 15, 1918, the American Red Cross offices in Halifax officially closed. The trip had cost them $19,244.43. Ladd's unit accounted for almost half. Based on their experience, J. Prentice Murphy, the secretary for the Boston Children's Aid Society and a Red Cross worker, concluded that the Red Cross would benefit from further specializing in disaster response. "The experiences coming out of Halifax suggest the organization of special Red Cross Disaster units . . . Each of the larger cities, like New York, Chicago, Philadelphia, Boston and Baltimore, should have organized from four to six of these units . . . each member of a particular unit to know of the special services he is to render and to be subject to call. . . . Each of the disaster units should have an emergency kit containing duplicate copies of all the standardized forms and blanks. . . . There should also be (this of course has been suggested by the medical men) a thorough organizing of medical resources for emergency disaster work."

For their efforts, the American Red Cross volunteers each received an official Red Cross Certificate of Appreciation.


ON JANUARY 22, 1918, the Halifax Relief Commission was sworn into existence. The commission was divided into four areas: rehabilitation, reconstruction, medical, and finance. A claims department was set up to deal with fifteen thousand claims for furnishings and clothing worth less than $100. Of the 328 streets in Halifax, claims were submitted from 229. Claimants were allotted ten minutes to make their case and checks were issued immediately upon the decision. The job of determining each family's loss became the committee's predominant work, creating another instant and vast network of social workers, home visits, paperwork, court decisions,

THE AMERICAN RED CROSS

PURSUANT TO A RESOLUTION ADOPTED BY THE EXECUTIVE
COMMITTEE AT ITS MEETING HELD IN THE CITY OF
WASHINGTON ON THE *29th* DAY OF *January 1918* I DO
HEREBY EXPRESS THE HEARTY APPRECIATION OF THE
AMERICAN RED CROSS TO

*Clara Devlin*

FOR HELPFUL SERVICE IN ADMINISTRATION OF RELIEF FOLLOWING

*The Halifax Disaster*

*W. Frank Persons*
DIRECTOR GENERAL OF CIVILIAN RELIEF

American Red Cross volunteers received a Certificate of Appreciation for their efforts.

and subcommittees to oversee every aspect of the survivors' lives, including
how much they drank and with whom they shared their bed. "If a woman's
morality came into question, she could lose her pension temporarily or permanently." In the words of Judge Russell, who wrote to the local paper, the
rehabilitation process suffered from "an overdose of 'business efficiency' and
social service pedantry."

The payments and pensions were based on the military pension system.
Widows who owned less than $3,000 worth of property received a pension
of $8 a month for every living child and between $40 and $65 in pension,
prorated against their pre-explosion income and not to exceed that income.
Those with a net worth between $3,000 and $21,000 saw their pension reduced by 20 percent to 100 percent. Even in Halifax, the pension was not a
living wage, but it was regular and it was guaranteed for life. Claimants also
had the right to reject the pension and accept a lump-sum payment of $500
instead. "It was a fairly well-established fact that those in receipt of regular
allowances had a higher life expectancy."

Three days after the explosion, the Canadian military, under Colonel
Robert Low, who was made the chairman of the Reconstruction Commit-

tee, began construction of temporary apartments.* Low's plan was to build temporary apartments that could be converted into barracks once the homeless were resituated. In the dead of winter, soldiers gathered on the Commons to build shelter for one thousand people, a feat that took less than a month. Two rooms rented for $5 a month, three for $7.50, and five for $12. The Governor McCall Apartments on the Exhibitions Grounds were more expensive, with four rooms running $12. These opened in March and accommodated more than two thousand people. The two-story buildings, made up of four or five units each and constructed from tarpaper on the outside with wainscoting and beaverboard interiors, were neither fancy nor particularly warm, but each unit had its own entrance, affording tenants some privacy, a welcome feature after so many had been sharing not only houses but beds with others. Although simple, some tenants found their new apartments cozy and inviting; some even preferred them to their Richmond housing. With the cooperation of customs, the Massachusetts-Halifax Relief Fund spent $500,000 on a warehouse where the dispossessed could go "shopping" for furniture—though everything was free. For those who had been at the mercy of others for months, to pick out furniture to suit their taste was as cheering as the furniture itself. They were allowed to keep everything they received. The Massachusetts-Halifax Relief warehouse furnished fifteen hundred homes and received almost as many thank-you notes. "I now write these few lines to try and thank-you for your great kindness in helping us to furnish a little home after losing all we had in the explosion of December 6, 1917. Words can in no way express our thanks to all concerned." Some people who had lost their sight wrote letters on type-writers supplied by the Relief Fund. "I am, therefore, now in the proud and happy position to once more be able to use the 'open sesame' which provides me with the means of personally corresponding with my sighted, worldly brethren and sisters. Of course my early attempt on the machine must appear very crude and amateurish so I must beg a little forbearance."

As in every disaster, rumors spread quickly and were accepted as fact. The most common claim was that some families were getting preferential treatment, jumping ahead in line for housing, and many people believed that their neighbors either bribed officials or pulled strings to get apartments. But that is not to say that the system was without prejudice. Social

---

*Permanent housing would have to wait until the ground thawed and construction workers could excavate.

The Massachusetts governor, in bowler hat, inspects the temporary apartments named after him with some of the tenants.

hierarchies quickly found their place in the process; disbursements were not quite as impartial as the formulas implied. Respectable families came out ahead of poorer people. Particular disdain was shown to the soldiers' wives, common-law wives of soldiers stationed in Halifax, and the residents of Africville. Although somewhat shielded by the hillside, the houses there were as damaged as those on the streets surrounding the devastated area—doors were knocked off their hinges, dishes lost, windows shattered. Often called a shantytown, Africville was a growing, if modest, community with a wooden church, a school, three stores, and many residents who worked alongside their Richmond neighbors on the railroad and at the dockyards. Their proudest export was "Little Chocolate," the first black boxer to win a world title (1890) and the most famous black man of his time until another boxer, Jack Johnson, usurped him and won the first world heavyweight title. There were other successes as well. James Johnstone, the first black man admitted to the prestigious Dalhousie Law School, kept an office on Hollis Street not far from the Legislature. But for the most part the two communities remained segregated.

Relief investigators concluded that only a few black families were affected

A warehouse filled with furniture donated by the Halifax-Massachusetts Relief
Committee. Survivors appreciated being able to choose their own furniture for their
new homes. More than $250,000 worth of furniture was given away.

by the ten deaths of black residents and that despite the community's prox-
imity to the explosion they should only be awarded 10 percent of their
losses instead of the 20 percent the rest of the population received. On May
17, 1918, investigator H. Tapp appraised the case of William Howe, a forty-
year-old laborer with three children, who put in a modest claim for $190.55.
He had made $160 worth of permanent repairs to his house, received a
blanket, some clothes, and a shipment of coal. He asked to be compensated
for a barrel of flour, twenty pounds of potatoes, ten turnips, one tea set,
glassware, one dozen cups and saucers, two platters, blinds, curtains, lamp,
pictures, a watch and chain, repairs to a gold watch, carrots, and lamps. His
signature was clear and steady and his spelling correct. Tapp valued Howe's
claim at $20—not enough to replace even the winter stores the family had
lost, much less pay for his house repairs or cover the loss of furniture and
food. Not satisfied with the low assessment, Tapp included a suggestion in
his remarks about how to handle the community's claims. "As recommended will cover damage. In adjusting Africville claims the courts should

pay about 10% of the claims. My experience is they are 90% stuffed, all alike." The Relief Commission took Tapp's suggestion even further.

> May 22, 1918
> William Howe, Esq.
> Fairview, P.O.
>
> Dear Sir:
>
> In consequence of the inflated claim that you have rendered the Commission has decided to defer the payment of same to you indefinitely.
>
> Yours very truly,
> Chairman,
> Claims Department.

Charles Duggan did better than most, with much of his claim going unchallenged. He met with his first medical-social worker on December 28 while still living with his sister on Creighton Street. He was given $12.25 for food. He had already received four blankets and two mattresses and $42 for the mortuary. Under plans for the future, the investigator wrote: "Impossible to say at present time." The suggestion as to what the Relief Committee should do was "Home and Ferry Boat replaced." On January 3 he received one summer-weight suit that did not fit him and which he gave to his nephew Jim, three pairs of socks, two pairs of summer-weight underwear, two shirts, one overcoat, one cap, one pair of boots, and one pair of rubbers to match. By January 11 he stopped accepting money for food, although he would not receive his full claim until July 17. He was awarded $58.50 for his clothes, $66.50 for his possessions, and $600 for his portion of the ferry business. Both he and Billy chose the lump sum of $500 over the pension, giving Charles a total of $1,225. On January 16, Miss Marion Rowe of the Boston Associated Charities visited Charles to make another order for clothes; he asked for winter underwear and a better suit as well as a sweater coat and working shirts. At the bottom of the request, she included a short note. "This man lost seven members of his family, we would like this order nicely filled." Then she kindly marked it urgent.

BILLY DUGGAN'S, or rather Lottie Duggan's, file was more complicated. Lottie's file was filled with more requests, more hospital visits, and more reports of nervousness and illness. In December the children were split up and sent to live with various relatives and strangers. Helena stayed with Mrs. Eaton for a time; Bessie was sent to her mother's friends on Lilac Street in Dartmouth, but she complained of not having any shoes or boots. Lydia and Kenneth joined Charles at the Quinns' house while Irene remained in the hospital, which listed her as "nervous and unhappy." Lottie complained that they were not feeding Irene nourishing food. In January Lottie sent four of the children to board with her brother in Dartmouth for $3 a week, while Irene, who was still weak, joined Lottie at the YMCA. The doctors X-rayed her head before discharging Lottie, but soon readmitted her. She stayed there through most of January. Billy tried to rent an apartment for the family, but found it difficult. He only had an hour or two after he got off the boat each night. The city was still under blackout conditions; it must have been hellishly difficult to tramp through the streets in the pitch-black cold with so many in competition for the few available spaces. He did not have much luck. Eventually, he moved in with family friends, the Swafflers on Pelzant Street, where the family was reunited when Lottie was finally discharged. On January 24 they were still there when an investigator from the Building and Shelter Department visited them. The report included just two sentences. "Family anxious to get house. Eighteen people are living in one house."

By February the Duggans had moved to 965 Barrington Street, just above the harbor between Gerrish and Artz Streets. Another social worker came to visit in response to Lottie's calls to the office, complaining that the mattresses they had been given were too small. The investigator found her in poor shape. "Woman was badly cut on head; suffers loss of memory and faints very easily. Has been trying to do housework, but had to go to bed when I called. Had just been confined three weeks before explosion; baby was killed and Dr. Little says woman has not yet recovered from shaking up and severe nervous shock. Will talk to Dr. Little re this case. Children all O.K. Were badly cut. Has been at house at 965 Barrington Street since 21st of February. Wants $^{1}/_{2}$ ton of hard coal. Has tried to burn soft, but stove smoked so badly that she had to put fire out. Had no fire when I called. And reconstruction men were working on house; windows out, doors open etc. Gave woman Relief telephone number and my own that she might get in touch with us if necessary as I do not consider her fit to stay alone with the children. Will call again on Monday."

No matter how bad her injuries, Lottie fought for her family, sending back unsuitable furniture and arguing for a higher wage for the woman she hired to help out at home. Although Lottie could barely leave her bed or take care of her children, she fought to get the girl an extra fifty cents a week. "Saw Mrs. Duggan. Told her that $4 a week was the utmost could be paid for woman to help with work. Strongly advised a permanent girl. Knew of one in Lunenburg and she promised to write tonight and thought she might be here on Friday. Told her $3 was quite a good wage for girl." When the investigator returned to the office to confirm Billy's pay, the Navy told him Billy received $60 a month instead of $55 plus an additional $25 monthly separation pay. Despite Lottie's or perhaps Billy's omission about his true salary, the Relief Office finally agreed on a stipend of $15 a month for the housekeeper.* In May Lottie submitted a second clothing claim, which the Relief Office ruled too late to accept but offered her clothes from the order department. Lottie, expecting the clothes to be sec-ondhand, refused them and threatened to "consult Mayor of Halifax at once." She got her way. The Relief Office also provided the family with fur-niture, including a piano and a sewing machine, most likely because both could be used to earn money. As late as August, they were still sending her furniture.

In June Lottie complained again of chronic head pain and fainting and returned to the hospital for an X ray of her face that revealed several sizable pieces of glass still lodged in her skull. There is no mention in her file of them being removed, but later that month Lottie felt well enough to take a trip to Cape Breton, although she continued to complain of severe pain across her forehead and dizziness. On July 17, 1918, a doctor from the Med-ical Board examined Lottie again.

> Physical Condition: Severe wound extending from an inch above the hairline down over right frontal bone, and over right side of nose to the ala. Fracture of the skull, and the nasal bones were fractured. She complains of dizziness and a queer feeling at the back of her head and neck. She is very nervous and easily tires, and the palms of the hands are perspiring. Feels absolutely unfit for work. Knee jerks are exaggerated. Complains of, a "catching" pain in the chest in front and towards, the "right side." States, however, that she had a similar experience last summer.
>
> Physical examination of chest: Impairment of resonance over right apex above clavicle and immediately below. There is increased vocal fremitus, and the expiratory murmur is decidedly prolonged, amounting to almost "blowing" breathing. There are no rales. There is no cough to expectoration. This is a case of healed or arrested Pulmonary Tuberculosis.

---

*Lottie's efforts won the girl approximately fifty cents extra each week.

Lottie Duggan in her later years

Diagnosis:
a) Healed Pulmonary TB
b) Traumatic Neurosis
c) Cerebral Concussion effects
Recommendation for treatment: Much rest, open air and sunshine, good feeding, judicious management and suitable mental occupation.

Prognosis: Able to resume former employment, if not, period disability: Housewife.

Estimated percentage disability: Total but this should not be considered a disaster-produced condition entirely.

They awarded Lottie $18 a month for six months. She received another $250 for loss of furniture and clothing. Billy received $605 for his claim, $400 for his share of the ferry, and $300 for the car. Like many survivors, Lottie continued to remove pieces of glass and wood from her face and neck for the rest of her life. It would start as a bump or a black spot and slowly work its way to the surface, until it expelled itself.

# Chapter Seventeen

# Proper Burials,
# Private Services

A WEEK AFTER THE explosion, hundreds of bodies and remains lay unclaimed in the basement of the morgue at Chebucto Road. Searchers continued to find bodies trapped beneath wreckage, and the back entrance to the school was seldom vacant for long. Those bodies, charred beyond recognition, were listed only by the address where they were found. Since many people had either gone outside to watch or been blown some distance by the air blast, the addresses were not always helpful. Others were adequately described but were not identified. "No. 927A FEMALE—About 8 months (possibly more). Light brown hair. Fair complexion. Good teeth. Plump body. Flannel waist and skirt and pink flannel underskirt. Wrapped in patch work baby's blanket." Some identified bodies stayed in the morgue, their families being so adversely affected by the explosion that they were in neither the physical nor financial condition to make funeral arrangements. Even sadder were the families left lying in the morgue, identified by neighbors and friends but with no relatives left to claim them. They could not stay above ground for too much longer. The Mortuary Committee, concerned about contagion and space, set December 16 as the last day for picking up bodies.

The city, which had already ordered four thousand coffins, agreed to pay for the funerals and the burials of both the unidentified and the indigent. The burial plot was to be in Fairview Lawn Cemetery, the city's nondenominational cemetery, an unofficial Potter's Field. It was here in 1912 that the city had buried many of the staff and crew of the *Titanic*. Their 121 headstones were laid out in two long low rows that curved slightly at one end, evoking the bow of a ship, but the explosion victims would not be buried next to them. Instead, Fairview offered a separate lot off Bayers Road, across from an outcropping of rock left over from railway blasting. The plot was an unglamorous square patch of neglected grass, set apart from the rest of the cemetery, but it was this same discreteness that allowed the victims, so many of whom knew each other in life, to remain together in death.

The military had already held their own service on Tuesday, just five days after the explosion. Instead of using the civilian morgue, the military had set up their own at the Naval Hospital Pier 2, which had been badly damaged by a twenty-foot-long piece of flying chain. Sailors like Fred Longland were sent out specifically to locate sailors and soldiers. The service was spare but emotional. "There was no funeral dirge, no muffled drums, no gun carriage and no solemn military pomp, though in a few cases friends had covered up the rough coffins with Union Jacks. . . . Capless sailors and soldiers, here and there a sprinkling of women and civilians listened attentively to the grey-haired Nova Scotia chaplain consigning the bodies to the earth and their souls to God, after which there followed a slow shuffling of feet and companions of the unfortunate victims lifted the coffins and carried them through tear-eyed throngs to the waiting trucks outside." These men were buried in St. John's Cemetery.

From Monday, December 10, to Christmas Day, between twenty and fifty soldiers and volunteers spent their days and part of the nights digging graves in private and public cemeteries across the city, but it was not enough. Even families with the resources for a private burial found themselves facing unfamiliar obstacles. One in ten Canadian men were overseas. Almost four out of ten Nova Scotia men were enrolled in the service and Halifax's remaining laborers were either injured, killed, or busy with their own families. Many people had to dig graves themselves. The next problem was finding someone to give the service. Church parishes were decimated and their clergy exhausted from assisting and burying parishioners. Kaye Street Methodist lost 167 people. Grove Presbyterians lost 170 members, while St. Mark's Anglican Church lost 200. The Duggans' church, St. Joseph's, had the heaviest loss—494 parishioners between the church and the school. Some clergymen simply remained in or near the cemetery during the day, performing funerals until it got too dark to read. One minister took a room next to St. John's cemetery. Others remained in the hospital performing last rites. St. Paul's, the Anglican church across from City Hall, which had been providing relief, held the city's first church service in the basement on the Sunday after the explosion, but other churches did not hold proper services until Sunday, December 16—the last day to claim bodies before the public funeral.

# Chapter Eighteen

# Monday, December 17, 1917

T HE FUNERAL FOR UNIDENTIFIED bodies was scheduled to start at 2:30 p.m. A crush of fedoras, wide-brimmed ladies' felt hats, caps, and military headgear bobbed between the fence and the house next door, overflowing onto the side streets until they surrounded half the school. The crowd lost its solemnity the farther it got from the schoolyard. "Some of the older folk may have come out of motives sincere and respect for the dead, but on the whole the crowd was like that which greets a St. Patrick's day procession." On the other side of the fence, three spindly striplings, planted the year before, divided the schoolyard into thirds. Wooden frames held them up on either side, subtle reminders of the frailty and youth of some of the victims. Past the trees a collection of soldiers, Salvation Army members, and reporters, including at least one newspaperwoman, milled about waiting for the service to begin. The 66th Princess Louise Fusiliers, dressed in long gray coats and peaked hats, set up in the corner by the entrance. The strap of their haversacks slashed diagonally from shoulder to waist in a bright red stripe that was dimmed only by their glinting tubas, trumpets, and French horns. The service was to be multidenominational, which in Halifax meant for Protestant and Roman Catholic.

The morning started out with another cloudless blue sky that eerily evoked the morning of the explosion. The crowd began to gather almost as soon as the soldiers arrived for work, lining up on the other side of a dull picket fence that ringed the schoolyard. By noon hundreds were waiting.

"Women brought their babies. Children skated on the sidewalks. Young girls ogled passersby of the opposite sex." By 2:00 p.m., three thousand people crammed onto the trampled-down snow that covered the ground, and the sun, which had been so bright, slipped behind a cloud, casting dreary light across an already dreary scene. The crabbed and knotty branches of a neighbor's tree reached up over the crowd's hats toward the winter sky in an exasperated silhouette.

The morgue staff spent the morning preparing numbered markers for the unidentified and going over the final details of the service. Each coffin was numbered three times, on a band of grass resting on the body, on the coffin, and on a slab to go at the head of the grave. The coffins were all different colors and sizes—brown-black, white, baby blue. Some contained single fragments, others the remains of six people. When the door finally swung open, two soldiers walked out carrying the first coffin accompanied by the Funeral March, which sounded "strained and thin." Men and women in the back leaned forward to see coffin after coffin set down on the cold ground after being checked off the list. When the two rows of ninety-five coffins—some tiny and white; others long, dark and fitted with bright brass handles; all with a sprig of fresh flowers—were laid out, the band stopped. "Only the dogs seemed to comprehend the enormous burden of our sorrow. They slinked among the coffins, their every movement betraying dejection."

The unidentified were laid to rest on December 17, 1917.

The Protestant service was first, starting with the band leading the crowd in a hymn.

> O God, our Help in ages past,
> Our Hope for years to come,
> Our Shelter from the stormy blast,
> And our eternal Home.

Six ministers stepped onto the dais—Anglican, Presbyterian, Methodist, Baptist, Lutheran, and Salvation Army. The archbishop of Nova Scotia, Clarendon Worrell, representing the Anglican Church, expressed the citizens' growing indignation with the accident.

"It is not by the hand of the Almighty these unfortunate human beings have suffered, but by the mistakes of others."

He might as well have mentioned Frank Mackey and CXO Frederick Wyatt by name.

After the last hymn, Father Charles McManus and Father Grey, both from the destroyed St. Joseph's Church, stepped onto a dais and read a service together. At least one viewer found the services inadequate through no fault of the speakers. "Words counted for little."

Over three thousand people attended the funeral for unidentified bodies.

At the end of the service, the crowd burst into "God Save the King" as a line of soldiers with coffins propped on their shoulders slid the first coffins onto a waiting truck. "No stately hearses with nodding-plumes and purple hangings . . . just trucks and flat wagons." And when those ran out, a policeman seized sleighs out of the street. The drivers could hardly refuse in front of three thousand people, and quickly accommodated the officers. The crowd began to disperse, some off to the cemetery, others lining Windsor Street to watch the funeral procession. When the last coffin was loaded, vehicle after vehicle started down Windsor Street. "One by one they rumbled off, jolting over the snowy ruts. Loaded high with their boxes of blue and brown and white, with silver trappings, they looked for all the world like a circus procession. The surging, neck-craning crowd which lined Windsor St., heightened the illusions. Only the blaring calliope was lacking." They had to hurry. They were losing the light.

One of the hearses got lost and arrived an hour after the others in the dark. At Fairview Lawn Cemetery, one of the trucks was still running, its lights pointed toward the trenches where the soldiers worked. They lifted the coffins off the trucks and wagons and onto their shoulders, cigarettes dangling from their mouths. The varying coffin sizes made lowering the coffins into the trenches difficult. When a position was secured for a coffin, a soldier carefully added it to a diagram of the coffins. He marked the number down beside it and mapped out a guide to the coffins buried in the lot, but by the time the last coffins were in place, it was getting late. "They would have to spend one more night under the stars and alone."

One of the reasons the soldiers had a hard time fitting the coffins into the Fairview Lawn trenches was that more bodies were delivered than expected. Half were supposed to go to Mount Olivet, the Catholic cemetery, but somehow they ended up at Fairview, and as twilight turned to night, Fathers Grey and McManus stood waiting in front of empty trenches. Just two coffins were delivered to them.

DECEMBER 17, 1917, was funeral day for the Duggans as well. Without any money, with four households destroyed, and with at least three families living in one house, they more than qualified for the public funeral. Charles still did not have proper clothes. Billy's family was split between five houses, and he did not have a hope of reuniting them for at least another month, maybe longer. Lottie was being transferred from Camp Hill to the YMCA, so that her head could be X-rayed. Irene and Bessie had been sent there the day before and were discharged that morning. Their church, St. Joseph's, had been destroyed and its parishioners were scattered across the province. Both Father McManus and Father Grey would have known the Duggan siblings—Charles, Billy, Ellen and Sarah—since they had all been baptized and married at St. Joseph's, but it was the Relief Fund that paid for the family's coffins. Vincent's was particularly nice, costing $5 more than the regular coffin. Chances are that the Duggans were in that crowded schoolyard. They were certainly at the cemetery on Monday when Father McManus performed the ceremony over their plot in the northwest section of Mount Olivet near Dutch Village Road. The gravestone was made of a light stone, the letters engraved on top, the Duggan family name embossed at the bottom. Charles Sr. and his wife Susie Hinch were listed on one side. Vincent and Evelyn on another. Charles's wife and son were buried together, their names—Theresa and Warren—etched into the western side, facing the trees. The Duggan children and grandchildren had lost more loved ones than most in the explosion, but as they left the cemetery that day, they were one of the families lucky enough to know who among their kin was being buried.

# Chapter Nineteen

# The Rules of the Road versus the Law of the Land

O N THE DAY of the funeral, another ritual was being played out across the city at the County Court-house on Spring Garden Road. Frank Mackey was on the witness stand under cross-examination. Exactly one week after the explosion, almost to the hour, the Honorable Arthur Drysdale of the Supreme Court of Nova Scotia had opened the "Investigation into the *Mont Blanc* and *Imo* Collision," better known as the 1917 Wreck Commission. "The setting was almost Dickensian. The Inquiry convened in a large room with twenty-five foot ceilings in the old courthouse. The windows had been blown out by the explosion and were boarded up. Power was unavailable and the room was dimly lit with two oil lamps. Drysdale peered down through the gloom from an elevated Victorian pulpit, flanked on either side by the master mariners who were to serve as his advisors." William Henry stood for the Dominion Government, Andrew Cluney represented the attorney general of Nova Scotia, Francis Bell represented the City of Halifax, while T. R. Robertson appeared on behalf of the Halifax Pilotage Commission. The owners of the *Imo* and the *Mont Blanc* had their own lawyers, each with dramatically different styles. Humphrey Mellish, who represented the *Mont Blanc,* was older, more established, and more polished. He was joined by Joseph Nolan, a lawyer from New York who traveled to Halifax at the request of the owners of the *Mont Blanc*. The *Imo* hired Charles Burchell, who was younger and more theatrical. Two nautical consultants, Captain L.A. Demers and Captain Charles Hose, not only advised Judge Drysdale, but also used their nautical knowledge to further examine witnesses in areas that were less familiar to the lawyers, sometimes drawing out small but significant details with regard to navigation and protocol. The Rules of the Road, as the international sailing rules were commonly known, had been standardized by the International Maritime Consulting Organization (IMCO), which was formed after the *Titanic* sank in 1912. Although the IMCO was meant to enforce the new regulations, the organization's mission had been disrupted by the war. It would immediately become evident at the investigation that the war had disrupted the chain of command in Halifax harbor as well.

On the first day of the investigation, William Henry, who assembled the commission at the request of the federal government, explained how difficult it had been to notify witnesses. They were hard to locate and, in the midst of a week's worth of severe weather and without proper telephone or telegraph services, even harder to contact. He requested that any witnesses who had not been contacted come forward. Then he called the first witness: Captain Aimé Le Médec. Mellish jumped to his feet and objected on behalf of Nolan, who, being from out of town, suggested that they begin with disinterested parties. He might as well have spit into the wind. There were no disinterested parties in Halifax, including the judge. The two ships blamed each other. The local harbor officials blamed their military counterparts, who blamed the pilots. As it was neither a criminal nor a civil trial, but a federal investigation, cross-examination was loose, objections few, hearsay given as fact, and speculation encouraged. And that was just inside the courtroom. The newspapers covered it like a criminal trial and inflamed the public with suggestions that the conditions that allowed the accident to happen were still in place, although no ship with such a cargo had ever entered the Narrows before. Drysdale refused Nolan's request. Burchell then stood and pointed out that as long as they were going to start with the ships' witnesses, he was at a disadvantage with his pilot and captain dead.

"It is a question of two pilots, whether both or one of the pilots are at fault—they are the men who are responsible for this whole accident, and of course, as is stated here by Mr. Mellish, Pilot Mackey is really on trial in this Court; but the other pilot unfortunately is dead, and cannot be put on trial; but in fairness to him I should think that somebody should be acting for him."

Robertson offered to represent Pilot Hayes, as he was present on behalf of the Pilotage Commission, but Mellish, his *Mont Blanc* counterpart, suggested Burchell. Burchell refused.

"There are some possibilities of question like that arising and I don't see how I could act for the pilot and owners of the *Imo* jointly. I could not undertake that dual position."

Drysdale instructed Burchell to act as Hayes's lawyer for the morning, then find another lawyer at lunch if he really thought it necessary. That the judge did not see that the *Imo* and the pilot were potentially at odds might have been the first indication that he had already made up his mind as to who was responsible for the accident. Perhaps sensing this inclination, Burchell never did find a replacement and remained Hayes's lawyer.

Henry again called Captain Aimé Le Médec. The courtroom was silent as the slight captain walked to the stand with his interpreter. Le Médec and the rest of the crew had been staying at the French consulate all week, where the captain refused to speak to reporters. "I shall make my statement to the Admiralty Court." After the worst week in the city's history, the public would finally learn what happened in the minutes prior to the explosion.

Much of the testimony dealt with the whistles. The whistles were important because the first ship to whistle controlled the navigation. Which ship whistled first was a matter of dispute, not only between the *Imo* and the *Mont Blanc,* but also between the witnesses. Burchell intended to argue that the first signal heard on the *Imo* was a two-blast whistle from the *Mont Blanc*—meaning they intended to cross—and that the *Imo* responded with a return signal of two blasts—meaning they agreed. The *Mont Blanc* witnesses testified that they heard the *Mont Blanc* give a short blast first, directing the *Imo* to return to her proper course, which the *Imo* returned with a double, a cross-signal. Some observers in the harbor said they heard the *Imo* whistle first but understood it to be directed at the tug *Stella Maris,* a fact the crew of the *Stella Maris* disputed. As for Le Médec, no matter how many times he was asked, he answered that not only was he the first to blow the whistle, but he moved his ship starboard to confirm his intentions and that in response he received a cross-whistle, the *Imo*'s two short blasts. He spoke through a translator who switched between the first and third person, sometimes translating directly, other times paraphrasing Le Médec.

Q: Did he receive any signal from the *Imo* in response to his one blast?

A: Yes sir, the *Imo* replied by two short blast.

Q: Which was the first signal given by either of the ships to the either?

A: It was me gave one short blast meaning, I am going to the right.

Q: Did the *Imo* change her course after giving the two short blast signal?

A: I think so; but it is difficult for a ship against the land to find out if she is moving in one direction or not. The fact of giving two short blasts of the whistle does not imply that the vessel itself will go to the right or the left—it might say I pass to the right or I pass to the left.

This last response emphasized both the difficulty of navigating in a stream by landmark and the nuance of navigation for the layman, a problem that cropped up repeatedly through the testimony. It also highlighted the local system of whistles, which was a slightly expanded version of the Rules of the Road. The Halifax pilots allowed more flexibility in how they interpreted the whistles. As evidenced by the *Imo* and *Clara* passing, the Halifax style was more conversational than International Law dictated.

LE MEDEC: I asked myself why the *Imo* was giving two blasts, because according to the International rules of navigation the *Imo* should have given a short blast meaning I come to the right, besides I was holding to my right and I was the first to signal my maneuvers when I am going to starboard. He should have replied by one blast that I am going to starboard, because I was commanding the maneuver having signaled first.

Q: He could not understand what the two-blast signal from the *Imo* meant?

A: He says I understood very well that the two blasts of the *Imo* meant I am heading towards the left; but I had the right, and he had no right to change my signal because I had given first one blast, meaning I am heading to the right, except in case of a collision to avoid a collision.

Q: And he kept on after that signal of two blasts from the *Imo* the *Mont Blanc* kept her course?

A: He [Mackey] accentuated the course towards the right.

Q: With the helm to the right?

A: His helm to the right.

Q: What kind of helm has he, right or left helm?

A: Like all the French boats. When it turns the wheel to the right, the rudder also goes toward the right.

Q: Starboard helm brings the vessel to starboard?

A: Yes sir, in France they don't use any more the words port or starboard, so as to have no confusion and they say right and left to avoid all sorts of mistakes they used these words right and left.

The discussion of whether or not the command of the *Mont Blanc* was tainted by language problems and confusion on the part of Mackey and Le Médec continued throughout the trial with lawyers and witnesses arguing the differences between French and English commands. Even with the assistance of the nautical assessors, the terminology of rudders, tillers, wheels, and helms often got the better of the lawyers, who erroneously used the words interchangeably.* At several points the Court itself seemed troubled by its own understanding of the differences in steering styles and instructions, and asked more than once for clarification both from witnesses and from the nautical advisors. During Mackey's testimony, Drysdale himself, who as the Admiralty Court judge in the most active port in the county should have understood the terminology perfectly, asked for a recap.

DRYSDALE: The porting of the helm of your ship puts your ship to port?

A: No, it puts the ship to starboard.

Q: The naming of the movement is different?

A: Yes sir.

MELLISH: We will straighten that out now—it is just the same as English ships?

A: Yes sir.

Q: There is really no difference in it?

---

*Tillers are handles used to steer small boats. A tiller's counterpart in a commercial ship is the wheel or the helm, which controls the rudder, a flat paddle that remains fully underwater when loaded, and partially exposed when in ballast. The rudder turns in the opposite direction as the wheel, but turns the ship in the same direction as the wheel.

DRYSDALE: I was under the impressions that it was opposite from our ships?

MELLISH: They use right and left—starboard your wheel your ship's head goes where?

A: The same as the wheel; but to the opposite helm.

Q: Starboard your helm?

A: The ship's head would go to port.

Q: Porting your helm the ship's head goes to starboard?

A: Yes sir.

Q: Is the same on this ship?

A: Yes sir.

Q: I got it right last evening—I found on this ship—I don't know how it is on other ships the head of the ship goes the same way as the wheel—the same as English ships.

HOSE: With the order to the helmsman hard astarboard he immediately puts the wheel to port?

BURCHELL: I thought on the French ships that if they ordered or wanted the wheel hard astarboard they put it hard astarboard.

HOSE: If you give the order hard astarboard to that Frenchman he would put his wheel hard astarboard?

A: If I said hard astarboard the helm would go to port, and the wheel would go to starboard—the same as the ship.

DEMERS: It is the tiller goes hard astarboard?

A: Yes sir.

Q: And your rudder goes to port?

A: Yes sir.

HOSE: Just the same on the Frenchman as our own ships?

A: Yes sir.

MELLISH: Sometimes they run the tiller aft of the rudder post and then the tillers goes the same way as the rudder. At all events when you ported this ship, her head goes to starboard?

A: Yes sir.

Q: The same as English ships?

A: Yes, when I port the helm.

It was too much for poor Mellish. He continued his line of questioning. When he examined Le Médec, he shifted the discussion to the Wednesday-afternoon cargo inspection, pointing out that the examination boat gave him no special instructions despite understanding the nature of his cargo, insinuating that the Admiralty shared some of the responsibility for the accident. When it came time for Burchell to examine Le Médec, he immediately questioned him about why they did not fly a red flag to warn other ships.

Q: Did the ship carry any red flag or anything to indicate she was loaded with munitions?

A: No sir, because the red flag, according to the international rules of the road indicates that they handle explosive powder on board ship, that they take on board or discharge munitions. The regulations don't say that it must be shown to anybody that the ship is loaded with ammunition, and under the present circumstances he [Le Médec] was of the opinion that it was preferable that everybody should ignore the nature of his cargo.

Four crew members and one officer from the *Mont Blanc*

Burchell twisted Le Médec's answer into a question, asking the captain if he knew of the custom to raise the red flag in peacetime, giving the impression that he had intentionally broken a rule. Le Médec corrected Burchell again by repeating that the red flag was used only to show that explosives were being handled onboard, and that was not the case with the *Mont Blanc*. Burchell turned to the evacuation of the ship, suggesting that in the twenty minutes between the collision and the explosion they had not warned anyone either on the water or on land, assertions that the papers were only too happy to repeat the next day, despite later testimony that this claim was false. Burchell played to the community's sense of injustice, presenting the French captain and crew as self-interested and careless, failing to acknowledge that they did not have the benefit of hindsight, did not know that they had twenty minutes, did not know that the ship would drift across the harbor under way. When they abandoned the *Mont Blanc*, it was with the understanding that it might explode at any second. The investigation, which was meant to determine the cause of the accident, was soon overcome by the need to affix blame. Burchell had an easy target with the French.

For the last year Robert Borden and his conservative government had involved the country in a bitter and divisive battle over conscription, finally passing the military service act in July. From 1916 to 1917, the number of men enlisting in the military had dropped from thirty thousand a month to five thousand, and Borden took up the rallying cry just as his party began to flag in the polls. Tens of thousands of men were already dead on the fields of Europe, and the Conservatives denigrated all those who rejected the call for the draft, including Quebecers, as unpatriotic and selfish. Four days after the explosion, the *New York Times* ran an article about the tension under the headline "French Canadians Called Seditious." The French complained of discrimination—their men were fit enough to serve but not fit enough to be officers—and railed not only against conscription but against the war in general, pointing out that enormous profiteering was taking place at home while men died abroad. The Conservatives sidestepped the domestic squabble about profiteering and positioned Quebec's arguments as an immoral political shirk, questioning why they would refuse to defend their own country, even if she were being attacked at a distance. That Quebec contributed fewer soldiers per capita than the rest of the country infuriated English Canada, whose citizens realized that more of their men would be required to make up for Quebec's shortfall. Conscription continued to be a bitter and ugly debate that entrenched an already deep rift between the

French and English. Ironically, after the explosion, conscription in Halifax was postponed until January 9. The election in Halifax was also postponed, although it went ahead in the rest of the country on the opening day of the Wreck Commission. Inflaming the mistrust between the French and the English paid off. Borden won easily. It did not take long for those prejudices to spread through the proceedings, although Burchell made no real headway with Mackey and Le Médec on the language issue. Both men insisted that they had understood each other on the bridge.

By trying to taint the *Mont Blanc,* Burchell unwittingly shifted the focus from the navy's responsibility to oversee the harbor traffic to the actions of the individual ships, which, as the lawyer for Pilot Hayes and the *Imo,* eventually worked against Burchell because it emphasized the ships' responsibility and diminished the government's.

LE MÉDEC'S DEMEANOR—stiff and respectful if somewhat distant—was later described as arrogant and, at least by some, perceived as evasive. He certainly did not offer any apology or show any remorse for his decisions.

> Q: Did he think of changing the helm to run the ship into some place where it would not be so dangerous to the city—did he think of running it up into the basin?
>
> A: No sir, he says that if the explosion was to take place ten metres one side or ten metres to the other side it was bound to happen.

Le Médec was wrong. Certainly the ship would have done less damage if it sailed to either the Dartmouth side or into the Basin. Even an extra quarter-mile would have reduced the force of the blast in heavily populated Richmond by approximately a factor of two. Under Burchell's questioning, Le Médec let it be known that he was, in effect, under house arrest and unable to go out in public, although that order was probably meant to protect the captain. Certainly by the time Burchell's examination ended, he needed protection to walk the streets of Halifax.

ON THE SECOND DAY of the investigation, Drysdale ruled that he would not be too strict about the rules of cross-examination as long as the lawyers were trying to get at the truth. Burchell grew increasingly more aggressive. "Repeatedly he browbeat and misled witnesses, disregarded all the rules of courtroom etiquette and, on a number of occasions, violated the standards of legal ethics to which lawyers must subscribe." He scoffed at testimony inconvenient to him and told witnesses that others contradicted them— others who were never produced. When the second mate of the *Imo*, Peter Antonsin B'Jonnas, testified that the *Imo*'s first blast, a single blast, was meant for the *Stella Maris*—not the *Mont Blanc*—Burchell was soon on his feet informing the judge that the *Imo*'s wheelsman John Johansen intended to testify that the first signal he heard was from the *Mont Blanc* and that it was two blasts. Burchell encouraged Drysdale himself to cross-examine B'Jonnas in light of this information—surely inviting a judge to interfere with a witness's testimony was a strange invitation for any lawyer. As Johansen was the only survivor of the *Imo*'s bridge crew, his testimony held particular weight, but even Johansen would later point out that he was not listening for whistles, but concentrating on the wheel. Burchell then complained to Drysdale that the military was treating Johansen shabbily by throwing him in jail after one of Ladd's nurses working at the Bellevue called to inform them that Johansen offered her $25 for a newspaper. The military and the public wanted to know why he was so desperate to read about what was happening in court if he was innocent. Burchell considered the arrest premature. "He might be the greatest criminal on earth, but I found he was on an American ship, the *Abicon;* he was in the American Navy employ, and if they want any information about him they could telegraph and get the information."

The judge responded dryly. "There is more or less hysteria and I have no doubt the military people are doing what is right."

For once Judge Drysdale got it right. At least the part about the hysteria. The military told reporters that when they arrested Johansen, they discovered a German book in his possession, setting off a fresh wave of speculation that the collision had been no accident. It made beautiful newspaper copy. Even after it was confirmed that his book was in Norwegian—not German—many people believed that Johansen had murdered Captain From and William Hayes and then set his wheel straight for the *Mont Blanc*. The military secretly transferred Johansen from the Bellevue to the City Prison, where he was kept in isolation under armed guard, a fact Burchell would not discover until after Christmas.

The crews of both ships disagreed on almost all points, including where the ships were in the harbor, where they collided, at what angle, how fast they were traveling, the demeanor of the *Mont Blanc*'s crew as they abandoned ship, if the *Mont Blanc* crew warned anyone of the potential for explosion, who whistled first, and the sequence of whistles. Neutral observers were just the same—one contradicting the next—a deeply dissatisfying situation for a community desperate for answers.

Frank Mackey's two-day appearance produced over 175 pages of testimony, more than double Le Médec's and quadruple Johansen's. For the most part, he verified Le Médec's and Glotin's stories, with the only real disagreement being whether Mackey or Le Médec was in charge of the whistle. Both said the other blew the whistle. The uniformity of the *Mont Blanc's* crew sounded suspicious in relation to the rest of the witnesses. Few could agree on anything, but the French crew seemed to agree on everything. As for Mackey, particularly damning were the words of Peter Johnston, the superintendent of lights and buoys, who met Mackey at the Dartmouth ferry later that morning. The superintendent testified that Mackey told him that he had put the helm amidships to stop the *Mont Blanc* from going into the Lorne Athletic Club. That Burchell tried to indict him with this testimony and that Mackey denied it was particularly odd, considering that if the ship had blown up closer to the Lorne Club, which was next to the North Ordnance magazine, the rumor of a second explosion might have proved true.* If the *Mont Blanc* had exploded there, it would have taken most of the dockyard, Wellington Barracks, the magazines, and much of the Canadian Navy with her. It did not matter; it made Mackey look like a liar.

After Burchell insinuated that Mackey was drunk, witnesses testified on Mackey's behalf. James Hall, a sheriff and chairman of the Halifax Pilotage Commission, said that he had known Mackey thirty years.

"We always looked upon him as one of the best pilots, sober, industrious and attentive to duties. We never had any reason to complain of his habits in any respect."

Captain Neil Hall, port warden of Halifax, said that he had also known Mackey thirty years, and had never seen him drunk. The only other criticism of Mackey aside from that of Burchell—and there was surprisingly little for a man who had worked the harbor for over a quarter of a century—came from the harbormaster, who said that before the war he had to speak to Mackey about running the red flag once or twice when piloting a petroleum ship, but Mackey told him the captain had been negligent.

---

*It would not be unusual for a person who had just experienced a trauma to make inaccurate statements and to later forget the whole conversation, especially someone who had possibly suffered a concussion.

Chief Examining Officer Wyatt also complained that Mackey had taken a ship out once without notice, but later called to apologize. During his two days on the stand, lawyers elicited flashes of pride and temper from Mackey, as when Burchell insinuated that he had acted out of fear.

"I was never frightened in my life."

But despite slight variations in his testimony and the false insinuations that he was drinking, what came through most in Mackey's testimony was that, as a result of his twenty-four-year career, he had an acute understanding of both of the harbor's water and its workings. Unlike other witnesses, most of whom were professional seamen, Mackey never pretended he did not know an answer out of convenience. He always provided a landmark or estimated a distance when the court requested details. Unfortunately, his understanding of French was not as deep.

Q. Can you give us in French, one word that is on the telegraph?

A: I cannot give it on the telegraph the proper pronunciation.

Q: Can you spell one single word that was on the telegraph instruments?

A: Yes.

Q: What word?

A: Tout.

Q: What is that?

A: Full.

Q: And another?

A: Demi-mitesse.

Q: Spell it?

A: I don't know if I can spell it correctly.

Q: Spell the first part of the word.

A: D-E-M-I.

Q: And the other word.

A: T-A-S-S-E.

*Demi-tasse* was not half-speed but half-cup. The word he was looking for was *demi-vitesse,* but it was not Mackey's lousy French that outraged the community, but the news that he was still working as a pilot, even as the investigation was under way. Instead of reassuring the population, newspapers seemed intent on driving people to greater hysteria. They openly sneered at Mackey. "And in the meantime Pilot Mackey, who brought in the ill-fated *Mont Blanc*, is STILL AT WORK and 'in a general way' the chairman of the Halifax Pilotage Commission had said that 'Since the disaster, a munitions ship coming up the harbor and piloted with Pilot Mackey had NARROWLY ESCAPED a collision with another vessel.' This same pilot had on one occasion previous to the disaster DISOBEYED the naval officer's instructions, 'but had subsequently apologized.' It is to tremble!" This rumor of a subsequent collision was nothing but exaggeration, but the public had a sudden interest in anything concerning the harbor, and the pilots, who were used to working autonomously and anonymously, had to bear the scrutiny of those still living in hospitals and railcars.

After a long holiday break, the investigation resumed and the focus switched from individuals to the Pilotage Commission and its relationship to the harbor management. Although the residents certainly were aware that the Admiralty had taken over the harbor when the war broke out, they soon learned the details and the characters involved. The papers were wild with accusations. They made the Canadian Navy out to be incompetents and the Admiralty arrogant double-dealers. It was as if the whole investigation were a spectacle produced to satisfy the public's suspicion that their leaders were incompetent rogues. Reporters had a lot of material—the Pilotage Authority's laxness, the chief examining officer's inability to control the pilots, the general disregard for the population of Halifax by the British. Chief Examining Officer Frederick Evans Wyatt testified that, a couple of months before the explosion, he had sent Captain Superintendent Edward Harrington Martin a letter complaining about the pilots' lack of cooperation in reporting outgoing ships.

"I would like to say that the last paragraph I put in there, in which I said I would not be responsible for any accident, was because for months and months I saw an accident or collision was coming and I could see there was somebody going to be made the goat for this and I did not wish to be made the goat—you can call it intuition or what you like; but that was my idea."

The papers demanded his resignation. The Navy did little to back up their man. Wyatt's boss, Captain Superintendent Martin, who did not even bother to show up to testify, replied by mail that he could not recall whether or not he had received Wyatt's letter. To reporters Wyatt's sudden ability to produce copies of letters in the midst of such chaos—his office on the *Niobe* was badly damaged—appeared more suspect than Martin's convenient amnesia. Plus, he won no friends by belittling the local harbormaster in a town that was notoriously sensitive to criticism. When asked how his decisions compared to Captain Francis Rudolf's decisions, he appeared insulted by the question itself.

A:  I know more about positions and berths than ever he would know in the whole of his life.

Q:  You are a better man?

A:  I think my records will show.

Of course his records most clearly did not show that. Rudolph was the only man who testified that he had made any special arrangements for ships carrying explosives; the biggest man-made explosion in history was on Wyatt's record. The very courtroom in which they were sitting—cold, blacked out, and filled with wounded—was evidence of his record. When it came out that Wyatt knew that the pilotage office was under the tutelage of the fifteen-year-old Edward Beazley and that Wyatt knew that Beazley had stopped reporting in the summer, the papers gleefully singled out a particularly devastating exchange and let their readers form their own opinion of the man responsible for harbor traffic.

Q:  The authorities left it to you and you left it to the boy; is that it?

A:  Yes.

Wyatt's testimony ended on January 28, 1918. His military career was over. Although never officially sanctioned, he was removed from Halifax and never given another assignment. Closing arguments began two days later. Burchell's closing argument was long, detailed, and as incendiary as his cross-examinations. He almost always referred to the *Mont Blanc* as "the French ship" and called Le Médec "a crazy Frenchman." He referred to Mayers, the sailor from the *Middleham Castle*, a man who posed no threat to his case, as "crazy Mayers" because he claimed to have been lifted to the top of Needham Hill by the blast, which was true. He attacked Mackey viciously, accusing him of perjury and calling the *Mont Blanc*'s actions that morning "erratic." The judge, now tired of the whole inquiry and seemingly having made up his mind at the outset, asked him to shorten his closing. In his usual fashion, Burchell agreed and then talked for three more hours. His argument rested on the fact that the *Mont Blanc* was in the *Imo*'s waters when the collision took place, making her responsible for the "stupid crazy collision." He sat down at 5:10 p.m.

Mellish closed the next morning, finishing before lunch, arguing that while the collision may have taken place in the *Imo*'s waters, the responsibility of the *Mont Blanc*'s being in those waters lay with the *Imo*. He blasted Burchell for the way he had gone after Mackey, and practically accused him of coaching witnesses. At this point, Drysdale interjected.

"You had your own proper side, why did you not hang on?"

This pronouncement must have shot Mellish through with dread. "Because the other vessel signaled she was going to come there too, and a collision was imminent. These vessels are close together—it is a question of 100 or 200 yards."

For twenty minutes Drysdale argued with Mellish about the *Mont Blanc*'s decision to port. The decision to port was crucial for two reasons. The first was that if she had not gone port the two ships would have remained parallel and passed without incident. The second was that by going port, the *Mont Blanc* crossed over into the *Imo*'s channel. Drysdale defended the *Imo*, fairly parroting much of Burchell's closing argument and reminding Mellish that the *Clara* and the *Stella Maris* had forced the *Imo* to the wrong side of the channel, even though the latter claim directly contradicted the testimony of Walter Brannen.

"All I suggested was there might have been good reasons for her being over there under the circumstances."

Mellish fought Drysdale's prejudice with logic.

"If there was a good reason for her being there, there was just the same reason for us getting there."

After that Drysdale let him continue his closing uninterrupted. At the end Mellish congratulated the Court for its patience—another shot at Burchell and possibly even Drysdale himself—and rested.

Robertson's defense of the Pilotage Commission came off as short and weak. He argued that because the Navy had not enforced the rule about outgoing ships, the Court could not the blame the pilots. He berated Commander Wyatt and Captain Martin, while chastising Burchell for making Mackey look like "a villain." Cluney and Henry's closings were more measured, better reasoned, and covered more territory. Attorney General Cluney reminded the Court that the inquiry was to decide the cause of not only the collision but also the explosion. He said that the people of Nova Scotia had no real interest in how the collision happened and that too much time had been given to ascertaining the details of responsibility. Cluney wanted to know how things would change to make sure that it did not happen again, calling the whole incident "a bitter lesson" resulting from misplaced trust, singling out Martin, Wyatt, and the pilots for abusing the public. He also suggested that in the future explosives be docked in an isolated cove outside the city.

Henry, who represented the federal government, believed that the *Mont Blanc*'s story was more consistent, but chastised the pilots for having a local version of the international rules on signals, citing pilots "using the whistles to communicate individual wishes as to whether the rules would be violated and broken." Describing Renner and Hayes's exchange of signals, he summed up their interpretation of signals as the Rules of the Road versus the Law of the Land. Henry contended that signals were meant to inform the other ship of the pilot's intentions, not to ask questions. When Renner answered the *Imo*'s single blast with a double, he was in effect asking a question: Can I cross starboard to starboard? The *Imo* answered with two blasts: Yes. Somewhere between these two practices, with Mackey abiding by the Rules of the Road and Hayes by the Law of the Land, the collision took place.

Henry was the only one to discuss the testimony of Willard C. Cope. Cope was an explosives expert who helped build the Panama Canal. Henry could not understand the Court's willingness to ignore the problem of picric acid despite its volatility. One of the curious aspects to come out at trial was that Le Médec did not seem to know, nor did anyone except Henry seem to understand, that the picric acid in the first hold was much more volatile than the TNT, which might have better withstood a collision. Perhaps it was because TNT was relatively new or perhaps because all explosions were measured in tons of TNT, but even after Cope testified that the picric acid was a more volatile explosive, making it the most likely cause of the chain reaction that set off the whole cargo, the Court, the lawyers, and the media seemed focused on the TNT. Ironically, if they *had* hit the TNT, the *Mont Blanc* might not have caught fire as quickly. Both Le Médec and Mackey stressed that they purposely arranged it so that the *Imo* would hit in the first hold, not the second, where the TNT was stored.

Fighting popular opinion, Henry also defended Wyatt by saying that not only was the commander not required to make special arrangements for explosives above and beyond what were covered in the naval rules, but it was beyond his authority to do so, just as it would have been for Wyatt to refuse the *Mont Blanc* entry into the harbor. When it came to Henry's friend Captain Superintendent Martin, he seemed genuinely disappointed that Martin did not ever positively deny seeing Wyatt's letter, something Henry found unbelievable. For the rest of the afternoon, he attacked Burchell for poisoning the public against so many, including Wyatt's young assistant Roland Iceton, whom Burchell had characterized as Wyatt's flunky. Henry blasted Burchell, an established, middle-aged man, for attacking a young man starting out on his career. Then he cleared up two last items. The first item was that the *Mont Blanc* was not a munitions ship in the strict sense. Munitions were nonreactive. One did not necessarily set off another. Hundreds of munitions ships entered the harbor, which was normal; only one ship laden with high explosives had ever entered. The second item dealt with two rumors that had traumatized the city—the accusation that since the trial began Mackey was involved in a collision of two ships in the harbor and a report that morning that a "narrowly averted collision" had taken place in the Narrows the day before between a petroleum ship and a munitions ship. While two ships had passed, Henry stated, there was no danger.

"There seems to be a determination to make the C.X.O.'s office and his subordinates a goat for the whole thing and as he said, he did not want to be the goat."

Wyatt did not have much to say about it. To the people of Halifax, Wyatt looked like a goat. Smelled like a goat. Must be a goat. Drysdale agreed. He read his decision on February 4, 1918. He did not even try to be impartial.

Having been directed by the Honourable the Minister of Marine to hold a formal enquiry into the cause of the explosion on the S.S. *Mont Blanc* on 6 December, 1917, I have to report as follows: That as directed I had associated with me as Nautical Assessors, Captain Demers of Ottawa, Dominion Wreck Commissioner, and Captain Walter Hose, R.C.N. of the City of Halifax. I began the enquiry on the 13th day of December, A.D. 1917, and having heard all the witnesses that could throw any light on the situation, and having conferred with the Nautical Assessors, I have reached the following conclusions and desire to report as follows:

1. The explosion on the S.S. *Mont Blanc* on 6 December was entirely the result of a collision in the harbor between S.S. *Mont Blanc* and the S.S. *Imo*.

2. Such collision was caused by violation of the rules of Navigation.

3. That the Pilot and Master of the S.S. *Mont Blanc* were wholly responsible for violating the rules of the road.

4. That Pilot Mackey by reason of his gross negligence should be forthwith dismissed by the Pilotage Authorities and his licence cancelled.

5. In view of the gross neglect of the rules of Navigation by Pilot Mackey, the attention of the Law Officers of the Crown should be called to the evidence taken at this investigation with a view to a criminal prosecution of such pilot.

6. We recommend to the French Authorities such evidence with a view to having Captain Le Médec's licence cancelled and such captain dealt with according to the law of his country.

7. That it appearing that the Pilotage Authorities in Halifax have been permitting Pilot Mackey to pilot ships since the investigation commenced and since the collision above referred to, we think the Authorities, i.e. Pilotage Authorities, deserving of censure. In our opinion the Authorities should have promptly suspended such pilot.

8. The Master and Pilot of the Mont Blanc are guilty of neglect of the public safety in not taking proper steps to warn the inhabitants of the city of a probable explosion.

9. Commander Wyatt is guilty of neglect in performing his duty as C.X.O. in not taking proper steps to ensure the regulations being carried out and especially in not keeping himself fully acquainted with the movements and intended movements of vessels in the harbor.

10. In dealing with the C.X.O.'s negligence in not ensuring the efficient carrying out of traffic regulations by the pilots we have to report that the evidence is far from satisfactory that he ever took any efficient steps to bring to the notice of the Captain Superintendent neglect on the part of the pilots.

11. In view of the allegations of disobedience of the C.X.O.'s orders by pilots, we do not consider such disobedience was the proximate cause of the collision.

12. It would seem that the pilots of Halifax attempt to vary the well known Rules of the Road, and, in this connection, we think Pilot Renner, in charge of an American tramp steamer on the morning of the collision, deserving of censure.

13. The regulations governing the traffic in Halifax harbor in force since the war were prepared by the competent Naval Authorities; that such traffic regulations do not satisfactorily deal with the handling of ships laden with explosives and we have to recommend that such competent Authority forthwith take up and make satisfactory regulations dealing with such subject; we realise that whilst war goes on under present conditions explosives must move but, in view of what has happened, we strongly

recommend that the subject be dealt with satisfactorily by the proper
Authorities.

Mackey and Le Médec were arrested that day and charged with
manslaughter in the death of William Hayes and Captain From. Wyatt was
added to the bill the next day. Mackey remained in the city jail behind the
courthouse, unable to make $6,000 bail. If it was heartbreaking to be charged
in his friend's death after participating in an accident that caused his city so
much suffering, Mackey never complained. Le Médec and Wyatt got out on
$10,000 bail. After a preliminary trial, where a judge found sufficient evi-
dence for the three men to go to trial, the men's lawyers filed a writ of habeas
corpus to petition their release. Provincial Supreme Court Judge Benjamin
Russell heard the case on March 15, 1918. He ruled to exclude the Wreck
Commission testimony, which had been given at an investigation, not a trial,
but entered the seven new witnesses. Russell, who seemed far less partisan
than Drysdale, could find no criminal evidence against the trio and called
their arrest a mistake. In his biography he recalled the trial, singling out
Mackey. "It seemed to me that, so far from being negligent or careless, as
charged in the information, the defendant had taken every possible care to
prevent the collision which was about to be caused by the conduct of the
*Imo* . . . I went so far in my decision as to say that I even doubted whether
any mistake of judgment had been made by the *Mont Blanc* considering the
manner in which she was being crowded over on the Dartmouth shore by the
course of the *Imo*. In any case, it surely cannot have been manslaughter for a
defendant to have done what was best in his judgment to prevent an impending accident even if, in spite of his best efforts, the struggle was unsuccessful." Russell's decision was unpopular. When one of his sons met a man
on the street the day the decision was announced, he told him that the judge
should be castrated.

Mackey, Le Médec, and Wyatt were free to go, but the Court was not
through with them yet. On March 19, a grand jury was convened to assess
Wyatt's criminal responsibility, and they held him over for trial despite Russell's advice against it. In a one-day trial on April 16, Russell again released
Wyatt, later referring to the indictment as "lunacy." In the meantime, they
appealed Russell's original habeas corpus ruling to three Nova Scotia
Supreme Court judges who declined to hear the case, citing lack of jurisdic-
tion. One judge dissented: Drysdale. One last attempt to try Le Médec and
Mackey came six months later, on October 2, 1918, when Police Chief Hanrahan, the man Deputy Mayor Colwell had met at City Hall that fateful

morning, signed an application to proffer a bill of indictment along with the new mayor, A. C. Hawkins. Dr. Hawkins had seen patients throughout the first day at his house, and now, almost a year later, still had a family living with him—against his wishes. The motion was denied and the two men released. Le Médec finally returned to France, where he was allowed to continue working as a captain. Mackey went back to work as a Halifax pilot.

JUDGE DRYSDALE, HOWEVER, was not finished. During the original investigation the owners of both ships made motions to sue and countersue each other for $2 million each. When the ships were sent to the Admiralty section of the Exchequer Courts, Drysdale heard the case. Not surprisingly, in his April 27 ruling, he ruled on behalf of the *Imo*. Hector MacInnis, who took over the *Mont Blanc*'s case when Mellish was made a judge, appealed to the Supreme Court of Canada. It seemed that the partisan politics would never stop. The two English judges upheld Drysdale's ruling. The two French judges dismissed it. The fifth judge, named Francis Anglin, thought both parties were equally responsible and dismissed the original case as having taken place in a poisoned atmosphere. Rather than call it a draw, which would have been a passive upholding of the ruling, the two French judges each then voted with Anglin that both ships were equally responsible.

In January 1919, Burchell appealed the Supreme Court's ruling to the Privy Council in London, the last measure of any Commonwealth lawyer. The *Mont Blanc* hired a British lawyer. For five days in February 1920, Viscount Haldane, Lord Dunedin, Lord Atkinson, Lord Justice Clerk, along with nautical advisors Sir Robert Nelson Ommanney and Commander W. F. Caborne, listened to arguments. They rejected both the previous evidence and the previous arguments, and instead focused on one maritime law. Both ships allowed themselves to get within five hundred feet of each other. Everything that happened after that was a consequence of breaking that first law. "A very serious question arises here, namely, whether having regard to the size of these ships, their speeds, courses and respective bearings of the one to the other, sound and prudent seamanship did not, if this evidence be accurate, imperatively require that each ship should have reversed her engines and gone full speed astern long before they were allowed to approach so close to each other as five hundred feet. . . . both Masters were to blame for not having prevented their respective ships from getting into it. So that beside the question which, if either, of the two ships is blameable for the maneuvers they resorted to in order to escape from the perilous position in which they found themselves almost in the agony of the collision, there is the other and anterior question whether they are not both blameable for the earlier and reciprocal omissions which created that position." The Privy Council's ruling neatly shielded the British Admiralty from any question of responsibility.

The trials were over. Although they provided plenty of details, little satisfaction accompanied the facts, and Halifax could never quite get over the suspicion that the collision had not been an accident. That so many factors conspired against them struck the port as impossible. If even one of the confusions had sorted themselves out—if either ship had made the nets that day, if there had been a rule about outgoing ships, if Beazley had let Wyatt know about the *Imo,* if it had been cold and cloudy, if one of the pilots had been less experienced and less confident, if they had hit the second hold and not the first—the list was long—the two ships might have passed without incident. But accidents on the scale of the explosion are rarely the result of one factor. If one thing goes wrong, an accident can usually be averted. It is the misalignment of three or four factors that causes accidents. Halifax had plenty to spare.

# Chapter Twenty

# The Tree at Boston Common

THE RELATIONSHIP BETWEEN BOSTON and Halifax continued long after the volunteers left. From 1918 to 1924 the Halifax-Massachusetts Relief Committee continued to work with the city to improve the lives of survivors and the general health conditions in Halifax. Ratshesky returned to Halifax in early January 1918 and devised the plan to provide the $500,000 worth of furniture (they only needed $250,000). The committee designated $25,000 to assist those newly blinded and provided the city with access to some of America's most experienced rehabilitation workers. In 1919 they promised $50,000 a year for the next five years along with $15,000 from the Canadian government and $10,000 from the Nova Scotian government to improve general health conditions, which focused on training more social workers and treating tuberculosis. In total, the Halifax-Massachusetts Relief Committee raised $716,000—all of it donated.

In 1918 when the Spanish flu hit Nova Scotia and Massachusetts, Nova Scotia sent a party of doctors down to assist, continuing the conversation between the cities. Then, in December 1918, Halifax sent Boston a Christmas tree to say thank you to the people of Massachusetts. The tradition was reinstated in 1971. In many large cities, including Boston, the local news covers the annual lighting of the Christmas tree as a festive kickoff to the holiday season. In Halifax, the ritual is a little earlier and a lot more sober, as reporters remind viewers of the explosion's devastation, but it is not all tragedy. They also cover the logistics of shipping a fifty-foot tree to Boston and the family who donate a tree from their land. Many people offer the tree to honor someone in their family. Others do it to be part of a tradition or just to say thank you. Either way, there is something poignant about watching a fifty-foot tree fall. In 2004 a stevedore told a local paper that the two-ton tree was the favored cargo. "This simple, beautiful tree touches us all. . . . No other container brings as much happiness to us. We all stop what we are doing and just focus on the tree." Each year on the first Saturday in December people arrive at Boston Common to watch the illumination of thousands of tiny blinking lights. It is funny how, more than 120 years after Edison invented the incandescent bulb, something as simple as turning on a light switch can still fill us with awe. Jim Mahar, a relative of Billy and Charles Duggan, once told a reporter that the act of remembering the explosion was a tribute to what he called quiet courage. "It's not the courage that allows you to run into a burning building. It's the kind that allows you to accept the unacceptable, bear the unbearable, keep going."

# Epilogue

ALL OLD SOLDIERS bear scars. Halifax has many, but the scar from the explosion is its worst. In 1918, what was left of Richmond was razed and turned over to city planners and Thomas Adams, a British town planner working out of Ottawa. Adams, who was put in charge of the redevelopment, was influential in the garden city movement, which believed that it was essential for a city's health to create small satellite cities that favored front lawns and boulevards. Adams softened the grid by adding a series of diagonal and rounded streets that ringed Needham Hill, making it easier for pedestrians, horses, and even cars to cross the steep hill. George Ross, a partner in the Montreal firm of MacDonald & Ross, designed the houses—six different styles each containing two, four, or six units. They were built of a new material called Hydrostone, a precursor to cinderblocks. By adding wood and stucco, porches and terraces, Ross gave the houses a Tudor feel more familiar to Montreal than Nova Scotia—but there was just enough of a British cottage look that they found their place in the city's architectural vocabulary, if not its heart. The new development of 324 houses, with its concrete sidewalks, planted boulevards, and paved roads, came to be known simply as the Hydrostone. The houses were clean, bright, and resisted fire. Halifax promoted the planned community as something new and progressive, two words Nova Scotians generally mistrust, but many survivors who took houses there were devoted to them. Some families continue to live there today. The Halifax Relief Commission fostered community events, such as gardening competitions, to help the survivors regain some sense of their lost community. From 1919 to 1921, displaced families began applying for rental units, and eventually the commission offered the houses for sale to their inhabitants. The Hydrostone, however, was only one part of Richmond and not the central part. At the core of the old neighborhood were the streets overlooking the harbor—Russell, Kaye, Young, Veith, Albert, Hanover, Ross, Kenny, Graves, Roome, Duffus. These streets were rebuilt too with MacDonald & Ross houses, but with other houses mixed in. Residents continue to find artifacts from the explosion. When my nephew moved from Vancouver to a house on Merkel Street in 1999, he complained to his neighbor that the house was built on landfill and every time he dug in his garden he came up with metal and glass. His neighbor informed him that it was the same throughout the neighborhood—all the result of the explosion. Another friend dug up a twisted fork and a heavy chunk of what he believes to be the *Mont Blanc*.

Curiously missing from the redevelopment was the name *Richmond*. It disappeared along with the Richmond Wharf, Richmond Street, and Richmond Printing. The absence of *Richmond* left the lower streets without a name and they were subsumed instead under the more general *North End*. Until I began to do research for this book, I had no idea where Richmond was. I had always pictured the explosion from the harbor, from the Dartmouth side. When I first walked through the streets looking for the houses of people whose stories I was researching, I was shocked by just how close the houses were to the har-

Building the Hydrostone. The new houses, built to resist fire, were assigned by the Relief Committee.

bor. The Duggan houses, torn down and replaced by the Halifax shipyard, were particularly close, nearly on top of the wharves.

Although Richmond technically started at North Street, the neighborhood did not really start until Russell Street, where Helen Clark lived, next to the lane leading to the Barracks flagpole. The explosion occurred where the dry dock is now, at the bottom of where Richmond Street used to be—where the Hillis boys watched from the window and where people lined the fences of the cattle pen. The shipyards, which were built afterward, tore out the low slope that ran to the water and installed a cement retaining wall along the edge of Barrington Street, an unnatural (and unkempt) division that separates the neighborhood from its industrial neighbor. Like Africville, which was torn down in 1970, little consideration was given to the North End by its industrial neighbors, even though many of its workers continued to live and work in both. Despite the high-tech equipment now installed in the updated shipyards, a rusty fence and the same crumbling cement wall give that section of Barrington Street a de- serted, uncared-for feeling, unlike the tight community of Richmond.

The MacKay Bridge, which opened in July 1970 and never fell down, marks the end of Richmond. The bridge, still called the new bridge, is named after the former chairman who oversaw the building of both bridges, A.

The Hydrostone was meant to rebuild both houses and community. Pictured here is a man standing in front of 17 Kane Place, the winning garden in a local competition.

Murray MacKay. Until her death in 2000, Helena Duggan was annoyed that the city had not named it the Richmond Bridge. I agree with her.

Although unhurt, Helena Duggan would awake at night frightened for much of her childhood: "After that I always was scared during the night. I'd often wake from a dream all shaken and ask my Mum if it would be daytime soon." Other survivors complained of the same trauma. Many children of survivors also had to learn to live with their parents' anxiety attacks. Some parents could not abide any kind of loud or sudden noises; others could not bear to be separated from their children. Some awakened their children and dressed them in winter clothes each time there was thunder. One doctor hanged himself after returning to his office in Cape Breton. At least one woman had to be admitted to a psychiatric hospital. Unlike her parents, who never spoke of it, Helena liked to talk about the explosion. "Sometimes I sit here and think about it and I make myself faint and I stop, you know." At eighty-two, she said, "I can still remember the explosion like it just happened yesterday." Helena Duggan died in Halifax in October 2000.

After the explosion, Lottie Duggan bore five more children with Billy but she never searched for the baby they had left in the basement. She told her youngest son, Harry, that she could not bear the disappointment of losing the baby twice. Harry remembers Lottie as an easygoing and gentle mother. Like so many other survivors, she was frightened by storms and loud noises, and bothered by her injuries. Billy, who lost all of his ribbons and medals save one, took a job running the city's boilers at City Field, where the family also lived until Billy's death in 1949. Kenneth, Helena's little brother, grew up to work as a mechanic for the city alongside his father. His ability to remain calm in a crisis was appreciated by his family. Harry described Kenny as "the family godfather . . . the guy you would go to." He certainly showed those qualities as a little boy, digging through rubble in search of his mother. Lottie Duggan died in 1965, shortly after her skin discharged its final piece of glass. She was eighty-three. She and Billy are buried together in the fourth section of the Gate of Heaven Cemetery on the Old Windsor Highway.

Charles Duggan sold the ferry business to George Dauphinee in Dartmouth. For much of his life, he supported himself by playing pool and cards. Perhaps he felt that, having almost lost his life, he could afford to gamble with it. He later remarried and had a son, Charles Jr. He is also buried at Gate of Heaven Cemetery beside his second wife Jean and not far from Billy.

The Mi'kmaq settlement as Turtle Grove was, as my father told me, devastated in the explosion. It was never rebuilt. By the time of the explosion, the land was already privately owned. There is some dispute as to the numbers of Mi'kmaqs killed. Alan Ruffman has found many names left off the original official list. William, Blair, and Madeline Paul were all taken to the hospital, where the baby Madeline would stay for eighteen months. She was permanently scarred on her leg and back. William was for the most part uninjured, but Blair had to have his leg and arm sewn back onto his body. Incredibly, their mother did not lose her pregnancy.

Helen Clark, the little girl with the red bow, moved to New York in 1929 and went to work on Wall Street. During World War II, she worked for the British Information Service as a stenographer and courier. When the war ended, she worked as a vice president of an insurance company. She married and had one son. She later taught at Acadia University in Nova Scotia, where she died in 1986 at the age of seventy-seven. In 1963 Helen wrote an animated letter to her cousin when she read about her grandmother in Michael Bird's book *The Town that Died*. "I remember so many things, since reading that book. Some of the things he speaks of at Camp Hill are before my eyes again. I have often thought that what went on there that day, and the blizzard next day, deserved a book by themselves." I hope that I have fulfilled her wish.

In 1918 Frederick McKelvey Bell used his experiences in the explosion as the basis for another novel, *A Romance of the Halifax Disaster*. It is told from the point of view of a young woman. It is a great loss that he did not write more about his own work organizing the medical response. In 1919 he left the service. He died in 1931 at the age of fifty-three.

Dr. William Edwards Ladd's experiences treating burned children in Halifax helped him to become an expert in fluid and electrolyte imbalances in children, confirming for him that the difference between adult and children's surgery was not only one of size but one of relationship. Ladd was promoted to instructor of surgery in 1918, to chief of surgical service in 1927, and made a clinical professor of surgery at Harvard in 1931. In 1941 he and Dr. Robert Gross published *Abdominal Surgery and Childhood*, a text that was soon found in the office of every pediatric specialist. The same year, Harvard established a chair of pediatric surgery in his name. According to Dr. Hardy Hendren, 85 percent of North American pediatric surgeons in the 1990 descended directly from Dr. Ladd, including my father-in-law, Dr. David Murphy, who brought Ladd to my attention and who interested me in the medical aspect of the story. Dr. C. Everett Koop, who met regularly with Ladd as a young doctor, said that Ladd never went into detail about his experiences in Halifax, except to say that he treated many burned children and that when he explained the early difficulties he faced in pediatric surgery, Ladd would always end his story the same way. "I confirmed all that with the fluid balance problems with children in Halifax." In Ladd's obituary in the *Journal of Pediatric Surgery*, Donald Watson wrote, "Dr. Ladd brought the diagnosis and management of surgical lesions of infancy and childhood into new perspective. Indeed, his pioneer efforts really initiated pediatric surgery as a separate discipline in the Western Hemisphere. Under his direction, and that of his immediate associates and pupils throughout the world, vast improvements in child health were realized through description and standardization of a wide variety of surgically correctible diseases and abnormalities." Ladd retired in 1945 and died in 1967 at the age of eighty-six. He is considered the father of pediatric surgery.

On July 25, 1919, Jean Lindsay sat at her desk and wrote out her account. "At the time I felt an obsession to write this account. I wrote it all at once, only stopping to eat one meal & when I reached this page apparently the obsession had ceased." She later married and moved to New Rochelle, New York, where she worked as a librarian. Charles Patrick Wiswell, the boy whose hands Jean Lindsay had held on the bed on her second night, the boy who "could not speak plainly but who swore fluently," died a week later from blood poisoning. He had lost his eye in a wound that traveled down the side of his face. His father searched for him at Camp Hill and, although he did not initially recognize him, reunited with his son shortly before his death.

Ginger Fraser worked the rest of the week of December 10 with the Relief Committee at the City Club, where he heard "many weird and true stories of the disaster." He reported later that even after his time at the morgue, he still found it hard to believe that "such a terrible thing had happened and that so many were killed." Everett Covey, with whom Ginger wandered around the city, died of meningitis shortly afterward. Fraser attributed Covey's exposure to the meningitis to their explorations that day. Covey, like so many others who died later from possible peripheral complications attributed to the explosion, is not included in the death toll. On a similar note, many survivors claimed that their friends and relatives died young, but to my knowledge no study has been done to prove or disprove anecdotal evidence. It would certainly be interesting to know if those who did live through the greatest explosion of their time, suffered injuries that shortened their life spans.

Billy Wells, the driver of the *Patricia*, was in and out of hospitals for eleven months. His house was wrecked, but his wife survived. His arm never recovered. When he returned to work in June as a taxi driver, he lasted only a summer because his hand and arm were too weak to change gears. In the winter he discovered that he could not drive in the snow either. Almost a year after the explosion, his files indicated that he was filling in at the fire station because so many men were out with the Spanish influenza, but he could not work overnight at the fire station because he could not dress himself. In 1919 he accepted a $1,000 lump-sum settlement rather than train at the Technical College in steam engineering. After Wells was discharged from the hospital, the Halifax Fire Department presented him with the steering wheel of the *Patricia,* which he kept until his death in 1971. It now hangs in the Lady Hammond Road Fire Station. He and Jack MacKeen, the teenager who first treated him, remained in contact for the rest of their lives.

May Sexton, vice president of the Halifax Red Cross, traveled ceaselessly across Nova Scotia giving lectures promoting the Red Cross until she died suddenly in 1923 from uremic poisoning, a complication of kidney disease. The Nova Scotia Technical Institute began admitting women in 1950.

The head of the VADs, Clara MacIntosh, went on to become a published writer and poet. Her plays were produced in Halifax, where she often appeared on stage, and her poems were published in the local papers.

Florence Murray, the fourth-year student who became the anesthetist at Camp Hill Hospital, was sent to Lockport, Nova Scotia, in 1918. The local doctor and much of the town were suffering from Spanish influenza. With most doctors overseas and the rest fighting the flu, the provincial health examiner asked her to go. When one Lockport man heard that a female doctor was coming, he complained that he would have "no petticoat doctor around him if he contracted the disease. He did, but by that time he had changed his mind about petticoat doctors." Murray traveled to Korea in 1921 and served as a missionary. In 1942, captured by the Japanese and held under house arrest, she wrote a memoir, which was confiscated and destroyed. The Japanese eventually bartered her life for prisoners of war, and she was freed. She returned to Korea in 1947, where she worked until 1969. When she returned to North America, she rewrote her memoirs and published them in 1974. She died in 1975.

Dr. George Cox continued his practice in Nova Scotia until he died on January 6, 1953, at the age of eighty-two. He was well-loved and respected as a man of science and medicine, who continued to practice in both Nova Scotia and, later, Florida. He was a member of the Nova Scotia Institute of Science and the Nova Scotia Historical Society. He wrote about science, history, and politics. In his obituary, the writer noted that the oyster, *Oystra coxae,* which he discovered off the coast of Florida, was named after him.

Elizabeth Fraser, the teenage girl who searched for her brother Arthur, picked up the paper on December 6, 1971, and read the memoirs of a soldier who mentioned a young girl searching for her brother. "I never knew who she was but to me she was a heroine." She recognized Donald Morrison as the soldier who had let her in to find her brother Arthur and wrote to thank him for his kindness.

The *Imo* sat grounded on the Dartmouth Shore until it was salvaged, returned to New York, and renamed the *Guvernoren*. She worked as a whaling ship until almost four years to the day after the explosion, December 3, 1921, when she wrecked off Port Stanley, in the Falkland Islands.

As for explosives in the Halifax harbor, it would take more than twenty years for the Canadian military to build a proper magazine outside the city limits. Magazine Hill, on the northern side of Tuft's Cove, continues to hold explosives and munitions. As Dartmouth has grown, businesses and houses have once again sprung up around the magazine.

The *Mont Blanc*'s anchor sits where it landed near the Northwest Arm. The gun, which landed at Albro Lake Road, was on display for many years in front of the Dartmouth Library, where I used to play on it as a child. It was recently returned to the beach where it fell that morning.

The unidentified bodies are buried on a modest patch of land on Bayers Road across from the rock outcropping that signifies the entrance to the South Shore. To enter the graveyard, visitors must park in the driveway to an apartment building and enter through the side gate. A modest monument sits in the middle of the field, but, unlike other memorials, there are no names to represent those buried there. Particularly now, when names have become the simple defining element of so many memorials, the modesty and anonymity leaves visitors with a terrible sense of injustice. Marked gravesites can be found in the Mount Olivet and St. John's cemeteries.

In July 2002, the Halifax Relief Commission Fund finally ran out of money, but the Canadian government continued distributing the pensions to the remaining survivors. In 2004, three people were still receiving a monthly check.

The official city memorial to the Halifax explosion sits at the top of Needham Park. Each year on the morning of December 6, survivors and the people of Halifax gather to participate in a memorial service. Survivors continue to attend. Standing in front of the bells and looking straight through the trees, one has a clear view of what used to be Richmond Street and Pier 6, straight across the Narrows to Dartmouth, where Charles Duggan landed in the field next to what was left of the *Grace Darling*.

# Acknowledgments

This book could not have been written without the formidable researchers and writers who preceded me. Between the libraries and archives in Nova Scotia, there are thousands of pages of original documents, and my predecessors' constant sifting helped to guide me to the proper documents many times over. In 1918 Archibald MacMechan, the official historian of the explosion, kicked off the preservation of the facts by interviewing hundreds of people connected to the explosion. The file of his rejection letters from publishers was one file among many in his holdings at PANS that broke my heart. I hope that I have honored his diligence by using so many details and accounts from the fascinating files he compiled. Janet Kitz's dedication to the subject and to the survivors is also particularly noteworthy. Kitz intervened between local inertia and time, interviewing survivors and publishing their stories. Without her, much of the history would have been lost. C.D. Howell and Alan Ruffman's commitment to getting the science straight has allowed me to walk in unannounced and steal all their hard-won numbers and facts, for which I am grateful. Their book, *Ground Zero: A Reassessment of the 1917 Explosion in the Halifax Harbour,* provided many insights and clarifications. I have bought many copies of out-of-print books since I started this project, many of them published shortly after the explosion, but *Ground Zero* proved the rarest book of all. Finally, I was lucky enough to borrow a copy from Carmen Moir of the Dartmouth Historical Society. I thank him. Jim Simpson took me on a guided tour of Richmond while I was considering writing this book. Walking down Russell Street, where Helen Clark and Helena Duggan ran, made me realize that I had been looking at the explosion from the wrong side of the harbor. A conversation with James and Rowena Maher reminded me many times that everyone I was writing about was not a fictional character, but my former neighbors. Harry Duggan graciously welcomed me, a stranger, into his home and shared his knowledge of his family's experiences with all the hallmark openness and friendliness of Atlantic Canadians. I hope that I have added to his family's story. The work of Greg King and the senior history students of Prince Andrew High School on the Halifax Explosion Research Partnership Project provided me with further details of Helena Duggan's day, recorded in interviews with Janet Kitz.

When I said that I was going to write this book, my father-in-law, Dr. David Murphy, immediately provided me with the information about Dr. W. E. Ladd, indirectly providing one of the most fascinating and least-known stories connected to the explosion. He and his wife, Dr. Sonia Salisbury, have both patiently answered all my questions about medicine and the body. Their friend and colleague Dr. Robert Replogle also provided insight into Ladd and his place in the world of pediatric surgery. Former U.S. Surgeon General Dr. C. Everett Koop kindly told me about his days as a young doctor and his luncheons with Ladd, and confirmed details that I was at a loss to confirm otherwise. Matt Murphy, my brother-in-law, gave up much of one summer to research the explosion. His keen instinct for story and character, and his patience, kept the chase as enjoyable as it was productive. It can be mentally exhausting to spend every day immersed in other people's worst moments. By sharing his favorite (and secret) swimming hole, he provided a welcome restorative to the end of each day. I still encourage him to write his own book.

All the archivists I worked with never failed to go a little further than I asked. Their commitment to and patience with the public always impressed me. In particular, the staff at the Public Archives with their labyrinthine minds provided instruction, direction, and photocopies, the last requiring much more skill and patience than it sounds. I am particularly indebted to Barry Smith, who took my phone calls, and Darlene Brine, who, on my last day of research, spent much of one afternoon to source one word in John Clark's letter and who asked if I wanted to see some MacMechan files she had come across that morning. Opening that box was a eureka moment and, needless to say, required that I stay in Halifax. Philip Harlting and Gary Shutlak also provided much patient direction and redirection.

At the advice of another relative, Michael Novak, I was able to consult with Pierre Pelletier, who took me through the ABCs of explosions. His knowledge, as a chemical engineer who works with military explosives and as a former member of the Canadian Forces Naval Reserve who sailed in Halifax, greatly guided me and provided me with some of the most interesting material. I thank them both. Drs. Deborah Warden and Charles Engel of the Defense and Veterans Brain Injury Center at the Walter Reed Army Medical Center answered my many questions about the mental confusion following the explosion.

My friends and family offered encouragement, support, and diversion while I was writing, particularly my readers—Geoff Rowan; my sisters Jennifer and Moira, who offered insights and helpful critiques; and my brother Adrian, who provided harbor and weather charts. I thank my adopted sister Debra Thier for her support over the years.

This book has seen the hands of various editors at different stages. Jake Klisivitch discussed writing a proposal. Chris Bucci bought it at HarperCollins before moving on. Publisher Iris Tupholme kept it alive. Michele Lee Amundsen and Jim Gifford brought much skill and patience to the manuscript. All I can say about publisher George Gibson is that he is exactly who I hoped to find. His skill and knowledge are matched only by his forbearance, enthusiasm, and integrity.

And finally I would like to thank Luke Murphy, who navigates tricky waters with grace, good faith, and a steady heart.

# Accident or Sabotage?

In June 1922 a report of a suicide in Seattle appeared in the Halifax papers.* The article claimed that a Finnish chemist named William Johnson, alias Mike Murphy, alias N. Prymatchenk, killed himself outside of Seattle in May 1922. The FBI was investigating his death because before his suicide he had confessed to causing an explosion in Halifax. " 'I had thirty five pounds of a more dangerous explosive than that left after we blew up three ships in Halifax harbor during the war,' Johnson is alleged to have said. 'If they had not discharged me, there would have been more ships blown up. We will be better prepared for them the next time they start a war.' " His suicide note read, "It's no use."

People immediately speculated that William Johnson was John Johansen, the wheelsman for the *Imo*. He could have easily killed Hayes and Captain From and then sailed the *Imo* straight into the *Mont Blanc*. The local newspapers discounted this theory because the trials provided consistent details about the lead-up to the collision. One of the more compelling facts was that Pilot Renner, who was navigating the *Clara*, recognized Hayes's voice minutes before the explosion. Plus Andrew Johansen, Captain From's steward, testified that he saw Hayes on the bridge after the collision. Reporters found no record of a man by the name of William Johnson in the local transports, although there were nine William Johnsons listed in the city directory. Plus there were only two ships involved, not three, and neither of them were British. For some reason, the reports failed to mention that John Johansen was only twenty-seven years old in 1922. William Johnson/Mike Murphy/N. Prymatchenk was forty. Without further information, the story faded, even if the feeling that the explosion was sabotage continued.

If there was a link between Germany and the explosion, Washington never found it. In 1939, the U.S. government published the results of the Mixed Claims Commission of

*For complete transcript of article, see Notes to Appendix A.

*Accident or Sabotage?*

USA and Germany, a commission that pored over all the German records during the war looking for evidence of sabotage. Although they quickly discovered that Black Tom and the Canadian Car foundry explosions were the result of sabotage, they found no evidence linking Germany to Halifax.

*Appendix B*

# Preparing for the Future

On November 21, 1918, ten days after Armistice was declared, the Massachusetts committee on Public Safety officially dissolved. It was the first state to start a Committee and the first to dissolve it. Hundreds of people from across the state volunteered to represent their towns, sit on committees, and to act in the event of an emergency. And while the explosion in Halifax represented perhaps its most dramatic effort, it was just a fraction of what could have been achieved if the war had taken a different turn and come to Massachusetts. Despite the suggestions by John Moors, who was part of the Committee of Coordination of Aid Societies as well as the Red Cross, and who recommended that a permanent emergency committee be formed, the government saw the committee as a wartime measure.

Governor McCall spoke at the committee's dissolution: "The Commonwealth contributed her share to a fitting victory; the victory has been won, and, as this was essentially a war committee, it has been suggested that the time has come for it to terminate its existence."

Over the next sixty years, U.S. disaster relief was run by states and volunteer organizations, resulting in a disconnected, messy approach that duplicated some efforts while neglecting others. The federal government, which had enacted separate pieces of legislation to deal with specific problems, such as flooding and hurricanes, did not empower a federal department to prepare and deal with disasters until 1979, when President Jimmy Carter amalgamated the work of more than one hundred separate agencies under the control of one: the Federal Emergency Management Agency (FEMA).

In Canada the federal government recognized the importance of emergency planning and response as early as 1957, but the programs were geared toward war-related events, weakly funded, and without much authority. In 1980 the Joint Emergency Preparedness Program (JEPP) was created to oversee programs and training in the provinces. JEPP is currently run by the Public Safety and Emergency Preparedness Canada Department, which deals with emergencies only at the request of provincial authorities.

Since the 1960s, disaster research departments have popped up at universities all across the United States and Canada where they study the Halifax explosion because to this day it it remains the biggest conventional explosion to detonate in the midst of a civilian population and because of the volume of testimony recorded by survivors. Halifax, with its old-world values, immediately appointed a historian, Archibald MacMechan, to gather facts. MacMechan interviewed hundreds of people—volunteers, military men, survivors, doctors, nurses, VADs, artists, and anyone who took the time to send in their story or who submitted to an interview. By preserving people's stories, MacMechan also preserved scientific facts that researchers and writers, including me, have used to re-create that day.

The explosion's most famous student is J. Robert Oppenheimer, who in 1942, using the data from 1917, extrapolated the numbers to calculate the aftereffects of a nuclear explosion. In an eerie coincidence, three years later when he detonated the first nuclear weapon in the Nevada desert, a group of politicians were invited to witness the historic explosion. Among them was the British ambassador to America, Lord Halifax. Two months later the United States dropped two separate nuclear weapons over Hiroshima and Nagasaki. Each bomb was five times more powerful than the *Mont Blanc* cargo. Since then more than 128,000 nuclear warheads have been built. There is still no firm data on what happens to our brains when exposed to air blasts; only recently have people begun to study the physical effects of these blasts.

*Appendix C*

# Francis Mackey Interview

Francis Mackey continued to work as a pilot in Halifax harbor for the rest of his life. In 1958 he gave a radio interview to the CBC. With the CBC's kind permission, I reprint it here.*

MACKEY: I came in on the *Mont Blanc*. The ship in the first place, a ship bound in was supposed to have the right of way. No other ship was allowed to pass her coming out and they did not know the *Imo* was in the port and that seems silly but that's exactly what [happened]. The reason they did not know—it was anchored in the sou'west part of the basin and she was behind the hill. Unless you went way up on the top of the hill or out in a boat, you couldn't see that ship. We arrived on the examination ground. Ships were only allowed into Bedford Basin in daylight. It was late in the afternoon. And the man from the examining boat came alongside as they all had to do to find out what the ship's cargo was and so on. Well I said, "Just wait a minute. You're standing on top of five hundred tons of TNT now, both of us. The rest of her cargo is picric acid, dry and wet. And benzol on deck. Now," I says, "that's a damned bad cargo." I said, "What I'd like you to do is ask the examining officer aboard the ship there. Ask or tell him there that I expect to get special orders for this ship through the night. Ask him if he can arrange it." Next morning, daylight came and I was ordered to get under way. I asked him, "Are there any special orders in way of protection of the ship?" And he said, "No sir." We come up, arrived up at the Narrows. We were coming up as slow as we possibly could [just steerage were on her]. And the other ship was coming down on his wrong side, answering my one blast with two, decidedly opposite to what he should do. He should have answered me with one and kept close to the Halifax side. Instead of that he had passed a ship on the wrong side up above in the basin, above the Narrows, and when he got down he kept up towards Tuft's Cove way. The water looked wider to him. When he got down a little further he found it was narrowing up across it, see and he got cold feet and pulled it full speed astern when he was on my starboard side and that's when he cut her into me.

*Courtesy of CBC Radio, originally broadcast on CBC in 1958.

CBC: That's when you hit?

MACKEY: Yeah, he cut her right into me. It was like taking a horse by the bridle and saying I'm not going that way, see. Well we stood there as long as we could. The fire on deck, the benzol was burning. The friction between the two plates of the two ships created a spark. We stood there until we couldn't stand there any longer. I said, "The only thing to do is save your crew." I said, "Get them in the boats." So we filled up one boat with about 20 men, 21. And the boat I was in and the Captain, last to go, we had about 20 men or 21, perhaps 22. And we pulled away from the ship. There was a navy tug going down past us and we hailed him and I waved to him, "Take us in tow." Hollered but you might as well as holler at a post. Nobody could hear. Too much racket. Chasing him the second time put us on the Dartmouth side. We had no room to maneuver to pile them in. The only thing was to get them on the beach, turn the men ashore. The Captain was driving his men and I went up on the banks, looking at the thing, expecting her to go off any time and the Captain come and put his hand on my shoulder. "Go on, boy, go on." So we both turned around to run and we did not get any distance. Just as quick as that we were knocked down. I had a raincoat on here and it was taken off the same as if you had a rusty knife and cut it right around here.

CBC: Right around your waist?

MACKEY: Right around. We were knocked right down until the tree fell over us, just like a miracle. The branches on it were bigger than my arm. He seemed to be between two and I seemed to be between another two. My cap was gone off my head that I had on. And his coat was gone off. I knew, I was smelling this stuff all the time, I knew I was alive and after a while I stood up. I guess I must have been down there ten or fifteen minutes.

CBC: How do you think the collision could have been avoided? What should have been done?

MACKEY: By not allowing the *Imo* out. He come out on his wrong side. Broke the rules come on the wrong side of a steamer on the wrong side up above in the Narrows and then come down on the wrong side again and struck me. He wasn't supposed to be coming out. There was no ship allowed to come out if the signals and all had been carried out by the dockyard. There was no ship allowed to come out when a ship incoming was bound in. Had the right of way myself but she come out.

CBC: Once the collision took place, could anything have been done to prevent the explosion?

MACKEY: No. No. The explosion she was out of business. Couldn't do anything with her. No one was throwing water on her.

CBC: Could she have been taken in tow?

MACKEY: Well it would . . . was just a question . . . you wouldn't have been time to take her in tow and take her anywhere.

# By the Numbers

Location: Halifax, Nova Scotia
Date: December 6, 1917
Time of Explosion: 9:04:35 a.m.
Total Explosives: 2,925 tons
Killed: over 2,000
Wounded: over 6,000
Homeless: 9,000
Fully Blinded: 41
Half-Blinded: 249

## Morgue Statistics—1918

*Known Dead and Missing*

| | | | |
|---|---|---|---|
| Male | 933 | | 58% |
| Female | 678 | | 42% |
| Total | 1,611 | | 100% |

| Age | Male | Female | Total |
|---|---|---|---|
| 0–14 | 264 (16%) | 218 (14%) | (30%) |
| 15–40 | 324 (20%) | 242 (15%) | (35%) |
| Over 40 | 211 (13%) | 155 (10%) | (23%) |
| Age unknown | 134 | 63 | (12%) |

*Race*

| | |
|---|---|
| Caucasian | 1,586 (98%) |
| African | 10 (1%) |
| Asian | 3 (0%) |
| Indian | 11 (1%) |
| Malay | 1 (0%) |
| | 1,611 |

## By the Numbers

### Marital Status

| | |
|---|---|
| Single | 820 (51%) |
| Married | 571 (35%) |
| Widowed | 64 (4%) |
| Not stated | 156 (10%) |
| | 1,611 |

### Religion

| | |
|---|---|
| Church of England | 437 (27%) |
| Roman Catholic | 538 (33%) |
| Presbyterian | 194 (12%) |
| Methodist | 121 (8%) |
| Baptist | 60 (4%) |
| Lutheran | 9 (1%) |
| Congregational | 2 (0%) |
| Other Denomination | 35 (2%) |
| Not stated | 215 (13%) |
| | 1,611 |

### Occupation

| | |
|---|---|
| Professionals | 13 (1%) |
| Tradesmen | 21 (1%) |
| Clerks | 43 (3%) |
| Farmers | 3 (0%) |
| Fishermen | 1 (0%) |
| Craftsmen | 120 (7%) |
| Miners | 1 (0%) |
| Laborers | 165 (10%) |
| Railwaymen | 39 (2%) |
| Housewives | 331 (21%) |
| Domestics | 10 (1%) |
| Students | 18 (1%) |
| Seamen | 113 (7%) |
| Soldiers | 21 (1%) |
| Miscellaneous | 85 (5%) |
| No Occupation | 627 (39%) |
| | 1,611 |

### Age

| Age | Male | Female |
|---|---|---|
| Under 1 year | 36 (2%) | 31 (2%) |
| One year | 23 (1%) | 18 (1%) |
| Two years | 29 (2%) | 20 (1%) |
| Three years | 19 (1%) | 20 (1%) |
| Four years | 22 (1%) | 14 (1%) |
| 5–9 years | 84 (5%) | 72 (4%) |

| | | |
|---|---|---|
| 10–14 | 51 (3%) | 43 (3%) |
| 15–19 | 61 (4%) | 43 (3%) |
| 20–29 | 142 (9%) | 108 (7%) |
| 30–39 | 121 (8%) | 91 (6%) |
| 40–49 | 100 (6%) | 60 (4%) |
| 50–59 | 55 (3%) | 40 (2%) |
| 60–69 | 33 (2%) | 29 (2%) |
| 70–79 | 16 (1%) | 18 (1%) |
| 80–89 | 6 (0%) | 6 (0%) |
| 90–100 | 1 (0%) | 2 (0%) |
| Not stated | 134 (8%) | 63 (4%) |
| Total | 933 (58%) | 678 (42%) |
| | 1,611 | |

*Other Statistics*

| | |
|---|---|
| Identified | 959 (60%) |
| Unidentified | 242 (15%) |
| Total buried | 1,201 |
| Bodies known to be missing | 410 |
| Total known dead a/o 1918 | 1,611 |
| Dead a/o 2004 | 1,952 |

# Wreck Commission Participants and Witnesses

Sources for Quotes from Witnesses Testifying at Wreck Commission, Appeals and Habeas Corpus: Unless otherwise noted, all quotes and observations about the events in the harbor on December 6, 1917, are taken from testimony at the Wreck Commission, Appeals (NAC) and Habeas Corpus Trial (HRL).

Abbott, George: coxswain, Despatch boat
Babineau, Joseph: chief steward, *Musquash*
Beazley, Edward: clerk, Pilotage Office
Bell, F. H.: lawyer who represented the City of Halifax at the Wreck Commision
B'Jonnas, Peter Antonsin: second mate, *Imo*
Brannen, Walter: first mate, *Stella Maris*
Brun, Louis: third engineer, *Mont Blanc*
Burchell, Charles: lawyer representing the *Mont Blanc* and William Hayes
Cluney, A.: lawyer who represented the office of Attorney General of Nova Scotia
Cope, Willard: chemist and explosives expert
Creighton, James: secretary, Halifax Pilotage Commission
Currie, Norman A: government steamship inspector
Demers, Captain L. A.: Dominion wreck commissioner and nautical advisor to Judge Drysdale
Dixon, George: McKeen Shipbuilding Co., Dartmouth
Drysdale, Arthur: judge, Supreme Court of Nova Scotia and Exchequer Court
Dustan, Henry B: terminal agent, C.G.R.
Eldridge, Captain George Bernard: naval intelligence officer
Flower, Edward N: assistant marine inspector and French Line translator for Aimé Le Médec
Freeman, Terrence: examining officer, RCN

## Wreck Commission Participants and Witnesses

Glotin, Jean Baptiste: first officer, *Mont Blanc*

Hall, Captain Neil: port warden, Halifax

Hall, James: chairman, Halifax Pilotage Commission

Henry, Bert: Burns and Kelleher

Henry, W. A.: lawyer who represented the Canadian federal government at Wreck Commission

Hose, Captain Walter: nautical advisor to Judge Drysdale at Wreck Commission (RCN)

Iceton, Roland, assistant to Commander Wyatt, Mate, RNCVR

Johansen, Andrew: steward, *Imo*

Johansen, John: wheelsman, *Imo*

Johnston, Captain Peter: superintendent of lights and buoys

Johnston, Thomas: boatswain, *Colonne*

Kayford, Alfred: third engineer, *Colonne*

Le Gat, Anton: chief engineer, *Mont Blanc*

Le Médec, Aimé: captain, *Mont Blanc*

Leveque, Joseph: second lieutenant, *Mont Blanc*

Lovett, Arthur G.: customs officer

Mackey, Francis: pilot, *Mont Blanc*

Makiny, John L.: commander, *Neried*

Martin, Captain Edward Harrington: captain superintendent of the Halifax Dockyard

Mayers, Charles John: third officer, *Middleham Castle*

Mc Crossan, Edward: able seaman, SS *Curacus*

Mc Gannon, Charles: former writer in CXO's office

McLaine, Daniel: master, *Douglas H. Thomas*

McKenzie Adams, Lieutenant Arthur: *Acadian*, naval control staff, RNVR

Mellish, Humphrey: lawyer who represented the *Mont Blanc*

Nickerson, William, second mate, *Stella Maris*

Nolan, Joseph: lawyer from New York hired to represent the *Mont Blanc*

Pasco, Frederick C.: acting captain superintendent, dockyard

Pelvadeau, Pierre: sailor, *Mont Blanc*

Price, Richard Henry: secretary to captain superintendent of dockyard

Renner, Edward: pilot, Port of Halifax

Richards, Byrn: third engineer, *Picton*

Robertson, T. R.: lawyer representing Halifax Pilotage Commission

Rourke, John Joseph: chief engineer, *Douglas H. Thomas*

Rudolf, Francis: harbormaster, Halifax

Russell, Judge Benjamin: judge who threw out charges against Mackey, Wyatt, and Le Médec

Serre, Alphonse: wheelsman, *Mont Blanc*

Smith, George: Pickford & Black agent

Smith, Ralph: marine engineer, Burns and Kelleher

Spence, Launcet John: superintendent, Halifax Dry Dock

Sullivan, John: Jutland, Burns & Kelleher

Whitehead, Herbert: RNCVR, duty boat

Wyatt, Commander Frederick Evans: chief examining officer, RCN

# Featured People

| | |
|---|---|
| Archibald, Bertha | assistant pharmacist, Victoria General Hospital |
| Beazley, Edward | young clerk at the pilotage's office |
| Blois, E.L. | provincial commissioner for dependent and neglected children |
| Borden, Sir Robert | prime minister of Canada |
| Brannen, Horatio | captain, *Stella Maris* |
| Brannen, Walter | first mate, *Stella Maris*, son of Horatio Brannen |
| Brooks, Colonel William A. | acting surgeon general of the Commonwealth of Massachusetts |
| Brun, Luis | third engineer, *Imo* |
| Brunt, Albert | volunteer fireman who slid off the side of truck |
| Carstens, C.C. | secretary of the American Red Cross Halifax Emergency Relief Committee and General Secretary, Massachusetts Society for the Prevention of Cruelty |
| Chisholm, Dr. Murdoch | Halifax surgeon whose death was erroneously reported |
| Clark, Helen | St. Joseph's student who jumped out window |
| Colwell, Henry | alderman and deputy mayor of Halifax at time of explosion |
| Condon, Chief Edward | fire chief |
| Covey, Everett | Morris School student who accompanied Ginger Fraser around city |
| Cox, Dr. George | New Glasgow ophthalmologist who performed most eye surgery |
| Dennis, Agnes | president of the Nova Scotia branch of the Red Cross, wife of Senator William Dennis, the publisher of local paper |
| Dickson, Dr. | Dartmouth doctor who operated on dining table on Queen Street |
| Duff, W.A. | assistant chief engineer, Canadian Government Railways |
| Duggan, Baby | second son of Billy and Lottie Duggan |

## Featured People

| | |
|---|---|
| Duggan, Charles | North End ferryman, younger brother of Billy Duggan |
| Duggan, Charles Sr. | father of Charles and Billy Duggan |
| Duggan, Evelyn | sister of Charles and Billy Duggan |
| Duggan, Irene | daughter of Billy and Lottie Duggan |
| Duggan, Kenny | firstborn son of Billy and Lottie Duggan |
| Duggan, Lottie | Billy Duggan's wife, mother of Helena |
| Duggan, Lydia | daughter of Billy and Lottie Duggan |
| Duggan, Reta | wife of Charles Duggan |
| Duggan, Susie | mother of Charles and Billy Duggan |
| Duggan, Vincent | brother of Charles and Billy Duggan |
| Duggan, Warren | son of Charles Duggan |
| Duggan, William "Billy" | former rower and ferryman, older brother of Charles Duggan |
| Endicott, Henry B. | chairman of the Massachusetts Committee on Public Safety |
| Faulkner, Nora | St. Joseph's student and neighbor of Helen Clark |
| Fraser, David | Dalhousie professor who compiled *Medical Aspects of the Halifax Disaster* |
| Fraser, Elizabeth | teenage girl who searched for her brother Arthur's body |
| Fraser, Ginger (R. L.) | Morris School student and cadet |
| Freeman, Terrence | examining officer who inspected *Mont Blanc*'s cargo |
| From, Hakron | captain, *Imo* |
| Gallaway, Alma | sister of Charles and Billy Duggan, wife of Patrick Gallaway |
| Gallaway, Patrick | husband of Alma Gallaway |
| Glotin, Jean | first officer, *Mont Blanc* |
| Graham, George | president, Dominion Atlantic Railway |
| Grant, MacCallum | lieutenant governor of Nova Scotia |
| Hanrahan, Frank | chief of police |
| Harrington, Captain Thomas | physician-in-chief, Massachusetts State Guard, found Martha Manter |
| Harris, Chief Justice Robert | judge who advised John Moors to provide compensation to victims |
| Hayes, C. A. | general manager, Canadian Government Railway |
| Hayes, William | pilot, *Imo* |
| Henneberry, Benjamin | private who confused Annie Liggins with his daughter |
| Hillis, Frank and Gordon | brothers who were at home with measles |
| Howard, C. K. | general agent for Canadian Railways |
| Iceton, Roland | assistant to Chief Examining Officer Wyatt |
| Jackson, James | division manager of Boston metropolitan chapter of the Red Cross |
| Johansen, Andrew | Captain From's steward, *Imo* |
| Johansen, John | wheelsman, *Imo* |

| | |
|---|---|
| Paul, William | boy who warned Turtle Grove of impending explosion |
| Pears, William H. | American Red Cross member from the Boston Provident Association |
| Persons, Frank | director general of civilian relief for American Red Cross |
| Phelan, James | banker and member of the Public Safety Committee who learned of explosion over the private banking wires |
| Quinn, Ellen | sister of Charles and Billy Duggan, mother of Kathleen and Jim, wife of Howard Quinn |
| Ratshesky, Captain Abraham "Cap" | commissioner in charge of the Halifax Relief Expedition, banker, former state senator of Massachusetts |
| Renner, Edward | pilot, SS *Clara* |
| Serre, Alphonse | wheelsman, *Mont Blanc* |
| Sexton, May | vice president of Halifax Red Cross, organized sewing room and dispensary |
| Simmonds, Colonel Ralph | officer in charge of devastated area |
| Smith, George | Pickford & Black agent representing the *Imo* |
| Smith, Stanley | journalist and author of *Heart Throbs of the Halifax Horror* |
| Stone, Professor R. N. | professor in charge of the morgue |
| Symington, Captain | USS *Tacoma*, lent his men to patrol streets on first night |
| Thomas, Dr. Lewis | doctor who saved Dr. Murdoch Chisholm's life |
| Thompson, Colonel W. E. | colonel in charge of street patrol the first night |
| Triggs, T. K. | commander, *Highflyer*, took naval lighter to *Imo* to warn Captain From |
| Upham, Constant | grocer who called fire station to warn of fire |
| Weatherbe, Paul | colonel who headed up early medical response for the city |
| Wells, Billy | fireman, driver of *Patricia* |
| Wyatt, Frederick Evans | chief examining officer of Halifax harbor |
| Yates, George | Prime Minister Borden's secretary |

# Ships

*Curuca,* British supply ship; flew across the harbor and sunk in Tuft's Cove, killing forty-five of her crew

*Douglas H. Thomas,* Dominion coal boat

*Grace Darling,* motorized ferry carrying Charles Duggan

*Highflyer,* British destroyer

*Hilford,* tug left stranded on top of Pier 9

*Imo,* Belgian Relief Ship that collided with *Mont Blanc*

*J.A. McKee,* coal carrier closest to the graving dock, awaiting repairs

*Jutland,* Burns and Keheler repair boat following the *Mont Blanc*

*Middleham Castle,* next to the *J.A. McKee*

*Mont Blanc,* French ship carrying high explosives that collided with *Imo* and which eventually exploded

*Musquash,* trawler turned minesweeper

*Neried,* naval tug

*Niobe,* training base for Canadian navy

*Niobe,* naval lighter/pinnace, small vessel sent to help put out the fire

SS *Clara,* American tramp steamer that preceded the *Mont Blanc* through the Narrows

*Stella Maris,* tug carrying load of stone which tried to help put out the fire

USS *Morrill,* the coast guard cutter that entered the harbor after seeing smoke

USS *Old Colony,* an American passenger steamer that the American army had acquired from the British navy, converted into a hospital ship with the help of the USS *Tacoma*

USS *Tacoma,* third-class cruiser returning from transatlantic escort when saw smoke and headed to Halifax

USS *Von Steuben,* armed troop transport; soldiers patrolled streets of Halifax

For a more complete list of ships, please visit the Web site of the Maritime Museum of the Atlantic at www.museum.gov.ns.ca/mma.

For more views of the explosion, please visit laurammacdonald.com or the Nova Scotia Records & Records Management Web site, www.gov.ns.ca/NSARM/VIRTUAL/EXPLOSION.ASP

*Archives*

BA: Bundesarchiv, Germany
BHS: Boston Historical Society
BPL: Boston Public Library
CBC: Canadian Broadcasting Corporation
CML: Countway Library of Medicine, Harvard
DHM: Dartmouth Heritage Museum
HRL: Halifax Regional Library
MCM: Maritime Command Museum
MMA: Maritime Museum of the Atlantic
NARA: National Archives and Records Administration
NAC: National Library and Archives Canada
NLM: National Library of Medicine
PA: Philadelphia Archives
PANS: Public Archives of Nova Scotia (Nova Scotia Archives and Records Management)
SCA: Simmons College Archives
SLM: State Library of Massachusetts

# Notes

Unless otherwise noted, all names followed by PANS, MG1, are taken from interviews with Archibald MacMechan.

## Introduction

2. Previous bridges: J. P. Martin, *The Story of Dartmouth, Halifax Herald*, May 2, 1985.

3. Chebucto and Safe Bay: When I went to school this was something every school-child learned. I was surprised to find almost the exact line in Archibald MacMechan's manuscript at the Public Archives of Nova Scotia after I had written the first draft of this manuscript. I left it in but acknowledge that, unbeknownst to me, he wrote it first.

3. Eastern and western passages: Interviews with pilots John Bull, Gary O'Donnell, and Captain Peter Davidson. I am particularly indebted to John Bull, who took the time to show me maps and helped me understand the nature of the pilot. Peter Davidson illuminated the difficulties of piloting out of the Basin into the outer harbor. More information was found in J. P. Martin, *The Story of Dartmouth;* T. M. Longstreth, *To Nova Scotia;* and correspondence with Adrian MacDonald, Environment Canada.

4. On the history of Halifax and Dartmouth, sources include A. Wentworth Hamilton Eaton, *Chapters in the History of Halifax, Nova Scotia*, vols. 10–14; H. Chapman, *In the Wake of the Alderney;* J. Fingard, J. Guildford & D. Sutherland, *Halifax, The First 250 Years;* M. Hadley & R. Sarty, *Tin Pots and Pirate Ships: Canadian Naval Forces and German Sea Raiders 1880–1918;* Mrs. W. T. Hallam, *When You Are in Halifax;* T. M. Longstreth, *To Nova Scotia;* A. MacMechan, *The Book of Ultima Thule;* G. Metson, *The Halifax Explosion December 6th 1917;* N. Metzler, *Illustrated Halifax;* J. P. Martin, *The Story of Dartmouth; The Canadian Annual Review of Public Affairs,* 1918; File of Local Council of Women, PANS, Reel 14723.

5. Benjamin Franklin's line in *1776* was "Rebellion is always legal in the first person, such as 'our rebellion.' Only in the third person, 'their rebellion' does it become illegal": S. Edwards & P. Stone, *1776,* 1972. Mark S. Cookman uses it to describe privateers on his website home.tampabay.rr.com/claviger/primer1.htm.

6. I am indebted to Judith Fingard's *The Dark Side of Life in Victorian Halifax* for much of the information on these two neighborhoods—Sailortown and Soldiertown—and the social problems that plagued Halifax. Other records consulted include police records available at PANS. Scattered throughout the files of the Halifax Relief Commission and

the Red Cross are numerous mentions of the soldiers' wives that show a general distrust of and disdain toward them. Further sources include A. Wentworth Hamilton Eaton, *Chapters in the History of Halifax, Nova Scotia*, vol. 13.

7. "a favorite station . . . Melbourne or Sydney": Captain Eldridge, PANS, MG1, vol. 2124, #46.

8. Samuel Cunard founded his steamship line in Halifax. Cunard ships stopped in port every two weeks, en route from London to Boston, bringing with them the first news from the continent, a scarce commodity before telegraphs and telephones. According to the April 1940 edition of *Dots and Dashes*, New York and Boston newspapers were so competitive that they tried everything from sailing crafts out to meet the steamers to releasing carrier pigeons from the steamer's decks to get the news to their readers first. In 1849 while the telegraph was being extended from St. John to Halifax, six papers in New York joined to create what would later become the Associated Press. The Halifax Express was a pony express that ferried the news from incoming steamers to St. John, New Brunswick, where it could be telegraphed to New York. Boston newspapermen were surprised to find the news that they paid to have sent across the Atlantic was already printed on the pages of New York papers even before the Cunard ships landed in Boston.

8. Harbor traffic and shortage of labor statistics: *The Canadian Annual Review of Public Affairs*, 1918.

9. Sources for the Zimmerman affair: National CounterIntelligence, www.fas.org; NARA www.archives.gov.

9. "The U-boats had much more difficulty . . . even a weakly escorted group": M. Hadley & R. Sarty, *Tin Pots and Pirate Ships: Canadian Naval Forces and German Sea Raiders 1880–1918*, p. 199.

10. Jody Shields brought the zeppelins and fear of airplanes to my attention in 2004.

10. Sources for sabotage on the Eastern Seaboard: H. Landau, *The Enemy Within;* J. Witcover, *Sabotage at Black Tom: Imperial Germany's Secret War in America 1914–1917; Mixed Claims Commission United States and Germany*. When the explosion hit Halifax, Colonel W. E. Thompson's first reaction was relief. "At last the war has come to us. I'm glad. People will know we're in it." Halifax Disaster Records Office, PANS, MG1, vol. 2124, #233.

13. "About ten years . . . by a City team": J. MacNeil, *The Story of Dartmouth*, p. 459.

13. Turtle Grove: J. P. Martin, *The Story of Dartmouth; The Mail Star*, December 8, 1964 & December 6, 1997; DHM, History File: Explosion of 1917, *MicMac News,* December 1977; *Micmac-Maliseett Nations News,* May 1991; *Dartmouth This Week*, September 15, 1983; J. Burke, "Investigation of MicMaq Settlement at Turtle Grove," DHM.

13. Effects of mustard gas: B. Shepard, *A War of Nerves*, pp. 62–64.

14. Canadians at Vimy Ridge: M. Hadley & R. Sarty, *Tin Pots and Pirate Ships: Canadian Naval Forces and German Sea Raiders 1880–1918*, p. 195.

14. For more information on domestic life in Halifax after the explosion: S. Morton, *Ideal Surroundings: Domestic Life in a Working-Class Suburb in the 1920s.*

## 1. Wednesday

15. Unless otherwise noted, all observations, thoughts, and quotes regarding the ships' navigation, the actions of participants, and the observations of witnesses are found

in trial testimony: "Investigation: *Mont Blanc* and *Imo* Collision," December 1917, NAC, RG 42, vol. 5, g6/7; "Writ of Habeas Corpus for Aimé Le Médec, Frank Mackey and Frederick Wyatt," Supreme Court of Nova Scotia, February 5, 1918, HRL: K1M6.2; Exchequer Court of Canada in Admiralty, January 17, 1917; "Appeal to Supreme Court of Canada"; "Appeal to Privy Council," 1919.

21. Sources for Belgian Relief and British Blockade: G. Gay, H. Fisher, *Public Relations of the Commission for Relief in Belgium.*

21. Seventy-one bottles of whiskey, wine, claret, gin, and liqueur: *Imo* Store List, Shipping Records, New York Harbor, August 23, 1917, NARA, NY.

22. Sources for Charles Duggan: J. Kitz, *Shattered City: The Halifax Explosion and the Road to Recovery;* J. P. Martin, *The Story of Dartmouth;* J. Payzant, *We Love to Ride the Ferry: 250 Years of Halifax-Dartmouth Ferry Crossings,* 2002; *The Acadian Recorder,* December 10, 1917; *The Evening Mail,* December 10, 1917; *The Morning Chronicle,* December 13, 1917; *The Nova Scotian,* December 5, 1987; Halifax Relief Commission file, PANS, MG36, Series "P," Pension Claims #3683, 1770; DHM History File: Ferries; interview by Janet Kitz with Helena Duggan, Halifax Explosion Research Partnership Project, December 14, 1983; interview with Harry Duggan by author, October 2004.

22. "They were a two-boat family": Interview with Harry Duggan by author, October 2004.

23. In interviews Helena Duggan claimed that her father was a world champion and that he lost hundreds of medals and ribbons in the fire. I could not find evidence of his being a world champion. His titles that I know of include 1902 Coronation Regatta Singles Champion, 1903 United Bankers Singles Champion, 1905 Maritimes Singles Champion, 1905 New England Singles Champion, 1906 State of Pennsylvania, 1907 Halifax Harbor Champion. Sources for William Duggan's rowing career are taken from papers given to me by Harry Duggan and undated newspaper clippings: Scrapbook #113, PANS, MG9; *The Mail Star,* Friday March 31, 1978.

## 2. *December 6, 1917*

27. Record of *Imo* in Philadelphia: R.G. 21, U.S. District Court of Delaware, Admiralty Case Number 927, Schmaal vs. Steamship *Imo,* October 9, 1917, NARA, Mid-Atlantic Region; RG 36, District of Philadelphia, Entry 1059, Inward and Outward Foreign and Coastwise Manifests, c. 1890–1918, PA, NARA, Mid Atlantic Region.

32. Mackey was a little confused when he spoke to Glotin. He told him it was the *Kron Prinz Wilhelm.* He meant the *Kaiser Wilhelm der Grosse.* I have taken the liberty of correcting him in the dialogue for clarity's sake. L. Paine, *Ships of the World: An Historical Encyclopedia.*

34. "It was a beautiful, sunny, warm day, more like September than December": Jean Lindsay Ross diaries, PANS, MG 27.

34. Ginger Fraser sources: R. L. Fraser, *The Atlantic Advocate,* January 1967.

34. Bertha Archibald sources: B. Archibald, *The Nova Scotia Medical Bulletin,* 1950.

35. Dr. George Murphy sources: George Murphy, Halifax Disaster Record Office Records, PANS, MG1, vol. 2124, #204.

35. Helen Clark sources: Helen Clark Gucker to Cousin Kate, January 7, 1963, MMA; M. Bird, *The Town That Died.*

35. Fred Longland sources: Fred Longland, Personal Account, MMA.

38. Mackey's thoughts about Hayes's actions: Frank Mackey, CBC Radio Interview, October 3, 1967. See Appendix C for full transcript.

38. "I was not in a position . . . he was making a mistake": Testimony of Frank Mackey, Wreck Commission, December 15, 1917.

39. That is not your order: Frank Mackey, CBC Radio Interview, October 3, 1967.

40. "I knew that . . . on that particular hold": Testimony of Aimé Le Médec, Wreck Commission, December 13, 1917.

41. "The collision was unavoidable. . . .": Testimony of Daniel McLaine, Master, *Douglas H. Thomas,* Wreck Commission, December 18, 1917.

41. "Quite a crash . . . heard all over the ship . . . A good hard crack": Testimony of Frank Mackey, Wreck Commission, December 15, 1917.

41. A government steamship inspector, Norman A. Currie, who inspected the *Imo,* presented the theory of the anchor at trial. The theory did not go unchallenged. Others thought that the plate found inside the *Imo* was blown through her hull during the explosion, but that doesn't explain the punctures in the *Imo's* hull before the explosion. On one photo of the ship, the dents are clearly visible.

41. I have used the testimony of Willard C. Cope, a chemist from New York, who testified at the trials to clarify what happened below the deck. Repeatedly writers have ignored the picric acid in favor of the better-known TNT, despite Cope's fascinating testimony about the importance of picric acid in setting off the explosion. I forwarded Cope's testimony to Pierre Pelletier, who works as a chemical engineer in the military explosive area. Pelletier has informally studied explosive accidents such as the Halifax accident and is a former member of the Canadian Forces Naval Reserve, who had sailed in the Halifax Harbor. Pelletier agreed with Cope. Much of my explanation of the explosion is due to Pelletier's kind assistance and instruction. Interview and correspondence between Pierre Pelletier and author, 2004.

## 3. *Black Smoke, White Smoke*

44. *P.V. VII* description: J. G. Armstrong, *The Halifax Explosion and the Royal Canadian Navy;* M. Hadley & R. Sarty, *Tin Pots and Pirate Ships: Canadian Naval Forces and German Sea Raiders 1880–1918.*

44. Constant Upham sources: *Acadian Recorder,* December 7, 1917; Halifax Disaster Record Office Records, PANS, MG1, vol. 2124, #225; *The Mail Star,* October 6, 1967; *Daily News,* December 3, 1992.

46. "We saw white . . . black smoke": Testimony of William Nickerson, second mate, *Stella Maris,* Wreck Commission, December 21, 1917.

46. Billy Wells sources: Halifax Disaster Record Office Records, PANS, MG1, vol. 2124, #20; Halifax Relief Commission file, PANS, MG36, Series "P," Pension Claims #777; *The Mail Star,* October 6, 1967; *The Mail Star,* December 6, 1967; *The Mail Star,* December 6, 1995; *Daily News,* December 3, 1992; *Firefighter's Digest,* vol. 2, No. 2.

49. "Explosion": Testimony of Ralph E. Smith, marine engineer, Burns and Kelleher, Wreck Commission, December 21, 1917.

50. "Before I had . . . side like rats": *The Morning Chronicle,* December 13, 1917.

51. "They wanted to . . . pier would catch fire": Testimony of Walter Brannen, first mate, *Stella Maris,* Wreck Commision, January 22, 1918.

51. This account differs from Michael Bird's account in *The Town That Died*. Bird has the *Stella Maris* try the five-inch hawser without results before they changed, but nowhere in the testimony of Walter Brannen or William Nickerson do they mention securing any line. In fact, when testifying on December 21, 1917, Nickerson denied ever seeing a line attached. "Q: You were talking of getting lines on board and towing her off; did you notice if anybody tried to secure a line to her? A: Not that we noticed." Without confirmation I relied on the testimony of Brannen and Nickerson. Herbert Whitehead, RNCVR, Duty Boat, testified on January 25, 1918, that he did see two men, one in a red sweater, onboard but that he did not see the *Stella Maris*.

51. "a fine big ship" and subsequent dialogue: Testimony of Frederick C. C. Pasco, captain superintendent, Dockyard, Wreck Commission, January 23, 1918.

52. "I am surprised . . . leave it in a body": Ibid.

53. Refinery workers on the roof: M. Bird, *The Town That Died*, p. 55.

53. Where the fire was: C. E. Creighton, Halifax Disaster Record Office Records, PANS, MG1, vol. 2124, #134; Captain Lorne Allen, Halifax Disaster Record Office Records, PANS, MG1, vol. 2124, #113.

54. "tongues of flames . . . light fleecy clouds": C. E. Creighton, Halifax Disaster Record Office Records, PANS, MG1, vol. 2124, #134.

54. "There was flames . . . burst in the air": Testimony of Charles John Mayers, third officer, *Middleham Castle,* Wreck Commission, December 12, 1917.

55. "Ship on fire": Fred Longland, Personal Account, MMA.

55. "They'll never put that fire out": Ibid.

55. "The ship was . . . a beautiful sight": Billy Wells, *The Mail Star,* October 6, 1967.

56. "Go back! Go back": Dorothy Lloyd, *Boston Globe,* November 24, 2001.

56. "The ship will . . . fire engine coming": Interview: Mr. H. Frank Hillis and Mrs. Hillis (Burbridge) with Janet Kitz, PANS, FSG, MF298, #171.

56. "Don't go out . . . Mrs. Bowen's house": Ibid.

57. "The ship is going to explode. Run. Run": *MicMac News,* December 1977.

57. "No confusion . . . on the ship": Testimony of Aimé Le Médec, captain, *Mont Blanc,* December 13, 1917.

57. Agnes March: M. Bird, *The Town That Died; Daily News,* 2004.

58. "A white man just warned me that the ship is going to explode": *MicMac News,* December 1977.

58. "A lurid yellowish . . . cloud of smoke": *The Morning Chronicle,* December 13, 1917.

## 4. *A Word on Explosions*

59. Classifications of explosions and resulting differences: Interview and correspondence between Pierre Pelletier and author, 2004; Colorado School of Mines, Detonation Physics, www.egweb.mines.edu.

60. "It was difficult . . . particularly safe": G. Brown, *The Big Bang,* p. 151.

61. Further definitions and history of nineteenth-century explosives: BBC www.bbc.co.uk; Royal Society of Chemistry, www.rsc.org.

61. "was so stable . . . quarries and mines": G. Brown, *The Big Bang*, p. 130.

62. 2,925 tons and subsequent facts regarding size and effects of the explosion: A. Ruffman & C. D. Howell, *Ground Zero: A Reassessment of the 1917 Explosion in the Halifax Harbour*, pp. 276–277.

63. "The concussion . . . Blowing": Interview: Mr. H. Frank Hillis and Mrs. Hillis (Burbridge) with Kitz, PANS, FSG, MF298, #171.

63. When the crew of the *Wave*: *Acadian Recorder*, December 13, 1917.

63. Eyes opened by blast: Interview: Kendal J. Partington to Kitz, PANS, FSG, MF298, #151.

64. Damage to Dartmouth: J. MacNeil, *The Story of Dartmouth*, p. 516; DHM, History File: Explosion of 1917.

64. "Look out": Testimony of Charles John Mayers, third officer, *Middleham Castle*, Wreck Commission, December 12, 1917.

65. "I tried to throw . . . a rubber coat": D. Johnstone, "The Tragedy of Halifax 1917," PANS, MFM, Micro J735.

65. "blinding flash, an awful shudder and a bang": Fred Longland, Personal Account, MMA.

66. Two small tornadoes: Lillian Griffin, Halifax Disaster Record Office, PANS, MG1, vol. 2124, #148.

66. "Like a grain field in harvest before a gust of wind": Halifax Disaster Record Office, PANS, MG1, vol. 2124, #284A.

66. Ships in the harbor: Captain Robie Frellick, *The Mail Star*, December 6, 1984; Reports on Services Rendered by Members of the Military Forces at Halifax on the Occasion of the Disaster, December 6, 1917, Halifax Disaster Record Office, PANS, MG1, vol. 2124, #249; D. Johnstone, "The Tragedy of Halifax 1917," PANS, MFM, Micro J735; A. Ruffman & C. D. Howell, *Ground Zero: A Reassessment of the 1917 Explosion in the Halifax Harbour*; J. G. Armstrong, *The Halifax Explosion and the Royal Canadian Navy*.

67. George Holmes: Halifax Disaster Record Office, PANS, MG1, vol. 2124; *Mail Star*, December 6, 1967; J. MacNeil, *The Story of Dartmouth*.

67. "a sense of oppression": Captain Newcombe, Halifax Disaster Record Office, PANS, MG1, vol. 2124, #207.

68. $35,000,000: The Canadian Annual Review of Public Affairs, 1918, pp. 646–656.

68. "I myself . . . like a stone": Charles Duggan, *The Morning Chronicle*, December 13, 1917.

## 5. Minutes Later

70. "Survivors complained . . . stimulus at all": For more discussion of these symptoms, see Note 5, Chapter 16. D. Fraser, "Medical Aspects of the Halifax Disaster," PANS, MG36, Series "C," Folder 19.

70. "Because at the time . . . mentioned a German": Compilation, Kitz, PANS, FSG, MF298; Hildreth Mason (Isnor) #4; Mary Elizabeth VanBuskirk #160; Mr. H. Frank Hillis and Mrs. Hillis (Burbridge), #171.

70. USS *Tacoma* sources: Report of P. Powers Symington, R. Hayes, Halifax Disaster Record Office, PANS MG27, Vol. 2, #31.

71. "The sight was awful . . . telegraph wires": Billy Wells, *The Mail Star*, October 6, 1967.

72. He held him in his arms until he died: Interview: Mr. H. Frank Hillis and Mrs. Hillis (Burbridge) with Janet Kitz, PANS, FSG, MF298, #171.

73. Elizabeth Fraser sources: Elizabeth Fraser, *The Mail Star*, December 6, 1972.

74. "Mother, where is Arthur"; "Arthur? Arthur": Ibid.

74. "I saw my aunt . . . did not know": Ibid.

74. Aunt Sophie: Halifax Explosion Remembrance Book, PANS website.

75. "My heavenly God . . . your knees girls": Halifax Disaster Record Office, PANS, MG1, vol. 2124.

75. "I clutched madly . . . she let go": Helen Clark Gucker to Cousin Kate, January 7, 1963, MMA.

75. "little heap of old snow in the corner by the steps": Ibid.

76. "Here's my handkerchief, put it to your neck": Nora Faulkner, *Halifax Daily News*, December 3, 1992.

77. "Nora, go home if you have one to go to": Ibid.

77. "Where will we go mister": Gus Crowley, *The Mail Star*, December 6, 1973.

77. "Stay clear of the buildings": Ibid.

77. "Dolly, look at the stove pipes flying in the air: Dorothy Lloyd, *Boston Globe*, November 24, 2001.

77. "Go home, girls": Ibid.

78. "Our father who art in Heaven . . . Hallowed be thy name": Helen Clark Gucker to Cousin Kate, January 7, 1963, MMA.

78. "I yearned . . . on fire too": Ibid.

78. "like the curls . . . was not a curl": Ibid.

78. "It was burning . . . waving and screaming": Ibid.

78. "In a little while . . . C O A L": Ibid.

79. "That's my house . . . some help": Helena Duggan, *The Nova Scotian*, December 5, 1987.

79. Helena Duggan sources: Ibid.; Helena Duggan with Janet Kitz, December 14, 1983, courtesy of Halifax Explosion Research Partnership Project, Janet Kitz, and the Senior History Students of Prince Andrew High School; PANS, MG36, Series "P," Pension Claim #1770.

80. "We had her . . . screaming and fire": Helena Duggan with Janet Kitz, December 14, 1983.

80. "I could see . . . me confused": Ibid.

81. "Don't do that. Don't do that": Ibid.

81. "We were . . . happen next": Elizabeth Fraser, *The Mail Star*, December 6, 1972.

83. Spruce trees: A. Mac Mechan, Halifax Disaster Record Office, PANS, MG1, vol. 2124, #173.

83. "I met a car . . . was wounded": Testimony of Aimé Le Médec, Wreck Commission, January 21, 1918.

83. "What caused the explosion": Testimony of Captain Peter Johnston, superintendent of lights and buoys, Wreck Commission, January 22, 1918.

83. "The ship I was on exploded": Testimony of Mackey quoted by Johnston.

85. Janette Baxter, also called Janet Baxter: *Acadian Recorder*, December 15, 1917.

87. Dickson and Russell Urquhart: Halifax Disaster Record Office, PANS, MG1, vol. 2124; Interview with Mollie Forbes, DHM, History File: Explosion of 1917; J. MacNeil, *The Story of Dartmouth*.

87. a dead horse: Interview with Mollie Forbes, DHM, History File: Explosion of 1917.

88. "A novel . . . school early": Ian Forsythe, quoted in Chapman, ed., *Dartmouth's Day of Anguish*, p. 16.

88. "half-denuded": Charles Duggan, *The Morning Chronicle*, December 13, 1917.

88. "Probably . . . own people": Ibid.

## 6. *Far from the Harbor*

90. "It was amazing . . . a helping hand": D. McMurray, "Four Principals of McGill," reprinted in *The Mail Star*, December 6, 1974.

90. "Doc's done it . . . have got us": R. L. Fraser, *The Atlantic Advocate*, January 1967.

90. "I think it . . . him very much": Ibid.

91. "They were people . . . carts and trucks": Ibid.

91. "What happened": Ibid.

91. "A ship . . . been killed": Ibid.

91. "That was hard to believe": Ibid.

92. "We did not . . . bleeding quite badly": Ibid.

## 7. *Scramble at City Hall*

93. City Hall: Relief Work Connected with the Halifax Disaster, PANS, MG36, Series 6, #88.12; G. Metson and A. MacMechan, *The Halifax Explosion; December 6, 1917 New York Times*, December 7, 1917; Halifax Disaster Record Office, PANS, MG1, vol. 2124; History of Halifax City Hall pamphlet, Halifax Regional Municipality.

93. City Hall sources: Minutes, Morning Meeting, December 6, 1917, Halifax Disaster Record Office, PANS, vol. 2124, #3; Minutes, Afternoon Meeting, December 6, 1917, Halifax Disaster Record Office, PANS, vol. 2124, #3D; Gillis to Bell re: Transportation Committee, January 31, 1918, Halifax Disaster Record Office, PANS, MG1, vol. 2124, #2; From Weatherbe to Chairman Exec. Relief Committee, December 28, 1917, Halifax Disaster Record Office, PANS, MG36, Series C, #120.3; Memorandum 2, PANS, MG1, vol. 2124, #283D #283D; Dougall MacGillvray, Halifax Disaster Record Office, PANS, MG1, vol. 2124, #196; Edmund Saunders, Halifax Disaster Record Office, PANS, MG1, vol. 2124, #196; G. Metson and A. MacMechan, *The Halifax Explosion*, December 6, 1917.

93. Poultry show: Harry Piers Collection, MG1, vol. 1047, 1918.

94. "water spout": G. Metson and A. MacMechan, *The Halifax Explosion*, p. 50.

95. "W.A. Duff . . . Canadian Government Railways": W. A. Duff, Halifax Disaster Record Office, PANS, vol. 2124, #51; G. Metson and A. MacMechan, *The Halifax Explosion*, p. 50.

95. "For God's sake . . . Mayor of Halifax": G. Metson and A. MacMechan, *The Halifax Explosion*.

96. Military response sources: C. A. MacLennan, Halifax Disaster Record Office,

PANS, MG1, vol. 2124, #201; Col. R. B. Simmonds, Halifax Disaster Record Office, PANS, MG1, vol. 2124, #225; Cadet Captain Kingsley, Halifax Disaster Record Office, PANS, MG1, vol. 2124, #162; Col. W. E. Thompson, Halifax Disaster Record Office, PANS, MG1, vol. 2124, #233; Lt. Ray Colwell and Lt. Arthur, Halifax Disaster Record Office, PANS, MG1, vol. 2124, #133; From Maj.-Gen. T. Benson to Secretary, Military Council, December 15, 1917, Halifax Disaster Record Office, PANS, MG1, vol. 2124, #250A; Lt. Col. Flowers, January 25, 1918, Halifax Disaster Record Office, PANS, MG1, vol. 2124, #253; Reports on Services Rendered by Members of the Military Forces at Halifax on the Occasion of the Disaster, December 6, 1917, Halifax Disaster Record Office, PANS, MG1, vol. 2124, #249; Richard Howley, Halifax Disaster Record Office, PANS, MG1, vol. 2124, #158; William Robinson, Halifax Disaster Record Office, PANS, MG1, vol. 2124, #220; Edward Orde, Halifax Disaster Record Office, PANS, MG1, vol. 2124, #211; Various, Halifax Disaster Record Office, PANS, MG1, vol. 2124; J. G. Armstrong, *The Halifax Explosion and the Royal Canadian Navy*. Armstrong's book gives a thorough account of the Canadian Navy's response to the explosion and the investigation into CXO Wyatt.

97. "The best fire I ever saw in my life": Lieutenant C. A. MacLennan, Halifax Disaster Record Office, PANS, MG1, vol. 2124, #201.

97. "My leg is all knocked to hell": Ibid.

97. "Fall in Company B": Ibid.

98. "To hell . . . medical orderly": Ibid.

98. "Get your kindling . . . no matches": Ibid.

98. "An honest-to-God fire": Ibid.

99. "Where is the fire": Ibid.

99. "On the roof": Ibid.

99. "An hour before I breathed normally": Ibid.

99. "Carry on.": Ibid.

100. Lt. Harrison and his father: Halifax Disaster Record Office, PANS, MG1, vol. 2124, #154.

100. "go up any minute": William Frank Lye, *Chronicle Herald*, June 12, 1972.

100. "One girl . . . continued her flight": D. Fraser, "Medical Aspects of the Halifax Disaster," PANS, MG36, Series "C," Folder 19.

101. "men in trousers . . . boudoir caps": Jean Lindsay Ross diaries, PANS, MG27.

101. "We finally landed . . . expected the explosion": Ibid.

101. "A large crowd . . . another dreadful explosion": R. L. Fraser, *The Atlantic Advocate*, January 1967.

102. "Quick decision . . . discussion": J. Byron Deacon quoting veteran disaster relief worker in *Disasters*.

103. Morgue sources: Morgue at Chebucto School, Halifax Disaster Record Office, PANS, MG1, vol. 2124, #203; Barnstead to Bell, Halifax Disaster Record Office, PANS, MG36, Series C, #127.15; Interim Report of Mortuary Committee, Halifax Disaster Record Office, PANS, MG36, Series C, #3; The Office, Halifax Disaster Record Office, PANS, MG1, vol. 2124, #282.

103. Rail sources: J. C. Gillespie, Halifax Disaster Record Office, PANS, MG1, vol. 2124, #149; Joseph Scanlon, "The Magnificent Railways," *Canadian Rail*, no. 461 (December 1997); H. Reid, "How They Got the Message Out, *The Atlantic Advocate*, January 1978;

*Canadian Rail* No. 461, 1997; "How the Government Railways Responded to the Call," Halifax Disaster Record Office, PANS, MG1, vol. 2124, #6A; Restoration of the Canadian Government Railways Property at Halifax, Halifax Disaster Record Office, PANS, MG1, vol. 2124, #8; F. Tapley, "Salvaging the Railway Facilities at Halifax, N.S.," *Railway Age,* Halifax Disaster Record Office, PANS, MG1, vol. 2124, #35; George Cutten, Halifax Disaster Record Office, PANS, MG1, vol. 2124, #5.

104. *Telegrams:* D. Johnstone, "The Tragedy of Halifax 1917," PANS, MFM, Micro J735. In full the telegrams Johnstone lists are as follows:

9:26 A.M. Amherst NS—American ammunition boat collided with another boat at Rockingham three miles from Halifax. A section of Halifax on fire.

9:50 A.M. Montreal—Reports reaching telegraph companies here indicate that the explosion near Halifax has affected their dynamos. All wire communication with Halifax and outside points severed.

10:03 A.M. Montreal—According to reports reaching here a number of people were killed when the explosion occurred in Halifax this morning.

10:13 A.M. Boston—The Postal telegraph Company's lines also down. The local offices stated that Montreal reported no wires working east of that city. One report was that an explosion of a bomb killing a number of men occurred at 9:30 A.M.

10:20 A.M. St. John NB—It is announced here that the censor has taken control of all wires at Halifax in connection with the explosion there this morning.

10:27 A.M. New York—Halifax has been cut off from all communication with the rest of the world, either by wire or cable, according to officials of the Western Union Cable Company in this city. All land wires are down, and the plant of the United States Cable Company at Halifax has been so damaged by the explosion that it cannot be operated.

10:35 A.M. Amherst NS—Hundreds of buildings were destroyed or damaged, scores of lives believed lost and certain sections of the city are in flames.

10:37 A.M. Ottawa—According to advices received here the Halifax disaster was due to the blowing up of a munitions ship in the harbor at eight o'clock this morning. All telegraph lines are down and the damage is very serious. It is believed a number of people near the scene were either killed of injured, including several telegraph employees.

12:05 P.M. Truro NS—It is reported here that the first estimate of the loss of life in the explosion in Halifax harbor this morning places it at fifty, while the number injured is correspondingly great.

12:26 pm Halifax NS (via Havana)—Hundreds of persons were killed and a thousand others injured and half the city of Halifax is in ruins as the result of the explosion on a munitions ship in the harbour today. It is estimated the property loss will run into the millions. The north end of the city is in flames.

104. Red Cross representative from the Department of Military Relief: Monograph 67, p. 51, Red Cross: Halifax Explosion, December 6, 1917; NARA, 891.1/08.

104. "Organize a relief train . . . casualties is enormous": B. Beed, *1917 Halifax Explosion and American Response*, p. 19.

104. Public Safety Committee of Massachusetts: *Morning Chronicle*, December 14, 1917; Report Massachusetts Halifax Relief Expedition: December 6–15, 1917; June 12, 1918: G. H. Lyman, *The Story of the Massachusetts Committee on Public Safety;* Red Cross: Halifax Explosion, December 12, 1917; NARA, 891.1/08.

105. "Understand that . . . me immediately": Report Massachusetts Halifax Relief Expedition, December 6–15, 1917; June 12, 1918.

106. Abraham Captain Ratshesky: Correspondence between author and A. C. Ratshesky Foundation, www.grantsmanagement.com/acrfhistory.html.

106. "Since sending . . . from you": Report Massachusetts Halifax Relief Expedition: December 6–15, 1917; June 12, 1918.

107. Military activities: From Major-General Thomas Benson to Secretary, Military Council, December 15, 1917, Halifax Disaster Record Office, PANS, MG1, vol. 2124, #250A.

107. Seizing cars: Lieutenant Colonel Flowers, PANS, MG1, vol. 2124, #253; Colonel Thompson, PANS, MG1, vol. 2124, #233. Thompson says that it was his idea. "Whenever you want a car or team, stop and take it."

107. "I asked him . . . driver on the seat": Stanley Smith, *Heart Throbs of the Halifax Horror*, 1918.

108. 250 and 300 cars: Transportation Report, Halifax Disaster Record Office, PANS, MG1, vol. 2124, #150.


## 8. The First Responders

109. "Halifax is on fire. . . . to Halifax": J. Scanlon, "The Magnificent Railways": Rail Response to the 1917 Halifax Explosion, *Canadian Rail*, No. #461, November/December, 1997.

109. "felt shock of the explosion near Rockingham": J. C. Gillespie, Halifax Disaster Record Office, PANS, MG1, vol. 2124, #149.

109. "Cold, barefooted and torn people": Ibid.

109. "There were a lot . . . baby in a bottle": Ms. Currie with Janet Kitz, PANS, FSG, MF298, #177.

109. C. E. Avery DeWitt: C. E. Avery DeWitt, Halifax Disaster Record Office Records, PANS, MG1, vol. 2124, #139.

111. "Get to Rockingham . . . the yards": Diary: P. W. Caldwell, PANS RG28, Series "S," vol. 26, #8.

111. "familiar with arrival . . . Nova Scotia": obituary, *The Eastern Chronicle*, January 8, 1953.

111. Dr. George Cox sources: George Cox, PANS, MG1, vol. 2606, #169; G. Cox to L. Wright, December 28, 1917, Red Cross: Halifax Explosion December 12, 1917, NARA, 891.1/08; New Glasgow Emergency Hospital, MG1, vol. 2124, #7; Obituary, *The Eastern Chronicle*, January 8, 1953.

112. "a noted surgeon" and "grand old man of medicine": *New York Times,* December 7, 1917.

112. "Why do not some of you go to Dr. Chisholm": L. Thomas, *The Nova Scotia Medical Bulletin,* 1950.

112. "We were in there but he's dead": Ibid.

113. Dr. Rice: G. Rice, Halifax Disaster Record Office, PANS, MG1, vol. 2124, #217.

113. "a grating rumbling sound": G. Murphy, Halifax Disaster Record Office Records, PANS, MG1, vol. 2124, #204.

114. "a dense, greyish . . . end of the city": G. Murphy, Halifax Disaster Record Office Records, PANS, MG1, vol. 2124, #204.

114. "It made movement . . . needed it most": Ibid.

114. "an arrow-shaped . . . moulding": B. Archibald, *The Nova Scotia Medical Bulletin,* 1950.

114. "Soon patients . . . comforted each other": Ibid.

115. "Someone walking . . . few steps": Ibid.

115. "Oh, do get me a bed"; "A bed"; "There isn't a vacant bed in the place": Ibid.

115. "We needed . . . surgical judgment": George Murphy, Halifax Disaster Record Office Records, PANS, MG1, vol. 2124, #204.

115. "I will stay where I am": Ibid.

116. VAD sources: MacIntosh to Copp, December 13, 1917, PANS, MG1, vol. 2124, #30; D. Fraser, "Medical Aspects of the Halifax Disaster," PANS, MG36, Series "C," Folder 19; various reports PANS, MG1, vol. 2124.

116. "Sixty-two members . . . necessary": D. Fraser, "Medical Aspects of the Halifax Disaster," PANS, MG36, Series "C," Folder 19.

116. Camp Hill history: *Camp Hill Hospital, 70 Years of Caring 1917–1987.*

117. "Can I do anything"; "Come right along in here": Marjorie Moir, Halifax Disaster Record Office, PANS, MG1, vol. 2124, #276d.

117. "As though some one had done it with a knife"; "Hold her feet": Ibid.

117. "Are you a V.A.D."; "No, I'm just an ordinary person but I'm willing to do anything I can"; "Nurse": Ibid.

117. Florence Murray sources: F. Murray, *At the Foot of Dragon Hill;* Florence Murray, Halifax Disaster Record Office, PANS, MG1, vol. 2124, #192.

118. "Has your class had instruction in anesthesia"; "Yes sir"; "In the army . . . questions"; "Go to the . . . anesthetics": Ibid.

118. "Use this . . . exhausted": Ibid.

118. "The first patient . . . not know": Ibid.

118. "Give it to someone who needs it more": Florence Murray, Halifax Disaster Record Office, PANS, MG1, vol. 2124, #192.

## 9. *Duggan Walks Home*

121. "Someone had . . . once again": D. Johnstone, "The Tragedy of Halifax 1917," PANS, MFM, Micro J735.

121. "Affected me . . . broken to pieces": Ralph Procter, Halifax Disaster Record Office, PANS, MG1, vol. 2124, #216.

121. "I had swallowed glass, I was pretty scared": Ibid.

122. "They didn't . . . time on one": Helena Duggan with Janet Kitz, December 14, 1983.

122. "Get back. Halifax is destroyed": Ibid.

122. "Shedding tears . . . smoldering coal": Helena Duggan, *The Nova Scotian*, December 5, 1987.

123. Upham's store: Halifax Disaster Record Office, PANS, MG1, vol. 2124, #225.

123. "like cordwood": Emily Brown, Halifax Disaster Record Office, PANS, MG1, vol. 2124, #118.

## 10. *Nightfall*

125. Harvey Jones: Harvey Jones, Halifax Disaster Record Office, PANS, MG1, vol. 2124, #161.

126. "I was feeling . . . clean up": Ibid.

128. "Mother. Mother": R. L. Fraser, *The Atlantic Advocate*, January 1967.

128. "Then I . . . my head off": Ibid.

128. "A nasty gash"; "Are you alright"; "Sure"; "Well you . . . bleeding": Ibid.

129. Cadets sources: J. H. Trefry, Halifax Disaster Record Office, PANS, MG1, vol. 2124, #36A; C. Gesner, Royal Canadian Army Cadets, Halifax Disaster Record Office, PANS, MG1, vol. 2124, #37.

129. "At least two . . . telegraph office": Interview: Kendal J. Partington to Kitz, PANS, FSG, MF298, #151.

129. City Hall activity: D. Johnstone, "The Tragedy of Halifax 1917," PANS, MFM, Micro J735.

130. "standing, gaunt . . . their kingdom": W. B. Moore, Halifax Disaster Record Office, MG1, vol. 2124.

131. "The rows of . . . witness it": Ibid.

133. "After vainly . . . looking for them": Dorothy McMurray, "Four Principals of McGill," reprinted by *The Mail Star,* December 6, 1974.

133. "A tangle . . . dental chairs": Ibid.

133. "One man yielded . . . wonderfully": George Cox, PANS, MG1, vol. 2606, #169.

134. "Here was the kind of thing . . . days and days ahead": Ibid.

134. McKelvey Bell sources: Telegrams NAC, RG 24, HQ 71-26-99-3, vol. I; Lt. Col. Frederick McKelvey Bell, Interim Medical Report, NAC, HQ71-26-99-3, vol. 2; Frederick McKelvey Bell, Military Records HQ6013-1, vol. 2; F. McKelvey Bell, *The First Canadians in France;* F. McKelvey Bell, *A Romance of the Halifax Explosion,* 1918; Red Cross: Halifax Explosion, December 12, 1917, NARA 891.1/08.

134. "His ability . . . was unfailing": J. P. Murphy Report, Red Cross: Halifax Explosion December 6, 1917, NARA, 891.1/08.

134. "he had never . . . in Halifax today": *New York Times,* December 7, 1917.

135. "Feeble old men tottering . . . they ran": F. McKelvey Bell, *The First Canadians in France,* p. 294.

135. "All hospitals . . . be expected": F. McKelvey Bell, Telegrams NAC, RG 24, HQ 71-26-99-3, vol. I.

137. "Is there anything we can do . . . Yes": Col. W. E. Thompson, Halifax Disaster Record Office, PANS, MG1, vol. 2124, #233.

137. "There were still moans . . . victims lying underneath": *The Mail Star*, December 6, 1967.

137. Dr. William Edwards Ladd sources: Halifax Disaster Records Office, MG1, vol. 2124, #315; Ladd to Zwiren, March 28, 1963; *Journal of Pediatric Surgery*, vol. 36, no. 10 (2001); *Boston Globe*, December 8, 1917; *Harvard University Gazette*, June 8, 1968; D. Watson, *Journal of Pediatric Surgery*, vol. 2, no. 4 (August 1967); H. Bill, "William E. Ladd: Great Pioneer of North American Pediatric Surgery," *Progress in Pediatric Surgery*, (1986); H. W. Clatworthy Jr., "Ladd's Vision," *Journal of Pediatric Surgery*, vol. 34, no. 5, Supplement 1, (May 1999); H. Hendren, "From an Acorn to an Oak," *Journal of Pediatric Surgery*, vol. 34 (May 1999); W. E. Ladd, "Children's Surgery and Its Relation to the Specialties," Arthur Dean Bevan Lecture, Chicago Surgical Society, October 7, 1941; T. H. Lanman, William E. Ladd Lecture at the Meeting of the American Academy of Pediatrics, Chicago, October 6, 1954; *Pediatrics*, vol. 14, no. 6 (December 1954); R. Goldbloom, *Pediatrics*, vol. 77, no. 5 (May 1986); "The Halifax Disaster," *CMAJ*, vol. 135 (October 1, 1986), reprint from *CMAJ*, vol. 8 (1918): 59–62; Dr. C. Everett Koop, Interview with the author: June 23, 2002; K. Ladd Fales, Interview with the author, June 2002; Correspondence between author, David Murphy, and Robert Replogle, June 2002, March 2005; NARA, Red Cross: Halifax Explosion December 6, 1917, 891.1/08; Telegrams NAC, RG 24, HQ 71-26-99-3, vol. I; Lt. Col. Frederick McKelvey Bell, Interim Medical Report, NAC, HQ71-26-99-3, vol. 2.

137. "A very unsatisfactory arrangement": Ladd to Dr. Zwiren, March 28, 1963 reprinted *Journal of Pediatric Surgery*, vol. 36, no. 10 (2001).

137. "The Children's was my very first and most permanent love": Ibid.

138. Boston Children's history sources: C. Smith, *The Children's Hospital of Boston: Built Better Than They Knew*.

139. Still undaunted by unconventional approaches: Hardy Hendren, "From an Acorn to an Oak," *Journal of Pediatric Surgery*, vol. 34 (May 1999); David Murphy, Interview with author, 2002.

139. "Tuberculosis . . . was unknown": H. Bill, "William E. Ladd: Great Pioneer of North American Pediatric Surgery," *Progress in Pediatric Surgery* (1986).

139. "Surgery was . . . well established": Ibid.

140. "In most hospitals, the . . . the range of 90%": C. Everett Koop, "A Perspective on the Early Days of Pediatric Surgery," *Journal of Pediatric Surgery*, vol. 34, no. 5, Supplement 1 (May 1999).

140. "The smaller . . . the tightrope": Dr. C. Everett Koop, Interview with the author, 2003.

140. "The physical signs . . . almost valueless": W. E. Ladd, Thirteenth Annual Arthur Bevan Lecture: "Children's Surgery and its Relations to the Specialties," Chicago, October 7, 1941.

140. Argument for specialized surgery: W. E. Ladd, "Progress in the Diagnosis and Treatment of Intussusception," *Boston Surgical Journal* (April 10, 1913).

141. "The autopsy table was his library": H. W. Clatworthy Jr., "Ladd's Vision," *Journal of Pediatric Surgery*, vol. 34, no. 5, Supplement 1 (May 1999).

141. "diminutive man or woman": W. E. Ladd & R. Gross, *Abdominal Surgery of Infancy and Childhood*, p. 3.

141. "the adult may . . . lead to disaster": W. E. Ladd, "Children's Surgery and Its Relation to the Specialties," Arthur Dean Bevan Lecture, Chicago Surgical Society, October 7, 1941.

141. "Anyone who can work . . . can operate on a child": Dr. C. Everett Koop, Interview with the author, June 23, 2003.

141. "iron gray": Halifax Disaster Records Office, PANS, MG1, vol. 2124, #315c.

141. "He'd pick up a baby and it fit right in his hand" Ibid.

141. "His hands . . . a child": Katharine Ladd Fales, Interview with the author, June 2002.

142. "an embarrassing . . . do anything": Lothrop to Persons, December 12, 1917; Halifax Explosion, December 6, 1917, NARA 891.1/08.

142. Red Cross relationship to Committee of Public Safety: C. C. Ely, *A History of the Boston Metropolitan Chapter*, American Red Cross, Boston Metropolitan Chapters, SCA, CCO28, 1919.

143. Weather: Neal to Milner: July 12, 1920, PANS, MacMechan files; NAV Canada, www.navcanada.ca; weather maps, Environment Canada.

Weather Record from Meteorological station from December 6–11, 1917:

- Thursday, December 6: Highest: 39.2; Low: 16.8; Cloudy

- Friday, December 7: Highest: 32.2; Low: 24.8; Blizzard conditions; 16.0 inches snow badly drifting

- Saturday, December 8: Highest: 29.8; Low: 24.8; Snow in morning; 1.2 inches

- Sunday, December 9: Highest: 50.4; Low: 14.0; Heavy rain from 1:40 a.m. till noon; 9.9 inches rain

- Monday, December 10: Highest: 34.2; Low: 16.8; Snow from 2:00 p.m. till 5:40 p.m.; 5.6 inches

- Tuesday, December 11: Highest: 18.2; Low: 6.6; Clear

## 11. *Friday Night and Folly Mountain*

144. "It was a heavy . . . well nigh impossible": D. Johnstone, "The Tragedy of Halifax 1917," PANS, MFM, Micro J735.

144. "The mercury . . . pairs of socks": D. G. O. Baillie, *A Sea Affair,* p. 54.

145. Symington's men: Report of P. Symington, Halifax Disaster Record Office, PANS, MG1, vol. 2, 31.

145. "One of the . . . the terminals": J. G. Armstrong, *The Halifax Explosion and the Royal Canadian Navy,* p. 89.

146. "I am sure I heard a moan a minute ago": D. Johnstone, "The Tragedy of Halifax 1917," PANS, MFM, Micro J735; *Boston Globe,* December 9, 1917; *Sunday Herald,* December 3, 2000; S. K. Smith, *Heart Throbs of the Halifax Horror*, p. 28.

147. "I'm going to find Arthur": Elizabeth Fraser, *The Mail Star*, December 6, 1972.

147. "Everything was covered . . . from another": Ibid.

147. "Heartbroken and lonely . . . to do": Ibid.

148. "I couldn't eat; I kept thinking of . . . my little brother": Ibid.

148. Baby found with collie: *Boston Globe*, December 9, 1917.

149. "Jessie Aitken . . . him at this address": *The Morning Chronicle*, December 14, 1917.

150. "That all parents . . . quickly as possible": *Acadian Recorder*, December 7, 1917.

150. "Regretting news . . . all aid": Ibid.

151. Clara MacIntosh sources: MacIntosh to Copp, December 13, 1917, PANS, MG1, vol. 2124, #30; Clara MacIntosh, Halifax Disaster Record Office, PANS, MG1, vol. 2124, #198c; D. Fraser, "Medical Aspects of the Halifax Disaster," PANS, MG36, Series "C," Folder 19; various reports, PANS, MG1, vol. 2124; Lillian Giffen, Halifax Disaster Record Office, PANS, MG1, vol. 2124, #148.

151. "I want a bath": Lillian Giffen, Halifax Disaster Record Office, PANS, MG1, vol. 2124, #148.

152. "We spread a . . . explosion was past": MacIntosh to Copp, December 13, 1917, PANS, MG1, vol. 2124, #30.

152. "Why not go offer your services": Clara MacIntosh, Halifax Disaster Record Office, PANS, MG1, vol. 2124, #198c.

153. "Am I to go on with this work": Ibid.

153. "Teams of women . . . food and clothing": MacIntosh to Copp, December 13, 1917, PANS, MG1, vol. 2124, #30.

154. "an old sergeant as orderly"; "a fine military nursing sister": Dr. George Cox, PANS, MG1, vol. 2606, #169.

155. "Eyelids were cut . . . larger were found": Ibid.

155. "Everyone, when . . . it was both": Ibid.

155. Cocaine: Interview with Ira Rutgow, July 13, 2004; I. Rutkow, *Surgery: An Illustrated History;* Dr. George Cox, PANS, MG1, vol. 2606, #169; L. R. Maguire, MG1, vol. 2124, #181a.

156. Jack MacKeen sources: John MacKeen, Halifax Disaster Record Office, PANS, MG1, vol. 2124, #197; *Mail Star*, December 6, 1967; MacKeen genealogy, www.rootsweb.com/-nspictou/elect_text/crerar4.htm.

157. Iodoform: *Columbia Encyclopedia Sixth Edition*, 2001.

157. Dakin's solution: I. Rutkow, *Surgery: An Illustrated History*.

157. "I thought . . . hate all sickness": Jean Lindsay Ross diaries, PANS, MG27.

157. "it seemed a small thing": Ibid.

158. "The door was guarded . . . at a time": Ibid.

158. "What sent me . . . sense not hers": Ibid.

158. "Our sealskin friend's car": Ibid.

159. "The double cases were particularly sad": George Cox, PANS, MG1, vol. 2606, #169.

159. "In one poor . . . in her arms": Ibid.

159. "But it was . . . needing attention": Ibid.

159. "If relief doesn't come soon, I shall murder somebody": D. Johnstone, "The Tragedy of Halifax 1917," PANS, MFM, Micro J735.

159. "The patients . . . other conditions": Dr. W. B. Moore, Halifax Disaster Record Office, PANS, MG1, vol. 2124.

160. "In a day . . . to see daylight": Dr. George Cox, PANS, MG1, vol. 2606, #169.

160. "My hands and feet were very cold, but I dared not stop": Elizabeth Fraser, *The Mail Star,* December 6, 1972.

161. "I stood . . . a foul smell everywhere": Ibid.

161. "Go in there and see what that is . . . I believe he is in there": Ibid.

161. "How I ever got there I will never know": Elizabeth Fraser, *The Mail Star*, December 6, 1972.

162. "a restful half light": A. MacMechan, Halifax Disaster Record Office, PANS, MG1, vol. 2124, #282d.

162. "What have you . . . the Thomas family": S. Smith, *Heart Throbs of the Halifax Horror.*

163. "Help. Help. Please help me": Donald Morrison, *The Chronicle Herald,* December 6, 1971.

163. "Oh please help. Will not anyone help me": Ibid.

164. "tumbled into the room": Ibid.

164. "Is my . . . find him": Ibid.

164. "She was sixteen . . . two days": Ibid.

164. "Body after body . . . was forgotten": Ibid.

164. "We went over to have a closer look": Ibid.

164. "I found you. I found you": Ibid.

164. "She cried as I have never seen anyone cry before or since": Ibid.

164. "Under ordinary . . . only human": Ibid.

165. "The most we obtained . . . the worse they sounded": A. C. Ratshesky, Report Massachusetts-Halifax Relief Expedition, December 6–15, 1917.

165. The complete list of supplies: Ibid.

*Public Safety Supplies*

564 fracture pillows
1,000 pillows
1,368 muslin bandages
53 splint straps
330 gauze compresses, 9 by 9 inches
4,000 gauze compresses, 4 by 4 inches
432 flannel bandages
1,196 bandages, 3 inches
2,694 gauze bandages
2,700 gauze compresses
1,200 gauze sponges
1,000 4-tail bandages
1,720 gauze rolls
204 flannel bandages
890 slings
8 Standard oil heaters
4 boxes lanterns, glass

21 pairs cotton blankets
36 gray heavy army blankets
6 litters
3 bedpans
4 urinals

*Medical Supplies*

50 tubes morphine sulphate—$\frac{1}{8}$ grain, hypodermic
5 tubes atropine, $\frac{1}{150}$ grain
100 salt solution tablets
1,000 aspirin tablets
500 calomel, $\frac{1}{10}$ tablets
500 cascara, 3-grain tablets
9 pounds ether, $\frac{1}{4}$ pound cans
9 pounds ether, $\frac{1}{2}$ pound cans
10 gallons alcohol
$\frac{1}{2}$ gallon tincture iodine
100 corrosive tablets
1 pint carbolic acid, 45 per cent solution
1 quart boracic acid, 4 per cent solution

*Red Cross Supplies*

498 sweaters
226 flannel pajamas
333 convalescent gowns
8,300 gauze compresses, 4 inches
9,354 bandages, 1 inch
1 crate gauze sponges
378 triangular bandages
1 box miscellaneous

*Additional list: Ibid.*

10 gallons alcohol
1 gallon tincture iodine
5 pounds cotton
5 pound, boric ointment
30 pounds vaseline
8 ounces tincture digitalis
500 caps camphor in oil
1 gallon aromatic spirits of ammonia
1 gross assorted catgut in tubes
11 skeins No. 1 white twisted silk
8 ounces 4 per cent cocaine
4 ounces 1 per cent atropine
1 pint olive oil

12 pairs dressing scissors
12 pairs dressing forceps
1 dozen 4-ounce tins
1 ½ dozen glass stoppered bottles (empty)
2 dozen rolls adhesive 7 by 36 inches
4 dozen rolls adhesive 2 by 60 inches
4 pints brandy
1 gross safety pins

166. Interpretation of the supplies: Dr. David Murphy, Halifax, August 2003.

166. "Governor McCall . . . given the world": *The Boston Globe*, December 7, 1917.

166. "Will you please . . . see daylight ahead": Ibid.

167. "For hours today . . . mission of mercy": Ibid.

167. "The welfare of the individual . . . no other way": J. Byron Deacon, *Disasters*, p. 167.

168. The relief trains from New York: D. Johnstone, "The Tragedy of Halifax 1917," PANS, MFM, Micro J735.

168. "Within the membership . . . emergency food supplies": J. Byron Deacon, *Disasters*, p. 212.

168. Previous American Red Cross disaster facts: Ibid.

168. May Sexton sources: May Sexton, Halifax Disaster Record Office, PANS, MG1, vol. 2124, #224; File of Local Council of Women, PANS, Reel 14723; Red Cross: Halifax Explosion December 6, 1917, NARA 891.1/08.

169. "Mrs. Sexton, knowing Halifax . . . Canada and the United States": J. P. Murphy Report, Red Cross: Halifax Explosion December 6, 1917, NARA 891.1/08.

171. "The Vice President . . . cleared as to first steps": McMahon to Lothrop, December 7, 1917, NARA, 891.1/08. Washington, Red Cross: Halifax Explosion, December 6, 1917.

171. "At every stop the size and consequences of the disaster increases": Ibid.

171. "wonderfully complete": A. C. Ratshesky, Report Massachusetts-Halifax Relief Expedition: December 6–15, 1917.

172. Photo of the canteen ladies: *Boston Globe*, December 7, 1917.

173. "We came into full force of the blizzard. It was a nightmare": Red Cross: Halifax Explosion December 6, 1917, NARA, 891.1/08.

174. "I pleaded . . . clear the track": A. C. Ratshesky, Report Massachusetts-Halifax Relief Expedition: December 6–15, 1917.

174. "The men realizing this . . . worked like Trojans": Ibid.


12. *Saturday: Reorganizing the Relief*

177. "Fallen houses . . . dangling over nothingness": S. Smith, *Heart Throbs of the Halifax Horror*, p. 26.

178. "Mr. C. A. Hayes, President of Canadian Government Railway": A. C. Ratshesky, Report Massachusetts-Halifax Relief Expedition: December 6–15, 1917.

178. McCall to Mayor of Halifax: Ibid.

179. "Just like the people . . . your service": Ibid.

179. "The private car of Sir Robert Borden, Prime Minister of Canada": Ibid.

180. "It was a gruesome start": Ibid.

180. "An awful sight . . . no order existed": Ibid.

180. "Our only orders . . . to everybody": John Hanlon Mitchell, Halifax Disaster Record Office, PANS, MG1, vol. 2124, #186.

181. "I never ate so much cheese in my life": R. L. Fraser, *The Atlantic Advocate*, January 1967.

181. "We did not wish to appear as intruders": A. C. Ratshesky, Report Massachusetts-Halifax Relief Expedition: December 6–15, 1917.

181. "Overwhelmed . . . long-range plans": C. C. Carstens, Red Cross: Halifax Explosion December 6, 1917, NARA, 891.1/08.

181. "The straightest-thinking people were far from normal": May Sexton, Halifax Disaster Record Office, PANS, MG1, vol. 2124, #224.

182. "Speaking as a Representative . . . it is yours": *Boston Globe*, December 9, 1917.

182. "We have come . . . to take charge": *Boston Globe*, December 9, 1917; Report of the American Red Cross Unit at Halifax, NARA, 891.1/08.

183. Centralized financial . . . Executive Committee: C. C. Carstens, Report of the American Red Cross Unit at Halifax, NARA, 891.1/08.

183. The committees varied slightly from the Red Cross's original priorities. They consisted of R. T. MacIlreith, the chairman; Mr. Justice Harris of the Nova Scotia Supreme Court, finance; J. L. Hetherington, a wholesale grocer, food; R. C. Beazley, a coal dealer, fuel; Colonel Robert S. Law, reconstruction; Agnes Dennis, clothing; W. S. Davidson, emergency shelter; Mr. McKeen, information; and A. D. MacRae, registration. Rehabilitation was not finalized because Moors urged this be deferred until more pressing matters were addressed.

183. "In my opinion . . . possible moment": A. C. Ratshesky, Report Massachusetts-Halifax Relief Expedition: December 6–15, 1917.

184. "Extending north . . . along the water's edge": J. P. Murphy Report, Red Cross: Halifax Explosion December 6, 1917, NARA, 891.1/08.

185. "In the hard shelled towns of Flanders . . . bombardment": Diary, George Yates, reprinted by S. Smith, *Heart Throbs of the Halifax Horror*.

185. "With sledge hammers . . . throw aside": Ibid.

185. "That . . . don't you think": Ibid.

185. "The other with . . . blood-stained": Ibid.

186. "That is all that is left . . . Windsor to bury them": Ibid.

186. "I begin to feel that I now know what war must mean": Ibid.

187. "Are you going . . . two more": Ibid.

187. "All the women's organized effort of the City is at your disposal": May Sexton, Halifax Disaster Record Office, PANS, MG1, vol. 2124, #224.

187. "On the second floor . . . many other articles": D. Johnstone, "The Tragedy of Halifax 1917," PANS, MFM, Micro J735.

188. "busy eye ward": Jack MacKeen, *Mail Star* (December 6, 1967).

189. "the type of operations etc.": Ibid.

189. Chloroform: J.T.H. Connor, "Chloroform and the Civil War," *Military Medicine*. Washington, D.C.: National Museum of Health and Medicine, Armed Forces Institute of Pathology: February 2004.

189. "Remarkable . . . flap hanging forward": Dr. George Cox, PANS, MG1, vol. 2606, #169.

189. "As if nothing had happened": Ibid.

190. "Oh, mother, it is so very dark": J. P. Murphy Report, Red Cross: Halifax Explosion, December 6, 1917, NARA, 891.1/08.

190. "Oh, that's . . . a Liggins": Interview: Anne (Liggins) Welsh to Kitz PANS, FSG, MF298, #169.

190. "What am I going to do with a baby?": Ibid.

191. "We got in . . . us in Ward L": Jean Lindsay Ross diaries, PANS, MG27.

192. "He was about 2½ . . . 'Tarlie' ": Ibid.

192. "I did not want to jump up for fear they'd think they got me to move on": Ibid.

192. "Sitting on patient's beds is not assisting in any way": Ibid.

192. "He kept a feeding cup hidden under the covers for fear he'd lose it": Ibid.

192. "Military Medical situation . . . on arrival": F. McKelvey Bell, Telegrams, NAC, RG 24, HQ 71-26-99-3, vol. I.

193. "No more dressings for me that morning": Jean Lindsay Ross diaries, PANS, MG27.

193. "How long have . . . Saturday night": Ibid.

193. "That man Chisholm. He was quite a man": B. Archibald, *The Nova Scotia Medical Bulletin* (1950).

## 13. Duggans Reunited, If Briefly

195. "I was glad to go with him": R. L. Fraser, *The Atlantic Advocate* (January 1967).

195. "That would be the first and last for a long time": Ibid.

196. Beaufort scale: Environment Canada, www.qc.ec.gc.ca/meteo/Documentation/Beaufort_e.html.

196. "No. 198 MALE . . . Glasgow, Scotland": S. Smith, *Heart Throbs of the Halifax Horror*, Appendix.

196. "No 480 MALE . . . marked 'P.L.' ": Halifax Disaster Record Office, PANS, MG36, Series "C."

197. "It is a mysterious . . . implements and vessels": Morgue at Chebucto School, Halifax Disaster Record Office, PANS, MG1, vol. 2124, #203; #282d.

197. "The attendants . . . passed around": Ibid.

198. Abandoned bodies: *Mail Star*, December 10, 1917.

198. "The streets were . . . the last straw": Rear Admiral Chambers quoted by J. G. Armstrong, *The Halifax Explosion and the Royal Canadian Navy*, p. 102.

199. "I can see the . . . hammer in his hand": Interview: Gertrude (Mercer) Rafuse to Kitz, PANS, FSG, MF298, #75.

199. "Some of the . . . out of here": Interview: Clifford Brown to Kitz, PANS, FSG, MF298, #165.

199. "My older sister . . . some body": Interview: Mrs. Catherine (Boudreau) MacDonald to Kitz, PANS, FSG, MF298, #99.

199. "So he went . . . I'll do this": Interview: Clifford Brown to Kitz, PANS, FSG, MF298, #165.

*Notes*

199. "The basement there was . . . quite a sight to see": Hilda Holloway, Interview: Edgar T. Holloway and Hilda Holloway with Kitz, PANS, FSG, MF298, #174.

199. "And he said . . . was on her face": Interview: Miss Maude Fenerty with Kitz, PANS, FSG, MF298, #71.

200. "One doctor . . . looked again": Helena Duggan with Janet Kitz, December 14, 1983.

201. "One of the sights . . . bury them like that": Donald Morrison, *The Chronicle Herald*, December 6, 1971.

201. "While going through . . . lost in the disaster": *Acadian Recorder,* December 17, 1917.

201. "Sad stories . . . humankind again": *Amherst Daily News,* December 21, 1917.

202. "a little metal . . . the numbers 29–29": *Morning Chronicle,* December 13, 1917.

202. "Thank God, then it has not happened yet": Halifax Disaster Record Office, MG1, vol. 2124, #172a; *Amherst Daily News,* December 21, 1917.

202. "Every effort . . . in the penitentiary": *Amherst Daily News,* December 21, 1917.

203. "Kept people away like the plague": Colonel R. B. Simmonds, Halifax Disaster Record Office, PANS, MG1, vol. 2124, #225.

203. "I'll admit . . . anything to help": R. L. Fraser, *The Atlantic Advocate,* January 1967.

203. "I would see . . . my head off": Ibid.

203. "with arms like a blacksmith": Helena Duggan, *The Nova Scotian,* December 5, 1987.

## 14. *The End of Emergency Relief*

204. John Clark letter: John Clark to William L. Clark, Norwich, CT, PANS, MG26.

206. "Are you going in the direction of Camp Hill": Jean Lindsay Ross diaries, PANS, MG27.

206. "She greatly disgusted me the night before. I was glad I was late": Ibid.

206. "She thanked me for coming very nicely": Ibid.

206. Trains over the weekend: Diary, P. W. Caldwell, PANS, RG28, Series "S," vol. 26, #8.

206. Line across the harbor: Neal to Milner, July 12, 1920, PANS, MacMechan files.

206. "Bostonians very appreciative": Halifax Disaster Records Office, MG1, vol. 2124, #177.

207. "Citizens deeply . . . further needs": *New York Times,* December 8, 1917.

207. Preparing for loading the ships: *Boston Globe,* December 9, 1917.

207. Blueberries: Correspondence between author and Wild Blueberry Network Information Centre, N.S.

206. *Calvin Austin* at Yarmouth: *The Morning Chronicle,* December 13, 1917.

208. "The windows . . . Debris was everywhere": Moors to Jackson, December 13, 1917, Red Cross: Halifax Explosion, December 12, 1917, NARA, 891.1/08.

209. "We had a pleasant . . . evening": Moors to Jackson, Red Cross: Halifax Explosion, December 12, 1917, NARA, 891.1/08.

209. Martha Manter: *Boston Globe,* December 12, 1917.

209. "What is the matter": A. C. Ratshesky, Report Massachusetts-Halifax Relief Expedition: December 6–15, 1917.

209. "The sight of . . . good to me": Ibid.

210. Contents of St. Mary's from Red Cross: Red Cross, Halifax Explosion, December 6, 1917, NARA, 891.1/08.

31 cases of sterilized dressings
1000 bed comforters
50,000 sterilized compresses and sponges
2500 gauze bandages
3000 convalescent gowns and robes
1000 pajamas
1200 surgical bed shirts
1200 sweaters
1100 mufflers
1000 pairs of socks
500 wristless gowns
628 trench caps
830 helmets
1 bale of absorbent cotton
1 case assorted bandages

211. "It was pleasant . . . Massachusetts could afford": Moors to Jackson, December 13, 1917, Red Cross: Halifax Explosion, December 6, 1917, NARA, 891.1/08.

212. "There were also . . . the dressing removed": Emily Brown, Halifax Disaster Record Office, PANS, MG1, vol. 2124, #118.

212. Of those 3,755 patients, 2,506 appeared at the dressing stations while 753 were treated at home. Another 496 dressings were listed without any location: Lieutenant Colonel Frederick McKelvey Bell, Interim Medical Report, NAC, HQ71-26-99-3, vol. 2.

212. Christian Science Train: Christian Science War Relief Committee, *Christian Science War Time Activities*, pp. 61–69.

212. "a strange contradiction": *Chicago Post*, quoted in *Christian Science War Time Activities*, pp. 61–69.

212. "an unusual spectacle": *Daily Times Journal*, quoted in *Christian Science War Time Activities*, pp. 61–69.

212. "happy and harmonious": Christian Science Train: Christian Science War Relief Committee, *Christian Science War Time Activities*, pp. 61–69.

212. "I enclose one . . . was not prepared": Ibid.

213. "No instances of neglect could be found": Gardner to Persons, December 12, 1917, Red Cross: Halifax Explosion December 6, 1917, NARA, 891.1/08.

214. Dartmouth's relief remained independent until August 1918: J. Kitz, *Shattered City: The Halifax Explosion and the Road to Recovery*, p. 127.

214. Canadian Red Cross Medical Supply Depot: Rehabilitation Committee Report to Executive Committee, PANS, MG36, Series "C."

214. State of infrastructure: Acton Burrows, Esq. to *Canadian Railway and Marine World*, December 31, 1917, Halifax Disaster Record Office, PANS, MG36, Series "C"; Superintendent of the Gas Department to *Gas Journal,* Halifax Disaster Record Office, PANS, MG1, vol. 2124, #218.

214. Captain Frederick Tooke: Captain Frederick T. Tooke, CAMC, "An Experience

through the Halifax Disaster," *Canadian Medical Association Journal*, vols. 59–62 (July 1918) F. T. Tooke, Military Records NAC HQ6013-1.

215. "The day was dark . . . city of the dead": Ibid.

216. "Mistress rubbed shoulder with maid . . . the same desire to help": Ibid.

216. "Practically every face . . . it could penetrate": Ibid.

216. "I have done so much work my instruments no longer cut": Dr. George Cox, PANS, MG1, vol. 2606, #169.

216. "I was tired and had had enough of a good thing for once": Ibid.

216. "Eyes were being removed without anaesthetics": Dorothy McMurray, "Four Principals of McGill," reprinted in *The Mail Star,* December 6, 1974.

217. "In many cases . . . luck was with us": Captain Frederick T. Tooke, CAMC, "An Experience through the Halifax Disaster," *Canadian Medical Association Journal*, vols. 1–115 (July 1918), 59–62.

218. "The inmates of that home are all gone": *Acadian Recorder,* December 19, 1917.

218. Contents of postcard: Ibid.

218. "December 10, 1917 [10:30 PM] . . . A.D.M.S. No. 6 (stop)": F. McKelvey Bell, Telegrams, NAC, RG24, HQ 71-26-99-3, vol. I.

## 15.  Cap Ratshesky Says Good-bye

219. "That is just what poor papa wants": Elizabeth Fraser, *The Mail Star,* December 6, 1972.

220. "I had a heavy load . . . to move into": Ibid.

220. "You, what are . . . your pass": Colonel R. B. Simmonds, Halifax Disaster Record Office, PANS, MG1, vol. 2124, #225.

220. "My name is . . . family is buried—": Ibid.

220. Man wedged between beams: *Acadian Recorder,* December 11, 1917.

221. Animal stories: *Acadian Recorder,* December 11, 1917.

221. "I had a little . . . got home": Interview: Keith Allen with Kitz, PANS, FSG, MF298, #90.

221. "The Capital . . . sister Provinces": A. MacMechan & G. Metson, *The Halifax Explosion,* p. 93.

221. One woman offered to record a tribute song: Helen Dixon to Ralph Bell, October 5, 1918, Halifax Disaster Record Office, PANS, MG36, Series "C," #25.17.

222. Donations from other governments and cities: J. Castell Hopkins, *The Canadian Annual Review of Public Affairs* (1918): 646–656.

| Canadian Government | $8,000,000 |
|---|---|
| UK | $5,000,000 |
| US Congress | $5,000,000 |
| London Lord Mayor's Fund | $800,000 |
| Australia | $250,000 |
| Province of Ontario | $100,000 |
| St. John's, Newfoundland | $50,000 |
| British Columbia | $50,000 |
| New Zealand | $50,000 |

222. "Further inquiry . . . being made here": Moors to Persons, December 15, 1917, Red Cross: Halifax Explosion, December 6, 1917, NARA, 891.01/08.

222. "Give this to some poor Halifax kiddie": *The Morning Chronicle,* December 13, 1917.

222. "A poor woman . . . women of Halifax": D. Johnstone, "The Tragedy of Halifax 1917," PANS, MFM, Micro J735.

223. "Mr. Endicott . . . for awhile": *Morning Chronicle,* December 14, 1917.

223. "That the heartfelt thanks . . . devastation of our city": A. C. Ratshesky, Report Massachusetts-Halifax Relief Expedition, December 6–15, 1917.

223. "Gentlemen, the resolution . . . sum of $1000": Ibid.

225. "I have never . . . the real facts": Codman to Woodbury, PANS, MG1, vol. 2124, #238C.

226. Red Cross discomfort: Moors to Persons, December 12, 1917, Red Cross: Halifax Explosion December 6, 1917, NARA, 891.1/08.

226. "from the point of view . . . down at the climax": Moors to Carstens, December 31, 1917, Red Cross: Halifax Explosion, December 6, 1917, NARA, 891.1/08.

*16. Playing Solomon*

227. Rehabilitation Committee a/o December 12, 1917:

*Chairman:*

Dougall MacGillivray (until evening of December 24), Manager of Canadian Bank of
    Commerce
J. H. Winfield (Chairman from December 25 on), General Manager of Telephone
    and Telegraph Co.

*Vice Chairmen:*

Judge J. B. Wallace, Judge of County Court
Charles H. Mitchell, Fish Merchant

*Others:*

W. H. Studd, Accountant, Representing Provincial Government
Philip Ring, Representing Labor
R. Anderson, Truant Officer
H. Murray, Representing S.P.C.A., Dartmouth
Major Creighton, Salvation Army
E. H. Blois, Superintendent of Neglected Children
Gavin L. Stairs, Stairs, Son & Morrow, Merchants
Dr. Eben MacKay, Professor of Chemistry, Dalhousie University
H. L. Hart, Alderman
Edward J. Murphy, J&Y Murphy, Wholesale Dry Goods
A. D. McRae, Royal Bank
Arthur C. Johnston, Former Mayor of Dartmouth
Mrs. Grant, Wife of Governor, Government House, Local Women's Council
Mrs. W. E. Dennis, Wife of Senator Dennis, President, Local Women's Council

Win. Schon, Proprietor of Ungar's Laundry
Mrs. John E. Wood, Wife of member of Wood Bros. Dry Goods
Mrs. Blackaddar, Wife of Dr. Blackadder
Miss Annie Chisholm
Miss Maria Stewart, Sister of Colonel John Stewart, doctor in Dalhousie Unit
Miss Mary Murphy, Sister of Edward J. Murphy
City Engineer: In an advisory capacity.
City Assessor: In an advisory capacity.

227. "It is the province of emergency . . . intelligent personal service": J. Byron Deacon, *Disasters*, p. 108.

228. Judge Harris, a Supreme Court judge: Moors to Persons, December 18, 1917, Red Cross: Halifax Explosion, December 6, 1917, NARA, 89 1.01 /08.

228. Early conflict: Halifax Disaster Record Office, PANS, MG36, Series "C," #89.33, 157.10, #88.12.

228. In 1918, Dr. David Fraser wrote a medical history of the explosion outlining some observations of the survivors. "Medical Aspects of the Halifax Disaster," PANS, MG 36, Series "C," Folder 19. This document contains no more fascinating entry than the passage "Slowness of the Healing of the Wounds": "Not a few surgeons reported a notable slowness in wounds healing during the first eight or nine days after the explosion. With this slowness of tissue repair was associated a mental condition of considerable inertness, not exactly lethargy, but a dullness or difficulty of responses. Dr. J. G. McDougall reported to the writer very fully on this condition. He regards the two phenomena, the slowness of tissue repair and the inertness of the central nervous system, as both of them expressions of one anterior condition. The writer believes that this view of the state of matters is a correct one. These persons had suffered a severe shock to the central nervous system in respect of the suddenness and the violence of the experiences through which they had passed. The suddenness and overwhelming character of the explosion, the noise, the commotion, the concussion, and, in many cases, immersion in the water of the wave that swept the North End, all contributed to this untoward condition of mind. These factors combined to produce a state of profound physical and mental weariness. The highest functions of the cortex cerebri, volitions and emotion were in abeyance. Dr. McDougall reported these cases as singularly of volitional activity or of emotional expression. There was a partial inhibition or paralysis of cortical function, somewhat similar to the condition for which the name 'psychasthenie' has been coined.

"These people were not the victims of shock in the usual surgical sense of that term; that is, they were not suffering from traumatic shook with its low blood pressure, pale extremities and anxious, alert expression. Their countenances were immobile; their replies were in monosyllables. They were as one might put it, too tired to talk, to look pleased or displeased; this was a condition of acute mental inertia or depression. They were dazed but not amazed. 'They did not complain of pain because the central apparatus for the perception of pain was depressed to each an extent that its perceptive powers were very feeble.' But the additional interesting thing is that during this inert or neutral period the wounds of those people healed very slowly. This we may take to be the peripheral expression of the deficiency of central innervation. No physician doubts the reality of this unconscious influence of the vital activity of the highest nerve centres on even the humblest form of tissue activity. There is the unconscious influence of mind on body: just as a pleasurable mental state can influence tissue changes for good so conversely can a disagreeable mental state influence them for evil, and so, analogously, a state of deficient intensity of central neural activity has its distant or peripheral expression in slow healing of wounds. The unconscious outflow of neural impulses is deficient in its potential, so that the tissues are correspondingly depressed in their vitality or power to repair themselves; for the *vix medicatrix Nature* is but the old name for this very old power.

"After eight days wounds began to heal, and exactly at that time the patients began to complain of pain and to evince some emotion. The psychasthenia was passing off and the tissue innervation beginning to be restored. This condition of central depression accounts for the indifference to pain and to their dreadful surroundings which the injured showed in the first few days, and which seemed to lay observers, the expressions a stoic heroism. It is not asserted that there was no stoicism on the part of hundreds of the heroic wounded, but much of the absence of complaining and even, apparently, of suffering was due to this mental dullness. The people were so dazed, that they did not realize the extent of their injuries. Many women and children badly injured and bleeding wandered away, not knowing where they were going, until they died of exhaustion and exposure by the roadside. There were, of course, cases where the element of true shock did enter in.

"The following may be taken as an example: An elderly man on the morning of December 6th was occupied in surveying a piece of land at the North End of the city when the explosion occurred. He remembers seeing the flame shoot up from the ship, and then nothing more till he found himself beside a burning house and saw the body of a dead man not far off. He struggled to his feet and managed somehow to walk to his office on Hollis Street, when he suddenly felt quite unlike himself and lay down. He became unconscious and remained so for a week, taking scarcely any food all that time. When he began to go about once more, he was conscious of severe pains all over his body.

"An example of an extreme degree of mental detachment is the case of a woman who lived on Roome Street, from where she was watching the burning ship. She remembers hearing a slight explosion, but the great one rendered her insensible and blew her bodily into Duffus Street, one block away. On regaining consciousness, she noticed the headless body of a child lying near her. Not far off she saw the head, and she remembers going over to it, taking it up, and, as she took it to the dead body, saying, 'Here, dear, here is your head.' One could scarcely have a better example of mental isolation from the objective side of the environment, of a lack of awareness as to external relations, of a greater degree of, detachment from the actual.

"The following, however, is probably a case of ordinary, surgical collapse. Dr. G. A. MacIntosh reported a case of a man about twenty-five years of age, a car conductor, who was struck on the head on Gottingen Street. He went to get his family out of their house, but after losing a great deal of blood he finally fainted near the Armories and was carried unconscious to Camp Hill. Here he received a saline injection per rectum, and for a long time was despaired of, being nearly speechless and of a dead white colour. About three P.M. he revived, began to talk a little, and was out in a couple of days.

Notes

"In some cases the effects of the explosion were exactly the opposite of shock, namely, stimulant. Several cases of neurasthenia were distinctly benefitted by the neural commotion engendered by the explosion and its concomitants. These were eases of a hysteroid order; and by the violence of the disaster were aroused from the lethargy of neurasthenia, to a life of normal activity. In certain households where neurasthenics had lain as incurable invalids for months and even years, this curative power of the explosion has been acclaimed by the rest of the family with expressions amounting to gratitude."

229. "One young woman . . . her a black dress": Janet Kitz, *Shattered City: The Halifax Explosion and the Road to Recovery*, p. 121.

229. "The whole department . . . scandal for a long time": C. C. Carstens, Red Cross: Halifax Explosion, December 6, 1917, NARA, 891.1/08.

229. talcum powder and toys: James Slayter, Halifax Disaster Records Office, MG1, vol. 2124, #226.

229. Food depots: Moors to Persons, December 18, 1917, Red Cross: Halifax Explosion, December 6, 1917, NARA, 891.1/08; C. C. Carstens, Report of the American Red Cross Unit at Halifax, Halifax Explosion, December 6, 1917, NARA, 891.1/08.

230. "Perhaps it is . . . not easily determined": John Moors, Red Cross: Halifax Explosion, December 6, 1917, NARA, 891.1/08.

230. Josie Crighton: Crighton to Wisdom, Halifax Disaster Record Office, PANS, MG36, Series "C," #157.3D-G.

231. Cases of people handicapped for life compiled by Hilbert Day: D. Fraser, "Medical Aspects of the Halifax Disaster," PANS, MG36, Series "C," Folder 19.

| Fractures, simple | 87 | 33.33% |
|---|---|---|
| Fractures, compound | 22 | 8.43% |
| Deep wounds | 46 | 17.62% |
| Burns of a serious nature | 21 | 8.05% |
| Amputations, upper extremities | 13 | 4.98% |
| Amputations, lower extremities | 12 | 4.60% |
| Septic wounds | 32 | 12.26% |
| Mental or nerve cases | 16 | 6.13% |
| Paralysis | 12 | 4.60% |
| Total | 261 | |

231. McKelvey Bell's conclusions: F. McKelvey Bell, Interim Medical Report, NAC, HQ71-26-99-3, vol. 2.

1. The linking up of all Voluntary Aid Associations such as the Red Cross, V.A.D.'s, St. John Ambulance Brigade, Victoria Order of Nurses, Independent Order of Daughters of the Empire, etc. with the medical services in order to obtain co-ordination of effort.

2. The Standardization of hospital equipment throughout Canada.

3. That complete units of 44 beds be ready for emergency call—the equipment to include the necessary stationary.

4. That supplies be packed, if possible, in stout plain wooden boxes with rope handles and screw-down lids of one-man load weight and contents plainly marked on all sides.

5. That a complete Emergency Medical & Surgical outfit of weight and bulk that could be carried on a passenger motor car together with an M.O., Nurse & Orderly be always on hand so that it might be ready for immediate use.

6. That a scheme for the organization of "First Aid Posts" and the mobilization of their personnel be prepared, their instruction to be carried out by the A.M.C. Training Depot.

7. The Registration of hospitals and public buildings together with their approximate accommodation so that they might be handed over to the Medical Authorities on demand.

8. That in the case of another such disaster it is most important that the A.D.M.S. should have full command of the medical situation both civil and military from the start.

231. Fred Kidd sources: Fred Kidd, *The Chronicle Herald,* December 6, 1974.

232. The problems of children: Carstens and McMahon to Persons, December 30, 1917, Red Cross: Halifax Explosion, December 6, 1917, NARA, 891.1/08.

232. Celia Brogan: Interview: Mrs. Cecilia (Brogan adopted as Power) Collen with Kitz, PANS, FSG, MF298, #134. "My foster father told me that my father was in the army and he went overseas as far as they know he never came back. Of course they wouldn't know because when I was five they took me to Sydney. I was brought up in Sydney. But mom told me my mother's name and my father's name . . . But I remember as a child one time I don't know how old I was—I must of been four or a little older, I was looking out the window and the soldier was walking up and down the other side of the street and my foster father took me and pushed my head down below the window so he couldn't see me. And I'm sure to God that was my father. Things like that keep haunting you."

232. "There was a . . . adopted him": Interview: Murial Chisolm Hebb with Kitz, PANS, FSG, MF298, #164.

233. "Out at 617 Robie Street . . . from the description given": *Morning Chronicle,* December 12, 1917.

233. "traveled for years . . . to put my mind to rest": Charlotte Moore (claim 3275), quoted by J. Kitz, *Shattered City: The Halifax Explosion and the Road to Recovery,* p. 101.

234. "A joint committee . . . training and education": Mrs. C. C. Ely, *A History of the Boston Metropolitan Chapter,* p. 30. This committee consisted of Edward E. Allen, superintendent of the Perkins Institution for the Blind of Boston; Mr. Edward A. Van Cleve and Mr. O. H. Burritt of the New York Association for the Blind; Sir Frederick Fraser, superintendent of the Halifax School for the Blind; Mr. Justice Robert Harris and George B. Ternan, Esq., both of Halifax.

234. 5,923 eye injuries: D. Fraser, "Medical Aspects of the Halifax Disaster," PANS, MG 36, Series "C," Folder 19.

234. Final tally of eye injuries: C. C. Carstens, Report of the American Red Cross Unit at Halifax, NARA, 891.1/08.

| | | |
|---|---|---|
| Totally blind | 41 | 5.93% |
| Both eyes doubtful | 44 | 6.37% |
| One eye doubtful | 136 | 19.68% |
| One eye blinded with other in good condition | 141 | 20.41% |
| Eye injured but both now in good conditions | 166 | 24.02% |
| Unable to locate | 84 | 12.16% |
| Out of town and address unknown | 50 | 7.24% |
| Not caused by explosion | 21 | 3.04% |
| Blind persons who have died | 8 | 1.16% |
| Total | 691 | |

234. Of the 41 . . . the ages of twenty-one and forty: Ibid.

234. Red Cross expenses: Ellis Russell to Persons, January 18, 1918, Red Cross: Halifax Explosion, December 6, 1917, NARA, 891.1/08. Dr. Ladd's unit was, by far, the costliest, totaling $8,447.58.

| | |
|---|---|
| Total | $20,009.83 |
| Balance sent to Washington | $765.40 |
| Total expended in Halifax | $19,244.43 |

| | Hotel | Transport | Salaries | Purchases | Printing | Office | Sundries | Freight | Packing | Total |
|---|---|---|---|---|---|---|---|---|---|---|
| Blind | 138.94 | 139.38 | | | | | 7.00 | | | 285.32 |
| Children | 144.95 | 46.25 | | | | | 12.28 | | | 203.48 |
| Med-Social | 198.78 | 692.90 | 108.92 | | | | 5.00 | | | 1,005.60 |
| Gen. Rehab | 731.85 | 330.45 | 682.00 | | 71.50 | | 13.35 | | | 1,829.15 |
| Gen Admin | 741.80 | 344.87 | 506.16 | | 65.60 | 391.25 | 53.66 | 176.87 | | 2,280.21 |
| Hospital | 197.71 | 4,808.92 | 5,351.45 | 3,002.61 | | | 159.98 | | 120.00 | 13,640.67 |
| Grand Total | 2,154.03 | 6,362.77 | 6,648.53 | 3,002.61 | 137.10 | 391.25 | 251.27 | 176.87 | 120.00 | 19,244.43 |

235. "The experiences . . . emergency disaster work": J. P. Murphy Report, Red Cross: Halifax Explosion, December 6, 1917, NARA, 891.1/08. C. C. Carstens wrote up his conclusions for publication in a monograph issued after the disaster: "The most striking fact in connection with the Halifax disaster relief was that within less than twenty-four hours the essential principles of calamity relief were accepted by the community, and the delaying of plans and the overlapping in the giving of relief or giving without suitable inquiry was due not so much to the failure to accept the principle as to the time it took to get the idea of rehabilitation understood and established in a community which had never given the subject of rehabilitation any thought. Out of the experience have come several points that are worthy of consideration as they bear upon other disasters.

1. The need of organizing a Civilian Relief Red Cross Squad in each division consisting of members with various capabilities, and beforehand definitely assigned to special tasks, to render service upon arrival in the general organization of relief work, in providing immediate shelter, food and clothing, in shaping a policy for permanent rehabilitation in children's work, in medical social service and in the use of volunteers.

2. In every undertaking for the relief of sufferers from disaster, the task of using to advantage the large amount of volunteer service offered, within as well as without the area in which the calamity has occurred, should be given to one specially trained for that purpose. It is an important work in vocational direction.

3. Much embarrassment would have been avoided and can be avoided in the future if the Red Cross Unit is definitely informed what its relation and its responsibility is to the medical units, not a part of the Red Cross organization who are sent to assist. Of the five medical units in Halifax only two were Red Cross Units, although the people of Halifax still believe that all five were Red Cross Units. A better coordination of State Guard Units with Red Cross Units is needed.

4. The relief work at Halifax is, as far as the writer knows, the first one where on any large scale the principle of restitution has been the guide rather than rehabilitation. Because of a conviction on the part of the people that they were suffering from the vicissitudes of war, and while far away from the real seat of conflict were as much entitled to consideration as those in the devastated area nearer the front, led to a considerable agitation in favor of complete restitution for all losses incurred. The large amount of money made available by the Dominion and Imperial governments must be regarded as a response to this request. A Public Commission of three persons was appointed by the Dominion government and the whole local work was placed in their hands. It will be helpful for making plans in later disasters that at the proper time the results of this policy of restitution in disaster shall have adequate examination and comparison with the policy of rehabilitation which, until Halifax, had held sway": Red Cross: Monograph 67, NARA, pp. 24–25, 89/.1/08.

235. Halifax Relief Commission: Report on the work of the Registration and Rehabilitation Committee, Halifax Disaster Record Office, PANS, MG36, "C," #157.3N.

236. "If a woman's morality . . . permanently": J. Kitz, *Shattered City: The Halifax Explosion and the Road to Recovery*, p. 181.

236. "an overdose . . . social service pedantry": D. Johnstone, "The Tragedy of Halifax 1917," PANS, MFM, Micro J735.

236. "It was a fairly . . . a higher life expectancy": J. Kitz, *Shattered City: The Halifax Explosion and the Road to Recovery*, p. 199.

237. Description of buildings: Carstens to Moors, January 4, 1918, Red Cross: Halifax Explosion, December 6, 1917, NARA, 891.1/08.

237. "I now write . . . thanks to all concerned": Massachusetts State House, MS Coll 90, Folder 13.

237. "I am, therefore . . . a little forbearance": Ibid.

238. "Little Chocolate": Canadian Boxing Federation, Ontario Black History Society Archives. His real name was George Dixon and, although born in Africville, he moved to Boston when he was a youngster.

238. James Johnston: B. Pachai, *Beneath the Clouds of the Promised Land*, 1990.

239. "As recommended . . . stuffed, all alike": H. Tapp, PANS, MG36, Series "P," Pension Claim #2064.

240. "In consequence . . . you indefinitely": Ibid.

240. "Impossible to say at present time": Charles Duggan file, PANS, MG36, Series "P," Pension Claim #3683.

240. "Home and Ferry Boat replaced": Ibid.

240. "This man lost . . . nicely filled": Ibid.

241. "nervous and unhappy": William Duggan file, PANS, MG36, Series "P," Pension Claim #1770.

241. "Family anxious to get . . . one house": Ibid.

241. "Woman was badly . . . on Monday": Ibid.

242. "Saw Mrs. Duggan . . . good wage for girl": Ibid.

242. "consult Mayor of Halifax at once": Ibid.

242. "Physical Condition . . . disaster-produced condition entirely": Ibid.


## 17. Proper Burials, Private Services

244. "No. 927A FEMALE . . . baby's blanket": S. Smith, *Heart Throbs of the Halifax Horror,* Appendix.

245. *Titanic*: Other *Titanic* bodies were buried in Fairview Lawn, Baron de Hirsch, and Mount Olivet.

245. According to Fred Longland's account, he worked in the morgue for much of the first day. After he returned to the ship, he was sitting in the wardroom sipping brandy to calm his nerves when the commander entered the room.

"Does anyone know of an officer called Longland?"

Longland jumped to his feet. "Yes, sir, that is my name."

"There is a man in Victoria Hospital Emergency ward, badly hurt and in his extremity keeps on calling out your name. Have you any idea who it is?"

"No sir, but I will go along and see."

Longland put down his brandy and returned outside to the gruesome landscape. An hour later he was walking past the rambling Victorian town houses of South Park, approaching the Victoria General. Inside an orderly took him to see a patient. He looked bad. Someone told him he had been calling for him since they brought him in.

"Fred, Fred Longland," he murmured.

Longland leaned over the man's face. They were about the same age, but Longland did not recognize him. Offering his apologies, he returned to the ship. He got another call from the hospital around Christmas. The patient who had called his name was awake after three weeks in a coma. Longland returned to the ward, but this time found the man sitting up in bed looking cheerful.

"Hello, Fred."

This time Longland laughed. It was the son of the postmaster in Waterloo, where

Longland had grown up. They had been boyhood friends. Longland asked him what happened and he told him that he had been serving on the *Picton* when the blast picked him up and ripped him through the air 150 feet. He landed in a field, naked aside from a boot and a sock. Longland was transferred to Esquimault, B.C., along with much of the Canadian Navy, and he sailed in the Pacific for the rest of his life.

The *Picton* was docked at the sugar refinery wharf and carrying ammunition, primarily shells. She did not have any high explosives on board. Nevertheless she did catch fire, and her cargo was in danger of exploding one shell at a time. Lt. Leslie Harrison, one of the men who rode down Barrington Street telling people to go south to avoid a possible second explosion, told Archibald MacMechan the story of his father's attempt to bring the *Picton* under control. "Just at entrance of Citadel in motor car when the explosion occurred. Shouted 'Take cover' and blew whistle. Took medical orderly and bandages and proceeded northward. Took first load of injured to the Victoria General Hospital about 9:25 and the second to the Infirmary about 9:40." In his third trip along Water Street he met his father, Capt. Harrison, agent for the Furness & Whithy & Co. Line, who said, 'Drive me North.' On reaching North St. Station they were stopped and turned back. Captain Harrison's object, though his son did not know it at the time, was to get on board the *Picton* lying at Brookfield's wharf, partially unloaded and consigned to his firm. In coming to the city the *Picton*, a steamer of 6,000 tons, had grounded and injured her stern post and runner. Her cargo was being put on shore to lighten her and make repairs. It consisted of general cargo—food, among other things—and fifteen hundred tons of shells. She was lying close to the burning sugar refinery and there was imminent danger of the munitions blowing up. Being unable to reach the *Picton* via Barrington Street, the Harrisons turned back and stopped at the corner of Jacob and Barrington, where Captain Harrison got out, his object being to get round to the *Picton* by water. . . . Captain Harrison went to the Furness, Withy & Co. wharf, got into motorboat, and ordered the man in charge to take him to the *Picton*, climbed on board fifteen minutes later by means of rope-ladder. A cook and another man helped him. Found naked bodies lying all over the deck to the number of sixty. There was rubbish on deck, burning with a thick, black smoke. The danger of fire and explosion was from the fire on shore of the sugar refinery. Captain Harrison got an axe and hacked at steel hawsers until they parted. It was about an hour's hard work and the heat from the burning building on shore was severe. As Capt. Harrison hailed one of G. S. Campbell's tugs, came and assisted towing the *Picton* into the stream. The rubbish on deck was still on fire. Captain Harrison had great difficulty in getting the motorboat crew to put him on board. The motorboat then stood off, watching him although it was in a dangerous position. Captain Harrison got on board about eleven-thirty. It was about four by the time she was anchored in the stream. Then men helped him to put the fire on the deck out, by throwing the burning rubbish overboard. Later Captain Harrison was ordered to tow the *Picton* to the Eastern Passage, as far as possible. This was done with great difficulty. In going through the submarine gate at George's Island, met a ship coming in, which seemed almost determined to ram him, and he was forced to alter his coarse in order to get clear. 'Never had greater difficulty' in avoiding collision. He obeyed the order and anchored the *Picton* in the Eastern Passage. In spite of the statements in the papers that the sea-cocks were open, she was not sunk."

Captain Harrison's story was recalled many times after the explosion as an example of heroism and the *Picton*'s presence used in the press to frighten the people of Halifax even more, suggesting that yet another explosion had been averted. The navy felt the *Picton* story was overblown and exaggerated. Shells did not explode in the same way high explosives did and, they felt, the ship was never in real danger.

245. "There was no funeral . . . waiting trucks outside": *Ottawa Citizen*, December 13, 1917; reprinted in J. G. Armstrong, *The Halifax Explosion and the Royal Canadian Navy*, p. 84.

245. Almost four out of ten of Nova Scotia men: J. Castell Hopkins, *The Canadian Annual Review of Public Affairs* (1918), p. 656.

### 18. *Monday, December 17, 1917*

247. "Some of the older . . . St. Patrick's day procession": A. MacMechan, Halifax Disaster Record Office, PANS, MG1, vol. 2124, #282d.

248. "Women brought . . . the opposite sex": Ibid.

248. Coffins: D. Johnstone, "The Tragedy of Halifax 1917," PANS, MFM, Micro J735; Arthur S. Barnstead, Interim Report of Mortuary Committee, February 4, 1918, PANS, MG36, Series "C," 127.20–20F; A. MacMechan, Halifax Disaster Record Office, PANS, MG1, vol. 2124, #282d.

248. "strained and thin": A. MacMechan, Halifax Disaster Record Office, PANS, MG1, vol. 2124, #282d.

248. "Only the dogs . . . betraying dejection": Ibid.

249. "O God, our Help . . . eternal Home": "O God Our Help in Ages Past," hymn by Isaac Watts.

249. "It is not by the hand . . . the mistakes of others": J. Kitz, *Shattered City: The Halifax Explosion and the Road to Recovery*, p. 108.

249. "Words counted for little": A. MacMechan, Halifax Disaster Record Office, PANS, MG1, vol. 2124, #282d.

250. "No stately hearses . . . trucks and flat wagons": Ibid.

250. "One by one . . . calliope was lacking": Ibid.

250. "They would have to spend . . . alone": Ibid.

### 19. *The Rules of the Road versus the Law of the Land*

252. Wreck Commission: "Investigation: *Mont Blanc* and *Imo* Collision," December 1917, NAC, RG42, vol. 596/7. Unless otherwise stated, all quotes from this chapter are taken from this transcript.

252. "The setting was almost . . . serve as his advisors": D. Kerr, Another Calamity: The Litigation, A. Ruffman and C. D. Howell, *Ground Zero: A Reassessment of the 1917 Explosion in the Halifax Harbour*.

254. "I shall make my statement to the Admiralty Court": "Investigation: *Mont Blanc* and *Imo* Collision," December 1917, NAC, RG42, vol. 596/7.

259. Conscription: A. M. Wilmms, *Canadian Historical Readings*: Conscription 1917, vol. 8.

259. "French Canadians Called Seditious": *New York Times*, December 10, 1917.

259. Conscription postponed in Halifax: *Acadian Recorder*, December 12, 1917.

260. Le Médec's demeanor: As much of Le Médec's testimony came in through a

translator, the author deferred interpretation to a more experienced court attendee, Donald Kerr, a lawyer whose excellent essay, "Another Calamity: The Litigation," is included in A. Ruffman & C. D. Howell, *Ground Zero*. Kerr describes the captain as "arrogant and evasive."

260. Factor of two: Estimate by Pierre Pelletier, correspondence with the author, August 6, 2004.

260. "Repeatedly he browbeat . . . lawyers must subscribe": D. Kerr, "Another Calamity: The Litigation," in A. Ruffman and C. D. Howell, *Ground Zero*.

264. "And in the meantime . . . is to tremble": *Evening Mail,* January 28, 1918.

265. Charles Mayers, the sailor who landed on Needham Hill wearing just a boot, recuperated from his injuries at the home of a man named W. T. Hart, who picked him up and brought him home on a sleigh on the day after the explosion. Mayers went on to become a river pilot in his hometown of Liverpool, England. The two men remained in contact for the rest of their lives: *Mail Star,* December 6, 1967.

270. Mackey and Le Médec arrest: "Writ of Habeas Corpus for Aimé Le Médec, Frank Mackey and Frederick Wyatt," Supreme Court of Nova Scotia, February 5, 1918, HRL: K1M6.2.

270. "It seemed to me . . . the struggle was unsuccessful": B. Russell, *Autobiography of Benjamin Russell.*

271. Further trials: Exchequer Court of Canada in Admiralty, January 17, 1917, HRL: RH 341.57 5727r; "Appeal to Supreme Court of Canada," PANS, K1M6.2; "Appeal to Privy Council," 1919 HRL: RH 341.57 5727r; D. Kerr, "Another Calamity: The Litigation," in A. Ruffman and C. D. Howell, *Ground Zero: A Reassessment of the 1917 Explosion in the Halifax Harbour*; *Halifax Herald,* November 1, 2003; D. Jobb, *Crime Wave: Con Men, Rouges and Scoundrels from Nova Scotia's Past.*

271. "A very serious . . . created that position": Appeal to Privy Council, 1919 HRL: RH 341.57#5727R.

20. *The Tree at Boston Common*

274. "This simple, beautiful tree . . . focus on the tree": *Saltscapes,* December 2004.

274. "It's not the courage . . . keep going": James Mahar, *The Record,* July 10, 1999.

*Epilogue*

278. Helena Duggan and the new bridge: As reported by Janet Kitz, telephone conversation with author, July 2002.

278. "After that I always . . . be daytime soon": *The Nova Scotian,* December 5, 1987.

278. "Sometimes I sit here . . . just happened yesterday": Ibid.

278. "the family godfather . . . the guy you would go to": Harry Duggan, interview with author, October 2004.

279. "I remember . . . a book by themselves": Helen Clark Gucker to Cousin Kate, January 7, 1963, MMA.

280. "I confirmed all that . . . with children in Halifax": Dr. C. Everett Koop, interview with the author: June 23, 2003.

280. "Dr. Ladd brought . . . diseases and abnormalities": D. Watson, *Journal of Pediatric Surgery,* vol. 2, no. 4 (August 1967).

280. "At the time . . . the obsession had ceased": Jean Lindsay Ross diaries, PANS, MG27.

280. "could not speak plainly but who swore fluently": M. E. Doane, Halifax Disaster Records Office, PANS, MG1, vol. 2124, #140C.

280. "many weird and true stories of the disaster": R. L. Fraser, *The Atlantic Advocate,* January 1967.

280. "such a terrible thing had happened and that so many were killed": Ibid.

280. Billy Wells: William Wells file, PANS, MG36, Series "P," Pension Claim #777.

281. "no petticoat doctor . . . petticoat doctors": F. Murray, *At the Foot of Dragon Hill.*

282. "I never knew who she was . . . a heroine": Donald Morrison, *The Chronicle Herald*, December 6, 1971.

## *Appendix A: Accident or Sabotage?*

285. "Special to The Evening Echo: SEATTLE, June 14:—Solution of mystery which surrounded the explosion of British ammunition ships and caused death and devastation in the city at Halifax, Nova Scotia late in 1917 is believed by government agents in Seattle to have come with the suicide of William Johnson, alias Mike Murphy, alias N. Prymatchenk, a highly educated Finn chemist whose body was found by an Indian on Bacon Creek, Skagit County, last month. Agents of the United States and Canadian government say the chemist confessed not only to responsibility for the Halifax disaster but also admitted the slaying of two men, one a captain of a British transport. Worry over his deeds and fear that came to him after he is alleged to have confessed are believed to have caused him to kill himself.

"Was In Halifax: It has already been established that Johnson was in Halifax in the British transport service. An address at which he later resided in Halifax is known to agents. Effects of the suspect found in a lonely cabin deep in the wood of Skagit County fifteen miles beyond Rockport off the line of the city of Seattle railway running to the city power project and others in a trunk traced to a cache near Bellingham will reveal names of accomplices, it is believed. Johnson, as the man was known to a few persons in Skagit County, lived alone in the secluded cabin where he experimented with acids and explosive formulas, it is alleged. His cabin was fitted with peep holes so no one might approach it unobserved. The only window was fitted with an opaque glass. The man is known to have been in the woods there since about March 1920. On one occasion an explosion burned him severely and neighbors a few miles away learned that he was experimenting with explosive materials in the manufacture of what it is supposed were bombs.

"Investigation Made: First information regarding the alleged confession and possibility of clearing up the Halifax blast mystery came from J. R. Cox, Watchman employed at Talc Mines on the Skagit River. Cox at the same time informed the officials and agents of the Department of Justice from Seattle went into the woods last month to investigate. In the cabin they found evidence that Johnson was well educated, a chemist and that he had been familiar with powder and other explosives. I.W.W. literature found in the cabin indicated that he had radical connections.

"The Investigators were at first handicapped, however, in finding that a trunk containing diaries and many personal papers had been carried away before his death by high water, which cut into a bank where the suspect was camping. It was while talking with Johnson some days before his death, Cox told Seattle agents, that Johnson alluded to the Halifax explosion. Cox had asked the chemist whether he could identify an unbranded high explosive powder. Johnson named it at once.

"Would Have Blown Up More: 'I had thirty five pounds of a more dangerous explosive than that left after we blew up three ships in Halifax harbor during the war,' Johnson is alleged to have said. 'If they had not discharged me, there would have been more ships blown up. We will be better prepared for them the next time they start a war.' Cox said that Johnson refused to tell him further details of the explosions but that he volunteered that he murdered the captain of a British vessel while returning from Australia to Canada. Johnson served as a conscript during the war, he told Cox. The suspect also told Frank L. Oakes, a prospector living in the Skagit woods, that he had murdered two men. Johnson was found dead on the bank of Bacon Creek, about a mile and a half beyond the point where the city railway crosses the stream, by Charles Moses, an Indian on May 20. His revolver, a weapon with unusually long barrel, was found in the waters of the creek nearby. His shirt was powder burned and he had apparently taken his own life. The only note left by the dead man, scribble on a piece of paper found in the cabin, which said, 'It's no use.' "

## *Appendix B: Preparing for the Future*

287. "The Commonwealth . . . terminate its existence": G. Lyman, *The Story of the Massachusetts Committee on Public Safety*, p. 529.

# Sources

Armstrong, J. G. *The Halifax Explosion and the Royal Canadian Navy.* Vancouver: UBC Press, 2002.

Baillie, D. G. O. *A Sea Affair.* London: Hutchinson, 1957.

Beed, B. *1917 Halifax Explosion and American Response.* Halifax: Self, 1988.

Bird, M. J. *The Town That Died.* Toronto: McGraw-Hill Ryerson Limited, 1962.

Boardman, M. T. *Under the Red Cross Flag at Home and Abroad.* Philadelphia: J. B. Lippencott Company, 1915.

Bradlee, F. B. C. *Boston and Lowell RR.* Salem, MA: Panoramic Publications, 1972.

Brown, G. I. *The Big Bang, A History of Explosives.* Thrupp: Sutton Publishing Limited, 2001.

Brown, R. R. *Halifax: Birney Stronghold.* Montreal: Canadian Railroad Historical Association 1964.

Burbidge, G. *Take My Hand.* Bridgetown: Self, 2000.

*Camp Hill Hospital, 70 Years of Caring 1917–1987.* Halifax: 1988.

Chapman, H. ed. *Dartmouth's Day of Anguish.* Dartmouth: Dartmouth Historical Association, 1992.

———. *In the Wake of the Alderney.* Halifax: Nimbus Publishing Limited, 2001.

*Christian Science War Time Activities.* Boston: Christian Science Publishing Society, 1922.

Deacon, J. B. *Disasters.* New York: Russell Sage Foundation, 1918.

Downey, F. *Disaster Fighters.* New York: Van Rees Press, 1938.

Dulles, F. R. *The American Red Cross: A History.* New York: Harper and Brothers, 1950.

Eaton, A. Wentworth Hamilton. "Chapters in the History of Halifax, Nova Scotia" (Self, 1921) (first printed in *Americana* magazine, 1915–1919).

Ely, C. C., Mrs. *A History of the Boston Metropolitan Chapter, American Red Cross*, Boston 1919.

Fingard, J., Guildford, J., and Sutherland, D. *Halifax, The First 250 Years.* Halifax: Formac Publishing, 1999.

Fingard, J. *The Dark Side of Life in Victorian Halifax.* Nova Scotia: Pottersfield Press, 1989.

Gay, G., and Fisher H. *Public Relations of the Commission for Relief in Belgium.* Stanford: Stanford University Press, 1929.

Goodchild, P. *J. Robert Oppenheimer: Shatterer of Worlds.* Boston: Houghton Mifflin, 1981.

Gosley, G. S. *The Story of the Dartmouth Park.* Dartmouth: 1985.

# Sources

Hadley, M. L., and Sarty, R. *Tin Pots and Pirate Ships: Canadian Naval Forces and German Sea Raiders 1880–1918*. Montreal: McGill-Queens University Press, 1991.

Hallam, Mrs. W. T. *When You Are in Halifax; Sketches of life in the first English Settlement in Canada*. Toronto: Church Book Room, 1937.

Hatfield, L. H. *Sammy*. Hantsport, N.S.: Lancelot Press, 1990.

Jobb, D. *Crime Wave: Con Men, Rouges and Scoundrels from Nova Scotia's Past*. Nova Scotia: Pottersfield Press, 1991.

Kitz, Janet F. *Shattered City: The Halifax Explosion and the Road to Recovery*. Nimbus Publishing Ltd., 1989.

———. *Survivors*. Halifax: Nimbus Publishing Ltd., 1992.

Ladd W. E., and Gross, R. E. *Abdominal Surgery of Infancy and Childhood*. Philadelphia: W. B. Saunders Company, 1941.

Landau, H. *The Enemy Within: The Inside Story of German Sabotage in America*. New York: G. P. Putnam's Sons, 1937.

LeBlanc, P. E. G. *From Tropical White to Battleship Grey*. Ottawa: Alone Publishing Enterprise, 1988.

Longstreth, T. M. *To Nova Scotia*. New York: D. Appleton-Century Company, 1938.

Lyman, G. H. *The Story of the Massachusetts Committee on Public Safety*. Boston: Massachusetts Committee on Public Safety, 1919.

MacLeod, M. *Nova Scotia Historical Review*, vol. 2, no. 2. Halifax: Nova Scotia Historical Review, 1982.

MacMechan, A. *The Book of Ultima Thule*. Toronto: McClelland & Stewart, 1927.

MacPhail, Sir A. *The Medical Services*. Ottawa: F. A. Acland, 1925.

Mahar, J., and Mahar, R. *Too Many to Mourn*. Halifax: Nimbus Publishing Limited, 1998.

Martin, J. P. *The Story of Dartmouth*. Dartmouth: 1957.

McKelvey Bell, F. *The First Canadians in France*. Toronto: McClelland, Goodchild & Stewart, 1917.

———. *A Romance of the Halifax Disaster*. Halifax: Royal Print and Litho Ltd., 1918.

Melzac R., and Wall, P. D. *The Challenge of Pain*. New York: Basic Books, 1973.

Metson, G., and A. MacMechan. *The Halifax Explosion: December 6th 1917*. Toronto: McGraw-Hill Ryerson, 1978.

Metzler, N. *Illustrated Halifax*. Montreal: John McConniff, 1891.

Miller, G. W. *The Work of Human Hands*. New Hampshire: Borderlands Press, 1999.

Monnon, M. A. *Miracles and Mysteries*. Halifax: Nimbus Publishing Limited, 1977.

Morton, S. *Ideal Surroundings: Domestic Life in a Working-Class Suburb*. Toronto: University of Toronto Press Limited, 1995.

Murray, F. J. *At the Foot of Dragon Hill*. New York: Dutton, 1975.

Pachai, B. *Beneath the Clouds of the Promised Land*. Halifax: The Black Educators Association of Nova Scotia, 1990.

Paine, L. P. *Ships of the World: An Historical Encyclopedia*. Boston: Houghton Mifflin, 1997.

Payzant, J. *We Love to Ride the Ferry: 250 Years of Halifax-Dartmouth Ferry Crossings*. Halifax: Nimbus Publishing, 2002.

Prince, S. H. *Catastrophe and Social Change*. New York: Columbia University Press, 1920.

Raddall, T. H. *Halifax, Warden of the North*. Toronto: McClelland Stewart Limited, 1948.

Rubin, S. E., and Roessler, R. T. *Foundations of the Rehabilitation Process*. Austin, TX: Pro-Ed, 1987.

Ruffman, A., and C. D. Howell. *Ground Zero: A Reassessment of the 1917 Explosion in Halifax Harbour*. Halifax: Nimbus Publishing Limited & Gorsebrook Research Institute, St. Mary's University, 1994.

Rutkow, I. *Surgery: An Illustrated History*. St. Louis: Mosby, 1993.

Russell, B. *Autobiography of Benjamin Russell*. Halifax: The Royal Print and Litho Ltd., 1932.

Shephard, B. *A War of Nerves*. Cambridge, MA: Harvard University Press, 2000.

Smith, C. A. *The Children's Hospital of Boston: Built Better Than They Knew*. Boston: Little Brown, 1983.

Smith, S. K. *Heart Throbs of the Halifax Horror*. Halifax: Gerald E. Weir, 1918.

Veedeer, B. S., ed. *Pediatric Profiles*. St. Louis: C. V. Mosby Company, 1957.

*Views of Halifax: The Empire Port and Eastern Gateway of Canada*. Halifax: McAlpine Publishing Co. Ltd., 1900.

Willms, A. M. *Canadian Historical Readings: vol. 8, Conscription 1917*.

Witcover, J. *Sabotage at Black Tom: Imperial Germany's Secret War in America 1914–1917*. Chapel Hill: Algonquin Books, 1989.

# Index

Note: Page numbers in *italic* indicate photographs

## Index

# Index

*Index*